JOHN LINGARD AND THE PURSUIT OF HISTORICAL TRUTH

In loving and grateful memory of my parents,
Lilian and Edwin Jones

John Lingard
and the Pursuit of Historical Truth

EDWIN JONES

With a Foreword by Norman Davies

sussex
ACADEMIC
PRESS
Brighton • Portland • Toronto

Copyright © Edwin Jones 2001, 2014.

The right of Edwin Jones to be identified as author of this work has been asserted in accordance with the Copyright, Designs and Patents Act 1988.

2 4 6 8 10 9 7 5 3

First published in hardcover 2001, reprinted in paperback 2014, in Great Britain by
PO Box 139
Eastbourne BN24 9BP

Distributed in North America by
SUSSEX ACADEMIC PRESS
ISBS Publisher Services
920 NE 58th Ave #300, Portland, OR 97213, USA

All rights reserved. Except for the quotation of short passages for the purposes of criticism and review, no part of this publication may be reproduced, stored in a retrieval system, or transmitted, in any form or by any means, electronic, mechanical, photocopying, recording or otherwise, without the prior permission of the publisher.

British Library Cataloguing in Publication Data
A CIP catalogue record for this book is available from the British Library.

Library of Congress Cataloging-in-Publication Data
Jones, Edwin.
John Lingard and the pursuit of historical truth / by Edwin Jones.
p. cm.
Includes bibliographical references (p.) and index.
ISBN 978-1-902210-93-3 (alk. : paper) —
ISBN 978-1-84519-046-0 (pbk.)
1. Lingard, John, 1771–1851. 2. Historiography—Great Britain—History—19th century. 3. Great Britain—Historiography. I. Title.
DA3.L7 J66   2001
941'.007'202—dc21   2001049381

Typeset and designed by G&G Editorial, Brighton.

Contents

List of Illustrations	vi
Foreword by Norman Davies	ix
Preface	xii
Acknowledgements	xxii
A Note on Editions and Text Conventions	xxiv

Introduction:	The Background to Lingard's Work	1
I	An Invitation to the Historian's Workshop	18
II	The Historiography of the Massacre of St. Bartholomew	39
III	The Collation of Sources and Lingard's Use of Public Records as a Tool of Source Criticism	51
IV	The Role of Private Sources and Their Use as a Tool of Source Criticism	72
V	The Great Step Forward: Pursuit of the 'Source of the Source'	98
VI	A Critical Apparatus for Prioritizing the Authority of Sources	123
VII	The Use of 'Forensic' Rules of Source Criticism	140
VIII	The Application of Lingard's Source Criticism to Some Celebrated Historical Problems	171
IX	Lingard's Place in English Historiography	198
Epilogue:	'Hic caestus artemque repono'	208
Appendix 1	The Development of Lingard's *History* through the Various Editions	211
Appendix 2	Lingard's System of Reference and Quotation	230
Appendix 3	Lingard as Literary Artist and Scientific Historian	234
Appendix 4	Lingard on St. Dunstan and the Tenth-Century Reforms	238
Notes		245
Manuscript Sources		288
Index		289

Illustrations

The author and publisher gratefully acknowledge permission to reproduce copyright material, as detailed below, and apologize for any errors or omissions. The publisher would be grateful to be notified of any corrections that should be incorporated in the next edition or reprint of this book.

The jacket/cover picture is a portrait of John Lingard, painted by James Lonsdale in 1834, when Lingard was sixty-three; the picture currently hangs at Ushaw College, near Durham. At the time the portrait was painted, Lingard had completed his first edition of the *History* and was preparing the next major revision. The idea, organization and financing of the portrait were undertaken by Lingard's friends, who presented it to him. One of them described it as a 'strikingly perfect' likeness. Lingard himself considered it the most accurate depiction of himself. The picture is reproduced with permission of Ushaw College; information concerning the circumstances of the portrait have been kindly supplied by the Rev. Dr. Peter Phillips, who allowed me oversight of his article on 'Portraits of Lingard' (2001).

1. *The Presbytery, Hornby, near Lancaster*
   (With the kind permission and help of Rev. Canon N. McArdle, the present parish priest at St. Mary's, Hornby)

2. *The Tomb of the Venerable Bede, at Durham Cathedral*
   (With the kind permission of the Dean and Chapter of Durham)

3. *Ushaw College, Durham*
   (With the kind permission of Ushaw College)

4. *Sir Thomas More (1478–1535)*
   (Courtesy of the National Portrait Gallery, London)

5. *Thomas Cromwell (1485–1540)*
   (Courtesy of the National Portrait Gallery, London)

ILLUSTRATIONS

6   *William Cecil, Lord Burghley (1520–98)*
    (Courtesy of the National Portrait Gallery, London)

7   *Gilbert Burnet (1643–1715)*
    (Courtesy of the National Portrait Gallery, London)

8   *David Hume (1711–76)*
    (Courtesy of the National Portrait Gallery, London)

9   *Thomas Hearne (1678–1735)*
    (With the kind permission of St. Edmund Hall, Oxford)

10 *John Lingard (1771–1851)*
    (Lonsdale portrait, about 1834, by kind permission of Ushaw College)

11 *John Lingard*
    (Skaife engraving, about 1847; when Lingard was 77, with close-fitting black wig. With thanks to the Rev. Dr. Peter Phillips)

12 *Sir Herbert Butterfield (1900–79)*
    (Reproduced with the kind permission of the Master and Fellows of Peterhouse, Cambridge)

13 *Lord Macaulay (1800–59)*
    (By kind permission of the Master and Fellows of Trinity College, Cambridge)

14 *Sir G. M. Trevelyan (1876–1962)*
    (By kind permission of the Master and Fellows of Trinity College, Cambridge)

15 *King John (1167–1216)*
    (Courtesy of the National Portrait Gallery, London)

16 *Scene from the Bayeux Tapestry – (eleventh century)*
    (By special permission of the Centre Guillaume-le-Conquérant, the City of Bayeux)

17 *King Henry V (1387–1422)*
    (Courtesy of the National Portrait Gallery, London)

18 *King Henry VI (1421–71)*
    (Courtesy of the National Portrait Gallery, London)

Illustrations

19 *King Richard III (1452–85)*
    (Courtesy of the National Portrait Gallery, London)

20 *Anne Boleyn (1501–36)*
    (Courtesy of the National Portrait Gallery, London)

21 *Henry VIII (1491–1547) and Thomas Cranmer
    (1489–1556)*
    (Courtesy of the National Portrait Gallery, London)

22 *Queen Elizabeth I (1533–1603)*
    (Courtesy of the National Portrait Gallery, London)

23 *Mary Queen of Scots (1542–87)*
    (Courtesy of the National Portrait Gallery, London)

24 *Sir Francis Walsingham (c.1532–90)*
    (Courtesy of the National Portrait Gallery, London)

25 *James II (1633–1701)*
    (Courtesy of the National Portrait Gallery, London)

26 *Edmund Campion (1540–81)*
    (Courtesy of the National Portrait Gallery, London)

27 *Charles I (1600–49) and the Eikon Basilike (1649)*
    (Courtesy of the National Portrait Gallery, London; and the Society of King Charles the Martyr)

28 *The Massacre of St. Bartholomew (1572)*
    ('An Eyewitness Account of the St. Bartholomew's Day Massacre' by François Dubois [1529–84], oil on wood, 94 × 154 cm, courtesy of the Musée cantonal des Beaux-Arts, Lausanne, Switzerland)

29 *William of Orange, 1650–1702 (William III of England,
    1689–1702)*
    (Courtesy of the National Portrait Gallery, London)

Foreword by Norman Davies

If one consults the latest version of the *Encyclopaedia Britannica* (1998) under the letter 'L', one finds that nothing exists between Lingaraja, Temple of and the Hindu sect of Lingayat. John Lingard (1771–1851) does not merit even the shortest of entries. Sometime after the famous Eleventh Edition of the Encyclopaedia in 1911, he was unceremoniously dropped. The omission speaks worlds about the established priorities of British historiography.

Similarly, if one examines any of the standard surveys of British and English history-writing, it is almost impossible to find a passing reference to Lingard, let alone a systematic analysis of his work. Specialists in the subject discuss everyone from the Venerable Bede to Herbert Butterfield and Arnold Toynbee and on to the post-modernists and their critics. Along the way, they find space for Camden's *Britannica*, Foxe's *Book of Martyrs*, William Dugdale's *Monasticon*, and, in the realm of source criticism, Henry Spelman's *Archaeologus* and possibly Henry Wharton's *Anglia Sacra*. Among Lingard's distinguished contemporaries, they devote great attention to Gibbon, Hume, Hallam, Carlyle, Froude, and Macaulay, but not to Lingard. When it comes to the rise of modern academic history in the late 18th and early 19th centuries, and in particular to the systematic study of documents and archives, virtually all the authoritative commentators from Lord Acton onwards give pride of place to continental scholars. Some praise the French School and the *Ecole des Chartes*. Still more praise Leopold von Ranke and the later Prussian School. But no-one praises Lingard. The assumption seems to be that academic history in Britain did not really begin before the days of Stubbs and Maitland. For Lingard has fallen into that strange category of people, (once formalised by the censors of the Soviet Bloc) 'who are not to be mentioned even to be denounced.' To all intents and purposes, he has become 'a non-person.' I myself graduated from the Oxford Faculty of Modern History in the 1960s without ever hearing of Lingard or seeing his works on a reading list. I don't think that my experience was unusual.

Yet Lingard was prominent enough in his own day. To British Roman Catholics, at least, which then included the Irish, he was known as the author of the most impartial History of England available and of various devotional works. He also wrote a ground-breaking study of the

Anglo-Saxon Church. To the public at large he was known as a minor polemicist who had dared to contest the views of Anglican bishops and to defend his position in a number of tracts and letters. In an age when religious disputations still stood high on the agenda, his views were often extremely stimulating. One did not have to agree with his line on The Massacre of St. Bartholomew or the Gunpowder Plot, to see that he produced much worth discussing.

What is more, the scale and success of Lingard's publications must have impressed even his most dogmatic enemies. His eight-volume *History of England* (1819–30) was more than twice the size of Lord Macaulay's and covered a far longer period. Over forty years it ran into seven editions. (The 4th edition of 1826–9 was reissued in enlarged ten-volume form in 1837–39, thereby turning the nominal Fifth and Sixth Editions into the sixth and seventh.) After Lingard's death, the massive ten-volume work was condensed into one single volume for the benefit of Catholic schools; and four separate abridgements were published, in 1855, 1867, 1912 and 1915. The last version to appear was prepared by its continuator, Hilaire Belloc, in the middle of the First World War, and was entitled *The History of England: from the first invasion of the Romans to the start of the reign of George V.*

More than two hundred years after Lingard's birth, however, it is the quality no less than the quantity of his scholarship which commands admiration. For he was a historical pioneer in two important aspects. For one thing, he was a true scholar's scholar, who based his judgements on the close critical study of documents. For another, he conducted research in French, Italian and Spanish archives, thereby putting British sources into dynamic juxtaposition with foreign ones. Born in Winchester, he had the great advantage of a continental education. Except for the inconvenient fact that he was a Roman Catholic priest in an era when Britain's Protestant Establishment remained fiercely intolerant, he must certainly have been hailed by his compatriots as one of the stars of the historical profession.

Edwin Jones is well equipped to tell Lingard's story, to examine Lingard's methods with true Lingardian meticulousness and to explain the circumstances of his intellectual ostracism. A pupil of the late Herbert Butterfield, who first exposed 'The Whig Interpretation of History', Jones has been familiar since his student days with the main battlelines of British historiography. As a Welsh-speaker and practising Catholic, he keeps his distance from the Anglocentric and Protestant traditions which until recently have underpinned so much history-writing in this country. And as the author of *The English Nation: the Great Myth* (1998), which examines the long pedigree of those traditions from Thomas Cromwell onwards, he is well acquainted with the formidable intellectual machine that he and Lingard have chosen to challenge.

FOREWORD BY NORMAN DAVIES

Yet, in the last resort, this book is deeply reassuring. It has been undertaken in a very positive spirit, confirming the view that the search for historical truth, despite the obstacles, is not a waste of time or effort. It restores Lingard to his rightful place in the pantheon of British historians. And it shows that the British historical tradition is even richer than most of us were led to believe.

Oxford
October 2001
Norman Davies
FBA, PH.D., MA (Sussex)

Preface

John Lingard (1771–1851) [PLATE 10] is hardly known to English people. His story is that of a lone Englishman who responded courageously and magnificently to the challenge of creating a new science in England – *source criticism* – to aid him in his personal pursuit of historical truth. It was to change the nature of English historiography. In so doing, together with other accompanying achievements, he became, in the view of this new study, the greatest English historian of the second millennium. At the beginning of this third millennium, we still have a great deal to learn from him – about the nature of historical truth and the attitudes of mind, together with the methodologies of source criticism, which are essential requirements for its successful pursuit.

Lingard rewrote the history of England in ten large volumes, based for the first time on original materials. He also set out to write as a 'citizen of the world',[1] so breaking the three centuries old tradition of anglo-centrism in English historical writing. His seminal work challenged a view of the whole English past – the 'Great Myth'[2] – which had been built up in the sixteenth century and continued to dominate both historical writing and the collective English psychology until the end of the twentieth century.

A new revisionist school of historians is now rewriting the story of the English past and is beginning to discover that the almost unknown Lingard had been there before them, nearly two centuries earlier. His achievement, in the words of Professor Norman Davies, author of *Europe* (1996) and *The Isles* (1999), was 'by any objective measure ... colossal'.[3]

This book reveals how Lingard was able to create a methodology of scientific source criticism which he applied to all the original materials covering the whole range of English history up to 1688. In so doing, he also created the conditions in which historical writing could become an independent discipline, concerning itself primarily with the pursuit and exposition of the truth about the past. In contrast, the other more celebrated historians of England in the eighteenth and nineteenth centuries – David Hume and Lord Macaulay – saw history as a branch of philosophy and 'fine literature', respectively.

The chapters that follow explore this 'scientific' methodology which forms the substructure of Lingard's monumental work, explaining how and why it was created and how it led to a radical reshaping of English history. The book is the result of original research, based on an intensive study of Lingard's work, together with insights from the fine collection of his letters deposited at Ushaw College, near Durham. It reveals, too, the contemporary culture within which Lingard was working and from which he was able to break free. The customary opinion until now has been that there was nothing in England at this time, to compare with the scientific advances in historiography on the Continent. Written as a long overdue tribute to the work of a truly great English historian, the work has radical implications for the history of English historical writing.

Lingard once answered a critic by saying that 'Time and Experience must decide between us'.[4] The year 2001 is 150 years after Lingard's death. It seems timely that historians should celebrate this anniversary by recognizing at last the nature and extent of his unique and 'colossal' achievement.

In 1956 I completed a research thesis on Lingard's pioneering techniques of source criticism in his *History of England* (1819–30).[5] My research began at University College, Swansea in 1954. In 1955 I was invited by Professor Sir Herbert Butterfield [PLATE 12] – perhaps the most distinguished English figure in the field of historiography in the twentieth century[6] – to continue the project under his supervision, at Peterhouse, Cambridge. I completed the project in the summer of 1956 and in 1957 Butterfield wrote in *George III and the Historians*:

> Now that we are beginning to study the ways in which critical techniques actually developed . . . some historians, like the Catholic Lingard, are acquiring an unexpected significance.[7]

I continued to widen my researches at Cambridge and completed my doctorate there in 1958.[8] Then, after being enthused by reading Jacques Maritain's *Education at the Crossroads* and for several other reasons, I decided to leave the world of research and enter the new and challenging world of Education where I remained for the next 36 years, retiring from my 30-year headship of a Comprehensive school in South Wales at Christmas, 1994.

After retirement I had the time and opportunity to turn to thoughts of publishing the results of my early historical researches. The idea of publishing the work was stimulated, too, by coming across a letter from Butterfield, written in 1967, in which he had urged that these findings should be 'given to the world', because 'your main thesis is so important and the purely historiographical revelations are so interesting'[9] He had died in 1979 and I felt now that I had a new job to do.

The first result of my publishing endeavours was the appearance in 1998 of *The English Nation: the Great Myth,* which included a long chapter on Lingard as a central and seminal figure in English historical writing. The chapter dealt mainly with the way in which Lingard had reshaped the history of England, destroying the 'Great Myth' of the English past, created initially by Henry VIII and Thomas Cromwell. This Myth claimed that England had never really belonged to Europe. It had been an 'Empire' – separate, independent, self-reliant and superior – from the beginning. England had always had its own Church, law and economic and political institutions; and had never had to borrow from or share with Europe. The Reformation had returned England to this marvellous, pristine state of splendid and independent isolation, after various papal ('foreign') attempts to enslave it during the medieval period.

This Myth had dominated English historical writing for most of four centuries. Lingard was intent on avoiding the anglo-centric approach adopted by all his predecessors and on writing from the viewpoint of 'a citizen of the world' as he himself put it.[10] His outlook made him the first English historian to pursue materials from the archives of other countries such as France, Spain and Italy, Malta and Portugal, instead of relying only on English sources.

The chapter in the *English Nation* also explained why Lingard's achievement was dismissed by his contemporaries and successors in the nineteenth and twentieth centuries. English historians, by and large, remained 'hypnotized' by the spell of the 'Great Myth' – a myth supported by the 'idea of progress' which characterized the whig interpretation of English history up to and including our own day. The work of the great 'propagandists' – Thomas Cromwell, John Foxe and Gilbert Burnet[11] – endured for four centuries. It is in the nature of propaganda that it remains highly effective as long as the political context in which it operates is one of triumph and success.[12] Success reinforces the first premise of the argument – false though it is. The 'Great Myth' was sustained by the political, commercial, industrial and imperial progress which brought England to the apogee of its position as a world power at the turn of the nineteenth century. Only in the later twentieth century, with the loss of Empire and world power, has the propaganda supporting the Myth began to be really questioned and probed by modern 'revisionist' historians. Only in this new climate can the real stature of English historians of the past be properly reappraised. Only now, for example, can the argument that John Lingard was a truly 'great' English historian, while David Hume and Lord Macaulay were not, receive a proper hearing.

Towards the end of the chapter on Lingard, I concluded that:

> I can think of no other English historian who has achieved so much. The significance and extent of his achievements have not been recognized by his country or by English historians of historiography. On a professional level

we may recall his words that 'time and experience must decide between us'; his time of recognition may yet come.[13]

I was pleased, therefore, to see that the reviewers of the book regarded the chapter on Lingard as one of its main strengths. Indeed, it seems to have achieved the objective of rescuing him from oblivion and establishing him as a forerunner of the modern revisionist historians who have come, nearly two centuries later, to many of his conclusions, interpretations and judgements.[14]

When the distinguished historian, Professor Norman Davies of London and Oxford Universities, published his innovative history of *The Isles* (1999), he wrote:

> It says much for the limited horizons of English historiography that Lingard never found his way into the company of the recognized 'greats'.[15]

Davies gave more attention to Lingard, to whom he devoted over eight pages, than to any other historian. Having written his own landmark study of *Europe: A History* (1996), he was in a much better position to appreciate the wider perspective which Lingard had brought to his own *History of England*. Davies acknowledged a 'special debt'[16] to *The English Nation: The Great Myth*, in the preface to *The Isles* and ended his account of Lingard's work with this estimate:

> By any objective measure, Lingard's achievement was colossal. There are not many historians who have succeeded in writing a ten or twelve-volume survey of their whole of English History and still fewer have seen their work run into several editions. There are still fewer who have based their conclusions on archival research in many countries, or who have produced an independent, unconventional interpretation. There are almost none who have not been accused by their rivals of serious errors. Yet Lingard passes all these tests. Lord Acton, who was no complacent judge, wrote: 'Lingard never gets anything wrong'. One is left, therefore, with a curious academic mystery. How could Lingard be so consistently overlooked? All those students who pass through the History Departments of Britain's great universities and who never find him on their reading lists should really be wondering why.[17]

It is therefore a great pleasure for me, at the beginning of the twenty-first century – a century and a half after his own death – that 'time and experience' seem to have decided in favour of Lingard after all; and that his time for recognition as one of the most important English historians may have arrived.

It is also a very interesting phenomenon in the history of English historiography that Lingard was so much ahead of his own time, that recognition has come only when a much later generation, benefiting from advances in knowledge over a century and a half, has been able to appreciate his work. Lingard's historical methodology is in contrast to the more celebrated English historians – Hume, Macaulay and Trevelyan – who expressed brilliantly the 'national mood' of their own times and consequently were extremely popular.[18] But they told people what they wanted to hear. There must surely be a more 'timeless' quality about the work of the 'great *historian*. He or she must, in some way, discover and express a kind of *historical* truth – other than 'philosophy' or 'fine literature' – which is of more than merely ephemeral significance.

It is on the basis of this belated recognition of Lingard's importance as a historian that I can now offer the present work as a subject of wider interest. It has been shown that his achievement was precisely to have discovered and expressed truths of lasting value. The next great question is: 'How was he able to do this?'. The task was made possible by the creation and employment of certain approaches to historical writing which were innovative and highly significant. I have mentioned his extension of English source material to the wider area of Continental archives. This provided perspective. Secondly, there was his decision to base his narrative on original sources, the 'fountain head' of historical truth, as he put it, rather than on the 'troubled stream' of secondary sources.[19] These aspects have been described already in *The English Nation: The Great Myth*.[20]

The third, and in some ways the most important of Lingard's major advances in English historical writing, was in the completely unknown field, in England, of source criticism. In short he developed a methodology of technical source criticism, as an auxiliary science to the writing of history. His methodology was consistently employed to form the substructure behind the narrative of the ten large volumes of his *History of England* from the coming of the Romans to 1688. Herein lies the reason for the almost 'timeless' quality of his historical work which placed it to a remarkable degree beyond the strictures of later critics in future generations.[21]

To Lingard, his methodology was simply a process of creating the tools needed to perform his task. He did not seem to understand the wider significance and importance of what he was doing. He was in fact taking the major and most decisive step in the advancement of English historical writing to its modern state as an independent discipline, in pursuit of historical truth.

Lingard believed, as did another great English historian – F. W. Maitland[22] – later, that the essential definition of the activity of being a historian is endeavouring to discover and portray the truth about what happened in the past. The first great step in setting the proper conditions for this enterprise had been taken by Jean Mabillon, the French Maurist monk who in 1681 produced his *De Re Diplomatica*, establishing the 'scientific' rules by which original documents could be authenticated. Mabillon's work was used extensively by English scholars at the turn of the seventeenth century, as the basis for their own superb editions of original documents.[23] Lingard himself made the first full and appreciative use of these original documents as a historian of English history.[24]

Mabillon's great work had in fact been simply his way of responding to a critic who had disputed the authenticity of a certain medieval document. He decided to display in book form the rules he had devised to prove its authenticity and sent this to his critic, who immediately capitulated. Mabillon did not think of the general import of a work which still stands as a foundation stone in the study of the auxiliary techniques needed to authenticate old documents.[25]

The next great step forward in English historiography was when Lingard, standing on the shoulders of Mabillon as it were, saw the need to devise the 'scientific' rules by which the *credibility* of an original document could be identified and assessed. He saw that it was not sufficient to demonstrate the authenticity of original sources, as Mabillon and the scholar-monks had done. There was a need also to get behind the original source and identify the 'source of the source', so as to establish its *reliability as a credible witness to the truth*. The need for this procedure may seem obvious now; but Lingard was the first English historian to recognize the necessity of such an approach and address it seriously. To place his initiative in proper perspective, we have to remind ourselves that the great Mabillon himself had not thought of taking this step.[26]

What made Lingard think of taking this great step forward in English historical writing? The truth is that he does not seem to have thought of it in this way. He was concerned primarily with discovering and presenting the truth about what happened in the past. To achieve this, it was simply necessary to deal with any obstacles that stood in the way. The great obstacle now was the difficulty in establishing the relative reliability or credibility of different and sometimes conflicting sources. He had to deal with this difficulty by establishing a critical methodology, using a range of 'scientific' rules or techniques, devised to establish a source's credibility. Moreover, he knew well that he was faced with a hostile audience; and this made it important for Lingard to show, in his footnotes and appendices, the processes by which he was establishing the truth. Both these factors are clearly present in his mind, as revealed in his private papers.

There was, I believe, a third factor, not shown in his papers, which must, I think, have constituted an important contributory factor in influencing – perhaps unconsciously – his approach to these matters. Lingard was unique among historians of England in having been educated abroad, at the Douai College in France. Here he was educated from his eleventh to his twenty-second year (1782–93) – a crucial period for his intellectual development. Douai was influenced by the great French tradition of critical scholarship established by Jean Mabillon and the other scholarly men of the Bollandist (Jesuit) and Maurist (Benedictine) Orders, who had first applied scientific methods to the authentication of documents – the first great step in the development of source criticism. The Philosophy course at Douai tended to be 'empirical with an element of critical doubt'; the emphasis in the physical sciences was 'definitely experimental'; and classical studies

> inculcated a passion for the study of the ancient past, a classical orientation that also marked the Renaissance and lay at the roots of modern historical consciousness.

Lingard did not commence his Theology course until 1791 and even here there was a leaning towards the critical study of sources. Scholarly criticisim in the elucidaton of old religious texts had long been a skill employed successfully by Continental theologians; and it was from these studies that critical skills were learnt later by the Continental historians.[28] At Douai, Alban Butler, known mainly to us by his *Lives of the Saints*, who died only a decade before Lingard reached the College, represented in his own work this cross-fertilization between theological studies and a scientific approach to the authentication of sources.

All this was part of the air that Lingard breathed at Douai, which had a fine library. There is no direct and material evidence of Lingard's imbibing the principles of Mabillon's *diplomatic* at Douai. All educationists know, however, that attitudes are more often 'caught' than 'taught'. Given an extremely intelligent pupil who is also a naturally inquiring scholar, it is difficult to imagine that Lingard did not benefit from the library, as well as from his courses. He always felt grateful for his education at Douai, so much so as to celebrate every year on the date commemorating his entry. In his own study of Lingard's *Anglo-Saxon Church*, Dr. Phillips mentions the *De Re Diplomatica* which established the new science of *diplomatic,* as something 'which surely underlies Lingard's own study of the texts and charters which furnish the sources'; and traces the 'principal inspiration' of Lingard's work back to this tradition.[29]

Certainly the training which Lingard received at Douai was not available in any English institution at this time. or indeed throughout the nineteenth century.[30] To Lingard, it would have been something which he took for granted, as most students do with regard to their own education.

All this was part of the background to Lingard's great and creative work in English source criticism. It was from the base of this tradition that Lingard went on to respond to the next great challenge. We know that the classical style of writing became the essential characteristic of

Lingard's own prose.[31] His natural approach to history was emphatically empirical rather than theoretical.[32] It seems fair to argue, then, that when he later turned to historical studies, his perception of the need for a critical methodology with which to approach historical sources, arose naturally from the way in which his mind had been trained during a long and formative stage in his intellectual development. As is usual in all great discoveries, the breakthrough did not take place in a vacuum, but rather because the appropriate person was in the right place at the right time, with the necessary ability and a caste of mind which had been prepared already in some way, to respond to the peculiar challenge of the situation.

Unlike Mabillon, Lingard did not write a book on the subject of his methodology of source criticism. He did produce, however, a hundred-page pamphlet when he felt it necessary to defend himself publicly against a violent attack, accusing him of prejudice, by the critic John Allen, in the *Edinburgh Review*. Lingard could not bear to be publicly accused of prejudice, which to him was a terrible offence against the responsibility of being a historian.[33] As it turned out, Allen did us all a service by provoking Lingard into publishing *A Vindication of Certain Passages in the Fourth and Fifth Volumes of the History of England* in 1826. Here Lingard sets out publicly the critical processes behind his treatment of the evidence in the case of the infamous Massacre of St. Bartholomew (1572) [PLATE 28]. This is so important because it was a particularly complex case in which historians know that Lingard's interpretation of the evidence was correct; whereas Lord Acton – a notable figure in English historiography – was completely misinterpreting the event up to fifty years later.[34] Even Ranke, the 'giant' among German 'scientific' historians, was not able to interpret the evidence properly until about 1880.[35] It is invaluable, therefore, to have this statement of the principles of source criticism which guided Lingard on this occasion; and I shall be returning to it in more detail below.[36] Apart from this one pamphlet, however, Lingard's rules of source criticism have to be unearthed from the minutiae of his private papers, letters and his working use of sources as revealed in a very in-depth study of his *History of England*.

Sir Herbert Butterfield had been invited to give the Wiles lectures at Queen's University, Belfast, in 1954. I was at these lectures as one of a group of scholars and researchers in the field of historiography, invited from various universities in Britain. The lectures were published in 1955 under the title of *Man On His Past*. They emphasized the importance of the German contribution to the development of 'scientific' history, which reached its height with the famous Leopold von Ranke (1795–1886). The only English 'hero' was Lord Acton (1834–1902) who became Professor of History at Cambridge University in 1895. Acton had at least appreciated the importance of the German contribution to 'scientific' history, though he published very little himself. His main thoughts on history and historical method had been left in manuscript form in a great collection of his 'cards' left to the University Library in Cambridge. Butterfield had spent a great deal of time researching these manuscripts and one of the key lectures in Belfast was devoted to 'Lord Acton and the Nineteenth-Century Historical Movement'.

There was no mention of Lingard in the lectures themselves, but Butterfield added to the later, published version of them, a chapter called 'Lord Acton and the Massacre of St. Bartholomew' which he had in fact published three years earlier. The publication was included 'in order to provide samples of the way in which the history of historiography may apply itself to specific themes'.[37]

The evidence surrounding this event was so complex that neither Acton nor Ranke was able to achieve completely the now-accepted version of it until well into the second half of the nineteenth century. The problem which baffled both Ranke and Acton, as the latter described it, was that 'no means existed of determining the credibility of the contemporary writers'[38] on this episode. The strange thing, however, which Butterfield noticed in his detailed research into the historiography of the massacre, was that the English historian, Lingard, had somehow been able to interpret the evidence completely accurately and had achieved a full modern understanding of the subject as far back as 1823.

Butterfield made no attempt to account for this at the time, because he knew hardly anything about Lingard at this stage. There must, however, have been some bell ringing in his agile and perceptive mind for he wrote that, when Acton mistakenly accepted certain evidence, Lingard 'had challenged' it 'over forty years before':

> When Acton quoted in 1869 a manuscript source in support of his view that the Massacre was premeditated he laid himself open to the criticism that he did nothing to establish either the authority or the date of the document. Lingard had been right back in 1823 in distrusting this whole part of the evidence: Acton was wrong in claiming – as he once did – that he had established its veracity.[39]

After one of the Wiles lectures in Belfast, Butterfield approached me – a complete stranger – to ask if I was the research student who was working on Lingard. After a discussion, involving a walk around the city centre of Belfast in the rain, he invited me to join him at Cambridge to pursue my research.

There is a continuous, if long interrupted, link between this meeting with Sir Herbert Butterfield in 1954, and the publication of the present volume in 2001 – the 150th anniversary of John Lingard's death. Lingard created single-handedly the methodology of source criticism in English historical writing – a very great achievement for which he deserves and should at last be given the full credit. It changed English historiography completely, providing the basis for the modern writing of history as an independent and fully professional discipline, in pursuit of the truth about the past.

Acknowledgements

I am pleased in the first place to acknowledge the help of people who encouraged my early interest in John Lingard, nearly fifty years ago. My thanks go to my parish priest in Swansea at that time, the late Fr. Pat Lenane, a former teacher, who presented me – a young student of history – with the ten volumes of the best edition (the sixth) of Lingard's *History of England*. These books have formed the basis of a lifetime's interest in Lingard's great work.

I thank Mr. Neville Masterman of the History Department at the University of Wales, Swansea, for our discussions at a very early stage; and the late Mgr. Philip Hughes, author of the three-volume *The Reformation in England* (1954) who had himself developed a great admiration for Lingard's work. I met him in London in 1954 and he confirmed my own growing respect for Lingard as a 'master historian'.

I met Professor Sir Herbert Butterfield, Master of Peterhouse and Vice-Chancellor of Cambridge University, at Queen's University, Belfast in November 1954, and he invited me to work with him at Peterhouse – an extraordinary opportunity to work with a modern master of historiography. During this three-year period I was able to begin to put Lingard's work into perspective within the history of historical writing in England and Europe. It gives me great pleasure to acknowledge my debt to Sir Herbert. He assisted me in many ways and in 1967, when I was in education, he encouraged me to get my work published and 'given to the world'.

In 1999 I met Professor Norman Davies of London and Oxford universities, who had read my first book, *The English Nation: the Great Myth* (1998) whilst in Australia and was good enough to contact me. From that time on he has encouraged me in more ways than he knows, to proceed to the publication of this present study of Lingard's work. I thank him for his considerable interest, friendship and support.

My thanks also to a new friend, the Rev. Dr. Peter Phillips, formerly of Ushaw College, who has provided me with photographs of Lingard and other information which has been of great use. He is editing a book of essays on Lingard to be published later this year.

I also thank Anthony Grahame, Editorial Director at Sussex Academic Press, for immediately seeing the importance of the book and giving me the opportunity of publishing it at the 150th anniversary of Lingard's

Acknowledgements

death. His editorial work has been extraordinarily painstaking and meticulous, and has contributed much to the book.

I dedicate this book, in grateful memory and with my thanks, to my mother and father who always gave me so much help and encouragement; and who guided me into History at a very early stage.

Finally, and most importantly, my sincere thanks to my wife, Andrea, without whose love and support the book could not have been written. In particular I am indebted to her skills in the field of Internet and computer technology. I am grateful to her and our family for helping me to keep things in perspective – an abiding need for all those who devote themselves to the sometimes solitary, if enjoyable, task of writing.

Edwin Jones, Easter, 2001

A Note on Editions and Text Conventions

John Lingard, *A History of England, from the first Invasion by the Romans (to the Revolution in 1688)*:

1st edition	(London, 1819–30), 8 vols
2nd edition	(London, 1824–31), 14 vols
3rd edition	(London, 1825), 14 vols
4th enlarged edition	(London, 1837–8), 13 vols
5th enlarged edition	(London, 1849), 10 vols
6th enlarged edition (& Memoir)	(London, 1854–5), 10 vols

Throughout this book, reference to Lingard's *History of England* will be to the sixth edition (with Memoir) (London, 1854–5, 10 vols), unless otherwise stated.

Reference will also be made to John Lingard, *The History and Antiquities of the Anglo-Saxon Church, containing an account of its origin, government, doctrines, worship, revenues, and clerical and monastic institutions*:

1st edition	(Newcastle, 1806), 2 vols
2nd edition	(Newcastle, 1810), 2 vols
3rd edition	(London, 1845), 2 vols

The text used in this study will be that of the 3rd edition, unless otherwise stated.

All references to the author's earlier work, *The English Nation: The Great Myth*, will be to the second edition of that work (Sutton, 2000), unless otherwise stated.

All text printed in italics (excluding note and reference material) is the author's use of italics for emphasis, unless otherwise stated. Lingard's various methods of source criticism are typographically distinguished (in small capital setting) throughout the text; the purpose is to demonstrate the pervasiveness of Lingard's methodology of source criticism as it relates to different historical periods and historical circumstances.

'My object is truth.'
John Lingard (1806)

'The truer history is, the more powerful it is.'
Lorenzo Valla (1407–57)

'Such has been the power and influence of the postmodernist
critique of history that growing numbers of historians
themselves are abandoning the search for truth,
the belief in objectivity, and the quest for a
scientific approach to the past.
For my own part, I remain optimistic that objective truth is both
desirable and achievable. I will look humbly at the past and
say despite them all: it really happened, and we really
can, if we are very scrupulous and careful and self-
critical, find out how it happened and reach
some tenable though always less than final
conclusion about what it meant.'
Richard Evans, *In Defence of History* (1997)

Introduction: The Background to Lingard's Work

'Piety and truth must never be considered as separable, for honest and genuine piety will never come into conflict with the truth.'
Jean Mabillon

'My object is truth ... through the work I made it a rule to tell the truth whether it made for us or against us.'
John Lingard

The Greek philosopher Pyrrho (*c.*360–*c*270 BC) is regarded as the founder of scepticism. He taught the doctrine of universal nescience – that we can have no certain knowledge of anything. His was fundamentally a doctrine of despair; for it meant that there was no possibility of discovering the truth in religion, philosophy, history, science, or anything else. While appealing possibly to a certain cast of mind or temperament, Pyrrho's approach could hardly be described as an incentive to the pursuit of truth.

Christianity taught a completely different view of the world. The Judaeo-Christian belief in *one* God contained the seeds of those principles of cohesion, integration and universality, which were to blossom in Western philosophy. The universe was now unified in a fundamental sense, as opposed to the fragmentation and inconstancy of the pre-Christian world, dominated by various and opposing gods.[1] Divine Revelation, through Scripture and the Church, mediated certain truths to mankind; but God-given reason was also a valid instrument for pursuing truth in all the various realms of human endeavour. The universe is intelligible to human reason. This is the fundamental basis for the activity of being a theologian, philosopher, scientist, historian, or indeed for any other pursuer of truth of any kind. It is a spur to the human intelligence in all its pursuits. It was the reason for the great intellectual advances in European history associated with scholastic humanism, the Renaissance and the huge development of modern science.

The history of human thought has witnessed, from time to time, a re-enactment of this perennial clash between these two opposing doctrines.

Introduction: The Background to Lingard's Work

In seventeenth-century France, Pierre Bayle (1647–1706) led a group of 'Pyrrhonistic' thinkers who declared that it was impossible to discover any historical truth. It seemed for a time that the subject of History as an academic subject might be invalidated.[2] It was not accidental that the great defenders of History as a discipline in pursuit of that truth emerged in two religious centres. A group of Jesuit scholars, working in Belgium on the *Acta Sanctorum* (editions of the lives of the saints and other scholarly texts) became known as Bollandists, after John Bolland who had produced the first two volumes of these texts in 1643. Led by the scholarly Fleury, they had become experts on investigating the authenticity of original texts. In France, a group of Benedictine scholar-monks, working originally in the monastery of St. Maur-sur-Loire, but later in Paris, became known as the Maurists. They produced, in the second half of the seventeenth century, fundamentally important works on the scientific methods of establishing the authenticity of old documents. These scholars included important names such as Papebranche, de Tillemont and Montfaucon, as well as the greatest of them all – Jean Mabillon, the scholar-monk who led the Maurists. These individuals provided the group work from which emerged the various critical sciences, auxiliary to the work of the historian. These sciences enabled them to establish beyond doubt the authenticity, or not, of original documents. Now history, for the first time, could be said to be founded on rock rather than sand. These religious scholars took the lead in Europe in saving the study of history as an independent and valid discipline, concerned with discovering the truth about what happened in the past, against the attacks of the contemporary Pyrrhonistic thinkers.[3]

These continental scholars of the seventeenth century also prepared the subject of history for the modern world in another way. They, like John Lingard later, had themselves been trained in philosophy, logic and metaphysics as part of their general seminary education, before they embarked on their specialist careers as historians. Again, like Lingard, they were able to make the necessary distinctions between the different aspects of truth pursued in these separate areas of knowledge. Mabillon had no difficulty, for example, in conceding that the science involved in the criticism of charters could not achieve 'metaphysical' or philosophical certainty; but then this was not the type of truth with which historians are concerned. Historical truth, like all scientific or empirical truth, is attained by distinguishing accurately between the probable and the improbable. Marc Bloch has pointed out in the twentieth century that historical criticism is like most other sciences 'except that it undoubtedly deals with a more subtle graduation of degrees'.[4]

Truth, in terms of historical criticism, is like the truth by which we all live our practical lives. The highest level of practical truth is that which distinguishes the infinitely likely from the infinitely unlikely. Marc Bloch

Introduction: The Background to Lingard's Work

uses the example that it is not *theoretically impossible*, but simply *infinitely unlikely*, that a monkey, given a typewriter to play with, could accidentally but consistently hit the right keys to produce Shakespeare's *Hamlet* as a finished product. It is this type of truth with which historians *qua* historians are concerned. It is the failure to make such distinctions which produced so many of the theoretical problems predicated in the work of post-modernist theorists at the end of the twentieth century. It is also the lack of training in the difference between metaphysical and practical truth which has made some practising historians unnecessarily diffident in stating their aims in pursuing historical truth. By making these distinction, Mabillon and his colleagues were setting the background for the eventual appearance of historical writing as a distinctive discipline, in search of a truth which is as valid as that sought after by other practical sciences, though having a 'more subtle gradation of degrees' of truth. This is a form of truth which is different from (though not opposed to) the truth pursued by theologians, philosophers and metaphysicians.

The main emphasis in the pursuit of historical truth by Mabillon and his colleagues in the last quarter of the seventeenth century was on the practical aim of establishing the authenticity of certain original sources such as documents, charters, inscriptions and manuscripts – involving the scientific examination of dates, paper, ink and signatures; as well as the various types of non-literary evidence such as coins, medals and artefacts of various kinds. Among the great scientific treatises produced at this time, in the fields of diplomatics, palaeography, numismatics, iconography and epigraphy, the most distinguished and influential was the famous *De Re Diplomatica* (1681), published by the brilliant young Maurist scholar, Jean Mabillon, to describe the methods for deciphering old writings and establishing their authenticity, including dates and signatures. A modern scholar A. Momigliano, has written with considerable feeling of appreciation and indebtedness, that 'We cherish the memory of Jean Mabillon' for his advocacy of the critical and impartial approach to historical sources.[5] Mabillon embodied the qualities of mind as well as the professional expertise which should characterize the historian in pursuit of the truth.[6]

Mabillon's work formed the cornerstone for the building of modern studies in this field of learning. Montfaucon, during the same period, extended Mabillon's palaeographical studies to Greek writing and gave to the new science its modern title – palaeographica graeca.[7]

In seventeenth-century England there were no great 'schools' of historical learning. The eminent Cambridge medievalist, C. R. Cheney wrote:

> As a result of the Reformation England was denied the direct benefit of such schools of learned discipline as the reform of the Religious Orders on the Continent provided. We had no Bollandists to inculcate sound principles of

Introduction: The Background to Lingard's Work

hagiology, no Maurist community to construct gradually a science of diplomatics.[8]

The only phenomenon in England remotely similar to the group-scholarship taking place on the Continent in the second half of the seventeenth century was the activity of the Non-juring scholars who did not live in community but did keep in fairly close contact with one another.[9]

The influence and inspiration of Mabillon and his fellow scholar-monks on the English scholars – especially the Non-jurors – of the late seventeenth and early eighteenth centuries, is one of the interesting findings of my research into their activities.[10] The question of the authenticity of the Gospels, for example, concerned all Christians and we find Mabillon being invoked by Archdeacon Nicolson in a letter concerning the assertion of 'the Doctrine of the Trinity by proving the text of St. John's Epistle authentic and canonical':

> The best rules for distinguishing the date of MSS. are to be had in F. Mabillon's learned treatise *De Re Diplomatica*. If you have that book, you need no further help.[11]

Here again, as on the Continent, we see the study of the scriptures by religious scholars leading to extremely important developments in the study of the scientific aspect of historical writing.

Between 1680 and 1730 the Non-juring scholars, such as Thomas Hearne, produced accurate editions of original documents which were later to form a sound basis for modern scholarship. These scholars, 'outlawed' and persecuted by the English establishment and society,[12] were inspired by continental influences. Dr. George Hickes, for example, was the greatest figure in Anglo-Saxon studies at this period. He had learned his craft from Mabillon's great work on diplomatics and his own *Linguarum Veterum Septentrionalium Thesaurus*, which began to appear in 1703, was literally an epoch-making factor in the history of Anglo-Saxon scholarship. His work earned the praise of the master. Mabillon said that Hickes was 'a truly learned Person – not one of those Writers who did not understand their Subject to the Bottom . . . that learned Man is one of ten thousand'.[13]

Thomas Hearne [PLATE 9] was another great English editor of original texts, who owed much of his inspiration to Mabillon. The French scholar was always the model present in Hearne's mind. Hearne used his work to indicate the errors in the work of others.[14] In 1721 he wrote to a friend, mentioning that he has not yet seen the second edition of Mabillon's *De Re Diplomatica*, and wondered, in regard to a particular point, whether there is anything to add to 'the original Ed' which he had by his side.[15] In another letter Hearne mentions that a certain scholar has evidently not seen Mabillon's views on a certain subject.[16] Indeed there are occasions

Introduction: The Background to Lingard's Work

when Hearne seems to be consciously seeing himself as a kind of English Mabillon or Montfaucon. Writing in 1713, he refers to a particular manuscript which he intends to print:

> Had either ... Mabillon, or Montfaucon seen this MS. they would without doubt (if we may judge from what they have done – what indeed is prodigious – for the promotion of Learning), have either transcribed it themselves, or at least have procured a Transcript of it, & forwith printed it, & that too, I believe, in Capitals, in the same manner as I do'.[17]

A modern authority tells us that 'Hearne had a respect for the sanctity of an original authority which had been shared by none of his predecessors and that he worked with an extraordinary accuracy, even when judged by the most rigid standards'. His editions 'set up new standards in the editorship of such texts' and constitute a 'work of national importance'.[18] We may well assume that Mabillon could be proud of his English protegée whom he had never met and who was ridiculed by the polite society of eighteenth-century England.[19]

Mabillon's *De Re Diplomatica* established the sciences of diplomatics and palaeography. Even now it is regarded as a classic text book for aspiring scholars. Together with his French colleagues and his English followers he achieved – in establishing the authenticity of original documents – the first great stage in the setting up of History as a valid professional discipline, equipped for the pursuit of truth, instead of a trivial, if pleasurable, kind of fanciful hobby. This stage was an essential prerequisite for the modern study of history and it was as far as they were able to go in the seventeenth century. It is a humbling experience for us, if we perceive it properly, that Mabillon lacked something which we now take for granted. He 'had little conception of the principle of "authority" in the use of a source other than the evidence of external criticism He failed to perceive the importance of the "source of the source"'.[20]

The 'source of the source' was going to be the second great stage in the development of historical research and writing into its modern form. It was going to be the great contribution of John Lingard to the development of historical writing in England. The fascinating aspect of the story is that nobody seems to have fully appreciated the extraordinary importance of Lingard's unique contribution in this field. Nor was his work taken up by other contemporary historians so as to become a recognizable stage in the development of historical writing in general in England. It was something which appeared long before its time and has not been properly understood. This situation was partly because of the unpopularity of the revisionist account of English history which Lingard's source criticism maintained; and partly because his scientific techniques of source criticism have had to be unearthed from the minutiae of his working papers, letters and footnotes. They were never published – with one

Introduction: The Background to Lingard's Work

exception – in the form in which Mabillon had presented his discoveries in the *De Re Diplomatica*.

When Lingard stated his intention of rewriting the history of England from original sources, he was proclaiming a new approach. It led him immediately to recognize the importance of the valuable editions of original documents produced by the antiquarian and Non-juring scholars of the seventeenth and early eighteenth centuries, which could be relied on for their authenticity.

Their work had been undervalued and even ridiculed in the eighteenth century. For example, one of the ablest of the editors of original documents, Thomas Hearne [PLATE 9],[21] had been derided by 'polite' society in the age of 'enlightenment and reason'. Those who were consumed with the idea of 'progress' looked down on anyone who bothered to study the 'dark ages' of the medieval period. By the time of his death in 1735, Hearne had become a figure of ridicule rather than a figure of persecution from which he had suffered earlier.[22] In 1736 there appeared a posthumous attack written 'by several Hands' in the *Impartial Memorials of the Life and Writings of Thomas Hearne*:

> *Hearnius* behold in Closet close y-pent
> Of sober Face with learned Dust besprent
> To *future* ages will his Dulness last
> Who hath preserv'd the Dulness of the Past.[23]
> [original italics]

When his beloved books were sold, a sheet was attached to the inside cover of his own manuscript catalogue, with the scornful words: 'Pox on't quoth Time to Thomas Hearne. Whatever I forgot You learn.'[24] He was ridiculed for the very qualities which we now regard as his greatest editorial virtues. He refused, for example, to change the original document in any way. He painstakingly copied words – as his critics scornfully noted – which were 'plainly redundant' as well as 'manifestly wrong' – though he added notes to show that he knew of the mistakes which he was faithfully copying. The *Memorials* concluded in summary, that 'after *wasting* not employing, a Life of Fifty odd Years, on the Tenth Day of *June, 1735* this *Studier* and *Preserver of Monkish Trumpery* gave up the Ghost'.[25]

Lingard seems to have been the first English historian to have fully recognized – and fully utilized – the importance of the Non-juring contribution to English scholarship. This is hardly surprising. Lingard's own work on old texts and charters, both in his *The History and Antiquities of the Anglo-Saxon Church* (1806) and in the *History of England*, shows sufficient evidence of his familiarity with the precepts and rules of the science of diplomatics which Mabillon had established in 1681 and which Hearne had eagerly copied in his scholarly editions of old texts.[26]

Introduction: The Background to Lingard's Work

Lingard wanted to rewrite the history of England, based completely on original sources; and here was a repository of such sources, based on unexceptionable standards of editorship. While preparing his *History*, he wrote to a friend in 1818:

> Now of the books I most want ... They are principally Hearne's publications. I have a few of his publications; and lately wrote to London to buy a few others. I had persuaded myself that an octave of two volumes would not cost above 30/-. What was my surprise, when I found from Booker that he could get none under five guineas. This was what my finances would not bear; and unless I borrow them, I must continue my journeys to Manchester to consult them.[27]

Similarly, Lingard made good use of Henry Wharton's great collection of medieval Church documents, the *Anglia Sacra* (1692), now recognized as a work which is:

> indispensable to the study of English monastic chronicles ... a work of the first importance ... with which the comparative study of English monastic chronicles for the first time became possible.

The *Anglia Sacra* was a collection of original materials which might 'subserve a scientific history of the medieval Church in England;[28] and in Lingard's hands – for the first time – it did.

Equally, Lingard used the collection of documents published by other Non-juring scholars such as Henry Gale and Sir George Hickes, for his work on the Anglo-Saxon period.[29]

Lingard shared the admiration which modern scholars have learned to have for the splendid editions of original texts, faithfully and rigorously produced by these earlier scholars. Inspired by Mabillon's expertise, they had replicated the latter's work on the Continent with their own accurate publication of documents in England. Lingard valued and used, also, the work of still earlier seventeenth-century scholars associated with the Society of Antiquaries, such as Sir Henry Spelman (the *Concilia*, 1639) and Sir William Dugdale (the *Monasticon*, 1655).[30] These seventeenth-century scholars had achieved the first great step forward in the development of modern scholarship in England, by retrieving and preserving original documents.

Like all great innovators, Lingard stood on the shoulders of his predecessors whose achievements he recognized and valued. We know that he had studied the work of Fleury, the Bollandist scholar; and that he had commended the importance of Bollandist and Maurist scholarship in his *Anglo-Saxon Church*, where he had used original sources and manuscripts in Anglo-Saxon and Latin.[31] It was from this basis that he accomplished the next great stage in English historiography – the science of source criticism. In his pursuit of historical truth, he realized that it was

Introduction: The Background to Lingard's Work

not enough to have established the authenticity of original documents. Though this was an essential prerequisite, it was only the first part of the challenge. Having established by scientific means, that documents were genuinely *authentic* and not forgeries, Lingard was the first Englishman to proceed to the next stage of asking whether or not they could be established as credible or reliable witnesses to the truth – again by scientific means.

He set out a proper questioning procedure. Were the authors in a position to know the truth? Were they likely to be prejudiced or interested parties? Did they have vested interests? From where did they get their information? This last question introduced the famous 'source of the source' technique as a key instrument in the historian's craft. Finally: what 'scientific' rules could be established by which the reliability of the source's information could be assessed? Such questions as these had to be answered in order to establish and prioritize the authority of authentic documents. Moreover, and very usefully for us, Lingard had to demonstrate this critical process to a potentially hostile audience, so that his readers, too, could be convinced by the evidence. He did this by an unprecedented use of footnotes (and appendices), in which he showed how he had arrived at his conclusions with regard to the necessary 'weighting' of the various pieces of evidence.

To place Lingard's work into perspective, we can contrast his approach with that of two of the most famous of English historians, one who preceded him and one whose work came slightly after him – David Hume [Plate 8] (*History of England*, 1754–63) and Lord Macaulay (*History of England*, 1848–62). Each was the most popular historian of his own day, portraying a highly acceptable account of the English past. Both are still highly esteemed in the English academic world, Hume's work being regarded as a prime representative of Tory historical writing, and Macaulay seen as 'unquestionably the greatest of the Whig historians'.[32]

Hume's *History* was the most prestigious work in England during the century following its publication. Two hundred editions of it have appeared since. But Hume was primarily a philosopher. His historical work was made to fit into the philosophical principles and theories which he held beforehand. He had no conception of the critical use of sources. He had an attitude of contempt for the medieval period, which was characteristic of the 'age of enlightenment and reason' in the eighteenth century. Like his contemporaries, he was 'so sure of being right on the subject of life and the universe'[33] and disrespectful to the people of the past – a major obstacle, therefore, to his historical understanding.

Hume simply repeated the view of his predecessors, that the 'Dark Ages' were dominated by ignorance, superstition and obscurantism. Here, ironically, we are truly in the 'dark ages' of English historical writing, if we regard it as an independent discipline. Hume, the philosopher, was not

Introduction: The Background to Lingard's Work

primarily interested in the historical truth or facts. He regarded history as a branch of philosophy, a view which was typical of his times. In his philosophical work, *Enquiry Concerning Human Understanding* (1748), he had indicated his views about the study of history:

> Its chief use is only to discover the constant and universal principles of human nature, by showing men in all varieties of circumstances and situations, and furnishing us with the regular springs of human action and behaviour.[34]

In the Preface to his *History of England*, Hume described his unconcern for original research and factual detail:

> I have inserted no original papers and entered into no detail of minute uninteresting facts. The philosophical spirit which I have so much indulged in all my writings, finds here ample materials to work upon.[35]

To move from Hume's account of the coming of Christianity to Britain to that of Lingard, for example, is to become aware that one is moving from one world to another in terms of the development of English historical writing. Hume writes:

> Christianity was introduced into Britain at an early period, in all probability however, not through Rome, but from the East ... The most probable tradition ascribes the adoption of Christianity in Britain as an established religion, to Prince Lucius, or Leuer Maur (the Great Light), who flourished some time in the second half of the second century.[36]

This old myth, that Britain was converted to Christianity originally by missionaries from the East, had been part of the great attempt at the time of the Reformation, to show that Britain had not been brought into the Catholic Church by its representatives from Continental Europe. This was an essential part of the 'Great Myth' and it continued to hold sway through the nineteenth century and into the twentieth.[37] Hume was content simply to repeat it.

Lingard's statement below, written in 1819 on the same subject, leaps ahead into the world of modern scholarship. It is based upon the same primary sources as those used by modern scholars:

> Nothing can be less probable in itself, nor less supported by ancient testimony, than the opinion that Britain was converted by oriental missionaries. The only foundation on which it rests is, that in the seventh century, the Britons did not keep Easter on the same day as the church of Rome. That, however, they did so in the beginning of the fourth century is plain from Eusebius (Vit. Con. iii. 19), Socrates (Hist. v. 22) and the Council of Arles (Spelman, pp. 40, 42) ...[38]

It is surprising that modern historians should have represented the Britons

INTRODUCTION: THE BACKGROUND TO LINGARD'S WORK

as holding different doctrines from those professed by the Roman missionaries, though these writers have never produced a single instance of such difference . . . Bede has related with great minuteness all the controversies between the two parties. They all regard points of discipline. Nowhere does the remotest hint occur of any difference respecting the doctrine.[39]

In quoting Bede's *Ecclesiastical History of the English Church and People* (731), Lingard was referring to a source which was generally out of fashion among English historians, because it was 'tarred with the Papist brush'.[40] Lingard himself rated Bede very highly, using him as a primary source,[41] and modern historians have learnt to do the same.[42] The eminent Anglo-Saxon scholar, Sir Frank Stenton, wrote in 1946 that Bede's work:

> belongs to the small class of books which transcend all but the most fundamental conditions of time and place . . . [Bede's] work can be judged as strictly as any historical writing of any time.

Bede's Preface 'reads like the introduction to a modern work of scholarship' and, in short, 'he had reached a conception of history'.[43] In 1995 D. Bates wrote that Bede's 'range of learning was prodigious and his scholarship rigorous'; his *History*

> is by far the best source of information for the conversion of the English to Christianity, not only because of the record of events it supplies, but also because of the care that Bede took to recount particular incidents in detail.[44]

In 1997 another modern scholar, A. E. Redgate, wrote of Bede, that 'his scientific scholarship was advanced' and 'modern scholars . . . depend heavily on him'. His book was 'well written and researched . . . subtle and complex'[45] [PLATE 2].

We can now fully appreciate Lingard's estimate of Bede: 'If the reader looks into his writings, he will be astonished at the depth and variety of his statements.'[46] Lingard's, however, was a lone voice contending against a long-established alienation from Bede, seen – according to the 'Great Myth' – as one of the 'papist' enemies.

Lord Macaulay's reputation was immense in the nineteenth century and remained so up to the end of the twentieth century [PLATE 13]. He told the English people what they wanted to hear – that they were a superior people and that their history demonstrated this.[47] He was also a very gifted writer and orator who believed that history was a branch of literature, rather than an independent discipline in its own right. He had a rather cavalier attitude towards the historical pursuit of truth or facts:

> My accuracy as to facts I owe to a cause. The past is in my mind soon constructed into a romance.[48]

Introduction: The Background to Lingard's Work

He stated that he wanted in his *History* to 'produce something which shall for a few days supersede the latest fashionable novel on the tables of young ladies'.[49] It is now recognized, even by those who most admire his other brilliant qualities, that a 'great gulf' separated him from 'the new German pioneers of historical method and source criticism'.[50] He regarded Sir Walter Scott, founder of the historical novel, as 'the master' in historical writing.[51] Sir Charles Firth, the editor and commentator on Macaulay's *History*, wrote:

> He treats history throughout as a part of literature or 'a department of literature' is his precise phrase . . . So long as history was regarded as an art, truth and accuracy were matters of minor importance compared to the artistic statement of facts or what were supposed to be facts.[52]

Macaulay made an attack on Lingard, accusing him of being one whose 'great fundamental rule of judging seems to be that the popular opinion cannot possibly be correct'.[53] Unfortunately for Macaulay, the occasion for this attack was a subject on which both Macaulay and his famous great-nephew Sir G. M. Trevelyan a century later have been proved to be wrong, whereas Lingard is now seen to have given the correct version.[54]

Lingard's private opinion of these two popularly-conceived 'greats' of English historical writing – Hume and Macaulay – was not very flattering. He was reacting against all that they stood for. In the Preface to his *History*, he attacked the idea, so characteristic of the previous age of 'enlightenment and reason', that history was a branch of philosophy. It is interesting to note that Lingard himself had been trained in Philosophy and Theology and was well-equipped to draw the proper lines between these subjects and history as an independent discipline. He writes:

> It is long since I disclaimed any pretensions to that which has been called the philosophy of history, but with more propriety be called the philosophy of romance . . . If they indulge in fanciful conjectures, if they profess to detect the hidden springs of every event, they may display acuteness of investigation, profound knowledge of the human heart, and great ingenuity of invention; but no reliance can be placed upon their statements . . . They come before us as philosophers who undertake to teach from the records of history: they are in reality literary empirics who disfigure history to make it accord with their philosophy. Nor do I hesitate to proclaim my belief that no writers have proved more successful in the perversion of historic truth than speculative and philosophic historians.[55]

Lingard does not mention Hume by name, for he never did make personal attacks on individuals. He devotes himself, objectively as always, to attacking the approach to history which Hume stood for. In private, however, he writes to a friend:

Introduction: The Background to Lingard's Work

> Why do you want the hallucinations of Hume? From me it is impossible that you can get them. I have never looked into Hume since I left Ushaw in 1811, unless on three occasions, for passages to which my attention was directed by others. I have not time to take and read for that purpose.[56]

Lingard, in fact, had clearly recognized a fault in such writing, which was to be the bane of much historical work in the nineteenth and twentieth centuries. Such ideas were at the heart of historicism – teaching that historical events are governed by 'laws'. This helped to spawn political ideologies – such as Marxism and Fascism – which created havoc and great loss of life in twentieth-century Europe.

One of Lingard's main rules of historical writing was that *the historian must always start with the facts, properly established and set in the proper sequential order. The historian must always be ready to be surprised by the facts. He opposed determinedly the approach of starting with ideas or theories, philosophical, religious or otherwise.*

The reason for this approach is set out quite clearly by Lingard in a letter written towards the end of his life explaining what lay behind the above-mentioned remarks about 'the philosophy of history'. In 1828, François Guizot (1787–1874), the French historian, had written his *Histoire Générale de la Civilisations en Europe depuis la Chute de l'Empire Romain, jusqu'a la Révolution Françoise*, which was an attempt to account for the rise and fall of European civilizations in theoretical terms, just as later Marx and Oswald Spengler were going to fit history into their ideologies. Concerning this, Lingard explained his opposition quite simply, in a way that now seems to us, with our knowledge of the effects of historicism, so obviously true; but which was something new and prophetic when he wrote:

> I saw plainly that every historical fact was distorted by him [Guizot] to make it support his own preconceived theory.[57]

For Lingard, it was essential that history should be 'earthed' to the facts; and the facts must be determined by the best 'scientific' methods available. Any cautious generalizations could arise only at a secondary stage of the historian's methodology; *after* a reflective survey of the established facts. They should not arise from preconceived theories which are then imposed on the facts. It was essential that the historian should be prepared to be surprised by the evidence.

It was significant, in this respect, that Lingard always showed great interest in archaeological findings and in the journal *Archaelogica*. He used these findings with good effect as very useful parts of his wide range of techniques of source criticism. The proven existence of a solid 'concrete' fact had its own fascination for him because he, like the scientist, realized its fundamental importance in the pursuit of truth. He was particularly

Introduction: The Background to Lingard's Work

pleased, at the end of his life, to be appointed vice-president of the British Archaelogical Association.

The modern professional historian would take exactly the same attitude about the subservience of theory to fact. However, he or she has the benefit of hindsight. Lingard was adopting this highly professional attitude in the first half of the nineteenth century. I have not come across any other historian in this period who saw so clearly the dangers of 'philosophic history' and expressed his opposition so vigorously.

Writing again near the end of his life, just after Macaulay's *History* was beginning to appear, Lingard wrote to another friend:

> It will not do. Macaulay does not write history. One half of the quotations from him are of no authority ... You might as well believe all the skits and witticisms & falsehoods which are prevalent during a contested election.[58]

This judgement of Macaulay's lack of historical method and source criticism was confirmed a century later;[59] but it was not until the very end of the twentieth century, in 1997, that a modern scholar, P. Ghosh, has dared to say that any enduring status for Macaulay can rest only on his literary work as an essayist, not on his *History*.[60]

Lingard was the first English historian to firmly establish the base on which history could stand as an independent discipline, concerned ultimately with the pursuit of historical truth, using its own methodologies and auxiliary sciences of source criticism. Style, for Lingard, was simply the vehicle within which historical truth could be best purveyed. Indeed his own style, based on a classical training, was ideal for this purpose – short, clear, well-crafted sentences which are a perfect model for the expression of meaning. As such his style has an artistic elegance and attraction of its own.

Interestingly, in his own day, Lingard was criticized for lacking the type of 'philosophical' and 'flowery' language to which the public had been accustomed at that time. Lingard's style is, however, timeless. His work can be taken up today and read with as much ease and clarity as it was in his own day. A distinguished modern historian has commented to me on this aspect of Lingard's work.[61] It seems to be the kind of style adopted by historians who have defined their purpose as being that of pursuing and expressing historical truth, as opposed to those, like Hume and Macaulay, who see history as a branch of some other activity. It is apparent again in the work of F. W. Maitland[62] at the end of the nineteenth century, or in that of Sir Maurice Powicke or Professor Dom David Knowles in the twentieth century.[63] In my view, style seen as essentially a vehicle for conveying historical truth is a mark of the true historian.

Lingard's own attitude to historical writing is completely in tune with his view of it as an independent discipline, in pursuit of the truth about what happened in the past; just as the scientist is in pursuit of scientific

Introduction: The Background to Lingard's Work

truth in the natural world and the poet is in pursuit of truth in the world of human feelings and emotions. Of course, the post-modernist critic will repeat the despairing message of Pyrrho, that they are all pursuing a mirage, because the truth cannot be found. Failing an acceptance of the validity of the human intelligence and the intelligibility of the universe, these critics may at least reflect on the fact that the great achievements and discoveries in all realms of human intellectual endeavour have been made by those who have so believed, and in doing so have brought great benefits to mankind.

At the very outset of his career as a historian, Lingard wrote in 1806, that: 'My object is truth'.[64] In 1819 he wrote to a friend just after the publication of the first volume of his *History of England*:

> Through the work, I made it a rule to tell the truth whether it made for us or against us.[65]

Consequently, when the *History* appeared it was attacked by some Catholics who had expected him to defend their 'side' always, in the manner of previous historians since the Reformation. He received a complaint, for example, that he had been prejudiced against the monks in his account of the dissolution of the monasteries, because he had accepted that some abuse had existed, though nothing on the scale alleged by Cromwell's 'interested visitors'. Lingard's answer to this was typical of his attitude:

> Perhaps he would have me deny the whole charge... To have met the charge by denying it would have been to have acted 'contrary to my conscience' since I believed it in many respects true.[66]

Lingard's scholarly and unprejudiced approach was something new in English historical writing. The Catholic, Mgr. Talbot denounced Lingard's *History* as a betrayal. Bishop Milner tried to get the Irish bishops to join in the condemnation. It was in answer to such attacks from some fellow Catholics that the values at the heart of Lingard's activity as a historian are revealed. He wrote to a friend in 1820, just after the first volumes of the *History* had appeared:

> Your friend thinks I should have occasionally assumed a tone of piety & betrayed something more of a bias towards the Catholic cause. I think that if I wished to do good, I ought to have written as an independent spectator. Time and experience must decide between us. Should their verdict be against me, no one will deplore my misjudgment more than myself.[67]

Lingard was following in the footsteps of Jean Mabillon, who had also been an avid pursuer of the truth. Both were men of great integrity. Both were devoted to the truth as well as to their religion. Indeed, for them there was no conflict between the two. We shall see in this study that

Introduction: The Background to Lingard's Work

Mabillon's words on the vocation of a historian are reflected exactly in Lingard's own words and working practises:

> If he [the historian] be honest; therefore he must present as certain, things certain, as false, things false, and as doubtful, things doubtful; he must not seek to hide facts that tell for or against either party to any issue. Piety and truth must never be considered as separable, for honesty and genuine piety will never come into conflict with the truth.[68]

The same quality is to be found in another great English scholar, F. W. Maitland (1850–1906) who has been described variously as 'By common consent one of the great British historians';[69] 'the greatest of Cambridge scholars';[70] and 'arguably the greatest of all historians of medieval England'.[71] Maitland described his main purpose in writing history, quite simply, as being to ensure that 'mankind should believe what is true, and reject what is false' in the field of historical knowledge.[72] Such a statement would seem ridiculously naive to our present-day 'post-modernists'; but there is no denying that such an aspiration inspired historical work of the very highest calibre. The pursuit of truth seems to have been a common denominator in the work of all great scholars and creative writers and scientists.

Lingard stated his own priorities as a historian. He wrote to a friend in 1819, the year in which the first volume of the *History* appeared:

> But style is become with me a secondary object. The task I have imposed upon myself of taking nothing on credit but of going to the original author, is so laborious that I have no time to throw away on the graces of style.[73]

Twenty-seven years later, referring again to his intense activity in preparing the last edition of the *History*, and intent on consulting all original materials which had become available since the previous edition of 1837–8, Lingard, at the age of seventy-five, wrote to another friend:

> But you must not expect me to attend to words unless it be accidentally. I have enough to do to attend to facts, dates, and references.[74]

Indeed we shall see that Lingard's insistence on getting the facts right, and then placing them in their correct sequence of time (dates), often enabled him to solve, quite simply, historical problems which had defied the complicated approaches of other historians. He was the fist English historian, for example, to interpret correctly the infamous Massacre of St. Bartholomew – and this before vital and conclusive documents, became available – by placing the correct facts in proper sequence, thus indicating the most probable answer.[75]

His preoccupation with facts did not mean, however, that Lingard's presentation was below par. True, he was criticized by contemporaries for lacking those general, philosophizing passages to which they were accustomed; and they judged him therefore as 'thus certainly falling short of the first rank among historians'.[76] But so, too, they would have judged the Venerable Bede and F. W. Maitland. The public had become used to regarding history as a branch of philosophy or literature.

For Lingard, the search for the truth about the past, resulting from scholarly research, came first. The best style, to him, was simply the one which conveyed the meaning of his historical findings most clearly and simply.

In the old debate as to whether history is an art or a science, my own view is that the arguments are based on a false dichotomy. History, Art, and Science are different ways of finding and expressing the truth about different areas of human experience. Each of them contains elements of the other two; but it is the difference in the proportional importance of the elements which decides whether or not the amalgam is good history, science or art. History is the attempt to discover the truth about the past. Science provides it with methodologies and techniques by which it can gain the correct information. Artistic skills are involved in correlating the facts, derived from a variety of sources, into a proper sequential order within a meaningful whole context. But it can only be judged as good history, in the end, if it is really telling the truth about the past; and in a way which can be understood and appreciated by other ages than its own. There must be a certain timeless element about it; a good standing when judged against the most rigorous standards of a later age.

It is part of the artistic skill of a good historian to bring forth, from the scientifically-established evidence and the complexity of the materials, a clear continuous narrative. But few historians reveal the process by which this takes place. In Lingard's case, we can observe the process by which the clear textual narrative above emerges from the extraordinary wealth of footnotes below, on the pages of his *History*. It is frequently an intriguing and always informative process to observe. From his eagerness to gain the confidence and 'partnership' of his readers, it happens that Lingard's *History* becomes a uniquely clear picture of historical writing in the making. Lingard's invitation to his readers to enter his history-making workshop means that we too, using the skeleton key of posterity, can enter. It is a workshop with which the reading public is still, at the beginning of the twenty-first century, too little familiar. For us, it also includes a fascinating opportunity to judge Lingard's *History* against the most rigorous standards of the present day – two centuries later. In this way it can be tested to see if it reflects simply the cultural ideas and standards of his own day, for, as we have been told recently: 'the key emphases of history have been defined by the dominant cultures and ideas of given periods'.[77] However, it can also be tested to ascertain if, exceptionally, it achieved a higher standard altogether by transcending these factors of contemporary culture. For it is in the achievement of a measure of 'time-

Introduction: The Background to Lingard's Work

less' truth that we can most readily identify the very highest level of human achievement in any field of intellectual activity.

Lingard was well fitted for the task. He knew seven languages, which brought the original documents of the Anglo-Saxon and medieval periods within his range of expertise, as well as documents from other European countries, needed to enable him to fulfil his stated function of writing as a 'citizen of the world'. He was acknowledged as 'the outstanding intellectual of English Catholicism'[78] and the 'sole systematic proponent of the Catholic Enlightenment in England'.[79] He, uniquely for an English historian: 'worked within the centre of European scholarly tradition'.[80] It has been said that, during his forty years of residence there, 'the intellectual centre gravity of English Catholicism rested in Hornby'.[81] [See PLATE I] This, then, was no ordinary Englishman.

We shall see in this study how Lingard pitted these factors, together with his other qualities of personality and character, against the whole weight of contemporary culture and historical tradition in England. There emerged from this conflict a work which achieved an unparalleled measure of that 'timeless' historical truth, when measured against the advance of historical scholarship and understanding in England during the second millennium. Thus stands the basis for my claim that Lingard was the greatest English historian of that millennium, as Bede was of the first.

Chapter 1
An Invitation to the Historian's Workshop

Seeking 'to find the truth, self-consciously aware of the inter-play of opinion and evidence ... using rigorously the best methods and techniques available to exercise a professional and objective judgment'.

Edwin Jones

Historians in England have rarely given us a picture of their professional craftsmanship. In 1951 one observer commented that:

> It must be admitted that historians are reticent about the ways in which they go to work, and that we are at present profoundly ignorant of the nature of historical thinking.[1]

The situation has not changed in the last fifty years in this respect.

It is usually impossible to observe the process by which the historian's narrative has been built up. Yet it is important in historical writing, as in all other spheres of professional activity, for new practitioners in the profession to be able to apprentice themselves to the master-historians. We are very fortunate, in the case of John Lingard, to be able to join him in his workshop, so to speak, and examine the processes and tools with which raw materials were turned into a narrative of the highest quality in terms of historical craftsmanship. This unique opportunity arises because of the peculiar circumstances in which the writing of Lingard's *History of England* (1819–30) took place.

John Lingard was born in the city of Winchester in 1771. He came from a family which had come from the North Wolds. His father was a carpenter, his mother the daughter of a small farmer, both of them Catholics. His mother's family had been impoverished by fine and imprisonment during the temporary revival of Catholic persecution after the 1745 rebellion in favour of the Stuart cause.[2] Lingard himself experienced as a young boy the anti-Catholic Gordon Riots of 1780 which followed the Catholic Relief Act of 1778. In 1782 the boy's exceptional intelligence and natural piety brought him to the notice of Bishop Challoner and his successor, Bishop Talbot. The young boy was given a bursary to enable him to go abroad, at the age of eleven, to the Catholic College of Douai in France where he stayed for the next eleven years. He was an outstanding scholar in the humanities course, before deciding to enter the school of theology. The French Revolution and the resultant declaration of war between England and France in 1793 brought an end to the College, which was occupied by the mob. Lingard saved himself from the revolutionary mob only by fleetness of foot, escaping to England with a group of fellow students.[3]

In 1794 Lingard became director of a group of ex-Douai students who settled at Crook Hall near Durham as a college community. He became vice-president, prefect of studies and head of the schools of Natural and Moral Philosophy at the College. He was ordained a priest at York in 1795. In 1808 the College moved to Ushaw, about five miles outside Durham, where it still stands as the major Catholic seminary of the north [PLATE 3].

It was during his time at Crook Hall that Lingard published his first work, *The History and Antiquities of the Anglo-Saxon Church* (1806), which has been described as 'an important event in the historical scholarship of the time'.[4] He used original sources in Anglo-Saxon and Latin. His friends now urged him to continue his theme and write a complete history of England. Lingard at first refused and his reason was significant: 'He hesitated to embark on an undertaking which might be injurious to the interests of the college'.[5] This was an early manifestation of that sense of extreme caution which his experiences of anti-Catholic prejudice understandably had bred in him.

Lingard remained at the College until 1811 in which year he left Ushaw and became parish priest of a very small and secluded parish at Hornby [PLATE 2], near Lancaster. Here he was to remain until his death in 1851, in spite of offers of the presidency of the Maynooth college in Ireland and of two vacant bishoprics. He had decided to confine himself to his pastoral work in the little parish there and to his historical studies. Apart from two visits to Rome and occasional visits to libraries in Manchester, Liverpool and London, Lingard lived for forty years at Hornby. Writing to help a priest, in trouble with his bishop in 1841, he remarks:

> I like to live in peace and am always glad to heal a quarrel. It has been my constant rule for these 20 years to abstract myself as much as possible from all the petty squabbles that agitate the catholic body.[6]

Another friend said that 'such a thing as a religious feud was never heard of during the whole 40 years he lived in Hornby'. Lingard was friendly with everyone, including, the Anglican rector, Mr. Proctor, and a

Unitarian minister, William Shepherd. He was a keen gardener, fond of nature and animals, especially his big Sicilian poodle called Etna and the tortoise, Moses. He planted an oak tree (brought from Lake Trasimene) which still flourishes in the garden of the Hornby Presbytery; and gave to friends some saplings from it on Easter Sunday 1851, a day before the start of his last illness. To his own parishioners, he was 'th'old doctor' from whose door nobody was ever turned 'empty away'; and whose catechism classes were influential.[7] When he died, the non-Catholic villagers of Hornby placed a plaque as a memorial 'from his friends', which is still there in their local Anglican church.

It was here in comparative isolation that creative work of primary importance for English historical writing took place. Important techniques were developed, by which the reliability of historical sources could be tested and evaluated. Moreover, his work is presented in such a way as to invite the reader to share the processes and methodologies by which he came to his historical findings. It becomes clear to the reader that Lingard's narrative is not based on prejudice or on repetition of what previous historians had written, but on a process of 'scientific' evaluation of evidence.

He used certain techniques and processes which can be repeated, in order to test the value of his source materials. Nobody had done this before in English historiography. How did it come about?

Lingard came from a recusant Catholic family which had suffered persecution. He wrote the first edition of the *History of England* (1819–30) at a time when the country was in ferment over the prospect of Catholic Emancipation which came eventually in 1829. Anti-Catholic feeling expressed itself in 'No-Popery' campaigns, meetings and petitions. The wise and witty Sydney Smith, 'enfant terrible' among his Anglican brethren in the early nineteenth century, vividly describes the contemporary 'No-Popery' fears and hatred[8] and makes the interesting comment:

> Few men will consider the historical view which will be taken of present events... What will be said of all the intolerable trash which is issued forth at public meetings of No Popery? The follies of one century are scarcely credible in that which succeeds it... If the world lasts till 1927, the grandmammas of that period will be far wiser than the tip-top No Popery men of this day.[9]

Historiographical legacies played a central part in all this furore. English people at the beginning of the nineteenth century had all that hostility to and fear of Catholicism which had been bred in them by three centuries of unmitigated literary and oral tradition on the subject. The tradition manifested itself in the Penal Laws against Catholics and in periodical outbursts of irrational hatred such as the Titus Oates Plot (1678) and the Gordon Riots (1780) which led to the loss of many Catholic lives.

In the 1820s the recourse to history took a primary place in the various tracts written against Catholic Emancipation, such as *The Accusations of History against the Church of Rome* (1825), *Christian Martyrdom: Being Authentic Accounts of the Persecutions Inflicted by the Church of Rome on the Protestants*. Also the *History of the Inquisition* (1826), and *Papal Pretensions or The Right of the Church of Rome to Power in Great Britain* (1826). Sydney Smith again made the perceptive comment:

> I have often endeavoured to reflect upon the causes which from time to time, raised such a clamour against the Catholics, and I think the following are among the most conspicuous: i. Historical recollections of the cruelties inflicted upon the Protestants ...

adding that 'The great object of men who love party better than truth is to have it believed that the Catholics alone have been persecutors'.[10]

Certainly the 'official' version of the reign of 'bloody Mary', the massacre of St. Bartholomew (1572) and the Irish Massacre (1641), all figure prominently in the anti-Catholic literature of the time. Catholic Emancipation was regarded as a great threat to the twin pillars of English security, prosperity and independence – the State and its Established Church. This feeling had for long produced a historical legend of its own, in the shape of an early British Church completely independent of Rome.[11]

Contemporary reviews speak eloquently of the suspicion caused by the publication of any work by a Catholic historian, which might counter the 'official' version as purveyed by generations of Protestant historians since the sixteenth century. The *Westminster Review* commented in 1827:

> A history of England by a Roman Catholic priest was assuredly destined to be met with coldness and suspicion. It required merit of a very high order to contend successfully against the prejudice of a nation of Protestants, glorying in the reformation of their ancient creed, and still eying with jealousy and apprehension the adherents of the once predominant faith.

And goes on to admit:

> We acknowledge that, on the first announcement of a History of England from the pen of a priest of the Roman Catholic faith, we did apprehend that neither the spirit of his religion, nor the habits of his profession, were calculated to prepare him for the composition of any impartial work.[12]

The *Edinburgh Review* warns in 1825:

> As the author approaches indeed to the critical period of the Reformation, it may easily be supposed that his partialities will not be less active, or his temptations to unfaithful statements and unfair conclusions less powerful.

We can discover, also, that his political predilections are almost as likely to suborn his accuracy as his ecclesiastical; and that he will require to be watched as closely in his account of our free constitution as of our Protestant Church.[13]

The *Edinburgh Review* looked back in 1831 and observed:

> he exhibited the fathers of the Anglican reformation, and all the circumstances of that great revolution in the laws and opinions of England, so unfavourably, and yet with so perpetual an appeal to authority, that, while many were startled to find their ancient prejudices disturbed without much power of resistance, the champions of orthodox Protestantism were quick to take up the gauntlet, and expose, if they could, the misrepresentation and sophistry which was dimming the lustre of its historical glory. The time drew more than usual attention to such a contest.[14]

Lingard knew very well the climate in which he was writing.[15] He had received a letter, for example, from the Anglican Dean of Peterborough, Dr. Kipling, who complained and threatened because of an earlier work of Lingard's in which he had referred to 'the new church of England' and 'the modern church of England'. These were, said Dr. Kipling: 'seditious words in derogation of the established religion', for which Lingard was 'amenable to a court of justice', since: 'the church as by law established in this country is so inseparably interwoven with the British Constitution, that whatever is calumny on the former must be calumny on the latter.'[16]

It is against the background of this sort of 'audience-reaction' that we can place into perspective Lingard's response to the great challenge that faced him – a nation of readers who would scrutinize every statement of an unpopular character and be only too ready to prove it incorrect or to attack anything resembling partiality in its presentation. In 1822 Lingard wrote to a friend in Rome describing the fate of a Catholic priest in Manchester – a Mr. Can – who had been so unwise as to publish a controversial pamphlet 'in which he displayed talent, though he did not write in a very gentlemanly style':

> But the bigots took the alarm. Pamphlet after pamphlet was published against him: weekly addresses to the labouring classes at one penny each continue to be printed: and at last neither he nor the other priests can walk the streets without insult, and the poor weavers etc. are often turned out of employment by their orthodox masters. To allay the ferment the bishop has requested Mr. Can to exchange Manchester for Wigan.[17]

To get anywhere near such an audience Lingard knew that he would have to write in a scholarly and impartial tone, appealing continually to the authority of original sources and avoiding anything which seemed like controversy or apologetics. He knew, too, that a sober and well-substantiated statement of the truth could do much to allay Protestant prejudices after three centuries of Protestant-dominated historiography in England.[18] It needed only a purely scholarly review of the history of religious persecution, for example, to show that such an ugly phenomenon belonged to a certain stage of history and was indulged in by all sides at that time; rather than being a unique peculiarity of Catholicism, which so many English people believed it to be.

Writing to a friend just after the publication of his first volume of the *History*, in 1819, Lingard explained:

> Through the work, I made it a rule . . . to avoid all appearance of controversy, that I might not repel Protestant readers . . . In my account of the Reformation, I must say much to shock Protestant prejudices: & my only chance of being generally read by them depends on my having the reputation of a temperate writer. The good to be done is by writing a book which protestants will read.[19]

The first step was to remove the prejudices of his audience:

> for prejudice in general indisposes Protestants not only from yielding to argument, but even from listening to it.[20]

To go through the Lingard papers and correspondence is to realize that it became almost an obsession with him to avoid any imputation of partiality or controversy in his work. For example, he had earlier written some religious tracts and now writes anxiously to his publisher, asking whether he thinks a re-edition of them might affect his good name as a historian.[21] He mentions certain things unnecessarily in his *History*, simply because to omit them might provoke the charge of prejudice;[22] and on one of these subjects he is criticized by a modern writer for being too harsh on the Catholic concerned.[23] Again, he finds an important charter in the Vatican archives and uses it to throw new light on the question of King John's homage to the Pope, which had none of those overtones of slavish servility to a foreign power, purveyed by the old official view.[24] In his first edition, however, Lingard failed to mention where he had found this document, and was accused of misrepresenting an altogether different charter. After putting the matter right in later editions, Lingard is rightly rebuffed by a friend for his studied obscurity in the first place – to which he replies:

> It is true, as he says, that I might originally have made the matter more clear by stating where I had found the charter: but I did not do that then. Why? Because it was an experiment: I was beginning my career as historian of England: I knew the host of prejudices marshalled against me: and I was afraid that if I had said that I found it in the Vatican it would immediately have been proclaimed a fraud &c &c.[25]

An Invitation to the Historian's Workshop

Lingard's realization of the need to explain how he had reached his conclusions is evident throughout the *History*. For example, referring to his treatment of the reports of Henry VIII's agents sent by him to gain 'favourable' opinions from various European universities on the subject of his divorce, Lingard says:

> That I may not incur the reproach of misrepresentations I purpose in this note to specify the reasons which have induced me to dispute the value of the answers returned by the universities.[26]

Then he referred to a wide range of original documents in showing that Henry had spent a considerable amount of money on bribery to get these 'favourable' opinions.[27] Lingard was breaking new ground in demonstrating this and had to be very careful in proving his point.[28]

Again, in revealing many new and significant facts concerning Wyat's Rebellion of 1554 against Mary Tudor, Lingard felt it necessary to prove his points up to the hilt:

> The reader must excuse the length and frequency of these notes. They are necessary to support a narrative which might otherwise be attributed to the imagination or the partiality of the writer.[29]

This particularly concerned the connection between the Princess Elizabeth and Sir Thomas Wyat, leader of the Rebellion against Mary.

The psychology behind the process of opening up to his readers the thinking behind his use of sources had its origin in Lingard's having to convince an audience which was known to be hyper-critical of what he had to say. But this psychology became transformed into a consistent methodology which Lingard applied throughout the *History*, irrespective of the subject.

To see this process working in areas where there was no fear of a hostile audience-response, we may take two instances which illustrate the difference in methodology between Lingard and two eminent twentieth-century historians, dealing with the same subject matter.

Concerning the coronation of King Harold in 1066, before the arrival of William of Normandy on the scene, Lingard writes:

> On account of the suspension of Stigand [Archbishop of Canterbury, suspended by Pope Alexander II], the ceremony [the coronation of Harold in 1066] was performed by Aldred, the archbishop of York.

It has the added footnote:

> Ingulf. 68. Flor. 633. Hist. Elien. 515. In a fact, which publicly took place in England, the native writers are more entitled to credit than foreigners. The Normans say Harold was crowned by Stigand (non sancta consecratione Stigandi – Guil. Pict. 105); and the statement is supported by the

figures on the tapestry of Bayeux (Lancelot, 421). But they give us only the reports prevalent in Normandy; and William, anxious to interest the religion of his subjects in his own favour, would readily countenance the notion that his rival had been crowned by a suspended prelate.[30]

Sir Frank Stenton, dealing with this same fact in his *Anglo-Saxon England* (1943), writes simply:

> the authority of the English evidence that Ealdred of York crowned Harold king outweighs the Norman assertion that he was 'ordained by the unholy consecration of Stigand'.[31]

Lingard gives us the *basis* of his evaluation of the evidence while Stenton is content to merely state the *result* of his.

Lingard relied on the impartiality of critical techniques in order to gain credence among his readers. It was important of course that these techniques should be used consistently. Lingard did this, showing, for example, that certain sources attacking Henry VIII's actions should come under the same rules. So, in noticing the opinions of disillusioned 'reforming' Protestants on the state of morality in England after the Henrician Reformation, Lingard observes:

> How far credit should be given to such representations may perhaps be doubtful. Declamations from the pulpit are not the best historical evidence. Much in them must be attributed to the exaggeration of zeal, much to the affectation of eloquence.

He goes on to state that a *conclusion should be reached only* 'when the invectives of Knox and Lever, of Gilpin and Latimer, *have been reduced by the standard of reason and experience*.[32] *The use of 'reason and experience' is in fact one of Lingard's abiding rules of source criticism,* as well as being part of his general outlook on life.

R. H. Tawney, on the other hand, in his *Religion and the Rise of Capitalism* (1926), deals with exactly the same material – the bitter words of the disillusioned and discontented 'reformers' – without mentioning in any way the reservations made by Lingard about evidence of this sort.[33] Yet Lingard's critical reservation is one that should be made in dealing with such evidence. Unlike many academics, *he always used his wider experience of life and 'common sense' – alongside his sophisticated techniques – to bear on the evidence.* It was part of his acute sense of perspective.

Lingard is aware that his references would be examined closely and inaccuracies sought for, so he provides the reader with the necessary guidance with which to interpret facts:

> Before I conclude I ought to observe, that, where, not to load the page with

a multitude of notes, I have classed several references in the same line, it is not pretended that each of them separately will fully authorise the statement to which it belongs. Some have furnished only particular circumstances; some may partially contradict the others; the text is the result from the comparison of them all, and should not be charged with inaccuracy, till all have been collated in their different bearings, and the value of each has been carefully ascertained.[34]

We find an interesting illustration of this statement in a letter from Lingard to his publisher, J. Mawman, in 1825. Referring to an attack made by the *Edinburgh Review* on the contradiction between two sources which he had used together, he writes:

Now in this respect instead of reproach I deserve the praise of candour. The work of Senatus was supposed to have perished. I discovered it in MS in the library at Durham, and finding in it a passage which seemed to contradict my opinion, I thought it a duty to give it publication, that nothing might be concealed from my readers.[35]

The idea of putting everything before the reader, of working with the reader, as it were, is manifest throughout the *History*. Lingard will explain why he has done something concerning the process by which the narrative has been built up;[36] or again he will explain why he has not done something – like mention a particular source or piece of evidence.[37] The reader is asked to use his or her own critical faculties in investigation and evaluation – to compare, contrast and decide;[38] and is referred to other material to look at.[39] Lingard once again reveals the workings of his own mind in the process of evaluation of evidence. We know when he is doubtful about something. There is quite frequent occurrence of such phrases as: 'if we may believe', 'probably', 'perhaps', 'if any credit be due to', 'I see no reason', 'I am inclined to believe', 'as far as I can understand'.[40]

Lingard conveys to the reader the sort of problems involved in historical research and composition: So:

if we may believe the unauthenticated accounts of some writers . . . We may however question their accuracy. Certain it is . . . .[41]

And in another matter where certainty cannot be achieved, he asks the reader to make his or her own judgement.[42]

Again, dealing with the claims of both sides during the Irish rising in 1641:

Nor is it easy for the impartial historian, in this conflict of passion and prejudice, amidst exaggerated statements, bold recriminations, and treacherous authorities, to strike the balance, and allot to each the due share of inhumanity and bloodshed.[43]

And, concerning the insurrection of the Protestant Vaudois in 1655, against the Catholic Duke of Savoy:

> It would be a difficult task to determine by whom ... the first blood was wantonly drawn, or to which party the blame of superior cruelty really belongs. *The authorities on each side are interested, and therefore suspicious*; the provocations alleged by the one are warmly denied by the other ...[44]

Then, in the matter of the civil and religious dispute in Scotland in 1679 between the Covenanters and the Government:

> Yet the historian who seeks to review these transactions with impartiality will generally find himself at a loss to determine what he ought to believe and what to reject. On the one hand, *the accusers are personal enemies, or men actuated by the wildest and most implacable fanaticism; on the other, the trial of Mitchell disclosed, on the part of Lauderdale and his associates, a scene of prevarication and depravity which inclines the mind to give credit to whatever may be alleged to their prejudice*.[45]

Lingard tells the reader where the evidence is conflicting[46] and where there is no evidence to decide something.[47] He indicates where the conclusion can be only a matter of personal judgement or inference, by such comments as: 'It has been of late a subject of dispute ... To me ...'; 'There have been many disputes respecting ... I think it plain from ...'; 'This is the inference I have drawn ... Some writers have come to a different conclusion'; 'This gentleman might be ... but I think he was'; 'The facts are certain; the reason here assigned is only that which appears warranted by the facts'.[48]

Concerning the question of whether or not Mary Queen of Scots was privy to the murder of her husband, Lord Darnley, in 1567, Lingard presents the difficulty in much the same way that a modern historian would do:

> Few historical questions have been more keenly or more obstinately discussed; but *her advocates, as well as her accusers, occasionally leave the pursuit of truth for the pursuit of victory; their ardour betrays both parties into errors and misrepresentations*; and the progress of the historian is retarded at every step by the conflicting opinions and insidious artifices of his guides. In the conduct of Mary, previously to the death of Darnley, I see nothing that can fairly impeach her character. There is no credible evidence that she was cognizant of the design, much less that she was the accomplice, of the assassins. But in her behaviour subsequently to that event, there is much of more questionable tendency, which, in the supposition of her guilt, will be considered as the consequence of her crime; in the supposition of her innocence, may be explained away by a reference to the difficulties of her

situation. I shall narrate the facts with impartiality; the reader must draw his own conclusion.[49]

Here, there is veiled warning against making the facts fit in with our suppositions, when there is really no proper answer. The matter remains to this day one of the unsolved problems of English history; and it looks as if may never be answered.

Sometimes the scene seems to change from that of a historiographical workshop to that of a seminar for apprentice historians. Lingard will sometimes inform the reader that there are two sides to a question.[50] Where he adopts one viewpoint, he will sometimes indicate another viewpoint, together with the evidence behind it.[51] He will occasionally anticipate the reader's question or supposition.[52] On other occasions, he will throw out a question of his own to the reader.[53] One such question draws attention to *one of Lingard's more important rules of source criticism*:

> *Were the minutes of this conversation committed to paper immediately, or after the Restoration? The credit due to them depends on this circumstance.*[54]

His method is reminiscent of the 'rules of evidence' used in our modern court of law, when, for example, the judge or magistrate will want to know if the police officer made up his or her notes immediately after an event, or, if not, how much time had been allowed to elapse. Such factors affect significantly the weight to be given to the evidence. In this particular case, Lingard was applying a critical test to an account in the papers of Whitelock (a lawyer and commissioner under Cromwell), of a private interview between himself and Oliver Cromwell in 1652 – but written up some unknown time later by Whitelock – in which the Lord Protector indicated his wish to have the title of kingship conferred on himself.[55] The dramatic event of the restoration of kingship to Charles II in 1660 was designed to change the outlook, attitude, behaviour – and possibly the memory – of many public servants.

In this sense, too, Lingard's work contrasts sharply with that of Macaulay, the most widely-read and popular historian of the nineteenth century.[56] Macaulay wrote dogmatically, as if he was completely certain about everything he said; part of his attraction was that his audience was pleased with what he was saying. He was purveying a view of English history which asserted the superiority of the English people. He did not have to be too careful, therefore, about his facts, since few people in England were likely to want to contest them. Sir Charles Firth, the sympathetic editor of Macaulay's *History*, was correct in this sense, when he wrote of the latter:

> The public likes to be told that the volume it is taking the trouble to read, does not want to have the labour of distinguishing between hypotheses and facts, and is not the least bit interested in the process by which the historian arrives at the truth. It demands a picture or a story. For students of history, however, the question how Macaulay got his facts, and what right he had to be so certain of them, should be as interesting as the picture or the story.[57]

Such an audience reaction may be true for the purveyor of an immensely popular and nationalist view of history. It is not true, however, for a writer like Lingard, who was presenting a completely new and unpopular version of the English past. The latter in fact turns many of his readers into historical students, since they will demand to know where he got his facts and what claims they have to be true – if only to overthrow them if possible. The paradox is that Macaulay, who was not good at establishing facts and who knew nothing about 'scientific' methods of source criticism,[58] was completely confident about everything he said; whereas Lingard, who represented scientific history par excellence, was quite prepared to admit that he could not prove *everything* beyond doubt.

After the publication of his *History*, Lingard felt strong enough to throw out a challenge to his critics:

> a jealousy has existed that he [Lingard] may occasionally be swayed by religious prepossessions. Nothing can be more easy than to throw out such insinuations: but he is not aware that any important error, calculated to justify the charge, has hitherto been discovered.[59]

He writes to a friend:

> Since my return from Rome my history has been noticed in two reviews, the quarterly in an article entitled 'the reformation' by Millman, and in Blackwood's last number in an article headed 'Dr. Lingard'. The first charges me with being an artful writer, but fixes on no particular passage as a proof of falsehood and misrepresentation: the second is nothing but rant about minds debased by superstition etc. and an exhortation to protestants to be on their guard, for the crisis is approaching and British papists maintain a weekly correspondence with the pope. I have reason to be content with each. For both show that they would bite, if they could.[60]

The *Westminster Review*, having acknowledged its initial misgivings on the subject of an English history written by a Catholic priest, went on to concede:

> Whatever be the process by which Dr. Lingard has become qualified satis-

factorily to discharge the duties of an historian, it is true, and his enemies admit it, that he must take his station among the most distinguished of the writers who have investigated the annals of this country.[61]

It was Lingard's belief that he could best serve the interests of his Church by following the maxims of independent scholarship and by pursuing 'the truth, whether it made for us or against us'.[62] He pinned his faith to his belief, against those who criticized him for following it. To him it was a matter of personal conscience.[63] He believed that historical truth is both achievable and sacrosanct. The truth was sacred, so he handled facts with great care. Truth and true religion, in his view, could never be at odds. But secondary to this, it was also his view that the truth was, in the final analysis, the *most expedient* policy to adopt in the defence of the Church of which he was a priest. He believed that, in the long run, the truth 'would out'.

Lingard's view of a fact as something sacred, in the sense of being an expression of truth, is characteristic of the long tradition inaugurated by Christian humanism, with its belief in the intelligibility of the universe and in the validity of the God-given human intelligence as the instrument with which to explore and investigate it. In opposition to this, there is the sceptical tradition inaugurated by Pyrrho and expressed by Bayle in seventeenth-century France, and now in the late twentieth century by 'post-modernist' figures such as Foucault, Sausurre, Hayden White, Derrida, Lyotard, Ermarth, Barthes, Ricoeur, Spiegel and Keith Jenkins. I mention these names because they significantly include no real historian. This is not surprising. If one holds the position that there is no such thing as an objective truth about the past and that such a concept is unattainable, then obviously one is not likely to spend one's time trying to discover it or to create professional skills which can help to make it attainable. If this position was acceptable, then historians might as well confine themselves to writing historical novels. Certainly there would be no good grounds for asking public bodies to fund any historical projects. There would after all be no truth to be discovered. The same argument, if it were to be really accepted as a working proposition, would bring the study of science to an end. In fact, practitioners of subjects as varied as science, history and theology have recently combined to assert their belief in objective truth as against the scepticism of post-modernists.[64]

Now, however, as one reviewer has put it very recently:

> Those historians who loathed postmodernism – or surely would do so if they knew what it meant – can take heart from an odd fact: that it is starting to go out of fashion among philosophers.[65]

He cites Martin Bunzl's *Real History: Reflections on Historical Practice* (1997) as an example of this, and also points to the logical flaw in Alan

Muslow's argument in his sceptical *Deconstructing History* (1997): 'there is no logical sequitur from his largely true statement that "nothing can be known unmediated" to his false conclusion that "nothing can be known objectively".'[66]

Lingard, trained in philosophy and theology, insisted that history was an independent and separate discipline, with its own skills, techniques and rules for attaining the truth in its own field of study. We have seen how he took his stand so clearly against David Hume and the 'philosopher-historians' of the eighteenth century, because he could see that the subject of history would run into the sand if it was left in the hands of such people.

Lingard's insistence on the importance of fact-finding was not the result of a dry and prosaic approach which could not see further than 'dry facts'. He knew, as do all practising modern historians, that the basis of the historical discipline is to establish the truth of facts and dates, and thus to be able to look at the correct *sequence* of events. This process in itself can give a sense of perspective where the truth of the larger picture can be discovered. Only in such a perspective can we discover, for example, the essential commonplaces or assumptions of thought which are the key to understanding the people of any age.[67] Facts connect historical investigation to the truth. One false fact can obscure the truth in history, as it can in forensic science or any other pursuit of truth. Facts therefore have an excitement of their own.

The opposite process was conducted by the 'whig historians' who created and relayed the old official version of English history. They started with the theory of 'progress', based on the assumptions of thought of the present, and then tried to fit all the facts into their theory, giving a totally false picture of the way in which people thought in the past.

Lingard was the founder of what we now call 'revisionist history'. He insisted on establishing the facts and dates, before beginning to talk about causes and results. He insisted, too, on starting from the facts, not from commonly-accepted theories. The results of this deceptively simple approach proved to be surprisingly 'explosive' in destroying age-old theories and myths in English historical writing.

Lingard did not believe – as did most English historians over nearly four centuries – that people in the past were divided into the 'winners' who supported 'progress' and the 'losers' who supported 'obscurantism'.[68] The people of the past were not able, for the most part, to look forward into the future and did not share our ways of thinking. Lingard understood, therefore, that it is central to the historian's task to be ready to be surprised by the factual evidence. He was able to see things, too, from the viewpoint of the people in the past; and so he could write:

> we often attribute to policy events which no deliberation has prepared, and which no foresight could have divined.[69]

And:

> it is not often that the adventurer discerns at the outset the goal at which he ultimately arrives. The tide of events bears him forward; and past successes urge him to still higher attempts.[70]

Or, again:

> for many of the improvements in the English constitution we are indebted more to views of personal interest than to enlightened policy.[71]

And:

> We are apt to attribute to the foresight of politicians those counsels which are in reality suggested by the passing events of the day.[72]

With regard to the Civil War, which whig historians saw as a great idealistic struggle between those who were consciously fighting for the idealist future (the 'heroes') and those who were against it (the 'obscurantist' villains of the story). Lingard commented:

> the controversy between the king and his opponents no longer regarded the real liberties of the nation.[73]

so there were no real heroes or villains in terms of what English historians usually saw in these struggles.

Lingard's approach was replicated nearly 150 years later when, in our own time, Conrad Russell and others made their concerted attempt to break free of the 'influence of hindsight' which had 'grossly distorted the story we have been told' about the English past. Russell pointed out that the modern International Commission for the History of Representative Institutions has demonstrated that England was not the unique creator of such institutions, so that it is difficult to sustain any longer 'the potentially offensive assumption that the survival of Parliament in England is due to any special virtue in the English'.[74]

The 'revisionists' have also been 'reluctant to assume as the Victorians did that England is always a special case.[75] Indeed to look at the following passages by Professor Conrad Russell, is to see how closely the revisionists are following in Lingard's footsteps:

> revisionism has always been directed against the historiographical assumptions Whigs and Marxists have held in common . . . the notion of progress [has led to] a tendency to use history as a way of explaining why events led to their ultimate conclusion . . .

And:

> the attempt to evade the influence of hindsight on the story has happened

in other fields of historical investigation, including the origins of the English Reformation, and in all of them, historians writing in the 1970s have been attempting to argue that hindsight has grossly distorted the story we have hitherto been told.

Revisionism, continues Russell, is:

> an attempt to avoid the pressure to assume, *a priori*, that the result we are investigating was inevitable . . . it has also been an attempt to restore the study of political narrative history. To let the search for causes or explanations take priority over the establishment of the correct story is to put the cart before the horse . . . we must establish the course of events by treating it as a subject worthy of study in its own right, and then and only then attempt to analyse its causes.[76]

Similarly Lingard's insistence on looking at English history from the viewpoint of 'a citizen of the World'[77] is only now, at the beginning of the new millennium, becoming accepted. English historians are now beginning to try to move away from the writing of history from the 'anglo-centric' point of view which has dominated English historiography for four centuries.

Amid all these important ways in which Lingard can be seen to have been so far ahead of his own time, this study seeks to highlight the processes, methodology and techniques of source criticism, which he created single-handedly and for the first time in English historical writing. These techniques were needed to establish the certainty of those facts and dates which form the basis of historical writing. He set out:

> to find the truth, self-consciously aware of the interaction of opinion and evidence . . . using rigorously the best methods and techniques available to exercise a professional and objective judgment.[78]

Lingard states quite clearly the basic tenets which should be part of the professional equipment of all historians. Indeed they express the standpoint, surely, of all modern practising and professional historians. In the last quarter of the twentieth century historians have been unduly on the defensive against another ephemeral appearance of the philosophy of 'nescience', expressed this time by the fashionable group of postmodernist theorists. Consequently some practising historians have tended to shrink from stating their professional tenets as clearly as Lingard did. It is refreshing, therefore, and even exhilarating, to look at Lingard's reflections on his own activity as a historian, in the preliminary notice to the sixth and last edition of his *History* in 1849:

> I have strictly adhered to the same rules to which I subjected myself in the former editions; to admit no statement on trust, to weigh with care the value

of the authorities on which I rely, and to watch with jealousy the secret workings of my own personal feelings and prepossessions. Such vigilance is a matter of necessity to every writer of history, if he aspire to the praise of truthfulness and impartiality. He must withdraw himself aloof from the scenes which he describes, and view, with the coolness of an unconcerned spectator the events which pass before his eyes, holding with a steady hand the balance between contending parties . . . Otherwise he will be continually tempted to make an unfair use of the privilege of the historian; he will sacrifice the interests of truth to the interests of party, national, or religious, or political. His narrative may still be brilliant, attractive, picturesque; but the pictures he paints will derive their colouring from the jaundiced eye of the artist himself, and will therefore bear no very faithful resemblance to the realities of life and fact.[79]

Such statements, of course, are of little value unless they are put into practice. That is why it needs an in-depth study of Lingard's use of sources, as provided in this study, to validate the statements which he makes about the historian's craft.

Lingard believed implicitly that it was his task to pursue, attain and express the truth about the English past. This alone, however, would not have made the present study possible, if he had not been faced with a more suspicious and hostile audience than had ever before confronted an English historian.

Lingard devised a methodology and an array of critical techniques with which to approach his sources. These were the instruments which he fashioned in his 'workshop', in order to achieve his aim of getting at the truth. These critical techniques were quite new to English historiography. They were to turn historical *writing* in England for the first time – apart from the editing of original documents by earlier scholars – into a 'science' as well as an art. That is to say that the historical narrative was now to be based on sources which had been tested by an array of techniques devised to ensure that they were credible. History was to be a branch of 'knowledge' (scientia), characterized by these critical techniques, which made it a separate discipline from that of literature or philosophy. At the same time its literary presentation would be in an art form characterized by a classically clear style as the best vehicle for its meaning. All this was devised by Lingard's need to find the truth, but partly also because he needed to be able to prove this truth to his readers. He had to substantiate his facts and judgements in order to overcome their prejudices against what he had to say.

Moreover, in order to gain the confidence and trust of his audience, he had to be able to *demonstrate* the process and methodology by which he had substantiated the facts which he was presenting. He had to invite his readers into his 'workshop' so that they could see the tools he was using and the processes by which he had come to his conclusions. He had promised that he would 'admit no statement on trust' and would 'weigh with care the value of the authorities on which I rely'.[80] Now he had to demonstrate how he was going to do this.

So it is that we are able to follow the processes and the rules of source criticism on which Lingard built 'the first modern narrative of the two critical centuries of English history'.[81] We can sit alongside Lingard and repeat the processes by which he constructed his narrative from source material which had been critically examined and evaluated in a manner unprecedented in English historical writing.

It seemed not to occur to Lingard to write a book himself, to explain these processes and techniques. He devised a new 'scientific' form of critical analysis of sources without apparently recognizing the general significance of what he was doing. As far as he was concerned, he was simply doing what had to be done, to find the truth, and to gain the trust and confidence of his readers. These readers would have to make a huge imaginative jump across the barrier of prejudice created by three centuries of constant repetition of the 'official' view of English history; and they needed to understand fully the basis on which his challenge was founded.

To the student interested in the craft of historical writing, Lingard provides an excellent subject for study. He provides a unique portrayal of self-revelation in the historian at work. He sets out to reassure and convince a manifestly hostile audience, by laying bare to its gaze the details of his methodology – those processes of collation, comparison, synthesis and critical evaluation of source material which lay behind the construction of the narrative.

I spent two years of research at this 'workshop', examining the methodology of source criticism used throughout the *History*'s ten volumes, but using the test-case of Lingard's treatment of the reign of Elizabeth I – one complete volume of 719 pages – for a specially intensive examination in detail of his use of original sources. The task involved going back to the original sources themselves, to examine how Lingard had used them in every case.

I commenced the research by going through the multitude of footnotes that supported each step of the narrative. I went to the original sources named in the footnotes and examined exactly how Lingard had used them. It struck me forcibly that this type of detailed work is the only sure method of assessing properly the professional craftsmanship of any historian. For, valuable as letters, and, to a lesser extent, prefaces, may be in throwing some light in a general way on the ideas and intentions of the historian, such material can be, after all, only an expression of self-proclaimed ideals and intentions. A detailed, structured study of the historian's critical abilities in using sources and creating a finished narrative based on them, is needed to discover the historian's working attributes and the real significance and importance of the work. The approach was useful, too, in giving me a grounding in the basic original sources for Elizabeth's reign as they existed in Lingard's day; because he kept strictly to his stated intention of writing wherever possible, from the original sources, throughout his *History*.[82]

Starting with a blank sheet of paper, I noted every instance, throughout the whole *History*'s ten volumes, where Lingard used a particular technique or rule of source criticism and evaluation. Its significance was proportional to the number and variety of occasions on which it was used. From the mass of evidence accumulated in this way, there emerged broad definite classifications and sub-divisions, which indicated a consistent recourse to particular techniques, which I was not at all aware of at the start. Some time after discovering these classifications, I was able to examine the personal papers and letters of Lingard deposited in the archives of Ushaw College, near Durham. Here I found direct confirmation of a deliberate use of important techniques which I had already deduced from detailed work on the original sources used in the *History* itself. I knew, then, that the techniques which I had discovered were the result of a conscious attempt to develop a methodology of source criticism which had never been seen in England before.

Though in this study I shall sometimes place, for reasons of neater presentation, the findings derived from the letters and personal papers before those deduced from the *History*, I should emphasize that the initial process by which the technique was discovered was the latter. This fact supplies better evidence of the actual use of a technique as a working instrument, while the study of the private letters and papers confirms that it was the result of a conscious activity on the part of the historian.

I also conducted a detailed examination of Lingard's quotation and reference system, using again the test-case period of Elizabeth I's reign. My examination involved checking back against the original source to discover the methodology and accuracy of Lingard's system of quotation and reference.

Finally, I undertook a detailed comparison of the gradual evolution of the *History* through from the first (1819–30), to the fourth (1837–38) and the last (1849) editions in order to examine the ways in which Lingard incorporated the evidence of new original material which was produced between the editions, to give added confirmation to some of his earlier findings, or sometimes to correct what he had written before in the light of the new evidence. Increasingly one came to admire his phenomenal industry in taking on board the mass of original materials, covering the whole range of English history, which became available between these editions. It was the quality of scholarship, however, which I particularly wanted to examine – the critical methodology, the 'scientific' techniques involved, and the artistic challenge of weaving the new material into the previous narrative.

An Invitation to the Historian's Workshop

As Marc Bloch, the French historian, commented in his *The Historian's Craft*, there is a fascination about studying the expertise of the professional historian in pursuit of documentary evidence:

> Despite what the beginners sometimes seem to imagine, documents do not suddenly materialize, in one place or another, as if by some mysterious decree of the gods. Their presence or absence in the depths of this archive or that library are due to human causes which by no means elude analysis. The problems posed by their transmission, far from having importance only for the technical experts, are most intimately connected with the life of the past, for what is here at stake is nothing less than the passing down of memory from one generation to another ... 'How can I know what I am about to say?'. I am persuaded that even the lay reader would experience an actual intellectual pleasure in examining these 'confessions'. The sight of an investigation with its successes and reverses is seldom boring.[83]

The story which emerged from my detailed research into the activity taking place within Lingard's 'workshop' proved to be of intriguing interest as well as of major importance for the history of historical writing in England. Work was taking place there which completely belied the idea that there were no important or significant developments in England in the field of scientific source-criticism at this time. Indeed, the quality of work was at least equal, in my view, to that achieved in the well-known centres of group-activity in certain German universities (especially Göttingen) at the time.[84]

Lingard was working in isolation. In England the emphasis was on historical writing as a branch of high literature, reaching its apogee in Macaulay's *History of England* (1849–61). Lingard did not consider that Macaulay was a historian at all, because he had no sense of source criticism and regarded history as a branch of belles-lettres. Nor is there any evidence of any contact between Lingard and the German scholars. Germany was the one continental country with which Lingard had no correspondence, though he did start to learn German in his sixties.[85] He makes an interesting and amusing general comment on German writers in a letter written towards the end of his life:

> Those whose labours are devoted to lexicography, or the the hunting out of passages in ancient writers, are above all praise for their industry and correctness: but [German] writers on politics, religion, science etc. are above or beneath my powers of understanding.[86]

German 'scientific' scholarship in history reached its apogee in the work of Leopold von Ranke (1795–1886).[87] On the one topic of European history which was not 'home territory' for either of them and on which they both brought to bear the full powers of their expertise in source criticism, there is no doubt, as we shall see in the next chapter, that Lingard proved to be the abler historian, better able to see 'the wood for the trees'. Moreover, it is also clear that Lingard's battery of critical techniques was more powerful, incisive and conclusive than that of the best representative of German technical scholarship.

My research showed that Lingard established, on his own, the second great stage in the development of historical writing, in England. The earlier English scholars, such as Henry Spelman, Thomas Hearne, Henry Wharton and George Hickes, had concerned themselves – following Mabillon – with the *internal* evidence on the basis of which their invaluable editions of original texts could be authenticated. They – like Mabillon again – did not look at the *external* evidence surrounding the document which could evaluate its credibility and authority. Lingard went on, for the first time, to look behind those original materials to the external evidence, in order to evaluate their credibility as sources. He devised a methodology which enabled him to do this.

Most of the chapters that follow are devoted to a description of this methodology and these rules of scientific source criticism. Lingard did not write a general textbook covering his activity in the field. He was provoked, however, to write a short pamphlet of one hundred and twelve pages, in defence of his completely new and 'shocking' account of the Massacre of St. Bartholomew (1572), which had been attacked severely. Having been accused of 'prejudice', which to Lingard was a terrible accusation, he replied in a small and obscure pamphlet. It contains some key passages in the creation of the second great stage in the development of source criticism in English historical writing. I shall now give some little time to the consideration of it, before looking at the main structure of Lingard's achievement in source criticism.

CHAPTER II
The Historiography of the Massacre of St. Bartholomew

'No means existed of determining the credibility of the contemporary writers.'

Lord Acton

The Massacre of St. Bartholomew (1572) [PLATE 28] in France was one of the most infamous episodes in modern European history, used perhaps more than any other single subject for polemical purposes. The popular version was that the massacre of Huguenots in Paris on that day had been 'premeditated': it had been planned and plotted by Pope Gregory XIII, with the aid of Catherine de Medici and her son, Charles IX King of France. It had been planned, said this version, as early as the meeting at Bayonne in 1565 between Catherine de Medici, her daughter (the Queen of Spain) and the Duke of Alva.

This 'Black Legend' in English historical writing had become something commonly considered to be self-evidently true. It had been used continuously in England as a rod with which to beat the Catholics who remained in the country. In particular, it was a mainstay in the arguments put forward against any alleviation of the harsh persecuting laws which 'kept them down' in England.

During the time when Lingard was writing his *History* – in the decade before Catholic Emancipation (1829) – this was one of the main arguments used by the vociferous opposition to that Act. One tract, written in 1826, for example, said that the conduct of the Catholic Church was 'too fearfully recorded in bloody, by the never-to-be forgotten Massacre of St. Bartholomew'[1] for it ever to be safe to allow Catholics the vote in England.

This subject is of particular interest to us in that its proper interpretation presented great problems to the historian. Indeed, as Lord Acton wrote much later in an extant manuscript note: 'no means existed of determining the *credibility* of the contemporary writers'.[2] It was therefore at the mercy of the propagandists until the coming of the second great stage in the technical advancement of historiography – the development of 'scientific' source criticism by which the real authority and credibility of contemporary writers could be judged.

On the Continent some developments had occurred in the eighteenth century. The 'Black Legend' had been taken up in France and used again, this time by certain writers of the 'Enlightenment' – including Voltaire – to attack the Church. In reaction to this in 1758, the Abbé de Caveirac dared to argue that the Massacre had been politically, not religiously, motivated; and that it was a panic measure, not premeditated. He made the significant point that extraordinary legends had arisen around the Massacre, and people were now afraid to oppose them in case they would be accused of supporting the Massacre itself. Indeed he was then violently attacked by the 'philosophers' of the 'Enlightenment' in just this way.

In Germany the first rudimentary stage of a more scientific approach to source criticism was taking place at the University of Göttingen (founded under the Elector of Hanover in 1734). In 1789 Ludwig von Spittler stated that he could find no basis for the notion that the Massacre of St. Bartholomew had been premeditated.[3] In England, however, there had been no such development. There was no 'school' of historical scholars and no movement in the universities towards a more scientific approach to historical evidence. Indeed, there seems to have been no awareness in England of what was happening elsewhere – limited though it was – at this stage. It is only with Lingard that we can trace the beginning of a change of interpretation on the subject of the Massacre in English historical writing. He was obviously aware of the novelty of his treatment, when he wrote in an appendix to his first edition (1823):

> The reader will observe that I have not adopted the usual hypothesis, that the massacre was the result of a premeditated plot, concealed with infinite cunning . . . but he may be assured, that my opinion was not framed till after a diligent perusal of the most authentic documents on the subject.[4]

Lingard stated that he had found no evidence to suggest that a plot had been concocted at the celebrated meeting between Catherine de Medici and the duke of Alva at Bayonne in 1565. The evidence of authentic sources told him that the Massacre was an opportunistic, panic-measure resorted to by Catherine de Medici and her son, Charles IX. It was to preempt the expected counter-attack by the Huguenots after Catherine's attempt to assassinate their leader, the Admiral de Coligny, had failed. Catherine had feared that they would turn on her and her son. This is now the accepted version of the episode.[5] Before examining the source criticism by which Lingard achieved his interpretation, it is useful to gain perspective by noticing how the best scholars in nineteenth-century England and Germany dealt with this subject much later.

HISTORIOGRAPHY OF THE MASSACRE OF ST. BARTHOLOMEW

Lord Acton (1834–1902), Regius Professor of Modern History at Cambridge (1895–1902), was reputedly the 'greatest man of learning in England' in his day.[6] He thought long and hard about this subject, studying the evidence intently from 1867 onwards, but 'rooting his history... in the world of ideas'[7] rather than facts. Until the mid-1880s, when European scholarship as a whole came to accept the case against premeditation, Acton believed the old version of the Massacre, in opposition to what Lingard had written as far back as 1823. In fact Acton repeated much of the argument used by John Allen in his attack on Lingard's account.[8] Acton failed to interpret accurately the importance of the evidence of Salviati, the Papal nuncio in Paris.[9] On the other hand, he attributed too much weight to the faulty evidence supplied by a 'mysterious' comment of Cardinal Bonelli.[10] Nor did Acton attempt to align the whole evidence with the immediately preceding context of events in France.[11] All this meant that he was still failing to understand what had happened in France in 1572, until some fifty years after Lingard's account.

Leopold Von Rank (1795–1886) was the greatest exponent of the German school of scientific and technical history in the nineteenth century.[12] He, too, was intrigued by the problem of the Massacre and brought all his expertise to bear on the evidence concerning the subject from 1835 onwards. He could not resolve two contradictory answers which the evidence seemed to yield to his questioning:

> He decided that history in itself could never solve the problem and that one must resort, therefore, to 'psychology'. It was Ranke's view that Catherine must have been preparing to act sincerely with the Huguenots and at the same time she must have been working out plans for their destruction.[13]

Ultimately, Ranke had failed to solve the historical problem; and he concluded that it was unsolvable in terms of historical evidence and methodology. In this, however, he was wrong; for the matter had been resolved already by Lingard in these terms.

After Lingard's treatment of the Massacre in his first edition of the *History* (1823), there occurred perhaps the most vitriolic attack he ever experienced, at the hands of John Allen, a writer for the *Edinburgh Review*. Allen was a sceptic in religion,[14] who seemed to have a personal grudge against Lingard.[15] He was also, however, a well-known scholar who had immersed himself in materials for the defence of the 'Black Legend' concerning the Massacre. He wrote with a manifest zest at being able, at last, to 'prove' Lingard's 'partiality' and 'infidelity'. It was with complete confidence that he led his attack:

> we had little doubt, that, if we selected for examination a more trying

period, where the credit and interests of his church were more directly concerned, we should see displayed in a stronger light the passions and prejudices of the author... We do not deny that... we are prepared for many errors and misrepresentations in this part of his work. And certainly we have not been mistaken in our anticipations. The harvest has been infinitely more abundant than we had expected, and our opinion of Dr. Lingard, as an historian, has in the same proportion declined... The supposition that the massacre of St. Bartholomew was planned a considerable time before it was carried into execution is 'unsupported' Dr. Lingard tells us 'by contemporary authority'. This we must confess, does strike us as a most extraordinary allegation... there is a degree of hardihood in the assertion that challenges admiration – with whatever other feeling it may be blended.[16]

It was against this passionate attack that Lingard published in 1826 a pamphlet entitled *A Vindication of Certain Passages in the Fourth and Fifth Volumes of the History of England*. It was a very cool, calm and detached account of the critical methodology which he had applied to this subject in order to come to the conclusion which had been so explosive in its results.

He began by explaining his general approach in writing his *History*:

I had imposed on myself a toilsome and invidious task. I foresaw that it would require habits of patient research and incessant application; that I should frequently be obliged to contradict the statements of favourite writers, occasionally perhaps to offend the political or religious partialities of my readers.[17]

In particular he had anticipated trouble over his account of the Massacre of St. Bartholomew:

I ventured to depart from the common opinion, that it was the effect of a preconcerted plan, and to consider it as the sudden result of an accidental and unforeseen event... I readily foresaw that the statement which I should make would excite surprise, and provoke contradiction. But the fact appeared to me a proper subject for historical inquiry; and the consideration that two centuries and a half have been allowed for passion to cool, and prejudice to wear away, determined me to commit my opinion fairly and fearlessly to the candour and discernment of my readers.[18]

Then Lingard began to demonstrate the rules of source criticism which he had employed in dealing with the evidence in this case. The main value of Allen's lengthy attack is that it made it necessary for the usually reticent Lingard to publish this document of some one hundred and twelve pages. It represents the first open statement of the principles underlying the second great stage in the development of historical writing in its modern form. It centres on the need to get behind the original documents, in order to evaluate their authority (credibility) by reference to external factors, as opposed to internal evidence. This was the step to which Mabillon and his English imitators in the late seventeenth century had not advanced; and which the critic, Allen, did not even comprehend.

Lingard begins with the fairly simple rule of criticism, that historians must have some real authority to back up their statements. Concerning the accepted version of the Massacre, he writes:

> Writers who asserted it were to be found without number; they were catholics as well as protestants: some took it for granted; others attempted to prove it. *But what was their authority? Nothing beyond suspicion, and report and conjecture.*[19]

Then came a specific rule of source criticism which derives from the distinction between a publicly acknowledged fact and a secret plot or design. The Massacre of St. Bartholomew was supposed to have resulted from a secret and premeditated plot. So, evidence concerning it had to satisfy a particular standard of proof. This rule was to protect Lingard against the 'false trail' of the 'Bonelli evidence' which later led Acton astray.[20]

> A broad distinction should be drawn between authority for a public fact, and authority for a secret design. The fact is a matter of notoriety: its truth may be easily ascertained ... But a design, supposed to have been formed and conducted in privacy and concealment, unless it be necessarily implied in the result, requires a very different proof. Its existence can be shown only by the confession of the parties, or by the testimony of those who have derived their knowledge from those parties. Such confession or testimony would be authority, and contemporary authority. But does any such exist? Was any such every known to exist? No.[21]

Lingard refers also to two other rules of source criticism, which have to be satisfied, when seeking credible evidence. One puts the question: *Was the source in a position to know?* The other asks: *Did the source have any reason for lying?* Therefore, concerning the planning of the attack on the Huguenots, allegedly promoted by the Pope, at a meeting between Catherine de Medici and the Duke of Alva in Bayonne in 1565, Lingard writes:

> In the correspondence of Walsingham, I found a denial on the part of Catherine de Medici, that any political business had been transacted at Bayonne: *but this I did not mention because she was interested in the denial.* In Strada I discovered the abstract of a letter from Philip of Spain to the archduchess [sic] Margaret, who governed the Low Countries ... *If we consider to whom and by whom this letter was written, we must admit it as authentic evidence* ...[22]

Philip II of Spain, as the Duke of Alva's master, *was in a position to know the truth*. Moreover he would have had no reason *to withhold it from the duchess Margaret, his Regent in the Netherlands*. Here was good evidence, therefore, to disprove the idea of the plot. It was in fact the later publication, in 1851, of Alva's despatches to Philip from the Netherlands, which 'made it certain that no extraordinary villainy' was agreed upon, or even proposed, at the Bayonne meeting in 1565.[23]

A centrally important feature of Lingard's methodology of source criticism is brought out in reply to Allen's accusation that Lingard had falsely claimed to have collated all the 'original' documents concerning the Massacre. Allen triumphantly recounted the names of contemporary writers whom Lingard had not brought into his evidence. Lingard's answer to this criticism reveals Allen's unawareness of the distinction between authentic (trustworthy or credible) and original (simply contemporary) documents. Allen could be excused, because this was the first time that such a distinction was being made in English historiography, as a key rule of source criticism. Lingard writes:

> I said that I had compared 'the most authentic documents'; he [Allen] makes me say that I compared the 'original documents'. The change may be unintentional, but it is not immaterial. *By the 'most authentic documents', I meant documents of sufficient authority to deserve credit, as coming from men, who either were the original devisors, or received their information from the original devisers, of the massacre. Such persons may be admitted as authentic witnesses. But the 'original documents' of the reviewer are not confined to such evidence; he extends the denomination to the numerous writings on the subject, published within a few years after the event; of which the far greater part proceeded from those who possessed not the means of ascertaining the real origin of the tragedy, and who wrote only from hearsay, conjecture, and passion. Such writings cannot be classified among 'the most authentic documents on the subject'.*[24]

For Lingard, however, the most important evidence concerning the nature of the Massacre of St. Bartholomew would be in the correspondence between the Papal nuncio in Paris, Salviati, and the Vatican in 1572. The Pope, according to the accepted version, had been the arch-plotter behind the premeditated massacre. Salviati, as papal nuncio in Paris, *would certainly have been in a position to know everything about a plot; and in his confidential correspondence with the Vatican, there would be no reason for duplicity*.

The French scholar, Chateaubriand, had made copies of the Salviati despatches from manuscripts which had been brought back to Paris from the Vatican as part of Napoleon's plans to bring all the European archives to this centre.[25] This was, of course, before the state archives of Europe had been opened for scholars.[26] Lingard contacted his 'agent' in Paris, a

Historiography of the Massacre of St. Bartholomew

Mr. Charles Brown Mostyn, who successfully communicated to him the findings of Chateaubriand on the subject of the Massacre, in a letter from Versailles in 1826.[27] This information indicated that there was no evidence in Salviati's letters to suggest that the Massacre was premeditated or that the Vatican had had any part in the affair. Passed on information was not, of course, an ideal state of affairs for Lingard because he had not been able to see the documents himself. However, in the light thrown on the subject as a result of his other rules of source criticism, Lingard was confident enough to state in his *Vindication* that:

> He [Chateaubriand] had the curiosity to search for the history of the St. Bartholomew where, if any where, the truth was to be discovered, in the archives of the Vatican, at the time when they where [sic] lodged in France during the reign of Napoleon. The several secret dispatches, written in cipher, and forwarded to Rome by the papal agents in Paris, were carefully examined, and the results of the inquiry proved most satisfactorily, that the St. Bartholomew had not been concerted beforehand.[28]

In the same year, 1826, Lingard wrote to his publisher, Mawman (a non-Catholic) to bolster his confidence after the fierce attack by Allen. The letter is interesting because it indicates another extremely important rule of source criticism which had been a guiding light to Lingard, in his first account of the Massacre in 1823, before any information had become available from the Salviati despatches. He writes:

> I was fully aware that the perception of the massacre provoked a belief that it had been long before determined and planned, and that this belief was admitted not only by the calvinists but by many catholic writers: but when I considered that none of them had adduced any convincing proof, and that *it was impossible to reconcile the supposition with the facts preceding the massacre*, I felt no hesitation in stating my opinion that the latter was not premeditated.[29]

The above demonstrates a key point in Lingard's source criticism, *It was only within a meaningful context of the established facts, dates and relationships between the parties involved before the central event, that the evidence concerning it could be properly interpreted*. The tool of 'contextual criticism' was a major feature of Lingard's craftsmanship. It also enabled him, for example, to interpret properly the content of certain medieval statutes for the first time in English historical writing.[30] There was no sign of it being used by any of his predecessors or contemporaries; and indeed, it has been a feature of only the best of his successors in the twentieth century.[31]

Lingard realized from the start, however, that the Vatican archives and the Salviati despatches in particular, would contain the final and complete answer to the Massacre problem; and he continued his pursuit of such

45

conclusive materials. In 1831, just before the appearance of the relevant volume of his second edition of the *History*, we find in the Lingard correspondence a letter from his 'agent' in Rome, Robert Gradwell, rector of the English College there (and a future bishop). Gradwell wrote from Rome:

> Above six weeks ago I had access to the secret archives of the Prince of Piombino in Rome, to search among the Buoncompani & Ludovisi papers, for documents serviceable to you, particularly for an allocation or other act of Gregory XIII respecting the affair of St. Bartholomew.[32]

And there is a reply from Lingard:

> I am much obliged both to him [Mgr. Capacini, another helper in Rome] and you with respect to the dispatches about the St. Bartholomew. If I can get one or two of them & be allowed to publish them they will silence the bigots who still pretend that the massacre was premeditated . . .[33]

But, by now, in a rather surprising way, the Salviati despatches had been published in England; just in time for Lingard to use them in his new edition. We know that Lingard had received information from Mr. Charles Browne Mostyn, his agent in Paris, in 1826, informing him of Chateaubriand's findings among the Salviati despatches. Lingard mentioned this in his *Vindication* (1826) and tells us, in a later letter of 1838, that:

> On account of my having referred to Chateaubriand in my 'Vindication', Sir Js. Mackintosh wrote to him, and obtained from him the transcripts which he had taken, while the MSS were at Paris. These have been published by Mackintosh in Lardner's Cabinet hist: of England, and are quite in my favour.[34]

We can only surmise why Chateaubriand was so obliging to Mackintosh. We know that the latter had supported the French in his *Vindiciae Gallicae* (1791) against Edmund Burke's *Reflections on the French Revolution*; and that he had contributed a long section on the French Revolution to Lardner's *Cyclopaedia*.

Lingard regarded the publication of these despatches in 1831 as the end of the matter. They provided the conclusive evidence that the Massacre of St. Bartholomew was essentially a panic measure of personal self-defence on the part of Catherine de Medici who had also involved her otherwise unwilling son, Charles IX of France. Neither the Papacy nor the King of Spain had been involved and there had certainly been no conspiracy or premeditation behind it. For Lingard, the debate was now surely settled for all to see:

Here, in the first edition, I introduced a note which led to an interesting controversy, whether the massacre was an accidental occurrence or the result of a premeditated plot. That controversy, as it appears to me, has now been set at rest by the publication (in the 3rd vol of Mackintosh) of the secret despatches of Salviati, the nuncio at Paris, to the cardinal secretary at Rome for the information of the pontiff.[35]

Interestingly, neither Lord Acton in England nor Ranke in Germany were able to recognize the decisive importance of these despatches to a proper interpretation of the whole matter.[36]

Lingard's treatment of the Massacre of St. Bartholomew provides an excellent illustration of the way in which a whole range of critical techniques were brought to bear on the sources for this subject. It was done to such good effect that he was certainly the first English historian, and perhaps the first European scholar, to set out the evidence for the modern understanding of it so simply, elegantly and completely; and with the utmost economy of style and presentation. His treatment of sources is at once comprehensible and acceptable to the most rigorous standards.

Sir Herbert Butterfield is the only modern English historian to have written in detail on the historiography of the Massacre of St. Bartholomew. His article on 'Lord Acton and the Massacre of St. Bartholomew' (1952) was later inserted as the last chapter of his *Man on His Past: The Study of the History of Historical Scholarship* (1955).[37] Interestingly, as an admirer of Lord Acton, Butterfield indicated the latter's chief weakness in dealing with this subject in 1869. Acton's account (nearly fifty years after Lingard's we might add)

> does not square (and did not square in 1869) with any possible diagram that could be made of the situation in France, or with any of the possible roles that could be formulated for the chief actors in the drama. Nothing could be more precise than the reasons for the massacre – and the predicament which drove Catherine de Medici to decide upon it ... Nothing could be more blurred than his own attempt to explain the logic of the whole affair – a piece of discourse which is remarkable from the start in that it refers primarily not to Catherine de Medici but to Charles IX.[38]

In fact, both Acton's and Ranke's[39] accounts were 'blurred' in this sense; whereas Lingard's much earlier account was clearly and accurately made to 'square' with the context of events preceding the Massacre.[40] It is also worth noting, in case Lingard's Catholicism is invoked as a reason, that Lord Acton was also a devout Catholic.

It is useful, here, to summarize the various rules of source criticism, devised by himself, which Lingard brought to bear on the solution of the Massacre problem. The whole matter brings out Lingard's place in the history of historical scholarship, when we compare his work in this field with the best English scholarship represented by Lord Acton and with the best German and continental scholarship represented by Ranke – both of whom worked after Lingard, and after the opening of the European archives.

In the first place, Lingard made it a rule *never to accept a charge made against anyone, where there was no convincing evidence provided to substantiate it*. This may seem an obvious point to us, but it had been the common norm before Lingard for English historians to repeat an accepted view which had been handed down for generations, so that it was eventually taken for granted. It was because Lingard followed this rule consistently that Macaulay accused him of being one whose 'great fundamental rule of judging seems to be that the popular opinion cannot possibly be correct'.[41] Lingard refused simply to follow the 'official' account of the Massacre as purveyed by previous historians. His first reaction was that 'none of them had adduced any convincing proof'.[42]

Secondly, as early as 1823 – nearly a decade before the conclusive evidence of the Salviati despatches had become available – Lingard had already rejected 'without hesitation'[43] the conspiracy theory of a premeditated Massacre. *This was because there was no convincing proof provided for it; and also because such a theory did not square with the known facts of the situation in France immediately preceding it*. These facts included, for example, the genuine desire of the young Charles IX to establish peace between the religious factions, his signing of the Edict of Pacification with the Huguenots (1570) and his known intention to strengthen this pacification by the marriage of his sister to the Huguenot King of Navarre. It was probably in this area of source criticism that Ranke lacked the ability to 'see the wood for the trees' in spite of his detailed knowledge of the documentation.[44] The ability to place events in perspective is crucial for the historian.

Thirdly, Lingard rejected outright the 'evidence of Cardinal Bonelli' which had led and was going to lead so many other historians – including Lord Acton – astray. The evidence had come from a message sent by the Cardinal from France to the Vatican on 6 March 1572, saying that he had important information to give the Pope privately. After the Massacre, statements were published, sanctioned by members of Bonelli's 'mission', which pointed to the Massacre (of 24th August) as the subject of that private information. These conjectures were immediately ruled out of court by Lingard because, in the first place, *if it was a 'secret design', Bonelli was not in a position to know*. Such 'evidence' did not meet the standard of proof required in such cases. Secondly these hints or suggestions were made later, with hindsight of the Massacre. *They did not constitute reliable proof*.[45] This is what Butterfield referred to in 1952, in noting that: 'Lingard had been right in distrusting this whole part of the evidence,[46] whereas Acton and others had been deceived by it.'

Fourthly, Lingard used *the rule of accepting only the evidence of someone who was in a position to know the truth and had no reason for concealing it*. Therefore he saw from the start the crucial importance of the despatches *in cipher* from Salviati, for conveying confidential information to the Pope. When these had been published, Lingard wrote:

> Evidence more satisfactory than this we cannot desire, if we consider the situation of the writer, the object for which he wrote, and the time, and opportunity which he possessed of correcting any error that might have crept into his previous communication.[47]

Salviati had written despatches *in cipher* on the 24th of August (the day of the Massacre) and again on the 22nd of September, the second confirming the first.

In his later editions, Lingard quotes in Italian from these despatches. They say that Catherine de Medici, jealous of the influence which the Admiral Coligni (the Huguenot leader in Paris) was beginning to exercise over her son, Charles IX (who wanted to live in peace with the Huguenots), personally designed an assassination attempt on the life of Coligni (22 August). When this failed, Catherine feared that her plot would be discovered because Coligny already suspected her of it. She therefore panicked, fearing the immediate vengeance of Coligny and the Huguenot party. She confessed what she had done to her son, and prevailed on him to consent to an immediate pre-emptive attack on the Huguenots (24 August). If Coligni had died in the assassination attempt, the Huguenots would not have been attacked. This is now the accepted version. The Massacre of St. Bartholomew was the personal crime of Catherine de Medici.[48]

It was no accident, then, that Lingard was able to make his historical judgement clearly, confidently and unequivocally on this matter, although he was breaking completely new ground in English historiography and expected his views to be met with incredulity and hostility. He had complete confidence in the methodology and the range of critical techniques which he was able to bring to bear on this and indeed on any other subject. He was willing to follow 'without hesitation' the results dictated by his objective tests of source criticism. His work, in this respect, contrasts strongly with that of both Acton and Ranke. Both the latter spent years turning the evidence over and over, changing their minds and only finally coming to Lingard's conclusion fifty years later, when the world of scholarship at large had agreed on it.[49] Lingard's approach to source criticism would appear to have been much more 'scientific' in his application of an objective methodology and then accepting decisively the results produced by it. The two vital factors accompanying his procedure, which reflect his true stature in English historiography, are that he created these objective tests himself and that, after nearly two centuries of later progress, we can look back and see that his final historical judgements, based on them, were right.

Lingard insisted that the interpretation of evidence should harmonize closely with the known historical context – the roles of people, their personal relationships and the known sequence of events. There is in his work an elusive quality brought about by his appreciation that the truth lies in perspective. He could always 'see the wood for the trees'. He was able to stand back and take the larger view within which historical detail took shape and meaning. The lack of such a perspective was, I believe, Ranke's weakness. His archival work was massive in the second half of his career and he was completely immersed in the detail. However, in the last analysis, Ranke fell short in 'breadth of mind and judgment'.[50] Interestingly, Acton left an early manuscript note in the Cambridge University Library, saying that Ranke's greatest weakness was 'in selection, in proportion and in perspective . . . He was "not guided by the importance of events" themselves'.[51]

The particular quality of seeing things in perspective and 'earthing' historical interpretation in the sequence of 'events themselves', informed all Lingard's work and his life in general. He could see English history within the greater whole of Europe. His detailed work in source criticism was meticulous, but he could also stand back to make sound judgements. More generally, the Catholic bishops relied heavily on these qualities when they sought and followed his advice in the campaign leading to Catholic Emancipation in 1829.[52]

Lingard had a fine sense of humour[53] which was part of his overall balance of mind. It was typical of him, for example, that when he noticed the stage coach stopping outside his residence for travellers to catch a glimpse of 'Dr. Lingard at work on his *History*', he made his large Sicilian poodle, Etna (an obliging animal) sit at his desk dressed in his own coat and spectacles, so that the astonished travellers could catch an amazing sight of 'Dr. Lingard' through the windows. The spirit of truth is very near the spirit of humour, both of them being related closely to an ability to see things in perspective. Henri Bergson, the French philosopher, wrote somewhere: 'laughter is above all a form of correction'.[54] We can laugh when we have the ability to recognize that things are grotesquely 'out of joint'. Humour was one of Lingard's most important qualities as a man and as a historian.

Chapter III
The Collation of Sources and Lingard's Use of Public Records as a Tool of Source Criticism

'The only sure way of coming at the truth, is to compare together the different letters in the several collections which allude to the same thing.'
John Lingard

Lingard did not publish an account of the rules of source criticism which he employed, apart from the one exception discussed in the previous chapter. Otherwise, his techniques of source criticism emerge only from his correspondence and private papers, and from the working practices revealed by a detailed study of his use of sources in his *History*.

The first and most obvious method which emerges is *the simple collation of evidence, used as a consistent technique*. Lingard saw that the truth of a historical episode was to be found by comparing, contrasting and evaluating a number of separate contemporary accounts. The truth would lie in the perspective which emanates from this process. It would be a prime method of overthrowing an 'official' and prejudiced view of the past that had relied on the repetition of an account based upon sources which expressed only one viewpoint. Because English historians had not wanted to look further than the official nationalist view which had satisfied them and their readers, they had not began to investigate the simple technique of collation of sources. Even this rudimentary step was therefore a very important innovation when Lingard began to use it consistently as an essential approach to evidence on diverse subjects. Thus Sir Cuthbert Sharp could write to Lingard in 1839 – while preparing his own *History of the Rebellion of 1569* – saying that 'Your's is the only History I can rely on' and that 'the herd of historians follow in the same track'.[1] Lingard wrote to a friend in 1821, referring to the various collections of state papers then becoming available:

> The only sure way of coming at the truth, is to compare together the different letters in the several collections which allude to the same thing.[2]

The Collation of Sources and Use of Public Records

Again, receiving a letter informing him that the Duke of Norfolk would give him the use of all the materials in his extensive library, Lingard writes to a friend:

> Before I had read half of it, I sprang from my chair & ran round the room exclaiming 'Vive le duc de Norfolk'. I shall now be quite set for a long time & trust that by collating so many original papers, I shall be able to make a history of Elizabeth etc something different from those which we now have.[3]

It is interesting here to compare Lingard's excited reaction to the opportunity of seeing new original material, with that of David Hume who was made a similar offer during the previous century. Hume wrote to Adam Smith, a philosopher-friend, explaining why he had not taken up the offer:

> Some push me to continue the 'History'... All the Marlborough papers are offered me... I am become too wise either to want censure or praise.[4]

Hume was a philosopher-historian whose interest was not so much in seeing new evidence or collating original material, but rather in applying already conceived theories to the data.[5]

There are other examples in the Lingard papers of his emphasis on the importance of being able to collate different sources dealing with the same subject.[6]

In Lingard's *History* itself there are innumerable examples in the footnotes of the collation of original source material. For example, referring to the execution of the Duke of Monmouth for his leadership of the rebellion in 1685 against James II, we get:

> See for all these particulars the Buccleugh MS... Account of the execution of the duke of Monmouth, signed by the four divines and the sheriffs; Somers' Tracts...; Letter from Lloyd, bishop of St. Asaph to Fell, Bishop of Oxford...; Barillon, 26 Juillet; Reresby...; Evelyn;...; Dalrymple...; Gazette 2052; Echard...; State Trials, xi. 1068–1083.[7]

Here we have eleven sources of original materials centring on this matter, including manuscript letters, contemporary tracts, diaries, news-sheets, contemporary historians and public accounts taken from the publication of State Trials and foreign despatches.

Again, referring to Charles I's escape from Hampton Court (1647):

> See Ashburnham's letter to the speaker on Nov. 26...; his memoir...; Berkeley...; Journals... Rush...; Clarendon...; Mem. of Hamiltons...; Whitelock... That a letter from Cromwell was received or read by the king, is certain (see Journals...; Berkeley...); that it was written for the purpose of inducing him to escape, and thus fall into the hands of the Levellers, is a gratuitous surmise of Cromwell's enemies.[8]

Here there are eight contemporary and original sources dealing with the matter, including letters, memoirs, an account of a contemporary historian and public documents in the form of Parliamentary Journals.

Apart from the continuous use of collation of evidence, there are various sub-sections of this rule of source criticism and appraisal. For example a very prominent technique frequently used by Lingard, is that of the DIRECT COMPARISON OF TWO DIFFERENT SETS OF EVIDENCE, USUALLY REPRESENTING TWO DIFFERENTLY INTERESTED PARTIES, ON THE SAME POINT. So, during the Cromwellian period, with its constant interplay of relationships between King, Army and Parliament, we find such footnotes as:

> Compare the narratives of Berkeley . . . ; Ashburnham . . . Ludlow . . . and Huntingdon (Journals . . .) with the proposals of the army in Charles's Works . . .[9]

Or,

> Compare Whitelock's narrative of this meeting . . . with Cromwell's in Milton State Papers . . .[10]

Or,

> These particulars may be fairly collected from Whitelock . . . compared with the declaration of the officers, and Cromwell's speech to his parliament . . .[11]

Or,

> Compare the narrative published by the army (Rushworth . . .) with the letters sent by the commissioners to the House of Lords, Journals . . . and Herbert's Memoirs . . .[12]

Other more specialized sub-categories of the general technique of collation in the *History* are the:

> *comparing of English with French, Spanish and Dutch sources when the subject involves England's relationships with these other countries.*[13]

The frequently used rule by which a source is:

> *devalued if its statements are not confirmed by a second source which could be expected to have known if they were true.*[14]

The extra authority given to a statement:

> *when two sources of opposing interests agree on it.*[15]

Or the greater weight to be given when:

> *two independent sources agree on certain questionable points without any sort of consort between them.*[16]

The Collation of Sources and Use of Public Records

Again, Lingard works on the premiss that:

> *any charge or accusation needs confirmation from another source of good quality, if it is to be taken seriously.*[17]

And the need:

> *always to hear the other side – to hear what the accused has to say for himself.*[18]

Another interesting technique, used within this general category, is the giving of:

> *added weight to the evidence where the despatches of two or more foreign ambassadors from different countries, agree on a common view concerning a domestic matter in England.*[19]

Such reports have the advantage of being 'outside the situation'; but they need to be compared in case there is any question of one ambassador wishing to give a particular slant to his report for his own purposes.[20] Lingard wishes to write as a 'citizen of the world'.[21] Therefore the use of foreign archives and the reports of foreign ambassadors played a large part in his effort to give a 'Euro-centric' rather than 'Anglo-centric' account of English history.[22] We are reminded of Lingard's unprecedented pursuit of such source material in the archives of France, Italy, the Vatican, Spain, Malta and Portugal; and also that he was the first historian to understand the importance of the Venetian ambassadors' reports, long before Ranke did.[23]

One can hardly overestimate a central and fundamentally important technique – a cornerstone of modern methodology – related to the collation of sources and used consistently by Lingard, for the first time in English historiography. The epoch-making tool in Lingard's restructuring of the English past was his:

> *use of public records as primary sources which could be used to check the credibility of other contemporary sources.*

For the Anglo-Saxon period, the *Anglo-Saxon Chronicle* is used in this capacity.[24] The editions of various collections of legal and Church documents, such as those of Wilkins' *Concilia* (1737) or Sir Henry Spelman's *Concilia* (1639), are used in the same way.[25] Interestingly, too, Lingard was the first English historian to recognize the extraordinary quality of Bede's *Ecclesiastical History* (737),[26] which made it a primary authority for checking and testing other sources. Bede and the *Anglo-Saxon Chronicle* are often used together for this purpose, in remarks such as: 'This appears the most plausible manner of reconciling Ethelward ... with the Saxon Chronicle ... and Bede ...'[27]

The Collation of Sources and Use of Public Records

So, too, as we saw above, Lingard was able to give the modern account of the coming of Christianity to England, as opposed to Hume's reliance on legends and fables, by using Bede's *History*.[28] Modern historians now use Bede and the *Anglo-Saxon Chronicle* in the same way – as primary sources with which to test others.[29]

The technique becomes even more apparent in Lingard's treatment of the chroniclers of the medieval period. Here there were more formal public records of various kinds to consult. Lingard uses Parliamentary Writs, the Rolls Close and Patent, as well as public instruments of various kinds with which to check the contemporary chroniclers such as Matthew Paris and Wendover who had particular axes to grind in a way which warped their contemporary accounts.

The use of this technique had a dramatic effect on Lingard's account of the medieval period. English historians had relied heavily and almost exclusively on the chroniclers. An edition of Matthew Paris's *Chronicle* was published by Archbishop Matthew Parker in 1571 and this was re-edited in 1640, to provide one of the mainstays of English historical writing on this period. The jaundiced view of Paris and Wendover was just the kind of source which Reformation propaganda found most useful in attacking the 'Dark Ages' and papal 'domination'. It continued to mislead some of our best historians until the middle of the twentieth century, when outstanding medievalists such as M. D. Knowles and C. Cheney demonstrated that they could not be relied upon as authentic sources.[30]

One classic example is the 'official' treatment of the relationship between King John and the Papacy. In 1205 the monks of Canterbury had chosen the very able Stephen Langton to be the Archbishop of Canterbury. The Pope ratified this choice, but King John rejected it. This caused the conflict between John and the Papacy, which lasted until 1213 when John finally submitted to Papal authority in this matter.

Relying on Paris and Wendover, English historians had used his reign to 'demonstrate the Protestant-nationalist theme of the tyrannical nature of papal interference' and the 'shameful humiliation' of the English king and his subjects.[31] Lingard proved conclusively the unreliability of these chroniclers by checking them against the official, public documents, published for example in the Rolls Close and in Rymer's *Foedera, Conventiones, et Acta Publica* (1704-35)

> In most narratives of this transaction so many errors are found, that I may be allowed to state the naked facts, as they exist in authentic documents still extant ... The foregoing statement, drawn from authentic sources, shows how little credit is due to Matthew Paris, and also to Wendover, whose work Paris copies and occasionally interpolates. The narratives of both these writers abound with errors.

The Collation of Sources and Use of Public Records

Lingard corrects even Rymer's editorship of the documents, showing from the documents themselves, that:

> the titles of the several instruments in Rymer seem to have been copied out of Paris, and are equally calculated to mislead the reader. They are evidently contradicted by the contents of the documents to which they are prefixed . . .[32]

The detailed scholarship involved in using the public records as a check on Paris and Wendover enabled Lingard to give a drastically different picture of the relationship between King John and Pope Innocent III. But, intriguingly, the old story continued, in spite of Lingard, until the intervention of three distinguished medieval specialist scholars in the twentieth century. In 1948 Professor C. R. Cheney finally expressed surprise 'that historians have not been more concerned about the difficulty of accepting this testimony of Wendover'. He showed that, by collating the various chroniclers with the public records:

> the details of Wendover's narrative cannot be other than the products of imagination . . . in the history of this episode, fiction has successfully masqueraded as fact for more than seven hundred years.[33]

Cheney, like Lingard, took away those elements which had been used from the time of the Reformation to prejudice the feelings of English people against the Papacy. Like Lingard, he placed it within a different historical context – of diplomacy and strategy within a European framework, rather than the narrow categories of nationalism and insular Protestantism which warped the views of later historians. As a result 'the terror-stricken tyrant and the domineering priest disappear from the story of well-calculated diplomacy by two men, each of whom had qualities of greatness'.[34]

However, Lingard had reached this position in 1819, by using the technique of testing the accounts of contemporary chroniclers against the public records of the medieval period.

In this way he dismantled in detail the old version of events in John's reign, which had become, by constant repetition, an assumption of thought in England. To take just one example of this we may look at the famous episode – highlighted in all the old histories – in which the papal legate, Pandulph, haughtily trampled under his feet the money offered by the 'humiliated' John as a token of his homage to the Papacy, at the time of his submission. Lingard dismissed this highly emotive scene in his usual very simple, effective and economical manner:

> Paris, moreover . . . describes Pandulph after the homage receiving the money, and trampling it in his pride under foot, though, as the reader has seen [from the public records], the money was not paid till several months afterwards.[35]

The Collation of Sources and Use of Public Records

But Lingard adds to this detailed source criticism a broad perspective which is not only Euro-centric, but adjusted to the norms and realities of the medieval period. In this way he was striking at the heart of the whig interpretation of history:

> Though the principles of morality are unchangeable, our ideas of honour and infamy perpetually vary with the ever-varying state of society. To judge impartially of our ancestors, we are not to measure their actions by the standards of the present manners and notions; we should transport ourselves back to the age in which they lived, and take into account their political institutions, their principles of legislation and government.[36]

This statement may be commonplace to us, but in Lingard's day it struck a completely new and revolutionary note in English historiography. The whig practice of reading the present into the past was to dominate English historical writing for another century and more. Lingard's statement was a seminal idea in the later development of modern 'revisionist' thinking.

Lingard proceeds to show that the stage of vassalage was not a matter of degradation in the thirteenth century. Many princes in Christendom had been in that position, including John's father (the very formidable Henry II) and brother Richard. John had entered into it with the agreement of the council of barons, showing that, in the circumstances, they did not consider it dishonourable to John or themselves. Also, it had meant that John – and his posterity on the English throne – would be defended by the Papacy against internal or external attack. The papal decision to ratify the appointment of the very able Stephen Langton as Archbishop of Canterbury, which had been the great subject at issue, was to be extremely important for English history. He was to play a very important part in the making of Magna Carta in 1215.

This perspective could only have been established by one who understood the medieval world, with the Papacy at the centre of a united Christendom and the European feudal institutions providing the background. Previous, contemporary and much later English historians, looking through the lens of English nationalism and Protestantism, saw events only in the light of a 'foreign and alien power', encroaching on the rights of an 'independent nation'. Lingard was attacked by critics who were 'a little astonished to find' that he had 'put in an elaborate plea to extenuate the infamy of John in this abject submission to the church of Rome'.[37] Lingard in fact had achieved a position of scholarly insight and understanding on this subject, which was not to be recovered again for more than a century.

The 'protestant-whig' view of this subject, maintained by Lingard's critics, continued to dominate English historiography until well into the twentieth century, when the combined specialist research work of three fine scholars, Sir Maurice Powicke (in his *Stephen Langton*, 1928), Dom

The Collation of Sources and Use of Public Records

David Knowles (in an essay on 'The Canterbury Election of 1205-6', 1938) and finally C. R. Cheney (in his essay on 'The Alleged Deposition of King John, 1948), combined to overthrow the old view. They showed, in turn, that Pope Innocent II was no power-mad foreign tyrant, but was simply concerned to carry out his duty in seeing that the Canon law of the universal Church was administered normally and that the normal rights of the Church in England were protected. The outcome – the final acceptance by John of Stephen Langton as the Archbishop of Canterbury – was in fact in the interests of England as well as the Church. Factual history had been sacrificed to the interests of propagandist causes for four hundred years, ever since the Tudor propagandists had exploited the jaundiced accounts of Wendover and Paris to the full, in pursuit of their own political interests. Powicke remarked in 1928 that:

> I doubt if the insularity of English historical inquiry . . . has had as misleading consequences in any matter as in its treatment of this quarrel between John and the Papacy.

And Knowles, in 1938 added that the highly influential medievalist, Bishop William Stubbs, had continued to lead people astray on the subject at the end of the nineteenth century:

> Amost all, whether scholars and specialists, or compilers of text books, who have written since the chief sources for the narrative appeared in Roll Series some fifty years ago, have followed very closely the account given by Bishop Stubbs . . . It is the purpose of this note to point out that a number of incidents in the narrative as given by Stubbs cannot be accepted as historical facts.[38]

Lingard, however, in isolation among English historians, had achieved the scholarly insights of these later medievalist scholars as far back as 1819. This had been achieved first by his sense of historical perspective, in placing English history within the framework of European medieval history, and secondly by his detailed techniques of source criticism in dealing with the medieval chroniclers.

There are numerous other examples of Lingard's critically important technique of checking medieval chroniclers against the public records, dealing with matters of purely secular history. These show that Lingard was not just using the technique to defend the interests of his own Church, but as a means of achieving the truth about the past in general. He writes, for example, concerning the position of Hubert de Burgh in 1232:

> The mistakes of the last writer [Matthew Paris] are to be corrected by the record Pat. 17. Hen III. m. 9.

And concerning disquiet in the Commons about the influence of Alice Perrers over Edward III, Lingard notes:

The Collation of Sources and Use of Public Records

> Rot. Parl. II. 329. Murimuth (p. 134) [chronicler] says they petitioned that she might be removed from the king's person; Walsingham repeats the same [p. 189], and most modern writers tell us that she actually was removed. But it appears from the rolls of Parliament that nothing more was done than is mentioned above.[39]

With regard to scandals surrounding the personal life of King John, Lingard refuses to be taken far from the reliable public sources:

> See Paris ... West [minister] ... Giral [dus] ... Heming [ford] ... These statements of the chroniclers may, after all, have no other foundation than the unauthenticated scandal of the day ... It appears to me from a diligent comparison of the dates to the entries on the rolls ... See Rot. Pat ... Rot. Claus ...[40]

Lingard is similarly unimpressed in general with the reliability of the chronicler Jean Froissart (originally from the Netherlands), when tested against public documents such as the Rolls of Parliament:

> Froissart may be accurate in his account of the sieges and battles [in the war 1383, between England and France] but it is evident from the Rolls and documents in Rymer, that he was misinformed as to the real object of the expedition.

And, again, concerning the impeachment of certain ministers in the reign of Richard II:

> Froissart, indeed, tells us ... but his whole narrative differs so widely from the authentic particulars contained in the Rolls. that it deserves no credit. It seems to be made up of every flying report which reached him.[41]

Lingard is reluctant to accept what is not confirmed by the rolls:

> I have neglected many circumstances mentioned by historians as I consider them mere fictions invented by the king's [Richard II's] enemies; the intention of indicting the framers of the commission [against Richard's opponents] I have admitted, as the indictment itself is still extant on the Rolls [p. 234].[42]

Sometimes the public records confirm the chroniclers' accounts:

> The testimony of the old chroniclers (Tit. Liv ... Wals ... Elm ...) is fully borne out by parliamentary documents, judicial records, and royal proclamations – Rot. Parl ... Rym ...[43]

But *the primacy of the public records is always made clear*; they outweigh the authority of a contemporary manuscript and a contemporary chronicle put together:

The Collation of Sources and Use of Public Records

> We are told . . . But this account must be erroneous. From several writs, which are still extant, it appears . . .[44]

> The contemporary author in MS . . . assures us . . . [and] Froissart . . . Both agree . . . But the Rolls of parliament declare.[45]

Often, Lingard's reliance on public documents saved him from attributing modern ideas to medieval people, by reading history backwards, which was what most English historians were doing up to the time of modern 'revisionism'. G. M. Trevelyan [PLATE 14], in his enormously popular and influential writing on the unique development of English institutions, for example, was often able to provide an inspiring story of the continuous progress of English freedom from medieval to modern times. His work was applauded commensurately by an admiring and thankful nation which rewarded him with the highest honours, academic and civic.[46]

Lingard was a very patriotic Englishman. Yet, by abiding closely to his own scholarly standards, sticking close to his 'authentic' sources, resisting any attempt to regard England as unique – a 'special case' in the world – or to read later ideas back into the past, he was able to make the necessary reservations which have been repeated in our day by modern revisionists.

So, writing of constitutional events in fourteenth-century England, Lingard comments:

> The opinion that the several estates sat and voted together derives no support from the language of the rolls . . . In the language of the time the law was said to emanate from the will of the king, at the petition of the subject. The reader, however, is not to suppose that because the petition was granted, the object of the petitioners had been obtained . . . the king, satisfied with the aid which he had obtained, dismissed the parliament, and thought little of the petitions which he had granted. Sometimes they were entirely forgotten; at others they were formed into statutes but never published; often they were so altered in the principal provisions as not to reach the grievance which they were originally designed to abolish.[47]

And:

> It was long before the advice of the latter [the Commons] was required by the crown; and when Edward III at last condescended to ask it, the sequel proved that it was a pretext to call upon them for money. They could not, he afterwards observed, refuse to aid him in the prosecution of those plans into which he had been led by their advice. Taught by experience, they sometimes declined the task.[48]

There are none of those glowing and 'inspiring' passages which characterized Trevelyan's work[49] in Lingard's account – only a sober narrative of the facts. Herein is the reason why Lingard was attacked by contemporary whig reviews for not being enthusiastic enough in describing the marvellous story of the continuous growth of English freedom through parliamentary development.[50] But it saved him, in fact, from falling into the whig interpretation of the English past – the reading of the future into the past – which dominated English historical writing until the late twentieth century.[51] Lingard's work is often more up to date with modern scholarship now than that of many of his twentieth-century successors.

Of course Lingard's *History* would not have served as a morale-raiser for the British spirit, as Trevelyan's did so notably in the 1940s,[52] when Britain was fighting against daunting odds in the Great War against Hitler. However, the aim of historical writing – and the criterion against which it must be judged – is simply to tell the truth about the past, not to serve as a morale-raiser for any cause. It is the truth which sets us free, in whatever realm we are pursuing it; and in the long run it serves us better. Here, then, is one of the most important lessons for all nations at the beginning of the new millennium. To establish peace among nations it is necessary for national history books to pursue the truth rather than serve any other perceived advantage.

Lingard's account of the English past serves us much better, for example, as a guide to important decisions concerning England's role in the world of the new millennium, than does Trevelyan's historical works; though Lingard has never, as yet, been honoured in England. Simply because he told the truth about the past, English history is placed in a perspective which corresponds more to the needs, realities and expectations of the world around us. We have to accept, for example, that the English are not 'special' in any sense which does not apply to other peoples; that the English are not independent, different in any fundamental sense, or superior to the rest of the world. England, of course, like other countries, has much to celebrate as well as to regret. Other countries have had their own parliaments. There are serious claims that Iceland had the first. England, for most of its history, has been part of the European community of peoples; all enjoying their own particular qualities and special achievements. Moreover, all of us share the dignity of being human and part of the human family. We are all 'citizens of one world' – Lingard's stated stance in writing his *History*.[53] His answer to critics was the calm and patient assertion that 'Time and experience must decide between us'.[54] Of all historians, he is the least susceptible to changing fashions in historian writing. He keeps to the facts and his style is perenially pelucid.

The sixteenth and seventeenth centuries have been called by G. P. Gooch, a distinguished student of history and historiography,[55] the 'two critical centuries of English history'; Gooch added that Lingard had provided 'the first modern account' of these periods.[56] One of the principal reasons for this was Lingard's use of the public and private sources for these periods, for the first time, as important complementary tools of source criticism.

With Lingard's treatment of the sixteenth and seventeenth centuries, we find the Journals of Parliament coming into prominence as primary records with which to check other secondary sources. The Tudor chroniclers had been dragooned into the propagandist cause of the Tudor monarchy[57] and were quite unreliable if used on their own. They had been taught to see English history from the viewpoint of the new Government. They became standard bearers for the 'official view' of the English past.[58]

Two other standard sources used by English historians as the basis for their 'Great Myth' of the English past[59] were John Foxe's *Book of Martyrs* (1563), one of the world's most effective pieces of propaganda, which had a massive influence on the thinking of the English;[60] and Gilbert Burnet's *History of the Reformation* (1679–1715), perhaps the most officially sponsored of English works[61] [see PLATE 7]. English historians used these two books as primary authorities. This fashion was completely in vogue in Lingard's time, when his contemporaries saw nothing wrong in simply quoting Foxe and Burnet as their authorities.[62] In the early nineteenth century these writers were generally regarded as:

> our ancestorial traditionary 'standard ecclesiastical authorities', accepted and received as Canonical Books.[63]

But with Lingard, for the first time in English historiography, Foxe and Burnet, together with the chroniclers such as Holinshed and Hall, and other contemporary writers and propagandists, were now to be tested by cool and detached references to the impersonal and coldly indisputable criteria of the official public records – Parliamentary Journals, State Papers, the Council book, Treasury documents and State Trials. This new technique, in Lingard's hands, changed the old type of propagandist warfare between writers of opposing sides[64] into the modern-style examination by source criticism. So, for example:

> If we believe Holinshed . . . and Hall . . . yet there can be little doubt that it is a mistake. For in all the public records . . .[65]

> On the testimony of Foxe we are told . . . (Foxe . . . ; Burnet . . .) but this statement . . . seems irreconcilable with the Journals . . .[66]

> Compare Foxe . . . and Burnet . . . with the Council Book, Harl. MSS . . . or State Trials.[67]

> Burnet . . . tells us . . . but it is plain from the Journals . . . that instead . . .[68]

> I have extracted these particulars from the original depositions in the Burghley State Papers . . . Several other particulars mentioned by historians I have omitted, because they are not supported by these documents.[69]

> Burnet has fallen into two errors . . . Journals . . .[70]

The Collation of Sources and Use of Public Records

It is important, however, to observe that this technique was used consistently by Lingard in his examination of all sources, not simply to deal with Protestant propagandists.[71] So, for example, Noailles, the French ambassador during Mary Tudor's reign, is found to be unreliable when tested against the public records:

> Noailles says that several bills proposed by the court were rejected . . . ; yet only one of them is mentioned in the journals of either house . . . It was unanimously passed by the Lords, but was lost on a division in the Commons Journals, . . .[72]
>
> According to Noailles . . . If it was so, the subject was not followed up. There is no mention of any such motion in the journals.[73]

Similarly the contemporary historian Polydore Vergil, who wrote his *Anglicae historia libri* (1534), is corrected:

> We are told, on the authority of Polydore . . . This is probably a fiction . . . Rym. xiii. 553. No more credit is due to the tale . . . Rymer xiii. 777.[74]

Here Lingard is using the public records published by Thomas Rymer, in his *Foedera* (1703–14), as a check on the account of Vergil, an Italian resident in England during Henry VIII's reign.

Similarly Sir James Melville (1535–1617) left a valuable account of his times in his *Memoirs* which were first printed in 1683. Lingard refers to this source but finds it unreliable after testing it against the public records:

> I do not believe Melville's story respecting Lord Herries . . . for that nobleman appears in every instrument about this time as a supporter of Mary and Bothwell.[75]

Again, the Lord Treasurer's Accounts proved that Riccio was never one of the Mary Queen of Scots' musicians:

> as is generally believed on the authority of Melville. But Melville's memoirs abound with tales, of which many are doubtful, many most certainly false.[76]

David Riccio (or Rizzio) was in fact royal French secretary to Mary, before he was murdered by Darnley, Mary's husband, in 1566.

In his treatment of seventeenth-century sources, Lingard follows the same methodology. Again, he tested the reliability of contemporary writers, historians, diarists and writers of Memoirs, against the evidence of public records: For example, Rushworth produced his *Historical Collections* between 1618 and 1648. Ludlow's *Memoires*, Bishop Kennet's *Register and Compleat History of England*, and Gilbert Burnet's *History of His Own Times* were other contemporary descriptions of

The Collation of Sources and Use of Public Records

events. Lingard tested all these against the evidence of the public records, especially the Journals of Parliament:

> It has been said by Rushworth . . . But this is a mistake. The Journals show . . .[77]

> Ludlow makes the present [to Richard Cromwell in 1659] tweny thousand pounds; but the sum of two thousand pounds is written at length in the Journals.[78]

> According to Kennet, the majority [vote in Lords, to proclaim William and Mary as King and Queen in 1689] was only twenty, to Clarendon twenty-five. But he numbers one hundred and nineteen peers as present, whilst the journals mention only one hundred and twelve.[79]

> Kennet tells us . . . but this is a mistake . . . See Lords Journals . . .[80]

> See the preceding references, and State Tracts . . . If the reader compare Burnet . . . with these authorities he will observe how strangely truth and falsehood are mixed up together in the narrative of the prelate.[81]

> Burnet says . . . Sir J. Lowther, indeed, seems to confirm Burnet . . . but both are contradicted by the testimony of the Journals . . .[82]

> Burnet's account of the trial [of Alicia Lisle, 1685] abounds with inaccuracies . . . he tells us . . . but of these three verdicts, there appears no notice either in the printed trial, or in the paper which Mrs Lisle delivered to the sheriffs at her death . . . This is a representation calculated to mislead the reader . . . [see] State Trials, xi, 355.[83]

> Burnet tells us [concerning the execution of the Earl of Strafford, 1641] N.B. . . . this is told very incorrectly [see] Journals.[84]

> Compare Rushworth with the Journals . . .[85]

The Public Records are used to support the testimony of contemporary manuscript accounts of the Gunpowder Plot, which had been sent to Lingard by the Jesuits from the Stonyhurst archives:

> This account is given both by Gerard and Greenway, and it is supported by the Journals . . .[86]

One of the most famous contemporary accounts of the Civil War period was that of Edward Hyde, Earl of Clarendon (1608–74), in his *History of the Great Rebellion*, published later in 1707. He was certainly in a position to know – being in a central position to observe events during this period – but his account is much diminished in *authority* (credibility) after Lingard checked it against the public records:

> If the reader compares the detailed narrative of these proceedings by Clarendon [with] the official account in the Journals . . . he will be surprised at the numerous inaccuracies of the historian. See also the State Trials . . .[87]

The Collation of Sources and Use of Public Records

> Whoever will compare the account in Clarendon ... with the Journals ... will be astonished at the inaccuracies of the historian. In five material points, including the principal part of his narrative, he is flatly contradicted by the testimony of the Journals ...[88]
>
> Commons Journals ... Lords' Journals ... Clarendon's statements cannot be reconciled with the Journals ...[89]

Contemporary tracts are also tested against primary sources, *showing an important distinction to be made in the use of sources*:

> Secret Consults ... This tract ... though it is often cited, is from frequent contradiction of more authentic documents, entitled to very little credit. *It may show what reports circulated in Ireland, but cannot be assumed as an authority for facts.*[90]

One of the most important aspects of Lingard's testing of such sources, is THAT IT IS DONE WITHOUT BIAS. Burnet, for example, was one of the most prominent whigs, while Clarendon was one of the very prominent tories in the second half of the seventeenth century. Similarly, the Catholic apologist Nicholas Sander's *De Origine ac Progressu Schismatis Anglicani Libri* was published in Cologne in 1585. Its republication in French was the spur to Burnet's retaliatory *History of the Reformation* (1679). The latter, together with John Foxe's *Book of Martyrs* (1563), formed the Protestant opposition to Sander in the polemic warfare between the two sides. Lingard was not interested in any of these as primary historical sources; but he knew very well that the 'official' view of English history had been built up mainly around Foxe and Burnet. Yet Lingard was able to use them as good evidence on the rare occasions when they satisfied another of his rules of criticism: *that it was good support for the truth of a fact if two writers of opposing sides agreed on it*:

> It has been said that ... but this again has been disputed by some modern historians, as depending only on the assertion of Sanders. It is, however, also mentioned by Foxe ... *I am indeed aware that the authority of Foxe is not one jot better than that of Sanders, but when two writers of opposite parties agree in the same statement, it may be presumed to have some foundation in truth.*[91]

It is possible – though there is no evidence for this in the Lingard papers – that the technique of testing 'private' sources against public records may have owed some of its original impetus to its usefulness in demonstrating that certain fundamental anti-Catholic texts, such as Foxe and Burnet, which formed the basis of the three-centuries old 'official version' of the English past, were not in fact trustworthy. If so, the technique seems almost immediately to have outstripped this more limited aim, to become an essential tool which Lingard used for pursuing the truth in history. *He* used it as a necessary instrument to test all secondary sources in all aspects of historical investigation. The methodology was undoubtedly seen as valuable in itself as a tool for pursuing historical truth. Lingard was demonstrating, for the first time in English historiography, what we would now call A 'SCIENTIFIC' APPROACH TO SOURCE CRITICISM in its full meaning.

To indicate its recognition by Lingard as a conscious part of his equipment as a historian, it is useful to observe the value of public records emerging in his private papers and letters at various stages of his working life. In a letter of 1822 to his publisher – when Lingard was preparing his volume on Elizabeth – he complained of a gap in the published Parliamentary Journals for the first year of her reign.[92] Again preparing for his last volume of the first edition on Charles II and James II, he wrote to his publisher in 1827:

> If Mr. Upcot is printing the debates, they may come out in time enough. I shall only want them to compare with what I have written and perhaps the alterations may not be great.[93]

And while preparing for his last edition, in 1849, he writes to a friend:

> In Vol. X of the journals of the house of Commons which you have, you will find the official account of proceedings on the 26 of Octr. 1689 . . . Now this answer I derive from Dodd . . . who copies Wood's Athenae Oxonienses. Now I fear to rely upon these when I may have an official account to consult. I will thank Dr. Tate to compare the above with the account in the journals themselves and to let me know whether my account differs, if differ it does, and that he would add from the journals any particular which he may think it important for me to know: which he may easily do by comparing the Journals with Dodd, iii. 456.[94]

And finally, in a letter written by Lingard, now aged seventy-nine – a year before his death – we find another reference to this habitual technique. He is here concerned with the subject of the unreliability of the despatches of Noailles, the French ambassador in Mary Tudor's reign. Although a contemporary source, Noailles has been tested against the public records and found to be deficient:

> The quotation from Noailles is placed there in contrast with the testimony of the journals to accustom the reader to consider him as totally unworthy of credit. There are several quotations from him for that sole purpose.[95]

THE GREAT VALUE OF PUBLIC RECORDS OF ALL KINDS AS PRIMARY SOURCES, TO BE USED AS TESTING INSTRUMENTS IN HIS BATTERY OF TECHNIQUES OF SOURCE CRITICISM, *remained uppermost in Lingard's mind throughout his career as a historian.*

If we are ever inclined to think of source criticism as a somewhat arid

The Collation of Sources and Use of Public Records

academic exercise, it was never that to Lingard. The conveying of the truth about the past was to him nothing less than the passing on of collective memory from one generation to another. False myths, buried in the collective memory of a nation, can be a real cause of prejudice, fear, hatred and strife between peoples. The truth can set us free from them even if it takes a long time to accomplish. One perfect example of this is Lingard's painstaking treatment of the 'Irish Massacre' of 1641. The 'memory' of this notorious and infamous episode, as conveyed by English historians for nearly two centuries before Lingard, was one of the major causes of English hostility and prejudice against Catholicism and the Irish people. This feeling was rife when Lingard was writing his *History*, because it was the era (1819-29) when the movement for Catholic emancipation was being hotly debated in England. Historical accusations against Catholics were being vigorously exploited by those who opposed emancipation.[96]

Lingard introduces his subject:

> The reader will be surprised that I have not alluded to the immense multitude of English Protestants said to have been massacred at the breaking out of the rebellion. I am perfectly aware that Clarendon speaks of 'forty or fifty thousand murdered before they suspected themselves to be in danger . . . that a nameless writer, copied by Nalson, says that the insurgents 'within a few days murdered an incredible number of Protestants, men, women, and children, indiscriminately' . . . ; that May asserts 'that the persons of above 200,000 men, women, and children were murdered, many of them with exquisite and unheard-of tortures, within the space of one month . . . ; and that the same has been repeated by writers without number. *But such assertions appear to me to be rhetorical flourishes rather than historical statements. They are not founded on authentic documents.* They lead the reader to suppose that the rebels had formed a plan to surprise and murder all the Protestant inhabitants, whereas the fact was, that they sought to recover the lands which, in the last and in the present reign, had been taken from them and given to the English planters. They warned the intruders to be gone; they expelled them from the plantations; they seized their goods and burnt their houses. That in the prosecution of this object many lives would be lost on both sides is evident . . . But that no premeditated design of a general massacre existed, and that no such massacre was made, is evident from *the official despatches of the lords justices during the months of October, November and December.*[97]

Lingard brought his techniques of source criticism to bear on the 'Irish Massacre' of 1641 for the first time in English historical writing and with interesting results. He checked the contemporary writer, Clarendon, and the later writers who followed him, against official public records. Lingard proceeded to use the despatches of the lords justices from Ireland, letters to the Privy Council, the Commons and the Lords' Journals, and concluded:

The Collation of Sources and Use of Public Records

> *If we consider the language of these despatches, and at the same time recollect who were the writers, and what an interest they had in exaggerating the excesses of the insurgents, we must, I think, conclude that hitherto no general massacre had been made or attempted.*[98]

The Lords Justices set up a Commission in Ireland to discover how many English Protestants had been killed in the troubles. Lingard notes:

> The commissioners accordingly took depositions from March 24 till October, 1644, and the examinations fill thirty two large volumes folio, deposited in the college library at Dublin.[99]

Lingard comments from an inspection of these documents:

> in infinitely the greatest number of them, the words *being duly sworn*, have the pen drawn through them, with the same ink with which the examinations were written; and in several of those where such words remain, many parts of the examinations are crossed out.[100] [Lingard's italics]

Inspection showed that *'the bulk of this immense collection is parole evidence, and upon report of common fame'*. As such THIS EVIDENCE WAS BASED UPON HEARSAY AND COULD NOT BE RELIED UPON. Lingard is able to take the matter further. For:

> Out of these examinations, therefore, the commissioners collected those statements which had been made upon oath, and consigned them to another book, attesting with their signatures that the copies were correct.[101]

FROM THIS ATTESTED AND SWORN EVIDENCE, *Lingard was able to make his judgement* that four thousand and twenty-eight Protestants were killed by the rebels; and about eight thousand died because of privations caused by the rebellion.[102] Lingard's judgement on the matter, in his *History*, was:

> That they [the rebels] suffered as much as they inflicted, cannot be doubted. But the blame of such barbarities should not rest solely with the perpetrators on either side; it ought to be shared by those who originally sowed the seeds of these calamities by civil oppression and religious persecution.[103]

He added in a letter to a friend that: 'I find the Irish less guilty than I had suspected and their adversaries at least equal to them in cruelty'.[104]

It is difficult now to recapture the bold originality, based on new techniques of source criticism, of these statements made in 1829, after two centuries of repetition of the official version. Lingard expected a violent reaction and wrote to a friend:

> Several small pamphlets etc. have been published against my account of the Massacre of St. Bartholomew. Perhaps as much may be said against the account in my next vol. of the Irish Massacre.[105]

The Collation of Sources and Use of Public Records

The reaction came and was expressed in a way which captures succinctly the spirit in which Lingard's scholarship was resisted by many readers. Contemporary historians, Henry Hallam and Thomas Keightley, ridiculed Lingard's challenge to what every one knew must be true because of its 'public fame'. They ridiculed

> Dr. Lingard's attempt to disprove by mere scraps of quotation, an event of such notoriety, that we must abandon all faith in public fame if it were really unfounded.[106]

In fact modern scholarship has completely vindicated Lingard's account of the rising in Ireland. A century after Lingard, the Stuart specialist, Sir G. M. Trevelyan, wrote:

> Land spoliation, social inequality and religious persecution which had so long been the lot of the Irish Catholics, at length ... produced the inevitable explosion. The general uprising of people ... maddened by the loss of tribal lands and rights, and led by an upper class ... goaded to frenzy by religious persecution, could not but result in terrible atrocities. *Some four or five thousand* Protestants perished by massacre, and a still greater number from cold, hunger, and ill-treatment. Rumour, crossing the channel, told tales yet more ghastly than the truth. While England was celebrating the memory of Guy Fawkes, she learnt that the Catholics of Ireland had massacred the Protestants. All Englishmen, equally ignorant of Ireland, were agreed that the task which Cromwell long afterwards accomplished must be set about at once.[107]

Another Stuart specialist, Geoffrey Davis, wrote in 1937:

> They [the Irish] were necessitated to take up arms, they say, for the preservation of religion ... and the natural and just defence of their country. It is safest to leave it at that.[108]

In 1996, John Morrill, a modern specialist on the Stuart period, stated succinctly that 'the rebellion was a pre-emptive strike by Irish Catholics, desperate to disarm the Protestant community before it launched a pogrom against them'.[109] M. P. Maxwell, writing in 1994 on *The Outbreak of the Irish Rebellion of 1641*, places the events within a wider context, summarizing the main conflict as 'England's nationalist expansion' against 'the Catholic religion's supra-nationalism'.[110] Lingard, typically, had confined himself to an accurate account of what had actually happened. No modern historian has done this better, or surveyed the whole of the evidence so well. One feels that, in a century ahead, Lingard's account will still be seen as the most up-to-date.

English nationalist and Protestant feelings had been exploited for centuries by a false history of this event. It helped to shape English attitudes in Lingard's day and has been part of that wide range of mutually incriminating memories which seems to have marked Anglo-Irish relations up to our own time when Tony Blair has made a public apology to the Irish for past mistreatment by the English Government.

The process by which a better perspective in which the truth lies is established by historical scholarship is not just a matter of an academic exercise. In its own way, by searching for and portraying the truth about the past, it can produce its fruits in creating a better understanding and relationship between peoples of different countries – albeit that the process may take a long time. The patient and laborious task of creating a true historical perspective is much more difficult and painstaking than the easy exploitation of prejudices, which lies at the heart of most nationalist myths. It is, however, a work which contributes significantly to what must be one of humanity's main aspirations in the new millennium – to learn better how to live properly with one another.

We are all enormously influenced by our 'collective memory'. It is important to dispel national myths which usually identify evil as that which exists in 'the enemy' nation or in this or that group of perceived 'aliens'. True history teaches us that evil is something which can divide every human heart. As a priest who spent much of his time hearing the confessions of other people, Lingard knew more about this than most of us. Unlike Lord Acton, Lingard was always interested in understanding the people of the past rather than judging them.[111]

Lingard was the first English historian to establish what is now taken for granted: that public records have an authority which establishes them as primary sources, against which the reliability of other contemporary writers – chroniclers, historians, diarists and writers of memoirs – can be tested. This is because, public records, by their very nature are public and objective witnesses of the factual truth of certain events, as opposed to the private or subjective witness of these other contemporary sources. In contemporary focus this is why, on certain important occasions, we have to produce public documents such as birth or marriage certificates as reliable proof of these publicly-attested happenings. And this is why, too, they are comparatively reliable – or as Lingard would describe them, 'authentic' – sources. I say 'comparatively' because, as we shall see in the following chapter, public documents, in certain circumstances, can themselves be manipulated by unscrupulous governments for their own purposes. Lingard knew this and had his own way of dealing with this situation.[112]

Recognition of the primacy in source value of official public records and its use as a critical tool for dealing with other secondary sources is of great importance in the history of historical writing. A cursory reading of the contemporary English historians in the early nineteenth century shows that none of them – Lingard apart – were remotely aware of this development. Sharon Turner's *History of the Reigns of Edward VI, Mary and Elizabeth* (1827), Henry Hallam's *Constitutional History of England* (1827) and Henry Soames' *History of The Reformation of the Church of England* (1839), not to mention the earlier but still most popular *History of England* (1754-62) by David Hume – all reveal the great extent to which they depended unthinkingly, and proudly so, on the famous secondary texts of Foxe and Burnet, supplemented by the selected documents of the Anglican John Strype,[113] for their source material. None of these writers checked these sources against public records. They were all purveyors of the age-old, 'official' version maintained by the 'Great Myth' of the English past.[114] And they were retelling a story which everyone had accepted for three hundred years. They were under no necessity to impel themselves towards any kind of invention or innovation of this kind.

Indeed the next historian to dominate the English scene, with his hugely popular *History of England* (1849-55), was Lord Macaulay – the 'greatest of the whig historians'[115] – who maintained the old whig interpretation, but expressed it in the attractively beguiling form of historical writing, seen as a branch of 'high literature' or the 'belles-lettres'. He was completely ignorant, while blissfully sure of his own certainties, of the revolution in terms of scientific methodology in source criticism introduced by Lingard. He was aware of – but only enough to ridicule – Lingard's rewriting of English history, which was based on source criticism. Lingard's new account, to Macaulay, was an attempt to deny things which 'everyone' else – particularly himself – 'knew' to be true because 'popular opinion' had supported a blinkered interpretation for centuries.[116]

CHAPTER IV

The Role of Private Sources and Their Use as a Tool of Source Criticism

---

'Confidential correspondence ... offers ... the most valuable assistance. It removes the veil ...'

John Lingard, 1819

'The ultimate disclosures are likely to be produced by the more unreserved communications which ministers or diplomats may have exchanged with one another behind the scenes.'

Sir Herbert Butterfield, 1955

While public records were used as a check on the reliability of other sources, Lingard was well aware that many matters of crucial importance would be discoverable only from private or confidential papers. Writing of the historian's task, Lingard observes:

> Among these sources of historical information there is one which deserves his peculiar attention; the confidential correspondence of persons in high and official situations. This offers to him the most valuable assistance. It removes the veil which policy has drawn before the counsels of princes, reveals the secret springs which set in motion the machinery of government, and exhibits kings and ministers in their true character, not as they affect to appear to the public eye, but as they really were in the privacy of their own houses, and in the circle of their familiar acquaintances. Without such documents history is an inert and spiritless mass; from these it may derive both life and vigour.[1]

Lingard's recognition provided a strong impetus to his pursuing private sources wherever possible. Many manuscript sources were still in private hands; some were eventually destined for public archives; others would be lost for ever. Lingard understood their importance, which accounts for his strenuous efforts to locate them. Manuscript sources in the form of despatches or private letters were provided for his inspection by Lord

Hardwick, the Duke of Hamilton, the Earl of Shrewsbury, the Duke of Northumberland, Sir Bourchier Wray, Lady Stafford, Philip Howard of Corby Castle and Mr. Butler at Burton Constable. We find letters in the Lingard correspondence pursuing manuscripts at a Scottish library, and to a Mr. Leigh, in Devonshire, who had 'several original letters between Walsingham & his underlings', found in the attic of his ancestral home.[2] Lingard's reaction here was: 'as I cannot prevail on him to let me have them I have urged him to publish them himself' – which Leigh failed to do.[3] Mr. Kyle, a Scottish bishop, had 'about 60 letters of Mary of Scotland, originals from her to the Archb. of Glasgow' in cipher. A friend, Henry Gillow, was sent to examine manuscripts in the Dean & Chapter Library at Durham. The Duke of Norfolk supplied a manuscript life of Philip Howard which the editor of *State Trials* had failed to secure.[4]

The Jesuits at Stonyhurst were asked for any 'information or documents which you may possess respecting Mary or Elizabeth of England, or Mary of Scotland'.[5] Lingard obtained from them two important manuscript sources concerning Jesuit priests who had been accused of complicity in the Gunpowder Plot (1605), by James I's Government. A modern historian comments that 'Until Lingard . . . historians made few attempts to increase our understanding of the Gunpowder Plot . . . he used two sources hitherto untapped'.[6] These two sources were the manuscripts at Stonyhurst. Lingard himself was able to write in his *History* (in a footnote):

> Before I proceed to the history of the gunpowder plot, I should inform the reader that I am indebted for many of the following particulars to two manuscript narratives in the handwriting of their respective authors: the one in English, by Father John Gerard; the other an Italian translation, but enriched with much additional information, by Father Oswald Greenway. Both were Jesuit missionaries, the familiar acquaintance of the conspirators, and on that account, suspected by the government of having been privy to the plot. They evidently write with feelings of compassion for the fate of their former friends; but they disclose many important particulars which must have been otherwise unknown.[7]

Then there was the unusual and intriguing case of a source which was at once 'public' and private – the Secret Treaty of Dover (1670) between Charles II and Louis XIV. No English historian had ever seen it. It was public knowledge in the sense that everyone knew of it; it was private in the sense that no one except the participants and certain members of Charles II's 'Cabal' really knew what it contained. So, whig historians used its supposed contents as one of the most powerful and inflammatory pieces of propaganda in English history from 1670 onwards. They said that Charles II had arranged, in this treaty, for a French army to come over to England and force Catholicism on the English people, after he

(Charles) had publicly declared his own Catholicism. Here, then, was a dire warning to the English people of what would happen if ever a Catholic came to the English throne; and it was soon made illegal for this ever to happen – as is still the case today. It made Catholics more unpopular than ever in England. No one could deny the rumour because nobody had seen the Treaty. It was perfect material for the whig propagandist view of 1688 as the triumph of English freedom (Protestantism) over despotism and rule by foreign tyrants (Catholicism).

The Secret Treaty had in fact been deposited in the archives of the Clifford family; for Sir Thomas Clifford had been one of the members of the Cabal. Lingard was given the original document of this Treaty by the Clifford family; and he printed it in full (in the French original) as an appendix to his last volume in 1830. It was headed with the remark: 'This important treaty was kept secret till the year 1830, when the late Lord Clifford permitted me to publish it from the original in his possession.'[8]

The Treaty actually says that Charles II intended to declare publicly his conversion to Catholicism. If, as a result, his enemies used this as an excuse to incite a rebellion to overthrow him, Louis XIV would supply him with soldiers to put down such a rebellion and enable him to keep his throne. In a modern edition of English documents, published in 1967, the Secret Treaty is published directly from Lingard's Appendix. Nothing is more eloquent of the remarkable fashion in which Lingard's work has been popularly ignored, than that the old version of the Treaty was still appearing in 1952 in a work used widely as a textbook – of a reputable professional who could not have read the text of this treaty; the mistake is repeated as late as 1995 in *The Companion to British History*.[9]

Lingard also used manuscript sources which were kept in great collections in some of the old library archives abroad as well as at home. He had a network of old friends, many of them priests from Douai and Ushaw, who were now scattered about Britain and the Continent. Friends were used to great effect in the pursuit of manuscript sources. For example, an old pupil of Lingard, and future bishop, was Robert Gradwell who became rector of the English College, Rome, in 1818. He was to become an important 'agent' for Lingard with regard to the Vatican archives. At the British Museum Library a number of helpers were used, including one 'Peter', a Mr. Kaye, Thomas Wright and Tierney. Henry Gillow was given work to do at the Chetham Library in Manchester. Mr. Whedall worked for him at the Oscot College library, and Mr. Kirk at Lichfield. Searches were undertaken for Lingard in the Library at Lancaster and in the library of Norfolk House. Mr. Upcot at the London Institution and Mr. Palgrave, 'sub-commissioner of records', were also very helpful to him.[10]

Lingard's personal impact on the State Paper Office was interesting. He wrote to a friend in 1827:

The Role of Private Sources

> You perhaps know that I had copies of some of the papers in the state paper office respecting the Gunpowder plot. Office copies of everything were made and sent to Mr. Peel by his order . . . Well, Sir, my researches have given birth to more; and now nearly a hundred papers on plot [sic] have been discovered.[11]

Lingard had gained permission from Lord Lansdowne to visit the State Paper Office. He was provided with an 'order' allowing him to study papers concerning the Commonwealth period. But he was not allowed to see anything concerning the Gunpowder Plot, since these papers 'were not comprized in Lord Lansdowne's Order'. Lingard noted that 'of Catholics they appear very jealous'. He adds, quite vehemently: 'It is my intention on my next visit to have these papers included in my order and to ascertain the truth.'[12] His determination succeeded. The relevant papers did in fact appear among the sources in Lingard's account of the Gunpowder Plot.

The story of Lingard's access, through his 'agents', to manuscripts in the archives of Rome, France, Italy, and Spain – and his attempts to gain such materials from Portugal, Malta and Germany – have been told already.[13] And all this, remarkably, was before the great national state archives in Europe had been officially opened to public scrutiny after 1860. Lingard was the first English historian to use these archives for English history.

Lingard was also the first English historian to use manuscript sources, such those in the Harleian and Lansdowne collections, in writing the history of England. It was nearly twenty years later that Ranke, celebrated as the German pioneer of 'scientific' history, came to understand that sixteenth-century history could not be written from the printed materials alone. In fact when Ranke came to produce the first volume of his *History of England Principally in the Seventeenth Century*, in 1858, he used Foxe, Strype, Hallam, Froude and Sharon Turner as authorities for the sixteenth century and did not use the Harleian and Lansdowne manuscripts as Lingard had done. Nor did Ranke recognize, as did Lingard, the major role of Thomas Cromwell in the Reformation movement in England.[14]

In the Lingard papers, we find him ever seeking the kind of material contained in confidential correspondence, especially that between the principal participants in any historical episode. He writes to Robert Gradwell in Rome to inquire after the letters between Henry VIII and Anne Boleyn which had been deposited in the Vatican archives;[15] and after a letter of Mary, Queen of Scots, to the Pope.[16] On the subject of the Divorce, he writes to Gradwell in 1819, while preparing his first edition of the *History*:

> Is there any life or are there any original memoirs of Campejo? Perhaps you

The Role of Private Sources

may find letters or dispatches of his giving an account of his proceedings respecting the trial of the divorce. They would be highly important.[17]

Cardinal Lorenzo Campeggio was the papal legate, sent to England to try the Divorce suit. Any letter between him and Rome would be of first-class value as historical evidence. Campeggio was certainly in a position to know, and he would have no reason for lying in his reports to the Vatican.

Again, in 1846, now nearing the end of his career as historian and preparing material for his last edition of the *History*, he writes to a friend:

> My first volume is not out. It is not even begun. We have been waiting for the publication of the letters of Hugo Nonant, chancellor in the reign of Stephen, promised to be out two months ago by the German booksellers. I thought they might disclose much, as we have nothing of the kind of that reign, and therefore prevented Dolman [his publisher] from beginning.[18]

We are reminded, here, again of the gigantic task which Lingard set himself – of writing the complete history of England, over seventeen hundred years, from original sources. No other English historian has ever attempted a task on this scale. To have succeeded in the attempt was an unparalleled achievement.

It is in the *History* itself, however, that we must seek the real evidence for Lingard's use of private sources, as for all of his critical techniques. Here, indeed, there is a mass of evidence to show how he used these private sources as a means of arriving at the hidden truths which often lurk beneath the surface of the 'official evidence'.

Although Lingard uses the technique throughout the *History*, there is no doubt that it comes in to its own as centrally important in his treatment of the sixteenth and seventeenth centuries. This is no accident. The work of Henry VIII [PLATE 21] and his first minister, Thomas Cromwell [PLATE 5], brought about the 'Tudor Revolution in Government', as described by Geoffrey Elton.[19] Here was the first step in the preparation of a form of government 'machine' suitable for controlling a modern centralized state, before the coming of a modern democracy. For the first time in English history we see phenomena such as an organized system of state propaganda and centralized forms of state control over education, cultural expression and the available 'media'.[20]

Thomas Cromwell was the first state minister of propaganda in European history. From now on there developed an 'official version' of the English past which dominated historical writing in England for centuries. It is what I have described elsewhere as the ideology of the 'Great Myth'.[21] It meant that public documents and official statements could no longer be unreservedly reliable sources for the historian, since they were often devised to manipulate and exploit public opinion. Historical writing in England was dominated for four centuries by a viewpoint on the past derived essentially from the Establishment's way of presenting it.

Lingard was the first English historian to recognize that private sources were now essential for getting behind the veil set up by government propaganda, which was a great obstacle in the pursuit of historical truth. He was the first, therefore, to make extremely effective use of the instrument of source criticism – checking public accounts and statements by testing them against the evidence of *authentic* private sources. A modern Peterhouse historian, Brian Wormald, stated in 1958:

> as from Lingard it became increasingly clear that scholarship endorsed many of the contentions on the Catholic side of the age-long argument whether or certain crucial events had occurred: for example (1) the Catholic contention that the marriage between Catherine of Aragon and Prince Arthur had not been consummated, and that lawfulness of Henry VIII's marriage had been generally endorsed; (2) the early entrance of Anne Boleyn into the situation governing Henry's actions (though not as early as Lingard thought) [sic]; (3) the existence of a draft licence sought from Rome by Henry allowing him to marry Anne despite his illicit relations with her sister Mary (a fact which can hardly fail to bear upon our judgement of the nature of the conscientious scruples over his relationship with Catherine); the use of bribes to gain verdicts from the European Universities favouring the King's view.

On these points, Lingard had got behind the veil of official justifications surrounding the central question of the Divorce and break with Rome, set out in the preambles to the acts of the Henrician Parliament (1529–36). Interestingly, too, we now know that Wormald was mistaken in his one attempt to correct Lingard.[22]

Lingard's account of the Divorce proceedings is informed by a wide range of private sources, which, together with the public documents, still form the best account available. These private sources are used time and again to get behind the Government-imposed veil of public documents. They include confidential letters between the main participants in the story. Letters between Henry VIII and Anne Boleyn come from English sources, together with seventeen which intriguingly 'had come by some unknown means into the hands of Campeggio', the papal representative, and were sent by him to Rome where they still exist in the Vatican Library.[23]

There is vital evidence from letters written by Henry himself to different people in England, taken from the State Papers; letters between Thomas Cromwell and Cardinal Wolsey from the Earl of Surrey to Lord Darcy; from Anne Boleyn to Wolsey and others; and letters between the Bishop of Bath and Henry, and from Richard Pace, one of the King's advisers, to Henry.[24]

Then, even more importantly, there is a range of important letters between England and the outside world, bringing a new dimension to the previously anglo-centric accounts. There are letters from Pope Julius to Henry VIII; between Pope Clement and Henry VIII; correspondence between Rome and England; despatches from the French and other ambassadors; letters from foreign observers who were also closely involved – such as the Bishops of Bayonne and Tarbes and the foreign agent, Joacchino. The private Journal manuscripts of Brienne are also used. The letters of Cardinal Pole, previously an informed confidant of the King and now writing to him from exile in 1535, remind Henry of things which they both know to be true. Again, private letters reveal the whole story of the way in which foreign universities were bribed to give favourable opinions of the Divorce. For example: 'The letters published by Le Grand have exposed the whole intrigue with respect to the University of Paris.'[25]

There is no better example, for the reader or for aspiring young historians, than Lingard's account of the Divorce proceedings, to reveal the way in which the historian can use private correspondence between the main participants to break through the defensive veil set up by public documents to hide the historical truth.

Again, Lingard is able to put in much better perspective the working relationship between Wolsey and Henry VIII in the light of 'the collection of letters in the Cotton Library, Cal. B. 1–viii'.[26] His treatment of this relationship is in line with modern scholarship, as reflected in J. Scarisbrick's *Henry VIII* (1968). Lingard writes:

> We are not, however, obliged to believe the tale so often repeated, that he [Wolsey] owed his elevation to the address with which he insinuated himself into the royal favour, by promising to take all the labour on himself, that his master might have more leisure to indulge in pleasure and dissipation. The multitude of letters still extant, all written by Henry to him, or by him to Henry, demonstratively show, that the king devoted a considerable portion of his time and attention to the cares of government. But Wolsey possessed the art of guiding his sovereign while he appeared to be guided by him, and, if ever he urged a measure of policy contrary to the royal inclinations, he had the prudence to desist before he had given offence, and entered into the opposite views of the king with as much industry and zeal, as if the new project had originated with himself.[27]

By turning to these private letters, Lingard was able to give a more realistic picture of the situation than that afforded by the conventional framework of thought on the subject, which had depicted a complete division in Henry's life between the utter irresponsibility of his early period and the close control of government seen in his later life. The neat kind of dramatic account which is most easily believed and repeated is in stark contrast to the research in depth necessary to bring out the truth. It also indicates that Lingard was using his technique of source criticism consistently – not simply to dispose of anti-Catholic propaganda.

Again, while giving due attention to the central role of Thomas Cromwell in English governmental affairs after 1530,[28] Lingard's description of the relationship between Cromwell and Henry and their mutual roles in government is much more like the now recognizably authoritative version of J. Scarisbrick in his *Henry VIII* (1968, 2nd edn, 2000), than the now somewhat dated version of G. R. Elton's *The Tudor Revolution in Government* (1953) – notwithstanding the important contribution to our understanding of Tudor government made by the earlier book. As Lingard depicts it, Cromwell had a very important role in all the great changes, but it was essentially servile. The King was always in charge. One experiences, as always, the uncanny feeling that Lingard's work is less susceptible to changing fashions than that of any other historian. There is, however, nothing mysterious about this, once one has unearthed and taken on board the sophisticated system of source criticism which Lingard invented and used consistently.

Lingard's account of Mary Tudor's reign achieves a balance which has only very recently been reconstructed in English historiography.[29] For four hundred years the period has been regarded in a completely negative light – a time of complete sterility when nothing good had emerged.[30] Lingard changed this picture, so that it is now very much up to date with current research on the subject. He accomplished this partly by the use of private sources which got behind the veil set up by the official accounts in which Mary Tudor has appeared as a 'grotesque caricature' of all that was sterile and negative – a view that prevailed until the last part of the twentieth century.

Lingard was unequivocally condemnatory about the 'barbarous executions' of Mary's reign, though he was able to place them in historical perspective:

> It was the lot of Mary to live in an age of religious intolerance, when to punish the professors of erroneous doctrine was inculcated as a duty, no less by those who rejected, than by those who asserted the papal authority.[31]

Lingard also showed that the reign saw the beginnings of the great trading and commercial expansion in Tudor times, increased support for the universities and creative reforms in the legal and financial areas.[32]

In his treatment of Mary's reign, Lingard made great use of the reports of foreign ambassadors, to break out of the closed system represented by the anglo-centric official version. He found in the Barberini archives in Rome in 1817, documents from the Venetian ambassadors containing 'a most ample and interesting account of England during the three first [sic] years of the reign of Queen Mary'.[33] This was used to provide new information, including the use of a reformed, creative system of taxation, which was brought to attention by John Guy in 1996.[34]

Lingard again arranged, through a chain of helpers,[35] to get information from the archives at Besançon, where the papers of Renard, the imperial ambassador in England during Mary's reign, were kept. Lingard sent a note to his publisher in 1823, for inclusion in the History: 'The whole of this part of the volume may be pronounced new to English readers, and an important addition to our history.'[36]

Much use was made by Lingard, too, of the letters of Cardinal Pole, some of which were deposited in the Vatican archives. The letters were the subject of an inquiry from Lingard to his 'agent' in Rome in 1821. They helped again to qualify the old one-sided caricature of Mary. So, for example, we find:

> Historians have indulged in fanciful conjectures to account for the shortness of this session in the 1553 Parliament. The true reason may be discovered in Mary's letter to Cardinal Pole of the 28th of October . . . It has been said, but groundlessly, that the queen had dissolved the last parliament on account of the refractory spirit of the Commons. Mary, in her letter to Pole, of Nov. 15, 1553, informs him of her intentions to dissolve it, because the session could not be prolonged at that time, and to call another in the course of three months . . .[37]

Again, on the question of the position of the English ambassador in Rome at the accession of Pope Paul IV, 1555, Lingard refers to a letter of Pole to Philip and Mary, showing that the English ambassador had been treated with 'kindness' and shown all the usual courtesies under normal protocol. Lingard writes:

> A very erroneous statement of the whole transaction has been copied from Frao Paolo by most of our historians: the above narrative is taken from the original documents furnished by Pole's letters.[38]

Another frequently used weapon in the armoury of anti-Catholic propaganda in England historiography, was that any turning back to Catholicism in England would mean that Church lands taken from the monasteries and sold to influential families of the English gentry by Henry VIII, would be returned to the Church.[39] Mary had in fact sanctioned only the return of those church lands which were still in the hands of the monarchy:

> Stat. iv. 275. Pole, v. 46, 51, 53, 56. Some writers have said that the queen sought to procure an act, compelling the restoration of church property, in whatever hands it might be. The contrary is evident from the whole tenour of Pole's correspondence.[40]

In his treatment of Elizabeth's reign, Lingard knew that the

The Role of Private Sources

Government was very much concerned with the propagandist value of official statements, in its struggle to achieve a united front against Catholics and Puritans at home, and Spain, in particular, abroad. *So, too, were contemporary chroniclers and literary figures pressed into the service of Government propaganda.*[41] *There was re-enacted in Elizabeth's reign all those strategies of organized state propaganda which had first seen the light of day in England during the 1530s, in the hands of Thomas Cromwell and Henry VIII.*[42] *Against this background,* THE USE OF MORE CONFIDENTIAL PAPERS AND PRIVATE CORRESPONDENCE BECAME OF PRIME IMPORTANCE AS A CHECK ON THE TRUTHFULNESS OF OFFICIAL STATEMENTS. 'Confessions', for example, drawn from those who were awaiting state trials, were very suspect in this climate.[43]

Thus contemporary chroniclers, such as Camden and Holinshed, and the later historians who followed them, were not to be given great weight on their own. Camden, Buchanan and Knox are all corrected in the light of private letters and papers.[44] A lie of Walsingham to the French ambassador is revealed by Burghley's private letters;[45] and a confession made by Morton and published by the Government, is qualified in the light of a letter from Mary, Queen of Scots, to Elizabeth.[46] The private letters of Elizabeth's ministers, written to each other, are usefully employed to indicate their attitude towards Mary,[47] and to illustrate the habitual irresolution of their sovereign on various topics.[48] A private letter is used to throw light on some signatures attached to an official document – to show that not all those who had signed it, shared knowledge of a secret contained in the document.[49]

A good example of getting behind official accounts by checking with confidential letters is provided in the use of a letter from Murray, the Scottish rebel, to Cecil, to devalue a statement made by the former before the French and Spanish ambassadors, for which he was rewarded by Elizabeth. He was made to say that Elizabeth had no part in the Scottish conspiracy of 1565 against the Scottish queen. But:

> Notwithstanding the farce enacted before the two ambassadors, there are several letters extant which prove, beyond contradiction, that Elizabeth was an accomplice in this conspiracy. I will cite only one from Murray to Cecil, of October 14 . . .[50]

CONFIDENTIAL LETTERS CAN 'GET BEHIND' THE LIES AND DECEITS PRACTISED *mutually among members of the same Government.* Referring to the military activities of Leicester in the Netherlands in 1585, for which he was severely chastized by Elizabeth for seeking his own aggrandizement, Lingard tells us:

> Besides the historians of the period, consult the original letters in the Hardwicke Papers . . . It would appear that Leicester had much to say in his

The Role of Private Sources

own defence, but that the advocates of peace had obtained the ascendancy while the earl was absent in Holland, and Walsingham was confined to his house by sickness.⁵¹

Once again we see the source technique being used consistently in all areas – not simply to deal with more controversial matters.

Lingard was very aware that, IN WAR, NATIONALIST PROPAGANDA WAS LIKELY TO AFFECT THE RELIABILITY OF OFFICIAL DESPATCHES – *when these were composed by leaders in pursuit of fame and glory. We find him using private correspondence, to get behind such official despatches.* Referring, for example, to the 1589 expedition to Portugal, Lingard writes in a footnote:

> Norris and Drake appear to have been proficients in the art of composing official despatches. They tell the council that in these battles, which were fiercely contested, they killed one thousand of the enemy with the loss of only three men ... But Lord Talbot writes to his father: 'As I hear privately, not without the loss of as many of our men as of theirs, if not more; and without gain of anything, unless it were honour, and the acquainting our men with the use of their weapons.⁵²

Also important is THE USE OF PRIVATE PAPERS AND CORRESPONDENCE *to get behind the Government's use of propaganda in its internal policies to entrap those perceived as dangers to the State.* Perhaps most significantly, Lingard uses private correspondence to reveal for the first time in English historiography the background activity of the various 'agents' used by Walsingham, the Queen's 'artful secretary'⁵³ [see PLATE 24] to ensnare potential opponents of the Elizabethan regime. Walsingham is shown to have been a past master at the utilization of 'agents provocateur'. He used a network of spies to infiltrate the ranks of potential 'trouble-makers', to encourage them in their intrigues until the time was ripe for him to strike and exterminate them.⁵⁴

Walsingham was particularly intent on using his agents to seek to entrap Mary Queen of Scots into revealing herself as a plotter against the life of Elizabeth. Lingard uses private correspondence to describe the extraordinary network of intrigue prepared to trap Mary. It involved the 'agent provocateur', Gilbert Gifford; the intermediary, Paulet; the decipherer, Thomas Philipps; and Arthur Gregory 'a man skilled in the art of counterfeiting seals, and of restoring them after they had been broken'. The letters between Gifford and Mary Queen of Scots were sent to Walsingham's office where they were 'opened, deciphered and transcribed'. After this: 'the originals, or the copies, occasionally perhaps copies falsified by interpolations, omissions, or additional postscripts' were returned through the same network. Mary was assigned to a house named Chartley in Staffordshire. Paulet was given a place in service there. They also secured the services of a 'carrier,

> a brewer, in the neighbouring town of Burton, known in the correspondence by the derisive sobriquet of the 'honest man', who on a fixed day of each week, was accustomed to send his dray to Chartley with a supply of beer for the inmates.

The 'honest man' delivered the parcels to Chartley and collected the return letters from Mary, to send on to Walsingham's agents.[55]

This particular spy network was maintained under Walsingham's ultimate control. His role would be known to us as 'Minister of Intelligence' or 'National Security'. It was used, in conjunction with the 'Babington plot', to successfully bring about the execution of Mary in February 1587.

Lingard provided the first full account of the Government's machinations to achieve its ends. He does so mainly by using a wide range of private letters, both printed and in manuscript form. He used the Hardwicke Papers, the Harleian manuscripts, many papers from the State Paper Office, original letters in the possession of Mr. Leigh, the Bethune manuscripts, the Egerton papers, a manuscript life of George, second earl of Shrewsbury; as well as the Courcelles Despatches in the Cotton Manuscript collection. He also used every available source of letters printed in a wide variety of published works and collections, including those of Murdin, Jebb, Strype, Camden, Von Raumer, Howell's State Trials, Ellis, Chalmers, Robertson, Lodge, Hearne, and Goodall. Some publications were not available for the first edition of Lingard's *History*, but became available in time for later editions. In 1838, for example, Thomas Wright produced his *Queen Elizabeth and Her Times*, which contained original letters that Lingard used for his fourth edition. Most importantly in 1844 Labanoff published his *Recueil des Lettres de Marie Stuart* of which Lingard made extensive use in his last edition of 1849. All these were used in addition to the public documents such as the Statutes of the Realm, State Trials and Journals of Parliament, but with the added purpose of 'getting behind' the latter so as to uncover the various 'secrets of state' which, of course, were not published openly.

Lingard was then the first to produce the first modern account of the intrigues of the Elizabethan Government in its finally successful endeavours in bringing about the downfall and execution of Mary Queen of Scots. Certainly Lingard's judgements on the issues involved are still secure in the light of modern scholarship. His main narrative, together with the detailed appendices on this subject, exemplify very well the high standard of Lingard's abilities in detailed source criticism and balanced judgement. It needed all his detached coolness to get through the labyrinth of ingenuity exercised by Walsingham and his agents in the legal proceedings against Mary. Walsingham's intrigues included the withholding of vital evidence for the defence and the inclusion and interpolation of vital incriminating phrases in Mary's letters as they passed through the hands of his 'technical' experts. It becomes clear that any proper court of law would have had to find the case of treason against Mary, unproven.[56]

It was a feature of Lingard's treatment of sixteenth-century sources that he DID NOT ACCEPT UNQUESTIONINGLY THE GOVERNMENT REPORTS OF ANY PARTICULAR EPISODE. He applied to them the same critical techniques with which he approached any other source – a new phenomenon in English historiography.

This procedure continued in Lingard's treatment of the seventeenth century. We find, for example, that an official but prejudiced account of the execution of Garnet, a Jesuit priest accused of participation in the Gunpowder Plot, is checked by the private letters of eye-witnesses.

> On the scaffold, according to the ambiguous language of the official accounts, he confessed his guilt; but if we may credit the letters of spectators, he denied all knowledge of the plot, except by confession [i.e. as a priest hearing confession]; and though he begged pardon of the king, he was careful to add that it was not for any participation in the treason, but for the legal offence of having concealed the general knowledge which he had acquired of some practice against the state, designed by Catesby.[57]

Private despatches from the Hardwicke papers are used to show the specious quality of the narrative given by Prince Charles and Buckingham to Parliament in 1624 as to their proceedings with the Spanish Government, during their visit there. The speech was designed to promote bad feeling against Spain, and two secretaries attended to 'read a few garbled extracts from despatches' to support it. But Lingard 'gets behind' the speech in a footnote:

> His highness the prince, says the lord keeper, upon very deep reasons, doubts whether it be safe to put all upon [i.e. fully inform] the parliament, for fear they should fall to examine particular despatches, wherein they cannot but find many contradictions. He wishes to draw on a breach with Spain with (out) ripping up of private despatches – Cabala. The despatches in the Hardwicke Papers show the prudence of this counsel.[58]

Private letters are used to refute 'popular' charges made against Archbishop Laud and the Earl of Strafford, in the reign of Charles I:

> It has been believed, on the credit of the charges against Laud and Strafford, that they were the real authors of the war against Scotland, 1639. It will, however, appear, from a careful examination of their private letters and other contemporary documents, that Laud dissuaded hostilities, and that Strafford's advice was not asked... See Laud's Troubles... Sydney Papers ... Strafford Papers...[59]

THE ROLE OF PRIVATE SOURCES

Contemporary writers or 'chroniclers' are also corrected in the light of private correspondence. This is seen, for example, in Lingard's treatment of the proposed treaty between Charles and Parliament in 1643 – an attempt which failed. Edward Hyde, Earl of Clarendon, had began writing his famous *History of the Great Rebellion* in 1646. Lingard writes:

> Hyde maintains that the king protracted the negotiation to give time for the arrival of the queen, without whom he would come to no determination; but *of this not a vestige appears in the private correspondence between Charles and his consort*; and a sufficient reason for the failure of the treaty may be found in the high pretensions of each party, neither of whom had been sufficiently humbled to purchase peace with the sacrifice of honour or safety.[60]

In 1825 Lingard wrote to his publisher, Mawman, saying that he had come across an important source of Charles I's private letters [PLATE 27]:

> Since I came down, the duke of Hamilton has sent his library, consisting of purchases while he had the book mania upon him . . . Among other things is a small MS vol: of the letters written by Charles I to his queen about the time of his flight to the Scots. They confirm my assertion, that he was not enticed to their camp by promises which they refused to fulfil.[61]

The *History* corrects the usual account of why Charles refused to yield to the Scots' demand that he should abandon episcopacy and take up the covenant:

> It was believed then, it has often been repeated since, that the king's refusal originated in the wilfulness and obstinacy of his temper; and that his repeated appeals to his conscience were mere pretexts to disguise his design of replunging the nation into the horrors from which it had so recently emerged. *But this supposition is completely refuted by the whole tenour of his secret correspondence with his queen and her council in France.*[62]

Lingard knew that a contemporary historian will often transmit an interpretation of events which is derived from popular report, itself often a product of the most influential group or successful party in the ascendancy at that time. Such a report, propagated by the interested party often becomes an unquestioned part of the historiographical framework, accepted automatically by later historians. This is certainly what happened in English historical writing from the sixteenth century up to Lingard, when historians by and large had repeated an accepted and popular story rather than test its findings with original documents and a science of source criticism. This was one of the chief causes for the success and durability of the 'Great Myth' and the whig interpretation of the English past over four centuries.

Here, then, we have PRIVATE LETTERS FROM THE PERSON IN THE BEST

THE ROLE OF PRIVATE SOURCES

POSITION TO KNOW *and with no reason to lie, being used to undermine one of those prejudicial and unfounded views* which were part of the whig interpretation of English history. According to that interpretation, all those who 'failed' (Charles I in this instance) were ipso facto not on the side of the future; they were not heroic and could not have been acting from noble purposes. In the end, it was only by detailed research that the old prejudices could be overthrown. Lingard played a significant part in the process by using his newly-created technical scholarship to test the evidence in detail.

The insurrection of the Vaudois in Switzerland (1655–6) against the Catholic Duke of Savoy had produced a famous influential sonnet of John Milton's in defence of the Protestant group.[63] Reports were sent out from Geneva by the Protestant ministers there, describing their plight. England was looked upon as the leading Protestant power in Europe, with a duty to intervene elsewhere on the side of Protestants. But Cromwell had sufficient problems of his own in England. Besides, were the reports accurate? He sent a special agent to report confidentially on the situation in Switzerland. Lingard used this agent's confidential information to correct the inflammatory reports:

> The infidelity of these reports is acknowledged by Morland, the protector's [Cromwell's] agent, in a confidential letter to secretary Thurloe. 'The greatest difficulty I meet with is in relation to the matter of fact in the beginning of these troubles, and during the time of war. For I find upon diligent search, that many papers and books which have been put out in print on this subject, even by some ministers of the valleys, are lame in many particulars, and in many things not conformable to truth' – Thurloe, iv. 417.[64]

The reports sent from Geneva were designed to gain the support of the Protestant powers, and so 'represented the duke of Savoy as a bigoted and intolerant prince, the Vaudois as an innocent race whose only crime was their attachment to the reformed faith'.[65] But the situation on the ground was more complicated and it was difficult, if not impossible, to assign more blame to one or the other side for the outbreak of violence.[66]

The use of private correspondence as a check on contemporary writers, also illustrates Lingard's rule of GIVING GREATER WEIGHT TO EVIDENCE PRODUCED CONTEMPORANEOUSLY WITH EVENTS, *as opposed to evidence written at a later stage when the source is looking back and relying on memory for what had happened.*[67] Sir William Temple, a distinguished English diplomat at the Hague, had played a part in negotiating the marriage between Mary, niece of Charles II, and William of Orange in 1777 which led up to peace negotiations between England, France and Holland in 1678. He later, from 1689 onwards, wrote his memoirs covering this earlier period. The Lord Treasurer, the Earl of Danby, had also played a leading part in the marriage negotiations. His private correspondence was available to Lingard as another source. Lingard considered both sources when dealing with the situation in 1678 when William of Orange, after persuasion by Charles II, made proposals of peace to Louis XIV. Here the particular rule of source criticism is applied again. *The evidence of a <u>letter</u> written by someone who was in a prime position to know and had no reason for lying, was superior to a <u>memoir</u>, written by an active participant, but only after some ten years had elapsed.* In the supporting footnote, we find:

> Temple, indeed, affirms that the king Charles II pledged himself to make war in case of a refusal on the part of Louis. It is, however, evident from the letter of Danby to the prince William of Orange of Dec. 4, that up to that day no pledge had been given ... *It may be, that Temple writing from memory has occasionally confounded dates and circumstances. Danby writing at the time, and to the prince, respecting a negotiation in which they were both engaged, could not be in error.*[68]

This same diplomat, Sir William Temple,[69] had been the source of the story, universally accepted in England, that the Triple Alliance of England, Sweden and Holland, negotiated against Louis XIV of France, in 1667, was another masterpiece of English political wisdom by which a European tyrant had been stopped in his tracks by English intervention. This was certainly the view taken by Lord Macaulay in the nineteenth century[70] and by his great-nephew, Sir G. M. Trevelyan, in the twentieth[71] – both classic representatives of the whig interpretation of English history in their respective centuries. Macaulay had dismissed Lingard's critical work on the subject, with the remark that the latter was one whose 'fundamental rule of judging seems to be that popular opinion cannot possibly be correct'.[72] Trevelyan, a specialist in the Stuart period, wrote in 1939, a century after Lingard, on the same subject:

> In 1668 an English diplomat in the Low countries, Sir William Temple negotiated with great skill the Triple Alliance of England, Holland and Sweden to check the French advance on the Rhine and in the Spanish Netherlands. The effect was instantaneous. Louis was compelled to accept the terms of the Treaty of Aix-La-Chapelle.[73]

It was only in 1949 that an outstanding modern specialist on the Stuart period, Sir George Clarke, 'reproduced' Lingard's now-accepted account. Clarke wrote that this Triple Alliance had long been mistakenly regarded as a 'master stroke of diplomacy', partly because the English diplomat Temple, who described it in his memoirs, was 'one of the best living writers of English prose' and 'took many opportunities of writing in his own praise'.[74] In 1952 another Stuart specialist, Maurice Ashley, added:

> But meanwhile the French king had arranged a secret treaty with the Emperor, head of the Hapsburg family. Louis XIV had good reason for being willing to make peace with Spain in the spring of 1668 (for why bother over a small part of the Spanish Empire if the bulk of it might be coming his way?) – and the Triple Alliance contributed little to his decision.[75]

And Thomas Munck, writing in 1993 on the European scene at the time of the Triple Alliance, notes that 'France had both the resources and the contacts to exercise a paramount influence on international relations'.[76]

Lingard's typically short, accurate and precise statement on this Treaty of Aix-la-Chapelle (1668) back in 1830 was:

> Much praise has been lavished on this negotiation, as if it had arrested Louis in his career of victory, and preserved the independence of Europe; but, in fact, it accomplished nothing more than the French king had offered, and was desirous to effect.[77]

This episode in an understanding of the past is very revealing since *it shows the application of a range of Lingard's methods of source criticism – including the use of private sources to get behind official accounts – brought together and focused on a particular subject.* It reveals the depth of research and source criticism which lies behind a very succinct statement in the narrative of what was a *general* history of England.

First, *Lingard compares foreign with domestic sources, as he normally does in dealing with an international question.* So his footnotes show a comparison of Temple's memoirs with the French account in D'Estrades and *Oeuvres de Louis XIV*.[78] In this way he avoided the common-place anglo-centricism of other English historians.[79] Secondly, Temple's memoir account was an 'interested' account and therefore not reliable on its own. Thirdly, Temple's memoir was written about twenty years later and was not as reliable as private correspondence between major participants written at the time. Lingard's uses letters written between Charles II and Louis XIV and another from Charles to his sister, the duchess of Orleans, to show the real motives behind Louis XIV's policies.

Lingard also used the *Oeuvres de Louis* to reveal the secrets of the 'eventual treaty', privately arranged between Louis and the Emperor Leopold, by which the possessions of the Spanish monarchy would be shared between the two of them, after the death of the King of Spain. Louis was very ready to restore Franche-Comté to Spain, because he had the expectancy of much greater gains in the future. As Lingard noted:

> Mr Macaulay . . . pronounced it unreasonable and ridiculous to suppose that Louis would have held himself bound by his former offers, if he had not been compelled by the triple alliance. To me, however, there appears good reason to suppose that he would have held himself so bound even if

the triple alliance had never existed; because he must otherwise have abandoned all hope of those splendid advantages which he had expected to derive from the eventful treaty.[80]

The episode indicates, as well, how well-versed Lingard was in European politics, because his approach was 'Euro-centric', or that of a 'citizen of the world' as he would have described himself. In this he stood far above any of his predecessors in English historiography and above most of his successors until the last decade of the twentieth century.[81]

The collection of writings – the *Oeuvres* – of Louis XIV formed a decisive source in revealing his motives in the Alliance episode. *Lingard's emphasis on the value of such papers in the prevailing circumstances, is a typical use of a tool of source criticism which was used consistently throughout his History.*

To conclude the chapter, it is worth showing how Lingard actually changed the general shape of English historiography in a fundamentally important period of English history in the seventeenth century – as he had done with the Reformation in the sixteenth century – by using private sources from home and abroad, and by bringing in the Euro-centric dimension, to remove the veil put up by the creators of the insular whig interpretation of English history and by those historians who followed them over the next three centuries.

Lingard and the 'Glorious Revolution' of 1688

The two great steps towards English freedom and supremacy in the modern world, according to the whig interpretation of English history, were the Reformation and the Revolution of 1688. Both these momentous changes were supported by a propagandist of genius. Thomas Cromwell led an enormously successful propagandist campaign to support the great Revolution in the 1530s; and Bishop Gilbert Burnet played an equally important part in the success of the Revolution in 1688.

I have shown elsewhere how Thomas Cromwell set up a total misreading of the English past in order to justify what he was doing in the name of Henry VIII. It was 'set in stone' in the preambles to the Reformation statutes,[82] and established the 'Great Myth' of the English past. Gilbert Burnet [PLATE 7] not only played a vital role in the events leading to 1688, but then proceeded to justify what had happened by writing pamphlets, preaching sermons, and especially by writing his celebrated *History of the Reformation* (1679–1715) in which he created the whig interpretation, built upon the previously established 'Great Myth', and added the 'idea of progress' and the dynamic interpretation of the 1688 Revolution.[83] It was the veil created by the superb propaganda of

The Role of Private Sources

Thomas Cromwell and Gilbert Burnet which Lingard had to draw from these events, in order to find and display the truth. We have seen something already of his work on the Henrician Reformation – using private sources to get behind the public documents and drawing on the European dimension to give a truer perspective.

The whig interpretation of the 'Glorious Revolution' of 1688 remained intact until the very end of the twentieth century. G. M. Trevelyan [PLATE 14] wrote of it in glowing terms in his *History of England* (1926) which went through innumerable new impressions and constituted one of the most popular history books of the twentieth century:

> It was only when the period of internal evolution had resulted in the settlement of 1688–89, that the new Parliamentary England, based on freedom in religion and politics, was matched . . . against . . . continental autocracy . . . It was the Revolution of 1688 that gave Great Britain freedom and efficiency . . . The political and religious tyranny of the monarch had been effectively curbed . . . For many generations to come the Revolution of 1688–89 was spoken of by our ancestors as 'the glorious revolution' . . . A written constitution is alien to the English political genius . . . the smooth development of our constitutional history . . . the good genius of English politics has often retrieved apparently hopeless situations. The last British Revolution is still that of 1688.[84]

The arrival of William of Orange on the English scene in 1688 was treated solely within an English perspective in the official version purveyed by the whig interpretation. It was an *English Revolution* – instead of a foreign invasion. William of Orange was the 'saviour' who had come, answering the call of the English, to save their freedom and Protestantism from 'Popery' and 'arbitrary government'. In 1996 Professor Black in his *History of the British Isles* (1996) observed that 'the Glorious Revolution is crucial to the Whig interpretation of British history, central to the notion of British uniqueness'.[85]

The tercentenary of the Revolution in 1988, in the meantime, stimulated modern academic research to new dimensions. In 1996 Dale Hoak and Mordecai Feingold, perhaps significantly two American historians, edited an epoch-making new study entitled *The World of William and Mary: Anglo-Dutch Perspectives on The Revolution of 1688–89*, published in the United States. Their book summarized the results of research done since 1988, providing a radically different picture of that famous event. An English reviewer of the work, John Spurr, summarized its findings very pithily in 1997:

> In 1688–89 William [see PLATE 29] conquered England and took the crown for himself. This simple fact, obscured by generations of Anglo-centric inter-

pretation, is glaringly obvious once the 'Glorious Revolution' is seen from a European perspective. And it has been one of the lasting achievements of the academic reassessment, prompted by the Revolution's tercentenary, to restore that European viewpoint.[86]

John Lingard, however, had reached this very same conclusion back in 1830. It was based, then, on two of his basic rules of source criticism. One was *his insistence on* USING CONTINENTAL SOURCES, *as well as English, in describing any episode which involved the relationship between England and any other European country. This established the European perspective.*

The second source technique was *his* USE OF PRIVATE PAPERS, *including the* DESPATCHES OF EUROPEAN AMBASSADORS, *as a means of getting behind the more official statements appearing in public documents – especially where the latter were subject to propagandist motivations and conclusions.*

In the second half of the seventeenth century, Louis XIV was the master player in the game of European politics and Paris was the central point of information. Lingard gave a great deal of attention to 'Continental Politics'[87] in his account of the reigns of the last two Stuart kings. He tells us in the preface to his *History*, how he had managed to get at the unpublished despatches of the French ambassadors during this period:

> During the reigns of Charles II and James II, the documents the most interesting to Englishmen are the despatches from the French ambassadors and agents, detailing their own proceedings, and the most important events in England and Holland. They had never yet been published . . . On this account Mazure, when he was preparing materials for his *Histoire de la Révolution de 1688 en Angleterre*, sought out every despatch appertaining to the subject, from whatever quarter it might come; and, as he possessed unrestricted access to the archives of the Ministère des Affaires étrangères de France, transcribed, for the sake of accuracy, every separate piece with his own hand . . . It will undoubtedly be noticed that, with respect to the same subjects, I repeatedly quote passages from documents hitherto inedited [unpublished]: and it may with reason be asked, from what source I procured them. I answer, from the very transcripts which were made by Mazure himself. After his death his papers came into my possession; and from them I was enabled sometimes to extract passages which he had passed over, because to him, a foreigner, they did not appear of so much importance as they must appear to a native; and sometimes to correct unintentional mistakes in Mazure's own history, when *he occasionally suffered his prepossessions to give to passages an interpretation which the words themselves in those particular circumstances could not bear.*[88]

At this time the European archives had not been opened to visiting scholars. In his private correspondence, Lingard enlightens us a little further, describing to a friend, how M. Mazure, the keeper of the archives at the Depôt des Affaires Etrangeres in Paris, had 'copied with his own hand the whole series' and 'at his death I purchased for £5 all his papers, and by that means became possessed of exact copies'.[89] This explains how Lingard was able to make such good use of the despatches of Barillon, Bonrepaus and d'Avaux, in constructing his own completely new description of the period.

Lingard's account indicates that, as early as 1674, William of Orange, a 'consummate politician',[90] was intriguing with a group of disaffected whigs for the succession to the English crown. The correspondence between them 'passed through the hands of Du Moulin, private secretary to Prince William. Lingard was here using the papers of d'Avaux (French ambassador at the Hague) as well as information from Burnet and Sir William Temple.[91] He also made considerable use of the letters of Barillon and Bonrepaus, ambassadors to England.[92]

These private sources revealed the secret activity of William in May, 1688, showing that:

> he had never lost sight of the great object of his ambition, [the crown of England].[93]

William 'silently prepared his expedition against England', pretending in all public documents 'to have no other object than the defence of the empire and his own country against the meditated aggression of France'.[94] The letters of d'Avaux revealed that William, 'under cover of this pretence', prepared a strong force for an attack on England:

> Orders were issued for the encampment of twenty thousand men between Grave and Nimeguen; fifty pieces of cannon, with the requisite supply of ammunition, were taken from the arsenals, and placed on flats to be conveyed to the rendezvous of the army; seven thousand men were raised for the naval, nine thousand for the military service; twenty-seven ships of war were added to the fleet of forty-four sail already in commission, and the squadron in the Zuider Zee received orders to proceed to the Texel, that it might be prepared to join the other squadrons at Helvoetsluys.[95]

Private sources – the Barillon despatches – again revealed that in September, 1688, William was in Minden: 'in close consultation with his German allies, who engaged to supply him with fifteen thousand auxiliaries, undoubtedly intended to supply the place of men who should accompany him to England'.[96] Still the public pretence was that William was preparing to resist Louis XIV of France.

Then, as the letter of d'Avaux revealed, in late September, 1688, William presented a public document from himself and the Estates, providing the 'public' reason for his expedition against England. It was:

The Role of Private Sources

a long and bitter invective against James [II], in the form of a memorial supposedly to be presented by the Protestants of England to the States, but composed under that name at the Hague by Dr. Burnet [now in exile with William].[97]

Burnet's vital role [see PLATE 7] as the main propagandist for the 'Glorious Revolution' has been detailed recently by T. Claydon in his *William III and the Godly Revolution* (1996). William brought his own printing press with him to produce thousands of propagandist leaflets in London after his victory. He was accompanied all the way by Burnet, who initiated a campaign of propagandist writings and sermons, in defence of the 'Revolution which had saved the liberties of England and Protestantism'.

Even now, at the last moment, William was acting under the public pretence that he was simply intending to protect the liberties and religion of the English people. He wrote to other Catholic powers, such as the Emperor and the King of Spain, on the eve of the departure of his expeditionary force:

> informing them that his voyage to England was undertaken at the request of the English nobility, and for the purpose of effecting a reconciliation between the king [James II] and his subjects; that he should take with him a small military force, both infantry and cavalry, *but solely for the protection of his person; that he had no intention of offering injury to the king or the rightful heirs, much less of advancing any claim to the throne, or occupying it himself.*[98]

Again, the papers of d'Avaux provide Lingard with details,[99] enabling him to get behind the public statements made by William.

At this point Lingard allows himself a rare personal comment:

> The history of diplomacy is in a great measure made up of attempts to beguile and to mislead: but never perhaps was falsehood so boldly and unblushingly put forward, as in these memorials [public statements] of the prince and of the Dutch States . . .[100]

Lingard states quite simply that 'William had . . . sailed from Helvoetsluys in pursuit of the English crown'.[101] His strong Dutch expeditionary force reached Torbay on 5 November 1688; the conquest of England was already almost completed.

Lingard makes clear that James's own mistakes played a major part in making the invasion possible[102] [see PLATE 25]. It might not otherwise have succeeded. As it was, when William sent four battalions of the Dutch guards and a squadron of horse under Count Solms to march into Westminster, there was at least a patriotic reaction. The details here were supplied by James's own memoirs, together with those of Buckingham and the despatches of Barillon:

The Role of Private Sources

The spirit of Lord Craven, the commander of the English guards, was roused; he declared that, as long as breath remained in his body, no foreign force should make a king of England prisoner in his own palace. James hesitated; but a moment's reflection convinced him that resistance against such disparity of numbers could only lead to unnecessary bloodshed, and by dint of entreaty, and some exertion of authority, he prevailed on the old man (Craven was in his eightieth year) to withdraw the guards from their posts, which were immediately occupied by the Dutch.[103]

Using private sources such as Buckingham's contemporary account, together with that of Kennet, Evelyn's Diary and the Ellis Correspondence, alongside James's own memoirs, Lingard adds:

> To most of the spectators it proved a mournful and humiliating sight. They felt that powerful impression which is always made by the spectacle of majesty in distress; and they could not behold without shame the king of England conveyed from his capital a prisoner in the hands of foreigners.[104]

Lingard feels able, after providing the evidence, to invite the reader to a conclusion:

> If the reader has carefully watched the conduct of the latter [William of Orange] during the last two years, he will have come to the conclusion that, whatever might be the pretexts set forth in his declaration, whatever the motives attributed to him by the policy or the partiality of his friends, *his real object from the beginning had been the acquisition of the English crown.*[105]

Lingard's historical judgement was based almost exclusively on private sources which were used to remove the veil, constituted by public statements and official documents issued by William's new Government after the conquest, which had concealed the true facts of the situation and continued to do so, as far as English historians in general were concerned, until the end of the twentieth century.

Revolutionary governments or those of victorious conquerors are particularly susceptible to using public statements and even parliamentary documents as means of propaganda to cover up the true nature of what has taken place. This is notably true of the Henrician Government and the Reformation Parliament (1530–36);[106] and also of the new Government which took over under William of Orange after the 'Revolution of 1688'.[107] In both cases a particularly adept exponent of propaganda – Thomas Cromwell in the first and Gilbert Burnet in the second – masterminded, under the direction of their masters, a highly successful campaign, using official documents and an abuse of history as powerful weapons with which to influence public opinion. In both cases, too, the propaganda of the successful side was powerful enough to determine the shape of historical writing in England on these events, up to the last part of the twentieth century.

Lingard's use of private sources and the confidential reports of foreign ambassadors was the only way, in these circumstances, in which the great historical distortions associated with the 'take-over' by the winning side could be corrected. His achievement was based also on an extensive knowledge of the state of politics on the Continent[108] during the time of these episodes in English history. Lingard's recognition of the primary importance of the French sources of information, in Paris, at this time when Louis XIV had skilful oversight over everything that was happening in Europe, was particularly important in providing Lingard with a Eurocentric view of what was happening in England.

It is a signally important demonstration of the power of private sources, to get behind public sources, that Lingard was able to produce a completely new interpretation of both the Reformation and the Revolution of 1688. He alone among his predecessors, contemporaries and successors – before the advent of revisionist historiography at the end of the second millennium – was able to do this. It is clear that he was able to do so because of his unique standpoint among English historians – the perception of himself as a 'citizen of the world'; and because he created a new methodology of source criticism which had never been used in England before and perhaps has never been used so skilfully again in the hands of any historian who has settled on the task of writing the whole history of England.

Interestingly, in the most recent account of James II, John Callow's *The Making of James II* (2000), the author, in surveying the historiography of the subject, comes only part of the way towards appreciating Lingard's contribution in this particular area. He is, after all, concentrating on the earlier part of James's life:

> John Lingard, an erudite and liberal priest, steeped in the culture and learning of the Enlightenment, whose *History of England* (Vols. VIII–X, London, 1855), did much to raise the tenor and quality of debate, while removing many of its more partisan overtones.[109]

He goes on to comment that later Catholic historians of the nineteenth and well into the twentieth centuries, lacked the status, historical skills and reconstructive vision with which Lingard had been able to establish a new framework and perspective, to challenge the old whig version of the subject. They were also more 'strident and sectarian', lacking the 'outgoing, receptive and conciliatory attitudes' which characterized Lingard's work.[110]

This chapter has brought into sharp focus the importance of historical perspective as a general tool of source criticism. Historical truth, in the last analysis, lies in perspective. Lingard certainly used this concept in his detailed work on the evaluation of sources. He insisted, for example, that the source had to be seen in the light of all the relevant external factors and relationships operating in the immediate historical context. These have to be weighted by a methodology of source criticism and then placed in their appropriate order of importance. Only then can the evidence be placed in perspective and the truth emerge. This process is shown very clearly in Lingard's treatment of the Massacre of St. Bartholomew.

There is also, however, the sense in which a whole period of a nation's history can take on a new meaning when placed within a wider contextual perspective. The whole medieval period, the Reformation in England in the sixteenth century and the 'Glorious Revolution' of 1688 in the seventeenth, are examples of important periods and movements which took on a different meaning in Lingard's hands, when placed, for the first time, within a European rather than an anglo-centric context. Until Lingard, the narrowly anglo-centric perspective had been all-pervasive in English historical writing. Wider vision, sustained by a wider range of sources, was needed to correct the distorted picture presented by other English historians.

It was part of Lingard's greatness as a historian that he saw the need for wider vision and perspective. Once this was exercised, the old facts fell easily into a new shape, quite different from that imposed by the straitjacket of nationalist propaganda created by Thomas Cromwell, Gilbert Burnet and the later Whig historians.

In the historiography of the third millennium, it will be essential for the historian to work increasingly within the context of global history, in order to provide a proper perspective for interpreting historical evidence from our 'global village'. Here, too, we have much to learn from Lingard, who stressed the importance of 'open-mindedness' and wide vision in constructing a proper sense of historical perspective. Even in 1837, Lingard was insisting that the historian must adopt the stance of a 'citizen of the world' rather than a citizen of the nation state, in his or her pursuit of historical truth.

❋ ❋ ❋

The next reference in English historiography to the importance of private sources occurs in a manuscript of about 1900 among Lord Acton's private papers, deposited in the Cambridge University Library. Sir Herbert Butterfield, who found it, remarked in 1955:

> He [Acton] puts forward the interesting point that there is one documentary source more close to the ultimate secrets than the more formal papers in official archives. The ultimate disclosures are likely to be produced by the more unreserved communications which ministers or diplomats may have

exchanged with one another behind the scenes. The private letters of such public figures constitute their ultimate exposure and few reputations survive the publication of these.[111]

Acton's manuscript note refers to: 'The unpremeditated self-revelation of correspondence – This is our great addition.'[112] Butterfield adds that his own teacher and predecessor as Master of Peterhouse, Cambridge, Sir Harold Temperley – who significantly was an expert in diplomatic history and international politics,

> while insisting on the primary important of official documents, was convinced of the change which a narrative was likely to suffer if the private papers also came under survey.[113]

Thus Lingard is shown to anticipate, a century earlier, a view of the importance of private papers, which was to be reiterated at Cambridge by such illustrious names as Acton, Temperley and, later still, Butterfield, who all seemed to think of it as something new.

Even then, though, Lord Acton, appointed to the Regius Chair at Cambridge in 1895, was preoccupied with the possibility of making moral judgements on historical persons and nations – his primary interest in using private sources such as correspondence and diaries.[114] Lingard, in complete contrast, was interested in private sources primarily as historical tools, which could be used to 'remove the veil' which often obscured the real springs of activity – the motives and nature of historical actions.

The historian must attempt to describe and explain what happened in the past and even, on occasions, make moral judgements about certain objective actions in history; but he or she would be gravely mistaken to attempt final moral judgements about people of the past, as of the present. Such a perspective is beyond the capacity and proper concern of professional historians. This was a view which Lingard shared with Ranke, the outstanding German exponent of 'scientific' history. In this way again, a great gap exists between Lingard and Acton – the later and much more famous Catholic historian; and it is Lingard's view which comes much nearer the professional attitude of the modern professional historian. One feels that Lingard's vocation and experience as a priest actually assisted him in his role of historian. The old theological maxim: 'love the sinner and hate the sin', applies to the historian's proper approach to the people of the past. It is no accident that Professor Dom David Knowles, the first Benedictine monk and priest to become Regius Professor of Modern History at Cambridge in 1954, said in his inaugural lecture at Cambridge, that: 'We must, I think, allow that Acton wished to give the historian a function that cannot be his ... The historian is not a judge, still less a hanging judge'.[115]

Chapter V
The Great Step Forward: Pursuit of the 'Source of the Source'

'Unfortunately for the credit of the historian, these letters are still extant and prove to be of an opposite nature.'

John Lingard

Lingard's central concern with the 'source of the source' is one of the most significant aspects of his work. It is a prime factor in the technique of the modern historian, but one which has emerged only in the modern age. It was not a feature, for example, in the work of the great Jean Mabillon – the founder of the modern study of diplomatics.[1] He concerned himself with establishing the *authenticity* of original documents. The activity of Mabillon and other scholar-monks in France, formed a vitally important first stage in the development of historical scholarship. But in 1681 Mabillon's view of 'authority' in sources was confined largely to establishing the genuineness of the original documents by the use of scientific techniques, applied 'internally' to the physical aspects of the documents – such as paper, handwriting, ink, signatures and seals. He did not investigate what we might call the 'external' questions associated with the *credibility* of these documents as witnesses to historical truth. Yet Mabillon represented the apogee of pre-nineteenth century 'scientific' history and his name lives properly as a major figure in the history of historiography. For nothing else could be done in building the modern structure of source criticism until the basic foundation of establishing the authenticity of the documents themselves had been established.

The second great stage in the development of technical historical scholarship took place in various parts of the continent of Europe, beginning in the eighteenth century, but emerging most conspicuously in Germany in the nineteenth century, reaching its peak with the work of Leopold von Ranke (1795–1886). It was marked particularly in German scholars by systematic and consistent work in the newly-opened archives of European states after 1860.² In the context of historical scholarship, the pursuit of the 'source of the source' was a central feature. It has been thought that little or nothing was achieved in contemporary England in this technical field, to compare with the work on the Continent. The main virtue of English historiography, it is still held, was its achievement in writing history as a branch of 'high literature' as characterized by such figures as Gibbon, Macaulay and Trevelyan, in the eighteenth, nineteenth and twentieth centuries respectively.³ The 'Great Myth'[4] of the English past owed much of its fascination and enduring power to the fact that it was enshrined in these wonderful examples of 'high literature'.

The work of the Englishman John Lingard in this field has remained generally unknown, for reasons which are themselves historically significant. One reason lies in the dominating force of the 'Great Myth' in English historiography. Anyone who challenged this 'official' view of the English past, accepted by the whole of English society, was unlikely to have the critical sub-structure of his work appreciated. Secondly, Lingard was a Catholic priest, when Catholics, though no longer 'outlawed', were still largely 'beyond the pale' in terms of social and political acceptability. They were not allowed, for example, to attend the Universities of Oxford and Cambridge. Lingard was the complete contrast, therefore, to Lord Macaulay, who was part of the English Establishment and enjoyed the privileges which accompanied such a position. In a land where the 'Establishment' counted for so much, Lingard was definitely not part of it. Indeed he was threatened with legal action because of his historical views, which were perceived as threatening the security of the Established Church and State.[5]

Thirdly, Lingard did not belong to a type of group scholarship which characterized the development in technical history associated earlier with the Bollandist and Maurist scholarship in France and with the contemporary universities, such as Göttingen,[5] in Germany. Lingard was an isolated pioneer in terms of his historical work. Fourthly, Lingard made no attempt to publicize his new methodology and range of critical source techniques, apart from describing how he had reached his conclusions in the *History* itself. He did not write a book on the subject, as Mabillon had done in his *De Re Diplomatica* (1681). Lingard's work in this field has had to be uncovered and 'resurrected', two centuries later, by detailed research into the minutiae of the critical scholarship which he took for granted.

Nevertheless, it was Lingard who created the second great stage of development in source criticism in English historical writing. It formed the sub-structure of his pursuit of historical truth. It was not sufficient to know that the original document was genuinely authentic. He went on to ask the vital questions: Where did this knowledge come from? How has the source come to know what it says? In other words he asked the epoch-making question: 'What is the source of the source'. The question of course was full of importance for English source criticism. It was the inspiration for much of Lingard's work in the field. But to Lingard – as to Mabillon with his great question: 'How can I know that a document is authentic? – the wider significance of the question did not seem to be apparent. It simply seemed the obvious question to ask, if he was intent on finding out the truth of what had happened in the past. Mabillon had written his *De Re Diplomatica* (1618) simply to prove to another scholar that a certain document was authentic.[7] Lingard created a methodology designed simply to overcome the obstacles and problems with which he was faced in his pursuit of historical truth. This methodology was needed to demonstrate that his new *History of England* was worthy of his readers' credibility, even though it was contesting popular views inherited over three centuries.

The German Ranke eventually applied himself to archival work in a much more systematic and consistent manner than Lingard could have done; but, interestingly, Lingard understood before Ranke that manuscript work was necessary to the historian.[8] Lingard was working before the opening of the European archives, which occurred from 1860 onwards. His activities in this direction were often indirect and sporadic – through a network of 'agents' whose archival work Lingard supervised closely.[9] His archival work was therefore not systematic; but he had an intuitive sense of knowing what secrets the archives abroad held, in his quest for a new and better understanding of English history. He prepared the right questions for his 'agents' and guided them to where the answers might be. They were thus able, under strict supervision,[10] to find answers in the documents of these archives, which played a significant part in Lingard's important discoveries in English historiography.[11]

It was in the actual treatment of sources, the methodology of source-criticism, however, that Lingard really 'comes into his own', revealing himself as a master of the science. In this field Lingard surpassed even the German exponents of technical history. And this why, even when working with a much smaller range of sources than the modern historian, before the great archives of Europe became open to all scholars, his judgements on historical issues are extraordinarily reliable when judged in the light of the most modern scholarship.

The search for the 'SOURCE OF THE SOURCE' is an abiding theme in the Lingard papers and letters. It is carried out through contact with a network of helpers throughout Europe. These contacts were English priests – many from Ushaw – who were at seminaries near the great archives, for example: in Valladolid, near Simancas in Spain and at the English College in Rome.

Lingard writes to Rome for the original letter from Rosetti, papal envoy to England in the reign of Charles I, of which he already has an abridgment in manuscript made about twenty years after it was written.[12] Robert Gradwell is required to search in the 'Archivium del Sant Officio di Roma' for the originals of Cardinal Pole's letters, used in a work by Pallavicini, which Lingard had consulted.[13] He wanted to check Pallavicini's use of the letters and to get more information.[14] Similarly Lingard is not satisfied with the publication in Hearne of some of Henry VIII's letters to Anne Boleyn. These were 'said to be copied from the Vatican M',[15] but Lingard doubts 'whether they have printed them all'.[16] He therefore wanted to have the originals examined.[17] Again, he receives a letter from Rome, informing him that a letter printed in Spondanus is a false print, this having been discovered after checking it with the original in the Vatican archives'.[18]

Lingard was using despatches published in a work by the French historian, Griffet, entitled *Nouveux Eclaircissements sur l'Histoire de Marie Reine d'Angleterre* (1766), when he discovers that the original despatches of Renard, the Imperial ambassador in England during Mary Tudor's reign, which Griffet had used, were deposited in the library archives at Besançon.[19] He determined to check Griffet with these originals and an agent was commissioned for the task.[20] In the list of inquiries sent by Lingard to the agent, we find questions concerning particular despatches, asking for their dates where Griffet had omitted them, inquiring whether Griffet had omitted anything else, and asking for a check on Griffet's account of certain particulars.[21] The publication of the *History* was held up to await the results of these inquiries.[22] Having received the answers, Lingard is satisfied and says that he will now be able to quote Griffet with more confidence.[23]

Lingard sought information in Rome about sources used by Gildas, the early British contemporary writer:

> I desired Flanagan to consult Dr. Wiseman whether the quotations in Gildas were from Vetus Itala or some other version. He answered that both Dr. Wiseman and Errington looked upon them as from Vetus Itala. *I wrote again to ask whether this was merely a conjecture, or a conclusion from the comparison of the quotations with Vetus Itala. It turns out to have been mere conjecture – therefore of no value to me* – I supposed that they would have Biancini's edition of that version in their library that came from Rome.[24]

We must turn, however, to the *History* itself, to examine the 'source of the source' technique as a working instrument. There are many illustrations of its use as a check on sources and we might begin with a look at its impact on Lingard's treatment of the medieval chroniclers, especially Roger Wendover and Matthew Paris, whose jaundiced accounts had misled English historians for centuries about the nature of Anglo-Papal relations in the medieval period.[25] Lingard was the first English historian to approach these chroniclers with an apparatus of source criticism – in which checking their statements against their own sources played a central part.

For example, with regard to the question of King John's submission to the Papacy in 1212, Lingard dealt effectively with the deficiencies and defects in the narrative of Wendover and Paris, BY TESTING THEM IN THE LIGHT OF THEIR OWN SOURCES. Indeed, he also criticizes the editor of the original documents, for not understanding the contents of these documents. He shows, too, that far from being independent and primary sources as they had always been accepted, 'Paris copies and occasionally interpolates' from Wendover, while both of them 'abound with errors'.

> They tell us that the 15th of May on which the proceedings with Pandulph the papal legate occurred was the vigil of the Ascension, whereas the Ascension fell that year on the 23rd of May . . . They pretend to give us copies of the charter granted by John, but imperfect and falsified copies which had led their readers into error. They affirm that John did homage to Pandulph; yet give as the form of homage the oath of fealty . . . I may add that the titles of the several instruments in Rymer seem to have been copied out of Paris, and are equally calculated to mislead the reader. They are evidently contradicted by the contents of the documents to which they are prefixed. Even the certificate of the King's absolution (Rym. 112) is no certificate; he was not absolved till several months afterwards, and the instrument itself contains not a word on the subject. There occurs in it a clerical error. By the omission of a word John is said to have done homage by oath and charter, whereas he only promised by his charter to do it.[26]

Here Lingard corrects the medieval chroniclers, and also Thomas Rymer's great collection of official documents, the twenty-volume *Floedera, Conventiones, et Acta Publica, an anno 1101* (1704–35) by the application of his 'source of the source' method.

The submission of King John [PLATE 15] to the Papacy in 1213, after refusing for eight years to accept Innocent III's decision in favour of Stephen Langton (who was to help in the making of the Magna Carta in 1215) as Archbishop of Canterbury, became a famous piece of anti-papal propaganda in English Protestant historiography after the Reformation. English Protestant historians depicted the Pope as a foreign tyrant interfering with the liberties of England and humiliating the English king John. Lingard challenged the testimony of Paris and Wendover in 1819, and proved them to be unreliable by testing them against their own sources. But the legend continued until the eminent medievalist Professor C. R. Cheney demolished their evidence again, using much the same methodology in 1948 that Lingard had used in 1819. By using his apparatus of source criticism – especially on this occasion the 'source of the source' technique – Lingard was able to achieve a scholarly insight which was

140 years ahead of his own time. This enabled him to place anglo-papal relations during the medieval period in a completely new context,[27] which was not recovered until the work of M. D. Knowles (1938) and C. R. Cheney (1948).

In case we are inclined to believe that such pursuit of historical truth is simply academic in its concerns, one reads in a recent work on *King John* (1999), that – 'since for the majority of the population, history begins with the Tudors' – the old version of John's 'humiliating' relations with the Papacy, forms one of

> the residual reasons for British hostility to Europe . . . a folk memory of which the details have been obscured, but nevertheless engraved upon the national consciousness . . . There is a direct link from this . . . to the Eurosceptics of today by way of the Tudor historians.[28]

It is important to note, however, that Lingard did not simply use these techniques to disprove anti-Catholic propaganda. He wanted to pursue the truth and after centuries of unabated repetition of the 'official' protestant version, it was natural that newly discovered truths often favoured the Catholic interpretation. However, Lingard used his techniques consistently, including episodes where the subject matter had nothing to do with the religious question. For example, concerning the Charter of the Forests, a section of Magna Carta which allowed people more freedom in royal forests, Lingard writes in a footnote:

> Chart. of Lib. p. 22–27. Annal. Burt. 271–278. Stat. at large, ann. nono Henry III. Paris tells us that two years later, when Henry came of age, he repealed of his own authority the charter of the forests (p. 283); but I have learned to doubt the assertions of that writer, when he is not supported by other documents. He has already told us that in 1223 the archbishop [Stephen Langton] had insisted on the ratification of the charters, that the king promised it, and by his letters ordered inquiries to be made in every county after the liberties enjoyed in the time of Henry II (p. 266, 267). *Unfortunately for the credit of the historian, these letters are still extant and prove to be exactly of an opposite nature.* The sheriffs are to inquire what customs and liberties John had in every county before the war, and to enforce the same for the benefit of the king – See them in Brady, App. No. 149, and the New Rym. i. 168.[29]

Mathew Paris is indeed a good example of Lingard's distinction between an 'original' and 'authentic' (reliable) source. This medieval chronicler was original, but certainly not authentic. Another chronicler, Gervase of Tilbury, also undergoes the same system of checking the 'source of the source': 'Compare the words of Gervase of Tilbury . . . with the correct extract from the MS. of the Sharneburn family, apud Wilk. Leg. Sax. 287'.[30] Again, with regard to Froissart (1337–1410), the French chronicler who visited England:

> The letters in Froissart are very different from the real letters published by Rymer. That amusing writer collected his information from hearsay, and of course was frequently the dupe of ignorant and deceitful narrators.[31]

On the subject of the impeachment of the Earl of Suffolk in 1386, we find the impeachment itself checked against its own source:

> But in the judgement pronounced against him, it was said that no confirmation of the grant could be found on the rolls; a direct falsehood, as it is entered there exactly in the same words as the grant to Gloucester, to which no objections were made ... Rot. Parl.[32]

The 'source of the source' technique is equally apparent in Lingard's treatment of the sixteenth and seventeenth centuries. For the reign of Elizabeth, for example, we find the historians Robertson and Von Raumer checked against their own sources and their interpretations questioned in the light of these sources.[33] The despatches of the papal envoys in England under Charles I, are used to reveal the deficiencies of a narrative account:

> At the end of Lord Nugent's 'Memorials of Hampden' ... is an account of the mission of Panzani, Conn and Rosetti, taken from the 'Guerre Civile' of Mayolino Bisacciono. But the comparison of that account with the despatches of those envoys show that Bisacciono was as ignorant of their real history as he was of the politics and conduct of parties in England.[34]

The inference drawn by a writer from a source is denied by Lingard who checks the source and can draw no such inference from it.[35] A comment made by David Hume upon a particular source is questioned and the reader is invited to examine a recent edition of this source.[36] Clarendon, who lived through the events concerned, is proved to be in error by reference to the sources which he himself used; and this leads to a negative assessment of his contemporary account in his celebrated *History of the Great Rebellion* (1702–4). In regard to this, Lingard gives an account of four bills based on the parliamentary journals as well as the King's papers:

> Journals ... Charles's Works ... Now let the reader turn to Clarendon, History ... He tells us, that ... *When this statement is compared with the real bills, it may be judged how little credit is due to the assertions of Clarendon*, unless they are supported by other authorities.[37]

Lingard was the first English historian to give the correct interpretation of the Secret Treaty of Dover (1670) between Charles II and Louis XIV. This was not surprising since he was the first historian to have seen this Treaty.[38] Yet a long line of English historians had written incorrectly about it without having seen it; and some were going to continue to misinterpret it up to the present day.[39] The mistakes made here had helped to inflame strong prejudices in England against Charles II, the French 'foreigners' and Catholicism.[40] The original source – the Treaty itself – is here used by Lingard to evaluate secondary sources which purported to give an account of it:

> It is plain, *from comparing the treaty itself with the account of it in the life of James*, that that prince, or the compiler of his life, was but ill acquainted with the true history of these transactions. He states erroneously . . .[41]

A later historian, Rapin de Thoyras, is checked by looking at the source of the source:

> Rapin tells us . . . that several Catholics were in the commission [to determine ecclesiastical causes, 1686], an extraordinary mistake, as is evident from the instrument itself . . .[42]

This was a reference to Rapin de Thoyras' *History of England*, first published at The Hague in seventeen volumes, the last of which was published in 1725. Rapin was a Huguenot who had arrived in England in 1685. Another contemporary writer is likewise examined in the light of his own source: 'We are told that "in the proclamation . . .". I can nowhere discover this indication. The words of the proclamation are these . . .'[43]

Even the Commons' Journals themselves can prove defective in the light of this method of source criticism:

> In the treaty between the English and Dutch, 1678, both powers agreed to compel jointly France and Spain to consent; but in article ix. the States assert that they have sufficient assurance of the consent of Spain (satis certi sunt), so that the treaty was in reality directed against France alone. *Yet this important point was concealed in the abstract of the treaty entered on the journals*.[44]

The above is a particularly significant example of THE PENETRATING POWER OF THE 'SOURCE OF THE SOURCE' *technique. For here, a primary source – the public record of the Commons Journals – is found to be faulty: because the Government wished to conceal something.*

We can see another example of this particular application of the technique when Lingard compares a letter of the Earl of Danby with the account given it in the Journals. It is evident in this instance that an important part of the letter has been suppressed. The critical technique in this instance produces historical insights of its own. Danby was Charles II's chief minister. He negotiated secret subsidies given to Charles by Louis XIV in return for English neutrality with regard to Louis' continental policies. Danby was impeached by Parliament and imprisoned. Some of his letters were produced in Parliament to incriminate him. Lingard uses a collection of Danby's letters and the Commons' Journals, together with the Parliamentary History. The 'source of the source' technique reveals an interesting and historically significant insight. *A deception can be practised which can leave even a public record faulty.* Deception can be hidden – for two centuries in this particular case – until a historian, intent on getting back to the 'source of the source', makes the discovery. Lingard's footnote reads:

> Danby says that the letters were not read (Danby, 102); but this, it appears from the journals (Dec. 20), is a mistake. They were moreover entered; and what is still more extraordinary, the entry of Danby's letters omits the very important postscript in the hand of the king, testifying that the letter was written by his order. Was this intended to keep this circumstance from the knowledge of the house? It has been answered no: that the letter, which had been read, and was entered, was a copy only, wanting the postscript; for Lord Russell said, 'Montague cannot come at the originals now, but he has a copy of them'. Whether that copy had or had not the postscript is immaterial; for Lord Russell spoke before the messengers were sent for the box, and meant to inform the house that, if the originals had been seized, yet there was still a copy at their service. But no use was made of that copy, because the messengers returned with the box, out of which Montague himself took the originals, and delivered them to the speaker, who read them to the house. Mr. Williams immediately asked: 'Will any member aver this to be the treasurer's letter?' Montague replied, 'I conceive it to be the treasurer's hand; for I have had several letters from him in the same hand' – Parl. Hist. iv. 1061. Hence it is plain that the original letters were read; and probably, that the postscript, as it was not afterwards entered, had been suppressed at the reading.[45]

On such occasions as this, the CRITICAL TECHNIQUE OPERATES AS A FACT-FINDING OR RESEARCH TOOL, *providing added historical insight as well as being a prime instrument of source criticism.*

Another aspect of the 'source of the source' methodology is *the evaluation of a source according to the type of source it is using.* Malmesbury, the medieval chronicler, is not 'safe' when he is basing his narrative upon 'traditional ballads'.[46] Matthew Paris's narrative of the reign of king John is not of great value, since he did not do much more than transcribe Wendover whose 'account of the period is very imperfect'.[47] Gilbert Burnet's *History of the Reformation* (1689–1715) is of little value when he is relying on the authority of William Thomas whose *Il Pereline Inglese* 'has led Burnet into a multitude of errors'.[48] On the other hand, Strada, the Spanish historian, is worth consulting on the subject of the Armada because he was able to use the original papers of the Duke of Parma – authoritative and original documents on the Spanish side.[49]

An intriguing aspect of Lingard's critical technique is THE ATTEMPT TO RECOVER SOME KNOWLEDGE OF AN ORIGINAL SOURCE WHICH IS NO

LONGER EXTANT, THROUGH THE WORK OF OTHER WRITERS WHO SAW AND USED IT. The idea is to reverse the methodology, so to speak, in order to recover some knowledge of valuable missing evidence. In this way Lingard discusses the value of a later document, called *Leges Henrici Primi*, for the treatment of the Anglo-Saxon judicature:

> On this I do not hesitate to appeal to the treatise called 'Leges Henrici Primi'. *Though compiled under the Normans, it gives in reality an account of the Saxon jurisprudence. This is asserted by the author . . . The same appears from the numerous passages which are evidently translations from Saxon laws still extant; whence it is fair to conclude that much of the rest has been drawn from other documents which have perished in the long lapse of seven hundred years.*[50]

The great legal historian, F. W. Maitland, nearly 90 years later, considered this source as the 'most valuable' of three Norman collections of laws, commenting that 'the main part . . . consists of passages from the Anglo-Saxon dooms translated into Latin'.[51]

Again, there is reference to an unknown 'one common document' from which the chroniclers Simeon, Hoveden and Westminster 'have copied the same words on a particular point'.[52] So, too, Lingard was able to get some information on a papal bull of the Tudor period, which is no longer extant: 'No copy of the decretal bull is extant. But that such was its purport is plain from the despatches in Strype.'[53]

Lingard was interested in showing that certain 'facts', taken for granted in English historiography, were not facts at all. We may take two examples of the way in which Lingard used his 'source of the source' methodology to establish a new factual basis for historical discussion on certain events which were central to the early history of the Reformation in England.[54]

The Question of the Validity of Henry VIII's Marriage to Catherine of Aragon

English historians had generally taken their cue from the Henrician Government's official line, arguing that the marriage between Henry VIII and Catherine of Aragon was not lawful and that Henry should therefore have been allowed to put Catherine aside in order to marry Anne Boleyn. An important part of their case was that the young Henry, at the age of fourteen, had 'protested' against the pre-contract made between the thrones of England and Spain for his marriage with Catherine. They argued that his 'protest', and the consequent delay of the contract, was because of his real doubts about the validity of the marriage.

Lingard showed that since a valid contract of marriage could not be made before the male was fourteen, a pre-contract was often arranged, which, however, either party could revoke on coming of age. It was often the policy of the parent or guardian, especially in cases where royal or dynastic marriages were involved,

> to instruct the party for whom he was interested, to seize the first opportunity of revoking the pre-contract, not with the fixed intention of preventing the marriage, but that he might extort more advantageous terms from the other party.[55]

Lingard wanted to look at the case within its proper historical context of the assumptions and conventions surrounding the vitally important area of royal inter-marriages, before the later events of the Reformation had entered the scene to cloud the real but more mundane issues involved at this earlier stage.

To understand the real reasons for Henry's 'protest' and for the delay preceding the marriage, it was necessary to see the correspondence between Henry VII and Ferdinand of Spain at this period, which would hold the key to the whole problem. Previous English historians had not done this. Their viewpoint was retrospective and anglo-centric. They read history backwards, wanting to find in the earlier 'protest' a reason to justify what had happened later in England when Henry VIII broke from the Church. Lingard approached the question from the viewpoint of the interested parties actually involved in the earlier events of 1509. He used the Euro-centric dimension to supply the political and diplomatic insights which lay behind the 'protest'.

Lingard's initial research enabled him to use a source, previously unexplored by English historians. His queries led him firstly to the findings of the sixteenth-century Spanish historians Mariana and Zurita,[56] for, as Lingard's 'agent' in Spain observed: 'I have no doubt that they consulted the original documents'.[57] These historians certainly confirmed Lingard's view of the case.

But at this stage Lingard was not satisfied. To clinch his findings *he needed* TO GET TO THE 'SOURCE OF THE SOURCE', TO GET BEHIND THE SPANISH HISTORIANS, TO THE SOURCES WHICH THEY HAD USED. His 'agents' in this matter were priest friends at the nearby seminary of Valladolid, about eight miles from the Spanish State Archives at Simancas. They were given the difficult task of investigating the original documents there,[58] though the Archives had not been 'opened' at this stage. In 1820 their findings were transmitted to Lingard by letter:

> A correspondence was carried on between Ferdinand and Henry VII till the death of the latter; the correspondence turns principally on the payment of Catherine's portion. Henry complained that the payments were not made at the stipulated times; Ferdinand in reply offered different excuses . . .

PURSUIT OF THE 'SOURCE OF THE SOURCE'

> Henry the seventh in a letter... 1507, tells him that he could get a far better match for his son than Catherine, twice as much money, but that he preferred her on account of her beauty and her virtue, and that he resolved to stand to his engagements (guardor los pactos) an evident proof that he had no doubt of the validity of Pope Julius' dispensation... The Protestation was evidently a political device intended to work on Ferdinand's fears. Henry pretended that he was at full liberty to conclude the marriage or not, just as he pleased; y corno tenia el aratte levantado. Ferdinand was obliged to accede to all his demands. This is the sum of what I have been able to find...[59]

It was evident from these Spanish documents that the delay in the marriage of Henry and Catherine, including the episode of the young Henry's 'protestation' (1509), was all part of a long drawn out piece of diplomatic wrangling between Henry VII and Ferdinand, to gain a tactical advantage in the terms of the proposed marriage, a situation which was perfectly in keeping with the thrifty character of Henry and the peculiar match-making ability of the Hapsburgs. The whole episode is reflected in Lingard's account of the subject in the *History*:

> The English historians seem entirely ignorant of the causes which for so many years delayed the marriage of Henry and Catherine. For the preceding narrative I have had recourse to the Spanish historians Zurita and Mariana, and have compared their statements with extracts from the original documents preserved among the records at Simancas, which have been copied for me by a friend in Spain.[60]

Henry VIII and Anne Boleyn

The second illustration of how Lingard used his 'source of the source' methodology to establish an important sequence of events is concerned with the question of when exactly Anne Boleyn [PLATES 20, 21] returned to England from her earlier stay in France. Was she on the scene in England before Henry had his 'scruples' about the validity of his marriage to Catherine? English Protestant historians had insisted that Anne Boleyn did not enter the scene in England until 1527. Lingard never allowed 'wishful thinking' to interfere with his critical rules of source criticism. His main intent was to get behind the historians, to get at the 'source of the source' – the ultimate documentation which would prove beyond doubt whether or not Anne was in England before 1527.

Lingard wrote to his friend, Tierney in 1831, indicating his determination to find the truth and his unwillingness to accept any evidence which lacked proper authority to clinch the matter:

You will recollect that you sent me copies of twelve letters from and to Lord Surrey, written in the year 1823... This passage will go far to show at what time Lord Henry Percy married Lady Mary Talbot, & is therefore of importance for [sic] following reasons. Cavendish, who was present at the court, informs us that Ld. Percy fell in love with Anne Boleyn, that Henry ordered the lovers to be separated, & that in consequence he was married to Mary Talbot, lord Shrewsbury's daughter. Of course it follows that, if this marriage took place in 1523, Anne Boleyn must have been in England, & at court in the previous part of that year. I have maintained that it is probable that she came to England in 1522, when Henry sent a peremptory order for her to quit France, & come to England. As, however, she might have disobeyed, & as Spelman says that after the death of Queen Claude (it happened in 1524) she entered into the service of the duchess of Alençon, protestant writers are all positive that she returned to England in 1527. Why 1527? Because then she could not have been the cause of Henry's wish to be divorced, as he had not before that publicly mentioned it. Now what authority Spelman had for saying that she entered into the service of the duchess, we know not: but were it true, it is as possible that she might return in 1525 as 1527: & Le Grand observes that she was at a ball at court in 1525... But for this he does not give any authority... The letter from Ld. Surrey which you sent me, goes far, as I said, to fix the marriage to the autumn of 1523. Yet it does not prove it entirely, for, though the chief baron was with Lord Northumberland 'to conclude it', there is a possibility that the negociation may have been suspended, and renewed at a later period. On this account I could wish to discover some document mentioning the <u>actual</u> celebration of the marriage... I cherish a hope that some notice of it may be contained in some of the other letters of Lord Surrey which you did not copy for me. If these are still accessible to you, may I beg you the favour to peruse them... In one of your letters you say 'the whole correspondence is in the possession of an old lady, I think at York'. Can you furnish me with the name of the old lady, or with a clue by which I might learn it? In that case I might perhaps obtain a sight of the other letters which were not copied.[61]

Another letter to Tierney in 1836 shows the investigation continuing.[62] Lord Shrewsbury has been approached for any help in the way of documents; but he has none. Evidence could probably be found in the despatches of the English ambassador in France; but these, Lingard fears, 'will be in the hands of the commission', presumably the Anglican Church commission to which he refers in another letter.[63] He disagrees with the editors of the State Papers on a point connected with the same subject. He hardly likes to ask the Duke of Northumberland for any materials which he may have on the subject, since 'your conservative peers' like Lord Lonsdale have not been very friendly in the past. Yet his reluctance to approach the Duke would seem to have been overthrown by his determination to pursue this point, for we find in a letter of the following year:[64] 'The Duke of Northumberland has ordered a search to be made but nothing has been found to fix the date of the marriage of Ld. Percy with Mary Talbot'. The Herald's College archives were searched for information, but to no avail; and there is another letter connected with the same subject from Mr. Holmes of the British Museum in 1841.[65]

Despite such frustration, Lingard finally believed that he had sufficient evidence to make a safe judgement as to the period when the marriage took place and when, therefore, Anne Boleyn had returned to England. Though not discovering the precise date of the marriage, he had brought together enough evidence from the letters of the Earl of Surrey, from the contemporary writer Lord Herbert, from an account of the English ambassador in France, and from the State Papers, to make the issue safe.

Concerning the marriage of Lord Percy with Mary Talbot, Lingard writes in a footnote to his last edition:

> I know not the day on which it took place, but I possess the copy of a letter from the earl of Surrey to Lord Percy, 'scribbled the 12th day of September' in the year 1523, in which Lord Surrey ... adds ... mentioning the ensuing marriage. We may therefore safely infer that it took place about the end of 1523 or the beginning of 1524; another proof that the historians who placed the return of Anne in the year 1527 are in error.[66]

With regard to the date of Anne's return to England, Lingard considered it safe, in the light of all the evidence, to say that:

> In 1522 she was recalled to England by Henry VIII, who had it in contemplation to put an end to the controversy between Sir Thomas Boleyn and Sir Piers Butler ... by giving Anne Boleyn in marriage to the son of Sir Piers ...[67]

> Though Spelman ... makes her remain in the family of the duchess of Alençon, who quitted France in September, 1525 ... it is plain that he cannot be correct. Lord Herbert assures us (and appeals to 'our records'), that she returned to England in 1522, 'at the time when our students at Paris were returned ...', and Fiddes informs us, that Francis king of France complained at the time to the English ambassador, that 'the English scholars and the daughter of Sir Thomas Boleyn should return home'.[68]

> This suggestion of marrying Anne to the son of Sir Piers came from Lord Surrey (St. Pap. ii. 57); and Wolsey was ordered by the king to bring about the marriage (ibid. i. 91). Now Mary Boleyn had been already married nine months; so that the daughter in question could only be Anne Boleyn. Wolsey undertook the negotiation in November, 1521, and the order for Anne's return reached Paris in the beginning of the next year.[69]

The whole matter of the date of Anne Boleyn's marriage is worth recording because it shows the importance of the accuracy of dates in historical interpretation and understanding. On the date of Anne's return to England from France depended the view that Henry knew Anne Boleyn well before he applied to the Pope for an annulment of his marriage to Catherine. The intended marriage between Anne and the son of Sir Piers Butler did not take place. The beginning of Henry's own interest in Anne, as is evident in his letters to her, says Lingard, 'must have begun at the latest in the summer of 1526, probably much earlier; at all events before the time assigned to the origin of his scruples respecting his marriage with Catherine'.[70]

Lingard's final judgement on the evidence was that Anne Boleyn had returned from France to the English court in 1522 – as opposed to the general view among English historians that she had returned in 1527. The discrepancy was vital to a proper interpretation of the Divorce question which was the central feature, the pivotal point, dictating the movement and process of the English Reformation. It led inexorably to the epoch-making statutes of the Reformation Parliament, the Act against Appeals (1533), the Act of Supremacy (1534), the submission of the clergy, the rejection of Canon Law, the dissolution of the monasteries and the execution of Sir Thomas More (1535).

Lingard's conclusions had been informed by his insistence on pursuing the 'source of the source' as far as he was able and indeed as far as anyone has been able to since. He had not been able to trace the 'records' mentioned by Lord Herbert. They had disappeared, perhaps significantly, and have never come to light. But Lingard's inference from Lord Herbert's reference to them, guided by the statements of other 'authentic' sources, was correct and contributed decisively to his original treatment of the matter.[71] Modern scholarship completely vindicates Lingard's judgement made originally in 1823. In 1997, Professor J. A. Cannon summarized the state of modern scholarship on the subject:

> The entanglement of personal motives with great political issues, which makes history both difficult and fascinating, is rarely more apparent... She [Anne Bolyen] has been accused of bringing about the Reformation single-handedly... Anne spent several years at the court of France. Returning in 1522, she was given a post the household of Catherine of Aragon. The king's interest at this time was in her sister Mary who, became his mistress. Anne was dark haired with large eyes, composed and cultivated, with a mole on her neck and a malformed finger. By 1527 Henry was initiating annulment proceedings against Catherine... Meanwhile her [Anne's] father had been given the Garter in 1523, created Viscount Rochford in 1825, and advanced to be earl of Wiltshire in 1529; her brother George was created Baron Rochford c.1530.

Professor J. Scarisbrick, in his authoritative, *Henry VIII* (1968), had confirmed already Lingard's date for Anne's return to England (1522), as well as his date for Henry's 'deeper and more dangerous attachment to Anne'.[72]

Pursuit of the 'Source of the Source'

One interesting branch of the 'source of the source' methodology is Lingard's CRITIQUE OF THE ULTIMATE SOURCE ITSELF, *in the form in which it has come down to posterity – in the light of statements made by certain contemporaries who were in a position to know the truth and had no reason for lying.* The source may have been tampered with for political expediency. Elizabeth's Government was particularly adept at this sort of practice. For example, the earl of Morton made a confession before his execution in 1581, of procuring Darnley's murder in 1567. Lingard suspected that the confession, as it has come down to us, may have been tampered with by government sources. It might well have contained evidence about earlier activities of English 'agents' intent on ensnaring Mary Queen of Scots, and in favour of Mary's innocence of the murder of her husband, Darnley. Lingard writes:

> See the whole confession, and the sequel, in Bannatayne's Journal... It has been contended that in this confession, published by the ministers, much was omitted out of tenderness to characters then living or for political purposes. Mary, indeed, in a letter to Elizabeth roundly asserts that, from the deposition of Morton, and from the depositions of those confronted with him, it was plain that all her misfortunes during her residence in Scotland, were caused by the suggestions and promises of the agents of the English queen... Camden also informs us that, according to Morton's real confession, he refused to act in the murder without a note from the queen; and Bothwell replied that such a note could not be procured because the murder must be perpetrated without her knowledge.[73]

The necessary evidence to decide this matter has never been found; but it is a reminder of Lingard's awareness that even the 'source of the source is not always sacrosanct, when in the hands of certain Governments'.

Lingard can be found pursuing the original source for statements made by later writers about the notorious massacre[74] of the Irish at Wexford by Cromwell in 1649–50:

> I have not quoted them, because they are not contemporary, but were written a century afterwards. It is on this account that I have not appealed to them: but their testimony shows that there does exist or did exist prior authority for the story... I dare say the original authority is among the friars [sic] letters at St. Isidore's at Rome. I wrote there, but got only a shuffling [indecisive] answer. For such researches you must get someone who feels an interest in the matter.[75]

Lingard's continual pursuit of this original document, from which later writers gained their information, is the subject of several letters in the Lingard correspondence.[76] Finally, in 1849, when he was nearing his eightieth year, he received some satisfaction from 'a paper' which 'has lately been discovered in the State Paper Office'. He describes this document which 'goes far to confirm' his statement on the subject.[77] We now know, in the light of present scholarship, that Lingard's description of the massacre was completely accurate. Cromwell's actions against the Irish inhabitants of Drogheda and Wexford are now regarded as 'savage' and 'ruthless... atrocities'.[78] In 1997, Professor J. R. Jones writes of the 'ruthlessness' and 'planned ethnic cleansing' for which Cromwell 'has been universally condemned'.[79]

> *A major aspect of the 'source of the source' technique is the* COMPARISON OF COPIES, TRANSLATIONS AND EXTRACTS, *taken from it, with the full text of the original source.* So, for example, referring to the document recording the last words of Cardinal Wolsey, Lingard notes:

> In the printed editions it is asserted that the cardinal poisoned himself, but ... it was an interpolation. The passage is not in the manuscript ...[80]

We now know that Wolsey died in Leicester, on his way to London, to answer a charge of treason. He certainly did not commit suicide.

Similarly, of Thomas Cranmer's secret 'qualifying clause' in his oath of obedience to the Papacy, on being appointed Archbishop of Canterbury in 1533, Lingard tells us: 'See it in the original Latin ... and not in the English translation which is very unfaithful.'[81] Again, significant omissions are noticed in the copy of a letter printed by the English Government, in the light of the original document.[82] The 'report' of a letter is checked, as are extracts from it, by reference to the letter itself.[83]

A good example of the comparison technique is provided by a footnote devoted to the question of Bishop Stephen Gardiner's attitude towards Elizabeth in Mary Tudor's reign. In this case Lingard demonstrates another aspect of the 'source of the source' critique: *revealing that the* PUBLICATION OF SMALL PARTS OF A LETTER MAY CONVEY AN IMPRESSION WHICH IS UNFAITHFUL TO THE TRUE MEANING OF THE WHOLE:

> In the beginning of April, 1554 during a conference between Renard the Imperial ambassador and Gardiner, in the presence of the queen, Gardiner is stated by the ambassador to have owned that 'as long as Elizabeth was alive there was no hope that the kingdom could be tranquil'; and to have said afterwards, that 'if everybody went as roundly to work in providing the necessary remedies as he did, things would go one better' – Tyt. ii. 365. It is a pity that this interesting letter has not been published, as well as others of much less interest. From the two short extracts copied above, it has been inferred that Gardiner really thirsted for the blood of Elizabeth. But no such inference can be fairly deduced from them; nor does the first of the two prove any thing more than that the wily statesman was willing to appear of the same opinion with the emperor. Of his real intention with respect to the princess we may judge from the fact that he continued after this conference

to shield her, as he had done before, from the repeated attempts of the ambassador to have her brought to trial, and put to death.[84]

This reveals not only Lingard's *insistence on* SEEING THE WHOLE DOCUMENT, RATHER THAN SELECTED PARTS OF IT; but also his realism in understanding that devious ways of speaking in certain situations must be CHECKED AGAINST THE KNOWN CONDUCT OF THE PARTY INVOLVED.

Again, dealing with the Hampton Court Conference (1604) between James I and the dissenting Puritan ministers, Lingard collates several pieces of evidence to show that a particular source does not do justice to the Puritans' case:

> Compare Fuller, cent. xvi. 1. x 7–24; Howell's State Trials, ii. 70–94, with Dr. Montague's letter in Winwood, ii. 14–16 and the bishop of Durham's letter in Strype's *Whitgift*, App. 236. It is plain that Barlow has greatly abridged, and often omitted, the arguments of the nonconformists.[85]

Perhaps the best example of this technique is provided by the *lengthy consideration of the differences between two secondary sources and the original document itself in an episode concerning the trial of Fr. Garnet, a Jesuit, for his alleged complicity in the Gunpowder Plot (1605)*. Garnet had in fact heard the confession of one of the conspirators, for which he was charged and executed for 'complicity' in the Plot. Lingard used two hitherto untapped original sources in his account, which was the first to develop our understanding of this Plot.[86] These were manuscript accounts written by the Jesuit priests, Fr. Gerard and Fr. Greenway.[87]

Lingard dealt with a letter from Garnet which was widely used for propaganda purposes on the part of the Government against Catholics. Dr. Andrews, Bishop of Chichester, published some extracts from it in his *Torture Torti* (1609). The same extracts appeared in a work entitled *Epistola ad Frontonem Ducaeum* (1611). In 1613 Dr. Robert Abbot produced a new version of it in Latin. Lingard proceeded, in an Appendix, to a collation of the three editions, and weighed them against the original manuscript source of the letter in the State Paper Office:

> That the reader may judge of the arts employed to confirm the conviction of the Jesuit, he may compare the parallel passages out of this letter in the following columns, the first taken from the more correct version of Dr. Abbot, the other from the false version of Dr. Andrews, published four years earlier.[88]

The above shows that 'the many erroneous renderings in the translation of Dr. Andrews are wilful, all being made for the purpose of aggravating the guilt of Garnet'.[89] Although Abbot's version 'has the appearance of being much more correct', 'yet he also seems not to have felt any objection to the employment of a little fraud, when its object was to blacken the character of a Jesuit'.[90]

The 'Jesuits', a strong force in the Counter-Reformation, had always been given a very bad press in English historiography. Lingard uses the original letters of Garnet and points out that 'these are still extant in the State Paper Office'.[91] Significantly Lingard was the first English historian to challenge the Government's version of the event, which had been accepted in its entirety as part of the 'official version' for more than two centuries.

Lingard received two manuscript accounts of the Gunpowder Plot by Fr. Gerard – one in English from the Jesuit archives at Stonyhurst, the other in Italian, from the Roman archives. He writes to a Jesuit friend at Stonyhurst:

> The Italian copy of the plot is not in father [sic] Gerard's hand I have no doubt that *your copy was written by himself and is therefore more authentic*.[92]

In the same letter, Lingard mentions a 'treatise on schism'. Here again we find his abiding need to find the 'source of the source'

> I have found the passage which made so much noise translated into Latin in Bridgewater's Concertatio . . . *But I should like to see the original*.[93]

Lingard admired Thomas Hearne's editions of original documents[94] and shared his instinct for presenting the original source in its entirety and in its original *form*. He wrote to Mawman, his publisher, in 1825, concerning a document which had been published incorrectly by another author. Lingard had sought and gained an exact copy of the original from the 'London Institution':

> Look at page 283. I wish to substitute the real words of Felton for those which Mr. Ellis has attributed to him. Have the goodness to see that the printer observe [sic] the stops, the comma, capitals &c of the MS. so as to make it resemble Felton's own paper as near as possible . . . I must thank Mr. Upcott who sent it to me. I have called him Mr. Upcott of the London Institution.[95]

Another category of the 'source of the source' methodology is found in those cases where *Lingard devalues a source if its own source is not stated or is unknown*. So, for example, we find him dismissing any claim to authority in such a source:

> But that life of Lord Shaftesbury 'lately edited by Mr. Coke' cannot be considered an authority: *for the documents from which it is said to have been compiled are neither quoted nor described by its author, nor have ever been seen by its present editor*.[96]

Again, a statement of the French ambassador in England in the reign of James II, cannot be accepted:

> That James believed in the existence of a plot to carry him off in 1688, is twice asserted by Barillon, *but we have no knowledge on what authority that belief was founded.*[97]

Another intriguing example of the same technique is found in Lingard's earlier work, *The History and Antiquities of the Anglo-Saxon Church* (1806). Lingard had a great respect and admiration for the Venerable Bede, author of *The Ecclesiastical History of the English People* (731),[98] now rightly regarded as the greatest English historian of the first millennium. But even this great historian and primary source for his own period had to satisfy Lingard's rules of source criticism.

Bede had given an account of the conversion of the British King Lucius to Christianity between 171 and 181. The story had in fact been repeated by other historians and had become an important part of the 'Great Myth' of English history, established by Thomas Cromwell and Henry VIII in the sixteenth century. Lucius had been 'nominated' as the first British king or 'emperor' who had ruled over Church and State in these islands – the predecessor from whom Henry VIII derived his own newly-established position as 'emperor', with authority over everyone and everything.[99]

It was long before the historical framework of thought supporting the notion of such an early British king crumbled.[100] All English historians, including the 'enlightened sceptic', David Hume [PLATE 8], accepted it. Lingard was therefore taking a brave step when he confronted, not only the 'official version' stemming from the sixteenth century, but also the vastly superior authority of Bede whom he really respected. Besides, Lingard had no means of denying it.

Lingard's answer was to deal with the issue by the usual calm application of two of his scientific rules of source criticism. He doubted the story, not because there was positive evidence against it, but because it simply did not satisfy his criteria. In the first place, *Bede had no first-hand knowledge of the event. He was writing of something which had taken place five centuries before his own time.* Secondly, THE HISTORIAN CANNOT ACCEPT THE EVIDENCE OF ANY SOURCE IN THESE CIRCUMSTANCES, UNLESS IT STATES ITS OWN SOURCE WHICH CAN ITSELF THEN BE TESTED BY OTHER RULES OF SOURCE CRITICISM.

As usual with Lingard, his own comment is terse, with the utmost economy of language, stating nevertheless quite adequately the grounds on which he cannot accept Bede's statement:

> This story itself is liable to suspicion, for we know not from what source Bede, at the distance of five centuries, derived his information.[101]

Pursuit of the 'Source of the Source'

In his *History of England*, volume I (1819), Lingard speaks of the uncertainty of the evidence for early British history:

> But their traditions have been so embellished or disfigured by fiction, that without collateral evidence, it is hardly possible to distinguish in them what is real from that which is imaginary.[102]

On the basis that certain happenings are 'confirmed by Bede', Lingard allows that 'we may believe' that Lucius was a high-ranking Briton who sent messages to Rome, though 'it is difficult to reconcile' Bede's dates for this with the date he gives for the accession of the Emperor Aurelius; but this may have arisen 'from the error of some copyist'. Lingard moves on quickly in his narrative, with the remark:

> But independently of such authority, we have undoubted proof that the Christian believers were numerous, and that a regular hierarchy had been instituted, before the close of the third century.[103]

Here he is much happier basing his work on original sources such as Spelman's *Concilia*, which informs us that at one of the earliest western councils, that of Arles in 314, three British bishops attended, from York, London and Lincoln.[104]

Lingard is obviously discomforted when having to deal with the vague British 'historians' of this early period, but is willing to give a half-hearted support to them, when they are supported by Bede. He is happy to leave this period and begin working on later original sources for Anglo-Saxon England with which he can come to grips and on which ground he feels that Bede himself becomes a primary and more sure authority. The final assessment is that Lingard pays a token respect to Bede's own views on this early period, but his main narrative recognizes that:

> At the distance of so many ages it is impossible to discover by whom Christianity was first preached in the island ... It is however certain that from a very early period there were Christians in Britain: nor is it difficult to account for the circumstances from the intercourse which had long subsisted between the island and Rome ... There is even evidence that the knowledge of the gospel was not confined to the subjects of Rome. Before the close of the second century, it had penetrated among the independent tribes of the north.[105]

Here he is on firm ground, using Tertullian as a source; and his narrative for the Christian conversion of Britain is along much the same lines as any modern account.

Finally, in this investigation into Lingard's technique of pursuing the 'source of the source', we can turn to his treatment of the contemporary German scholar, Friedrich von Raumer (1781–1873) who had published his *Beiträge zur neueren Geschichte aus dem Britischen Museum und*

Reichsarchive in five volumes in Leipzig (1836). Von Raumer's work was a collection of long extracts from British documents, 'all these strung together with hardly any commentary – exactly the kind of book that would be used as a quarry by later writers'.[106] An English translation appeared in London in 1836–7.

In 1837, while preparing his fourth edition of the *History*, Lingard wrote of Raumer's work:

> I know nothing more of Raumer than I have gleaned from reviews: but from them I saw that it was necessary for me to have him before the next edition of my work. I know not, if I am correct, but I have the notion that he has translated into German all the original letters and monuments which he quotes, and therefore that in the English edition we have them only in a second version, and on that account perhaps a very faulty version. Do you know if in the German the original documents are to be found in the original language in which they were written? In that case I would purchase it . . .[107]

With greater knowledge of Raumer's work, Lingard's critical awareness comes into play. He writes to a friend:

> I shall notice Von Raumer once or twice. A very great number of his documents have been published in collections in England: but published at length and fairly. He in general gives only parts, such as suit his own views, and passes over everything else – or if he gives a whole document, gives it in a very free translation, which we have translated again into English from the German, so that very often no one would conceive that the original & version were meant to represent the same document.[108]

Coming to the particular application of his critical methodology to Raumer's collection of documents, Lingard is suspicious of his version of a document entitled 'the confession of Curle', Curle being one of Mary Queen of Scots' secretaries, allegedly involved in the Babington conspiracy (1586) against Elizabeth.

There is a very telling letter in the Lingard correspondence, from a Mr. Holmes of the British Museum, who is answering a letter of query and investigation from Lingard into the reliability of the document:

> Your question has led to another proof, if such were wanting, of the inaccuracy not to say unfaithfulness of Mr. Von Raumer's compilations. I thought at first as you did, judging from the variation in the two extracts, that they were translations from one French original, such however is not the case. Curll's [sic] confession was evidently made in <u>English</u> and the copy certified by Nau, Mary's other secretary, under his own hand is still existing in the Cotton MS. Calig. D. 1. From it I have made a transcript for your use adding from the Harl. MS. 4647 portions wherein the Cotton original is deficient having somewhat suffered from fire. These additions and a few

trifling inaccuracies in the Harl. MS. I have marked in red ink. Now Von Raumer either could not read the Harl. transcript or has chosen wantonly to modernise the language and alter the sense. (He evidently did not know of the existence of the Cotton original); yet he prints his synopsis as if it were a transcript. You will now be able to judge of his faithfulness.[109]

Von Raumer's documentation, while representing the best efforts of German 'scientific' history at this period, does not seem to have measured up to Lingard's standard of source criticism as evidenced in his 'source of the source' technique. Lingard writes again to a friend in 1837:

> I have been reading Von Raumer ... I am surprised at this learned German ... the misfortune is that he publishes only fragments of letters, and those selected here and there out of the entire correspondence, so that the reader is more likely to form a false than a correct notion of the real transaction ... Raumer has been very unjust to her [Mary, Queen of Scots], having strung together a series of extracts from documents against her without reference to the character of the writers, the authority of the documents, or the real meaning of the language.[110]

Lingard is really describing here deficiencies in Raumer's source criticism, when measured against Lingard's own standards.

A summary of this matter is to be found in a footnote to a long appendix in Lingard's *History*:

> a copy of this confession of Curle, but strangely metamorphosed, and dated the 7th of August, is in Mr. Von Raumer's vol. iii, p. 327. The above was copied for me by Mr. Holmes, from the original (Cot. MS. Cal. 1) compared with the Harl. MS. 4647, which has supplied a few words in places where the original has been damaged by fire.[111]

The above example illustrates the two great stages in the development of historical source criticism. The first stage is demonstrated in Lingard's determination to get at the most *authentic* version of the original source – in this case Curle's confession – showing the type of concern for the 'internal' evidence in a source, which Mabillon had demonstrated in the seventeenth century. He goes into the second stage of source criticism, which he had established himself by an investigation into the 'external' factors surrounding the original source which would affect its *authority* as opposed to its *authenticity*.[112] The confession of Curle itself might have been an authentic document; but the context in which it was gained and exploited took away its authority as a reliable source.

In this chapter we have witnessed something of extraordinary importance in English historiography. It may seem difficult now to imagine the importance of Lingard's work in pursuing the 'source of the source'; but he was the first English historian to have set out to do so as part of his systematic methodology of source criticism. It is difficult to compare his work in the field of technical history, with what was going on in Germany, completely independently, at this time. We know that August Ludwig Schlözer (1735–1809), who worked at Göttingen University, had been conspicuous for asking the same sort of questions concerning German history; 'Where does our knowledge come from and how has it reached us?';[113] and he, too, examined the sources used by the medieval chroniclers in Germany just as Lingard was to do in England, though Lingard applied this technology to the sources of all English history. But there was no contact whatsoever between them. Lingard worked completely independently in the field of historical research. Any influence on Lingard had come from the French tradition of historical scholarship at Douai College.

In the second half of the eighteenth century a German reviewer of Edward Gibbon (1737–94) admired him for the scope and style of his work on *The Decline and Fall of the Roman Empire* (1776–88), but remarked on his inferiority when compared with the German interest and advances in source criticism.[114] Gibbon, like all the 'great' English historians, was famous as an exponent of historical writing as a branch of philosophy or 'high literature', rather than as practitioner of a disciplined attempt to discover the sober truth about what happened in the past.

Lingard, it is true, could not match the systematic and consistent archival work achieved by Ranke during his later period in the 1860s. But this was a different era, for it was after 1860 that the great state archives of Europe were opened fully for use by historians.[115] It must be remembered that Ranke's first work, written in 1824, contemporaneously with Lingard, had relied solely on printed sources, while Lingard was using for the first time, for example, the Harleian and Lansdowne manuscript papers. It was only from about 1840 – two decades after Lingard's first edition – that Ranke came to realize that sixteenth-century history could not be written from printed sources alone; and it was not until the 1860s, when the archives became readily accessible, that Ranke began his important task of working systematically and methodically through the manuscript materials[116] My view is that Lingard is supreme, even when compared with the Germans, in the field of source criticism and the scientific methodology associated with it. It is no accident that we have seen him pointing out the flaws in the work of Von Raumer on original documents[117] and interpreting evidence at a higher level than Ranke himself.[118]

Ranke eventually wrote a *History of England* (1859–68), based on unprecedented archival work; and Lord Macaulay's celebrated *History of England* (1849–55) superseded Hume's *History* as an example of 'high literature' in England. But significantly, it is Lingard's *History* (1819–30), which in the considerable opinion of G. P. Gooch in his survey of *History and Historians in the Nineteenth Century*, produced the 'first modern narrative of the two critical centuries of English history'.[119] The present study now shows that this was undoubtedly because of the superior source criticism which informed the unprecedented technical substructure of Lingard's *History*. It was so good, in fact, that it produced an account which was both more revisionist and more durable in value than Ranke's, even though the actual mass of original archive material used by Ranke was much greater. The achievement is even more remarkable when we remember that Lingard was writing a complete *History of England*, while Ranke's *History of England* was confined principally to the seventeenth century; and Macaulay's to the even shorter period of 1685–1702.

Lingard's achievement in writing the whole *History of England From the First Invasion by the Romans, to the Accession of William and Mary in 1688*, in ten large volumes of between five hundred and twenty and seven hundred and twenty pages each, based on the pursuit and scientific examination of the source of the sources used, has never been equalled in quality and quantity in the history of historical writing in England. His achievement makes him worthy of the name of the greatest English historian of the second millennium – the greatest in fact, since Bede.

Chapter VI
A Critical Apparatus for Prioritizing the Authority of Sources

'To understand these letters the reader should observe . . .'
John Lingard

There emerges from a detailed study of Lingard's work a clearly discernible attempt to indicate the type of critical apparatus which should be brought to bear on certain sources. Many sources may not be first class in authority or reliability, but they can still be very useful to the historian if he or she has the necessary critical apparatus with which to interpret them. It is necessary to understand the strengths and weaknesses of the source and to make appropriate adjustments in order to get the best information possible from it.

One aspect of this methodology is an indication of the relative value of different parts of a source when there are factors operating which make some parts more trustworthy than others. So, referring to the medieval chronicler William of Malmesbury's account of the reign of Athelstan (924–39), Lingard informs us:

> In Malmesbury we have three different accounts of Athelstan which should be carefully distinguished. The first he compiled himself from documents within his reach. The second he abridged from the longer work of a contemporary poet, whose extravagant praise of his patron he reduced to the standard of probability and common sense. The last is a collection of facts for which no written authority could be found; but which were mentioned in Anglo-Saxon songs transmitted from one generation to another.[1]

William of Malmesbury (1095–c.1143), a monk of that abbey, was the best English historian since the Venerable Bede and the most reliable of the medieval chroniclers;[2] but he still needs to be read with the critical reservations established by Lingard.

Referring to a seventeenth-century compilation entitled *Memoirs of James II*, Lingard places a critical proviso:

Where the compiler of the Memoirs of James refers to the writings of that monarch, I shall, as I have done above, add the word (Memoirs), because such passages are of higher authority than other parts of that work.[3]

Lingard's judgement is corroborated by a modern master of the Stuart period. G. Clarke tells us that the source 'is of very unequal value. The best parts throw much light on his policy; but especially after the Revolution much is untrustworthy'.[4]

We are told when a source is deficient in the sense that it provides accurate information, but does not reveal all that it could. So, for example, concerning the Irish Rebellion in 1641, Lingard tells us:

> See, for most of these particulars, MacGuire's relation ... He may perhaps conceal some things, but I have no doubt of his accuracy as far as he goes.[5]

The following relates to another seventeenth-century source, which was published as an appendix to a book by Welwood, a contemporary writer:

> That this journal [*Monmouth's Journal*] is authentic, as far as it goes, I have no doubt. It bears its origin on its face, and agrees with every credible document. That it is considerably mutilated is acknowledged by Welwood himself, who was unwilling or afraid to publish passages which might be thought to reflect on certain characters.[6]

Acts of Attainder are generally not to be regarded as good evidence, to be accepted unreservedly. Herein lies Lingard's unwillingness to be deceived by government propaganda – as most previous English historians had been.[7] An Act of Attainder was a convenient method of convicting political opponents of treason, without having to bother going through a court of law. Those named in such an act were ipso facto declared guilty, lost all their civil rights and property which went to the Crown, while their descendants were disinherited. Originally, attainders were attached to punishments inflicted by a court of law; but during the Wars of the Roses between the Yorkists and the Lancastrians and then during the Tudor period, the new form of attainder was used by the monarchy as a convenient and summary way of dealing with 'rebels'. Both Henry VIII and Elizabeth I made use of this essentially unjust measure against opponents, which was not abolished until 1870. Dealing with the aftermath of Lord Lovell's rebellion against Henry VII in 1487, for example, Lingard writes:

> The first care of the parliament was to supply the wants of the conqueror by a grant of money, and a bill of attainder, which included almost every man of property engaged in the late insurrection.

Lingards adds, in a footnote:

Rot. Parl. v, i. 386, 400. I have said 'almost every man of property', for by mistake or design lord Lovell was omitted. But the omission was discovered eight years afterwards, and a new bill of attainder was passed to include him (Rot. Parl. vi. 502). The number, however, of the insurgents had then dwindled from eight to five thousand, *a proof that we are not to trust to acts of attainder for more than the substance of the offence.*[8]

Some sources can be used only as evidence for reports that were current at a particular period and not as reliable authorities for facts. Such a source is the tract called *Secret Consults* for the reign of James II. Lingard warns:

> This tract, which was written by a warm partisan of King William at the time in which James was in possession of Ireland, though often cited, is, *from its frequent contradiction of more authentic documents entitled to very little credit. It may show what reports circulated in Ireland, but cannot be assumed as authority for facts.*[9]

An important part of the critical apparatus established by Lingard, is THE PROCESS BY WHICH AMBASSADORS' DESPATCHES AND REPORTS OUGHT TO BE APPROACHED. This is especially important in light of the fact that Lingard stressed the general importance of materials that could supply a more objective account of happenings, in England, taken from the viewpoint of outsiders. Lingard was always searching for such materials. He realized, for example, the importance of the reports of the Venetian ambassadors, long before Ranke came to the same conclusion.[10] Often such reports provide an excellent means of cutting through the bias and prejudice of 'internal' accounts, written by people representing different sides in domestic controversies.

Yet, as with all sources, Lingard argued, great care must be taken in their use. This type of source contained its own 'pitfalls' which the reader must learn to recognize. *Governments, for example, are sometimes* INTENT ON DECEIVING THEIR FOREIGN NEIGHBOURS AND MAY SOMETIMES ARRANGE FOR THE SENDING OF MISLEADING DESPATCHES ABROAD. We cannot, therefore, accept the charges of treason against Cardinal Wolsey simply 'on the testimony of the despatches sent by his enemies to ambassadors abroad', because:

> such despatches with general charges were always sent on similar occasions to justify the government in the eyes of foreign princes.[11]

Wolsey had in fact pleaded guilty to what is now regarded as an 'absurd' charge of praemunire, in 1529, and had 'dabbled unofficially in diplomacy in the summer of 1530'.[12] But anyone who opposed or even displeased Henry VIII was likely to be accused of 'treason'.

Prioritizing the Authority of Sources

Similarly, in Elizabeth I's reign, we are reminded more than once,[13] of her first minister Cecil's habit of SENDING DESPATCHES ABROAD VIA AMBASSADORS, FOR PROPAGANDA PURPOSES:

> It should, however, be observed, that the despatches of ambassadors are to be read with caution. They contain statements which, whether true or false, that wily minister [William Cecil, Lord Burghley] wished to be circulated in foreign courts.[14]

Of course, ambassadors' reports from other countries are also susceptible. Noailles, the French ambassador in Mary Tudor's reign, is guilty of falsehood on several occasions: 'sometimes by order of his sovereign'; and he is sometimes charged to keep certain things secret.[15] Lingard makes great use of ambassadors' reports but his technique is to approach them with a critical apparatus which takes account of the deficiencies and deceptions which may be present in them.

SUCH DESPATCHES MUST BE APPROACHED CRITICALLY, too, *from the viewpoint of the ambassador's personal propensities for bias or exaggeration, in sending back information to his own government.* So, the despatches of Noailles, for example, lose much of their value during the later part of his period in England. Mary Tudor's decision to marry a Spanish monarch meant the failure of Noailles' plans:

> This ambassador found that he had failed in the object of his mission, in his intrigues with the discontented, and in the predictions with which he had amused his court. After this, his chagrin and hatred of the queen, and her advisers, betray themselves in almost every page of his despatches, and detract much from the credit which might otherwise be given to his misrepresentations.[16]

Fénelon, the French ambassador in England in Elizabeth's reign, could be led astray by the exaggeration of his informant, 'that wily minister', the Bishop of Ross, who wanted to give the French monarch an exaggerated idea of Catholic strength in England so as to encourage the latter to lend his material support to a proposed uprising.[17] Lingard says of Fénelon:

> I must not conceal my suspicion that in his secret despatches to Catherine, the queen-mother, he may occasionally indulge in fanciful embellishments on matters connected with the private life of the English queen.[18]

And this despite the fact that Lingard himself had his own suspicions on the matter, which modern scholarship has tended to substantiate.[19]

James I, the first Stuart king, was disliked by Tillières, the French ambassador, because of his 'partiality for Spain, and the Spanish match'. James was planning a match between his son and the daughter of the King of Spain in 1521. All this was 'a constant source of vexation' to Tillières and 'prompted him to exaggerate and misrepresent' the personal weaknesses of James I.[20] So, with regard to the scandals told about James, we must distrust 'the reports which reached a foreign and discontented ambassador', making allowance for the colouring given to the picture by his prejudices or those of his informant.[21]

Barillon, the French ambassador sent by Louis XIV to the court of James II, must be read with equal care – this time for an opposite reason. Lingard tells us that he 'appears to act the part, not of an indifferent narrator, but of an advocate pleading the cause of his client [James II]'[22] and:

> puts into the mouth of James, not the language actually employed by that prince, but such language as might, by flattering the vanity and policy, obtain the good-will and consent of Louis.[23]

THE PERSONAL WEAKNESSES OF AMBASSADORS MUST ALSO BE CONSIDERED IN ASSESSING THE RELIABILITY OF THEIR REPORTS. Lingard was able to give the first modern account of the Triple Alliance (1667) between England, Holland and Sweden, against Louis XIV,[24] because he did not accept at face value the interpretation set on it by the English diplomatic representative, Sir William Temple. Lingard compared Temple's account with the published papers of Louis XIV, before coming to the now-accepted conclusion that the Treaty really changed nothing. In this case, it was simply the 'writing in his own praise' by Temple, 'one of the best living writers of English',[25] which had misled and was going to mislead all other English historians, including Lord Macaulay in the nineteenth century and Sir G. M. Trevelyan in the twentieth, for the next hundred years of historical writing in England.[26]

Another rule in Lingard's methodology of source criticism was that ONCE A SOURCE HAD PROVED TO BE DELIBERATELY UNTRUSTWORTHY, IT COULD NO LONGER – ON ITS OWN – BE GIVEN FULL CREDENCE. So, qualifying a statement made by Cecil, Elizabeth I's chief minister, to Throckmorton, after a failed attempt to capture Mary Queen of Scots on her journey from France to Scotland in 1561, Lingard comments:

> The men who fabricated so many falsehoods to conceal the object of Winter's expedition to the Frith, could easily fabricate others to excuse their uncourteous conduct to the Scottish queen.[27]

Winter was the English Admiral, sent unsuccessfully, to intercept Mary on her journey from France to Scotland in 1561. Referring to the letters of Mary, Queen of Scots, which passed through the hands of the Government agents, Philipps, 'the noted decipherer' and Gregory, the counterfeiter, during the events surrounding the Babington Plot (1586), Lingard provides 'a plain instance' of provable 'falsification' and concludes, therefore:

Prioritizing the Authority of Sources

> Whence it plainly follows that entire and implicit credit ought not to be given to any of the other documents which have come down to us from that laboratory of fraud.²⁸

Again, during his lengthy treatment of the Gunpowder Plot (1605), Lingard comments on Sir Thomas Percy's claim to have been duped by James I earlier into thinking that the latter would remove penal laws against the Catholics; and James's later denial of this:

> As for the denial of James, it is undeserving of credit. There are too many instances on record in which he had denied his own words.²⁹

Generally speaking, Lingard believed that A CLEAR DISTINCTION MUST BE MADE BETWEEN THE EVIDENCE OF CONTEMPORARY WRITERS AND THAT OF LATER HISTORIANS *whose evidence should not carry the same weight.* For example, with regard to the events surrounding the murder of Arthur, nephew of King John, who might have been a contender for the throne, in 1203, Lingard writes:

> It is unfortunate that at this interesting crisis we are deserted by the contemporary annalists, who led us through the preceding reigns, and are compelled to rely on the authority of writers, who lived at a later period, and whose doubtful notices cannot furnish a connected or satisfactory narrative . . . It is singular that the works of Diceto, Benedict, Gervase, Newbrigensis, Brompton and Hoveden, should all end about this period. Paris is the next in time; but at John's succession he was so young that he can be hardly termed a contemporary writer. He transcribed, indeed, Wendover; but Wendover's account of this period is very imperfect.³⁰

Arthur had suddenly disappeared, after being kept prisoner by John in Rouen. Lingard's judgement was:

> If the manner of his death could have borne investigation, John for his own honour would have made it public. His silence proves that the young prince was murdered. Report ascribed his fate to the dagger of his uncle; but the king of England could surely have hired an assassin . . .³¹

Lingard here *employs one of his rules of source criticism,* USED WHEN THERE IS NO DIRECT EVIDENCE AVAILABLE. *He comes to a conclusion* BASED UPON INFERENCE FROM THE KNOWN FACTS *(including the known character of the personages involved)* WHICH COULD NOT OTHERWISE BE SATISFACTORILY EXPLAINED.

Interestingly, a recent scholar, Dr. S. D. Lloyd, writes in 1997, that:

> modern scholarship has also strengthened some . . . charges against him [John]. Perhaps the most infamous charge, that he murdered – or caused to

be murdered – his own nephew, Arthur of Brittany, now seems virtually certain.

Lloyd also refers to the unreliability of the chroniclers, Roger of Wendover and Matthew Paris: 'In this century, the unreliability and ulterior purposes of many of these chronicle sources has [sic] been sharply exposed.'[32] But Lingard had already done this in 1819.

Lingard will also, where necessary, provide the literary and or linguistic apparatus with which certain sources have to be approached for a proper interpretation. So the reader is told how to read the letters of Lord Holland to Buckingham in the reign of Charles I:

> To understand these letters the reader should observe, that by the figure of a crown is meant the king of France, by that of an anchor the duke of Buckingham, high admiral, and by that of a heart his sweetheart, the French queen.[33]

Lingard uses letters of Elizabeth's courtiers to skilfully tease out elements of her character, which played an important part in Elizabethan politics; but sometimes these letters need interpretation. For example, a letter from Lord Henry Howard states:

> The queen is a lady that rather hears than compares, numbers than weighs, and by consequence would make all probable that is poetry.

Lingard interprets for the reader:

> It requires some acquaintance with the enigmatical style of this writer to understand him. He means to say, that Elizabeth believes all that is told her; it is sufficient that a thing may happen, for her to be convinced that it will happen.[34]

This aspect of Elizabeth's psychology would be an important factor in the downfall of Mary Queen of Scots. It enabled both Cecils, William and his son Robert after him, and Walsingham to frighten Elizabeth into doing things – such as executing the Duke of Norfolk in 1571, Mary Queen of Scots in 1587 and the Earl of Essex in 1601 – which she might not otherwise have done. Walsingham, Principal Secretary to Elizabeth, was a strong protestant of 'Puritan instincts'. He warned Elizabeth in 1568 of a European plot – which did not exist – against her and in favour of Mary. One of his favourite sayings was: 'there is less danger in fearing too much than too little'.[35] The effect of this sort of adviser on a person of Elizabeth's temperament would be a strong factor leading to Elizabeth's eventual agreement to the execution of Mary and others.

Again, in order to understand the letters between Queen Elizabeth I and Sir Christopher Hatton, we need to know that:

> Originally the queen gave to Hatton the name of her 'Mutton' which was afterwards changed into her 'Belwether', probably because he was captain of the guard. Raleigh was called 'Water', perhaps from his passion for maritime adventure and voyages of discovery.[36]

Sir Christopher Hatton, nicknamed 'the dancing Chancellor', was appointed Elizabeth I's Lord Chancellor in 1587. His 'good looks and graceful dancing' had originally brought him to Elizabeth's attention.[37]

We are told by Lingard when a source must not be taken literally.[38] Again SOME SOURCES BLEND TRUTH WITH ERROR SO THAT THEY ARE EITHER TO BE GIVEN NO CREDIT AT ALL, OR ONLY INSOFAR AS THEY ARE SUPPORTED BY OTHER AND MORE TRUSTWORTHY DOCUMENTS.[39] Gilbert Burnet's *History of My Own Times* (1724–34) falls into this category:

> There is, however, in Burnet's narrative, so much unquestionably false, that it is difficult to judge what may be probably true.[40]

Burnet's work was used by Lord Macaulay in his *History of England* (1849–55); but modern scholarship agrees with Lingard, that as a source, it is 'informative but partisan' and 'a mixture of history, autobiography and anecdote'.[41]

Lingard treats the Earl of Clarendon's *History of the Great Rebellion* (1702–4) in the same way. Edward Hyde, Earl of Clarendon, one of Charles's advisers, had gone into exile in 1646 and drafted his *History* during the period of Cromwell's rule in England. He later spent time writing the book in France. He died in 1674. The book was not finally published until 1704. Lingard writes of it:

> Clarendon's narrative is so frequently inaccurate, that it is unsafe to give credit to any charge on his authority alone ... Clarendon ... professes to have derived his information from Charles, and other actors in the same transaction ... yet whoever will compare it with the other accounts will see that much of great interest has been omitted, and much so disfigured as to bear little resemble to the truth. *It must be that the historian, writing in banishment, and at a great distance of time, trusted to his imagination to supply the defect of his memory.*[42]

Lingard supplies several illustrative examples.[43] Yet Clarendon's book is still regarded today as 'one of the most important contemporary accounts of the Civil Wars and the Interregnum'.[44]

Prioritizing the Authority of Sources

Lingard broke the anglo-centric tradition of English historiography by MAKING CRITICAL USE OF THE WORK OF CONTEMPORARY HISTORIANS OF OTHER COUNTRIES, including the Spanish historians Gerónimo de Zurita (1512–80) and Juan de Mariana (1532–1624). Zurita in particular was an expert 'in the search and use of manuscripts' and a founder of 'critical scholarship in Spain'.[45] Lingard found that both historians were good authorities for their account of Spain's relations with England during the reign of Ferdinand and Isabella. On the other hand, he was able to make a critical assessment of Meteren, the Dutch historian who wrote *L'Histoire des Pays Bas* at the end of the sixteenth century. The work was translated into French in 1670. Lingard found blatant errors in Meteren's work, once he wandered outside the history of his own country, and concludes:

> Meteren, when he refers to matters not concerning his own country, betrays the most profound ignorance or insincerity.[46]

The extension of sources to include the writers of other countries in their accounts of English history was in itself quite extraordinary at the time.

Lingard makes a very important and significant evaluation of Matthew Paris, the medieval chronicler who had been a favourite source for the English medieval period since the Reformation, for his perceived attacks on papal authority in England:

> Of these writers, the most querulous is Matthew Paris, a monk of St. Albans, partly the author, partly the compiler, of the ponderous volume which, with Rishanger's continuation has been published under his name. It contains many original and some valuable documents; but the writer, accustomed to lash the great, whether clergy or laity, seems to have collected and preserved every malicious and scandalous anecdote that could gratify his censorious disposition. It may appear invidious to speak harshly of this favourite historian; but this I may say, that when I could affront his pages with authentic records, or contemporary writers, I have in many instances found the discrepancy between them so great, as to give to his narrative the appearance of a romance rather than a history.[47]

The twentieth-century biographer of Paris repeated in 1958 Lingard's assessment – well over a century earlier – of this favourite medieval chronicler. Richard Vaughan writes of him:

> It is high time that the ghost of Matthew's anti-papalism was laid. He did not understand politics, though he was keenly interested in them, and his anti-papalism is by no means ideological. He never thought about the theory of papal power; he merely had a grudge against authority. He resented all

attempts at interference with his own material interests, and the king suffers just as much from his tirades as does the pope.[48]

It was Lingard's true assessment of Matthew Paris and of Roger Wendover, both of whose works 'abound with errors' when weighed against 'authentic' sources, which enabled him to make important interpretations of medieval history which were not to be repeated until the mid-twentieth century.[49]

Assessing another medieval chronicler, there is a glimpse of Lingard's ironic humour: 'Babour was a poet, and evidently avails himself of the privilege of his profession'.[50] Froissart[51] and Malmesbury[52] are also assessed, and the general inaccuracy of medieval chroniclers with respect to dates described.[53]

Lingard provides the important critical apparatus with which to approach the work of the twelfth-century Welsh writer, Gerald de Barri or Giraldus Cambrensis, as a source for the state of Ireland in the last half of that century:

> In three books on the topography, and two on the subjugation of Ireland, he has left us the detail of all that he had heard, read and saw. That the credulity of the Welshman was often deceived by fables, is evident; nor is it improbable that his partiality might occasionally betray him into unfriendly and exaggerated statements; yet the accuracy of his narrative in the more important points is confirmed by the whole tenor of Irish and English history, and by its accordance with the accounts which the abbot of Clairvaux had received from St. Malachy and his disciples.[54]

Lingard assesses the attempt of Lynch to overthrow this source:

> I have attentively perused the Cambensis eversus of Lynch, a work of much learning and ingenuity. In several instances he may have overturned the statements of Girald; in the more important points he has completely failed.[55]

Modern scholarship has come to the same view as Lingard on Gerald as a historical source. Gerald had accompanied Prince John on a tour of Ireland in 1185. The two books in question, the *Exugnatio Hibernica* (*The Conquest of Ireland*) and *Topographia Hibernica* (*The Topography of Ireland*) were written from first-hand observation after that Tour. Gerald was a 'keen observer'.[56] We are told in 1998, that the first book 'reveals his ability to arrange facts and shape a narrative full of memorable portraits'. The second 'gives a description of Ireland and its people which is a fascinating mixture of detailed, realistic observation and completely groundless beliefs'.[57]

Lingard gives an important critical analysis of Gildas, the only extant contemporary source for the early invasions of Britain by the Anglo-Saxons during the fifth and sixth centuries, in his *History and Antiquities of the Anglo-Saxon Church* (1808):

> The *historiola*, as the name imports, is very brief, and on that account very unsatisfactory, written too in a declamatory instead of an historical style. Gildas possessed, as he complains, no British documents; and if he consulted foreign writers, disfigured their narratives by mixing them up with the traditions of his countrymen. Towards the close he becomes more interesting, by unfolding to us the real state of the natives, after the departure of the Romans, and during their wars with the Picts and the Saxons. Here in every page he writes with the spirit of a Briton. If he blames his countrymen – and he often blames them most severely – it is yet in a tone of commiseration; but when he speaks of their enemies, he is at a loss for words to express the utter detestation in which he holds them. The earliest mention of these writings of Gildas occurs in the great work of Beda ... The works of Gildas are mentioned in Alcuin, who zealously recommends them to the notice of his countrymen. From these passages it is plain that the works now attributed to Gildas, were well known to literary men in the seventh and eighth centuries, and were taken by them for the genuine productions of the British writer, whose name they bear.[58]

Seven pages of an appendix are devoted to the description, evaluation and discussion of the authenticity of Gildas, which was widely questioned in Lingard's day. Lingard's account of the *De Excidio et Conquestu Britanniae* (c. 541) is the first modern assessment, which has been confirmed by recent scholarship. Gildas's is an important source. As it is the only contemporary description of the period it needs to be treated very carefully. His work is 'impoverished by unsufficiency of dating and ignorance of the Anglo-Saxons'; 'a polemical work, which castigates the sins of contemporary British society'; but it 'constitutes a crucial historical source for an understanding of conditions in Roman Britain'.[59]

Lingard recognized the outstanding quality of the Venerable Bede's *Historica Ecclesiastica Gentis Anglorum* (731) [PLATE 2], which had usually been denigrated by English historians since the sixteenth century, as 'tarred with the Papist brush'.[60] Lingard confirms Bede's place as the primary source for this early period of English history and he uses him as such, alongside the Anglo-Saxon Chronicle.

> Bede and Alcuin, Northumbrian scholars, whose literary superiority was acknowledged by their contemporaries, and to whose writings and exertions Europe was principally indebted for that portion of learning which she possessed from the eighth to the eleventh century ... He [Bede] had studied every science which survived the ruin of the Roman Empire, and if the reader looks into his writings, he will be astonished at the depth and the

variety of his attainments. Of his works the most valuable is the 'Ecclesiastical History of the Nation of the Angles', which, while it treats professedly of the establishment of Christianity in the different Saxon Kingdoms, incidentally contains almost all we know of the history of the more early princes ... His works were quickly transcribed and dispersed among the nations of Europe, and the applause with which they were received induced the Anglo-Saxons to consider him as the ornament and pride of their nation.[61]

The place of Bede as a truly great English historian and a primary source for Anglo-Saxon history has been fully accepted by modern authorities such as Sir Frank Stenton in his *Anglo-Saxon England* (1947).[62]

Lingard has an interesting observation on Shakespeare's depiction of the young prince Henry, later to be the celebrated Henry V [PLATE 17], in the Play of that name:

Probably the reader's recollection has already transported him to those pages, in which the frolics and the associates of the prince have been portrayed by the inimitable pencil of Shakespeare. It may be, indeed, that the particular facts, and personages are the mere creatures of the poet's imagination; but it cannot be denied that they are perfectly in unison with the accounts of the more ancient writers, and the traditionary belief of the succeeding century.[63]

Lingard accepts Henry's strengths and the 'glory' of military victories, which gave rise to posterity's admiration:

The splendour which conquest in France threw around the person of Henry during his life still adheres to his memory four centuries after his death.

But at the same time Lingard wishes to make some reservations:

Success, however, gave a tinge of arrogance to his character. He did not sufficiently respect the prejudices, nor spare the feelings of his new subjects in France ... Continually engaged in war, he had little leisure to discharge the duties of a legislator ...[64]

Recent scholars have the same sort of reservations John Gillingham wrote in 1995:

in 1415, he captured Harfleur, then marched through Normandy to AGINCOURT, winning enormous acclaim at home ... He led a second army to France in 1417 and methodically and ruthlessly conquered Normandy ... as Shakespeare's *Henry V* makes plain, for centuries posterity regarded him as England's perfect monarch – as indeed, some historians still do. Yet doubts remain. Some have wondered whether his ambitions did not finally

1 *The Presbytery, Hornby, near Lancaster (chapel adjoining to left; and Lingard's oak tree rising above)*

Lingard lived here for forty years (1811–51). This was where he wrote the *History of England* in 'comparative isolation', but with a mind which, like that of the Venerable Bede nearly a millennium before, 'ranged far and wide across European scholarship'. This, too, is where the judges on the northern circuit made a point of calling to see and talk to him.

2 *The Tomb of the Venerable Bede, at Durham Cathedral*

Bede (673–735), a monk who lived all his life at the monastery of Monkwearmouth and Jarrow, wrote *The Ecclesiastical History of the English People* (731). Like Lingard later, he received information from all over Europe and his 'range of learning was prodigious'. He was the first Englishman to reach 'a conception of history'. He was the greatest European scholar of his day; and the greatest English historian of the first millennium.

3 *Ushaw College, Durham*
Founded in 1568 at Douai, France, by Cardinal William Allen; and re-established in 1808 at Ushaw to train priests for the English mission. Lingard had been a pupil at Douai (1782–93) where he experienced a standard of source criticism which was unavailable in England at this time. He left Douai, which was attacked by the French revolutionaries in 1793, and later became vice-president and Head of the Schools of Natural and Moral Philosophy (1808–11) at Ushaw.

4 *Sir Thomas More (1478–1535)*
He is generally accepted by all as a *very intelligent man* of the *utmost integrity*. He was to meet his own death by refusing to lie about his own beliefs which he had shared with the majority of English people. He was also in a *good position to know the truth* about the murder of the 'Princes in the Tower'. He satisfied therefore several of Lingard's requirements of a good historical witness and Lingard used him as one of two main sources in his account of the 'Princes in the Tower'.

5 *Thomas Cromwell (1485–1540)*
He created the 'Great Myth' of English history, in order to disguise the true nature of the Reformation as the greatest Revolution in English history. He manufactured a new 'collective memory' for the English people, cutting them off from any real understanding of their past as part of European Christendom. Cromwell built this mythical past into the preambles of the Reformation statutes (1532–6) and promulgated it by the first example of organized state propaganda in English history, backed up where necessary by terror tactics.

6 *William Cecil, Lord Burghley (1520–98)*
Chief governmental minister of Elizabeth I, he was the main force behind the Elizabethan Settlement (1559). Strongly Protestant, he patronized historians such as William Camden who, at his behest, wrote the *Annals of Queen Elizabeth* (1615). This identified Elizabeth with England's national glory and became the basis of all future eulogistic accounts of her reign. His *The Execution of Justice in England for the maintenance of public and Christian peace against certeine stirrers of sedition* (1583) was the classic statement of Government propaganda in the battle to persuade the English people into a new 'mind-set'. It was the source of all later accounts of Elizabeth's reign, and provided the Elizabethan Government's viewpoint only – until the late twentieth century.

7 *Gilbert Burnet (1643–1715)*
Author of *The History of the Reformation* (1679–1715), which added the whig interpretation and the idea of progress to the 'Great Myth' of the English past; and adapted it to the 'needs' of this later period. He was also one of the main instigators of the 'Glorious Revolution' (1688–89), returning to England with William III as the main propagandist 'genius' of the new regime. He was highly influential in the politics of his own day and on the later historiography of the Reformation, in which his work was regarded as a 'canonical work' and a 'standard authority'.

8 *David Hume (1711–76)*
Philosopher and historian of the age of 'Enlightenment' and 'Reason', he saw history as a branch of philosophy ('philosophy teaching by example'). His atheistic and sceptical outlook added a secular interpretation to the 'Great Myth', but did not change its basic structure. His *History of England* (1754–62) was dominant in English historiography during the next century. Lingard criticized the 'philosophical' approach to history and did not regard Hume as a true historian.

9 *Thomas Hearne (1678–1735)*
He represents the fine, but inhibited scholarship of the Non-juring scholars at the turn of the seventeenth century. Much of their work had to be 'underground', left in manuscript form, because it was critical in some respects of the 'Great Myth'. Hearne represents, at its best, the accurate editing of original documents, inspired by the model of Jean Mabillon on the Continent, which characterized this group. Hearne was persecuted by the Establishment and ridiculed by the people of the 'Enlightenment'; but he is now recognized for his fine editing of original texts: 'a work of national importance'. Lingard was the first narrative historian in England, to recognize the importance of Hearne's editions and to build upon them.

10 *John Lingard (1771–1851)*
His *History of England* (1819–30) was the first modern account of the English past. He dismantled the 'Great Myth' and the 'Whig interpretation'. He was the first English historian to base his work on original documents (from the 'fountain-head' instead of the 'troubled stream' as he put it); the first to write as a 'citizen of the world' and seek help from a range of foreign archives; the first to create a methodology of scientific source criticism which formed the basis of the modern study of history as an independent subject, rather than a branch of philosophy or literature. He is the 'father' of modern revisionist history. All this forms the basis for the claim that he is the greatest English historian of the second millennium.

11 *John Lingard*
Lingard was now struggling against infirmities of various kinds, but working hard and courageously to retain his scholarly faculties and complete his last and thoroughly revised edition of his *History*. This revision was based on all the important original documents (published and manuscript) which had appeared since the previous edition of 1837–8.

12 *Sir Herbert Butterfield (1900–79)*
His *The Whig Interpretation of History* (1931) was the first direct and conscious attack on the whig interpretation of English history. It was one of the most powerful and influential essays in the history of English historiography; and it was to lead historians in new directions and to new insights in the second half of the twentieth century. He has been called, one of the two greatest English historians of the twentieth century.

13 *Sir G. M. Trevelyan (1876–1962)*
He was the last of the immensely popular and influential Whig historians, stressing the continuous and progressive story of England's unique greatness and superiority in the world. His *English Social History* (1944) was 'one of the best-selling books of all time'; and he had a huge cultural influence on his own time. Grand-nephew of Lord Macaulay, the greatest honours of the day were awarded to him by a grateful nation. But, in the light of revisionist history and modern research, Lingard had been right where Trevelyan was wrong, in their historical interpretation of the English past.

14 *Lord Macaulay (1800–59)*
He was 'unquestionably the greatest of the whig historians' and a great establishment figure in the nineteenth century. He was the most popular and influential English historian in the great age of Empire. The burden of his song was 'the superiority of the English people', as illustrated in their history. He saw history as a branch of fine literature; and had little or no concept of source criticism. He accused Lingard of believing that the 'popular opinion cannot possibly be true'. Lingard's private view was that Macaulay 'does not write history'.

15 *King John (1167–1216)*
In 1190 Richard I had nominated his nephew, Arthur of Brittany as his successor; but on Richard's death in 1199, his brother John took the throne. In 1202, John captured his nephew, Arthur and imprisoned him at Rouen. Arthur was never seen again. Rumours had existed before, but Lingard applied his rules of source criticism to evidence that John had in fact murdered the young Arthur in 1203, a verdict which is now accepted by modern scholarship.

16 *Scene from the Bayeux Tapestry (eleventh century)*
(By special permission of the Centre Guillaume-le-Conquérant, the City of Bayeux)
The Bayeux Tapestry, one of the finest pieces of fabric embroidery from the medieval period, was for long considered to have been made by Queen Matilda, wife of William the Conqueror. Lingard subjected this tapestry to a battery of his rules of source criti-

cism and came to the conclusion that it was made for Bishop Odo of Bayeux, by some of his own followers. The most conclusive evidence came from a comparison of this tapestry with the evidence of Domesday Book, when three men named in Domesday as 'homagers of Bishop Odo' also appear in prominent places – for otherwise inexplicable reasons – in the Tapestry itself. Lingard's conclusion has recently been confirmed.

17 *King Henry V (1387–1422)*
Lingard gave the first balanced account of Henry V's reign. His military successes, as acclaimed by Shakespeare, are given full weight; but Lingard had the same reservations as modern historians have come to have, about his being 'the perfect king'. Lingard points out that his military adventures in France meant neglect of legislative duties in England' while 'a tinge of arrogance' was shown in his treatment of his new French subjects. Lingard even anticipates a modern insight by ascribing to this 'European' king, a possible crusading motivation – to free Jerusalem from the Saracens – which, however, he never undertook.

18 *King Henry VI (1421–71)*
A mystery had long surrounded the death of Henry VI in 1471. Lingard indicated the faults and mistakes in the work of previous historians who had exonerated Edward IV. His more sophisticated range of source criticism showed beyond doubt that Henry VI had been murdered by order of Edward IV. Modern scholarship has accepted this completely.

19 *King Richard III (1452–85)*
Richard III is one of the most controversial characters in English history. Shakespeare immortalized him as 'evil personified'. A modern Society of Richard III has been set up, dedicated to clearing his name and showing him as a man to be admired. Did Richard, then, murder his nephews, the two boy princes, in the Tower in 1483? Lingard dealt with a mass of evidence which had deceived other English historians, in a way which indicated clearly his unprecedented skills of source criticism. He proved Richard's guilt in this matter, for the first time, in a way which has never been bettered, or equalled. Modern scholarship is left simply to confirm his findings.

20 *Anne Boleyn (1501–36)*

She changed, indirectly, the course of English history. Lingard was able to show, for the first time, that she had attracted Henry's personal attentions, before the epoch-making public action of the 'Divorce Question' began. He did this by painstaking research into private letters and documents from home and abroad which 'removed the veil' from Henry's public statements designed to conceal the truth. It was, too, a signal example of his methodology of pursuing 'the source of the source', even to the Spanish state archives at Simancas.

21 *Henry VIII (1491–1547) and Thomas Cranmer (1489–1556)*
Henry's determination to dissolve his marriage to Catherine of Aragon and marry Anne Boleyn, led unavoidably to the Reformation – the greatest Revolution in English history. The epoch-making Act against Appeals (1533) and Act of Supremacy (1534), made Henry supreme head of his own Church and prevented any appeals against his will, to a higher Church court in Rome. These acts separated England from European Christendom, to which it had belonged for nearly 1500 years; and changed the nature and course of English history. Lingard was the first historian, writing in England, to treat this from a 'Euro-centric', rather than an anglo-centric viewpoint; and to deal with it from the perspective of Henrician contemporaries.

Cranmer was to be instrumental in enabling Henry VIII to achieve what he wanted. Lingard was attacked severely for pointing out that Cranmer had taken a public oath of obedience to the Pope, in order to obtain his consecration as Archbishop of Canterbury in 1533 – but made a private reservation before chosen winesses, that he was not going to keep it. Lingard was also attacked for saying that Cranmer had played an important part in the condemnation (leading to the burning) of Protestant 'heretics' in Edward VI's reign; and also for planning the same fate for Catholics as 'heretics' in the same reign. Modern scholarship, however, has now accepted these facts.

22 *Queen Elizabeth I (1533–1603)*
Queen Elizabeth I was made to personify the national glory of England, by the propaganda machinery of her Government, led by William Cecil, Lord Burghley. This glorified image of her was maintained for four centuries of repetitive and uncritical English histories. Lingard recognized her strengths, but was the first historian writing in England to look critically and objectively at the Queen and the events of her reign; and the first to adopt a viewpoint different from that of her Government and to place events within a wider European perspective. He looked behind the facade of public statements and chroniclers' accounts, making critical use of private and other sources, to achieve an interpretation which is only now beginning to be recovered by modern revisionist historians.

23 *Mary Queen of Scots (1542–87)*
Lingard recognized all her weaknesses, but used his powers of source criticism, with particularly good effect, to show that there was no real evidence of the crimes – criminal implication in the murder of her husband, Darnley and criminal involvement in the plots to kill Elizabeth – for which she was relentlessly pursued and finally executed by the Elizabethan Government. However, the Government is shown, for the first time, to have been criminally involved in tampering with the evidence against her for reasons of 'state security'.

24 *Sir Francis Walsingham (c.1532–90)*
The very able, strongly Protestant, minister, closely allied to Cecil, Lord Burghley, who became principal royal secretary to Elizabeth. Believing 'that there is less danger in fearing too much than too little' (and instilling his fears in Elizabeth), he was perfectly suited to become the first 'minister of intelligence and national state security' in English history. He organized a network of agents at home and abroad, to detect 'Catholic conspiracies' of any sort. Lingard revealed for the first time, the underground, ruthless and unscrupulous nature of his activities, particularly in his determination to convict and eliminate Mary Queen of Scots and to brand any Catholics (especially priests) as ipso facto traitors to the State, according to the new Government-inspired 'mind-set'.

25 *James II (1633–1701)*
Lingard accepted the part played by James's own mistakes and weaknesses in his own downfall and loss of his crown in 1688. He was also, however, the victim of a premeditated, concealed, powerful and successful plan by William of Orange (assisted by the propagandist genius, Gilbert Burnet) to invade England and seize the English crown for himself, as part of his own greater designs against Louis XIV, within a European context. This was a new insight on the part of Lingard, derived from his use of private papers, to get behind official statements; and also from his ability to place the 'Glorious Revolution' of 1688–9 within a European perspective. These new insights and interpretations were not recovered until the last decade of the twentieth century, when they became clear as a result of academic research initiated by the tercentenary of the Revolution in 1988–9.

26 *Edmund Campion (1540–81)*
A brilliant scholar at Oxford, poet and historian, he converted to Catholicism in 1569 and went to Douai College in France. He became a Jesuit priest, returning to England in 1580 on a mission to serve the spiritual needs of Catholics. He was caught, tortured and executed by the Government in 1581. Lingard showed that he was completely non-political and that he was martyred simply because he was a Catholic priest. For the first time Lingard demonstrated that his trial was the dramatic clash between the traditional Catholic view (having allegiance in spiritual matters to God, and in political matters to 'Caesar') and the new mind-set of Tudor Government (total allegiance in all things to the King and national Government). Modern scholarship confirms: 'Trumped-up charges of conspiracy to overthrow the queen, and an unjustly conducted prosecution, brought conviction of treason and hanging at Tyburn [for Campion]'.

27 *Charles I (1600–49)*
Charles I was executed in January 1649, an action committed by the Army leaders, but inspired by Oliver Cromwell himself. Within days, the 'King's Book' or 'Royal Image', appeared, purporting to be Charles's own devotions and meditations on religion and politics before his death. This was the famous *Eikon Basilike*, in this version produced in Holland (and reproduced on p. 195). It was a hugely successful best-seller, creating the image of Charles as a martyr for the Anglican cause; and was to be much invoked at and after the Restoration of the Stuart Kingship in 1660. The initial engraving was by

William Marshall who had to re-engrave the plates eight times. There were forty-six editions needed in the first year. Further engravings were made about 1700 and in 1711. It remained popular in the eighteenth century. Perhaps the most dramatic effect came from the woodcut, used as a frontispiece, showing Charles at his devotions; and likening his agony to that of Christ in the Garden of Gethsemane. Lingard demonstrated that it was written mainly not by Charles, but by his chaplain, John Gauden, who was well rewarded for it after the Restoration – findings now accepted by modern scholarship.

28 *The Massacre of St. Bartholomew (1572)*
This infamous event had been blamed on the Pope and the King of Spain (together with Catherine de Medici, Queen mother of Charles IX of France) who were supposed to have premeditated and planned it as far back as 1565. This story had been commonly believed and used as propaganda against Catholics on the Continent and in England for three centuries. Lingard was the first English historian to show, using his new and

sophisticated techniques of source criticism, that the infamous event was the personal and political crime of Catherine de Medici. She had ordered it, as an opportunistic panic measure, to pre-empt an attack on herself by the Huguenots in Paris, which she feared, following her own failed attempt to assassinate the Admiral Coligny. Neither the Papacy nor the King of Spain were involved, as modern scholarship accepts.

29 William of Orange, 1650–1702 (William III of England, 1689–1702)
The whig interpretation of English history included an anglo-centric approach and the process of reading history backwards. It depicted the events of 1688–9 as the 'Glorious Revolution' by which England's freedom and greatness had been saved by William of Orange, who had been invited by the English to come to their aid. This interpretation remained intact until the last decade of the twentieth century. Lingard used his knowledge of continental politics, together with a wide range of private sources and his own highly-developed methodolgy of source criticism, to get behind the veil expertly set up by the revolutionary Government to disguise the true nature of the 1688 Revolution. His interpretation was only to be recovered and confirmed more than 150 years later, with the publication of *The World of William and Mary: Anglo-Dutch Perspectives On the Revolution of 1688–9*, edited by Dale Hoak and Mordechai Feingold and published in the United States in 1996. This crystallized the research, stimulated since, 1988, by the tercentenary of the Revolution. It confirmed Lingard's account, 170 years earlier, that in 1688–9 William of Orange conquered England and took the crown for himself.

Prioritizing the Authority of Sources

exceed those of his subjects – at the end of his reign, ADAM OF USK wrote of 'the smothered curses of the taxpayers' – or whether his brilliant exploitation of opportunities did not lead him into conquests that, in the longer term, would have proved impossible to maintain.[65]

Indeed one modern scholar, writing in 1997, concludes her account of Henry V with the statement: 'It is possible that all Henry's efforts with regard to France and the papacy were ultimately directed towards his plans for a crusade, which he never undertook'.[66] Lingard foreshadowed this observation, with his report of the words of the dying Henry V: 'that it had always been his intention to visit Palestine, and free the holy city from the yoke of the Saracens';[67] he follows with a footnote:

> That he actually meditated a crusade against the infidels, is shown by the survey of the coasts of Egypt and Syria made for him by Gilbert de Lannoi – See Archaeol. xxi. 281.[68]

Lingard, in opposition to the main tradition in English historiography, recognized the 'European' rather than simply 'English' nature of Henry's thinking – as a member of European Christendom.

What is interesting here is Lingard's treatment of Shakespeare's account of the young prince Henry, his recognition of posterity's estimate of the character and policies of the mature Henry V; and the way in which Lingard's judgements are being repeated by modern scholars at the end of the twentieth century.

Lingard can be very firm in expressing his views on a totally worthless source. After describing the short-lived plan of James II [see PLATE 25] to establish a Catholic episcopate in 1688, Lingard turns to an error-littered biographical account of one of the proposed new bishops:

> In 'the account of the family of Ellis', prefixed to the 'Ellis Correspondence', is a most ridiculous biographical memoir of Bishop Ellis, adopted on the authority of an article in the Gentleman's Magazine ... Now it is plain that the author of this memoir knew nothing of the real Bishop, who was not a Jesuit, but a Benedictine monk from Douai ... The whole of this worthless memoir abounds with the grossest errors, and is altogether unworthy of a moment's attention.[69]

He has forbearance, however, towards historians who are doing their best. There is a rather amusing example when Lingard has to inform his readers that the 'glowing description of Anne Boleyn as the life and ornament of the French court, said to have been extracted from the memoirs of the viscount Chateaubriand, a contemporary in the court of Francis I', and used as such by Miss Agnes Strickland in her *Queens of England* (1849), is not worthy of credit:

Prioritizing the Authority of Sources

> I am acquainted with only one passage corroborative of these reports [unfavourable to Anne's moral character, during her stay at the French court] and claiming original authority ... The fact, however, is that this extract is not taken from memoirs written by a contemporary of Anne, but by a contemporary of our own, by the bibliophile Jacob, who in 1837 amused himself with composing certain parts of a novel to be called the Memoires of madame of Chateaubriand (Françoise de Faix) Mistress of Francis I.[70]

Lingard adds chivalrously:

> There can be no doubt that in this extract the accomplished historian of England's Queens was misled by error of some foreign correspondent. It was, however, necessary to mention the mistake here, otherwise this imaginary description might hereafter, on the authority of Miss Strickland's name, have been received as a real and authentic document.[71]

We know from the Lingard letters how he had come upon this 'hoax'. One of the network of his continental 'agents' had been put to work. Lingard wrote to his friend Walker in 1846:

> Miss Strickland has published a passage from the unedited [unpublished] memoirs of the Viscount of Chateaubriand (a courtier in the time of Francis I) respecting Anne Boleyn. I wrote to a friend in Paris to make extracts from the same MS. for me. I have the answer today. The MS. est une chimère ... composed in part but never published by a man named Jacob – in 1837. What a hoax on Miss Strickland. It was a historical novel.[72]

The full significance of Lingard's critical approach in taking various sources and showing how they should be treated becomes apparent only when we consider the way in which these same sources were used by his predecessors and contemporaries. There was no evidence at all of any of these showing the least interest in or awareness of, any form of source criticism. Earlier English historians had generally adopted a polemical approach, repeating arguments of previous generations. In the eighteenth century Hume was just as polemical, but in a new way. He was keen to express secularist values at the expense of religious beliefs. In the nineteenth century, Lord Macaulay was the most celebrated of many who wrote history as a branch of high literature, extolling English superiority and the British empire. It was in only in the last quarter of the nineteenth century that history became a serious subject of study – with Honours Degree courses – in the Universities of Oxford and Cambridge. It was a long time after this again, that a type of source criticism appropriate to an independent discipline developed in the twentieth century.

Lingard's immediate contemporaries, such as Henry Soames, Sharon

Turnet and Henry Hallam, had no idea of source criticism as we have come to know it. They based their work on the old Protestant proto-types of John Foxe and Gilbert Burnet, with John Strype's interested selection of documents to provide support. They were the main pillars of the 'official version' of English history. There seemed to be no reason, as far as they were concerned, for any critical examination of traditional sources.

Henry Soames – an exact contemporary of Lingard – produced his *History of the Reformation of the Church of England* in 1826. In his preface to the work, he gives an account of the sources to be used. There could be no greater contrast to Lingard's own preface, which would not be out of place in any modern historical work, reviewing the new and original sources that have become available. One is immediately aware that Soames is in an entirely different 'world' as far as historical writing is concerned.

Soames refers to one of his main sources, John Foxe, as the 'venerable martyrologist' who has 'presented us with a series of valuable documents and important statements'. On the other hand, the Catholic Nicholas Sander, who wrote in exile against the English Reformation in the sixteenth century, was 'a plotting English Romanist', some of whose statements 'are so monstrous that they shock belief'. Soames considered even the *History of the Reformation* (1661) by the high-Anglican, Peter Heylyn, to be suspect, because it was written:

> with something of an unfriendly feeling against those who had disturbed an established order of ecclesiastical affairs even for the purpose of introducing a system allowedly superior.

Heylyn's work therefore had not been popular in England. It had 'justly failed to satisfying his countrymen'. This, to Soames, was a proper reason for denigrating it. The labours of 'the indefatigable Gilbert Burnet' however provided such popular results, in his *History of the Reformation* (1679–1715), that they 'entitled him to the public gratitude'. Then 'A further confirmation of Burnet's integrity was soon afterwards indirectly furnished by the diligent Strype'.[73] Soames ends his proud description of these Protestant writers: 'From the documentary evidence accumulated in the supplemental volumes of Burnet and Strype the present work has chiefly been compiled'. He then triumphantly concludes that there:

> can be no doubt that an attentive perusal of the evidence published in illustration of England's defection from papal Rome will generally lead to a conviction that her ecclesiastical Reformers attained important, and even also necessary ends, through wise and unexceptionable means.[74]

Similarly, Sharon Turner, an enthusiast for Icelandic and Anglo-Saxon literature, had found some original materials for his *History of the Anglo-Saxons* (1799–1805); but in his later *History* of sixteenth-century England (1829), he relied on the standard ecclesiastical 'authorities' – Foxe and Burnet – with no awareness at all of the need for a critical approach to sources. We find page after page of lengthy footnotes, consisting mainly of quotations from these writers, which supply a kind of parallel narrative to the text itself, rather than giving any indication of how the text had been built up.[75] Turner's book was written at a time when Lingard was demonstrating the unsatisfactory and unreliable nature of these same sources.

Again, Henry Hallam in his *A View of the State of Europe in the Middle Ages* (1818), had no idea of the value of Anglo-Saxon sources, especially Bede. In some ways his work typifies the view of the period adopted earlier by writers of the 'Enlightenment' and the 'Age of Reason'. He could hardly conceive that there could have been any worthwhile learning during that period.[76] He was quite prepared to acknowledge his ignorance of writers such as Bede and Alcuin, with whom 'I wish it to be understood that I pretend hardly any direct acquaintance'.[77] Hallam's attitude is reminiscent of Burnet's boast of similar ignorance of the medieval period back in the seventeenth century.[78]

The medieval chroniclers had long been available to English historians. Editions of the *Flores* of Matthew of Westminster, the *Historia Major* of Matthew Paris, the *Vita Elfridi Regis* of Asserius, and the *Historia Brevis* of Thomas of Walshingham, had appeared under the direction of Archbishop Matthew Parker in the Elizabethan period. An edition of Florence of Worcester was published in 1592 and that of the *Historia Nova* of Eadmer in 1623. But these had been published only as convenient weapons, when used selectively, with which to attack the medieval Church and the 'Dark Ages'.[79] They were part of a propagandist approach which characterized English historical writing during this period and for the next three centuries. No one before Lingard had approached these chroniclers with the appropriate critical apparatus of source criticism, with which the real meaning of their texts could have been discovered.

Henry Soames, for example, like all his predecessors, and contemporaries – and his successors for the next one hundred and thirty years – eagerly accepted Matthew Paris at face value as 'the most spirited, copious and interesting of monastic chroniclers' who 'confounded Romanists, and astonished everybody by bold reflections upon papal avarice and corruption', so that 'papal readers of his valuable history must be contented to wince.[80] It was not until the mid-twentieth century that the best of English scholars of the medieval period became aware of the unreliability of such sources;[81] though Lingard had demonstrated this very clearly in 1819. He had used the very same methods of source criticism then, that the modern specialist, Professor C. R. Cheney was going to apply to the medieval chroniclers in 1948.[82]

Henry Hallam was not so involved in religious propaganda. His bias was more in the direction of being anti-religious in his approach to the past. He, too, however, regarded Matthew Paris as 'one of the most respectable of that class' of medieval chroniclers.[83] He used Paris[84] and Walsingham[85] on their own as authorities. Interestingly, because of his own background as a lawyer, he deserves credit for using also the rolls of Parliament on their own. But very significantly, it never occurred to him to use the latter in order to check the former – the technique which Lingard was already using so effectively. The idea of source criticism, in the way in which Lingard used it, simply did not presented itself to Hallam or to any of his contemporaries and successors for another century and a half. Nevertheless, Hallam in his *Constitutional History of England* (1827) is less prejudiced than most other writers of the time, and, using his lawyer's training, approached Burnet and Strype, for instance, with a degree of critical acumen.[86] Indeed, he seems to have learnt from Lingard and uses him often as a source, sometimes in opposition to these others.[87]

Like most important new developments and discoveries, it is difficult afterwards to understand how intelligent people could have failed to see the importance of source criticism in the context of the pursuit of historical truth. It now seems so obvious to us. The answer may well lie in the fact that these historians had not developed Lingard's and the modern historian's view of historical writing as essentially *a pursuit of the truth of what had happened in the past*. It was on the premiss of this definition of historical writing as an independent discipline with its own professionally appropriate 'rules of working', that an objective apparatus of critical source criticism became an essential concomitant.

It was because Lingard was the first English historian to come to this conception of the profession of a historian, that he was also the first to develop the 'source of the source' and all the other techniques which he recognized as essential requisites to the whole undertaking. In the history of creative achievements there has been a much longer delay than usual – a time lag of one hundred and eighty years – before a proper appreciation of his lone achievement has taken place. In many ways, his discoveries have had to be repeated in the second half of the twentieth century by modern historians who knew little or nothing about Lingard's work.

Chapter VII
The Use of 'Forensic' Rules of Source Criticism

'I think I may call it a forgery...'
John Lingard

Lingard had many of the qualities to be admired in a High Court judge. Interestingly, among his visitors were the judges on the northern circuit – Pollock, Scarlett and Brougham – who made it a habit to break their journey by calling on him:

> Pollock, the uncompromising Tory, Scarlett, the equally uncompromising Whig – until his opposition to the Reform Bill drove him into the ranks of the Tories – and Brougham, the future chancellor, gathering round the table of the Catholic priest in his village presbytery, afford a picture which makes us sigh with regret that no echoes of their conversation, except the tradition of its excellence, have come down to us.[1]

Lingard's common sense, good judgement, detachment, insight and critical perception were employed by those who frequently consulted him for advice on important questions concerning the struggle for Catholic emancipation, as we see in the correspondence between him and Bishop Poynter.[2] He prepared the petition, for example, which was presented to the House of Lords on this matter. In such important political and legal matters of his day he was wise, balanced, diplomatic and sensible. Cardinal Wiseman wrote of him, some eight years after his death:

> it will never be known till his life is really written, and his correspondence published, how great a share he had in the direction of our ecclesiastical affairs in England, and how truly he was almost the oracle which our bishops consulted in matters of intricate or delicate importance.[3]

Here, then, is a description of the type of mind which Lingard brought to bear on his rules of source criticism, some of which we might well categorize as 'forensic'. These rules include the same processes involved in the

The Use of 'Forensic' Rules of Source Criticism

cross-examination' of sources as those which characterize modern criminology and the legal process in a modern court of law. Some parts of Lingard's examination of sources are reminiscent of that kind of legal work which is concerned with the unravelling of particularly complex cases of detection. In Lingard's case, however, these methods are applied to the solution of difficult historical problems, centuries after the events had taken place. Moreover, we can now look at his work and evaluate it with the considerable hindsight of nearly two centuries of further developments in modern scholarship.

One of the most dramatic changes in Lingard's reshaping of English history in the Tudor period took place because he was the first English historian, resident in England, who did not automatically look at events from the viewpoint of the Tudor government. Tudor chroniclers had been taught to do just this, and later writers simply followed the same path, until the latter part of the twentieth century. J. B. Black, who contributed *The Reign of Elizabeth* (1936) to the prestigious and influential series of *Oxford Histories of England*, was more frank than other historians:

> we have been compelled to observe events predominantly . . . through the eyes of the English government . . .

He added that 'the paramount necessity' has been to put 'the reader at the standpoint of the queen and her ministers', which 'has prevented a rigorous following out of the principle of always considering other viewpoints'.[4] Sir John Neale, in his *Queen Elizabeth* (1934), A. L. Rowse, in *England under Elizabeth* (1950) and Conyers Reade in *Lord Burleigh and Queen Elizabeth* (1960), all followed the pattern of seeing things exclusively through the eyes of the English Queen and her Government.[5]

Lingard, in dealing with Elizabeth's reign, followed a rule which, he insisted, is a matter of necessity to every writer of history:

> to admit no statement merely upon trust, to weigh with care the value of the authorities on which I rely, and to watch with jealousy the secret working of my own personal feelings and prepossessions. Such vigilance is a matter of necessity to every writer of history, if he aspire to the praise of truthfulness and impartiality. He must . . . view with the coolness of an unconcerned spectator the events which pass before his eyes . . .[6]

It was from this premiss of the essential nature of the historian's role that Lingard proceeded to construct critical rules by which he could achieve an objective viewpoint.

It is not surprising, therefore, that in dealing with the reign of Elizabeth I in an unprecedently neutral manner, Lingard makes much use of *the technique of* CHECKING THE EVIDENCE BY A CRITICAL APPROACH TO ITS

The Use of 'Forensic' Rules of Source Criticism

'INTERNAL' CHARACTERISTICS – *taking into account such factors as content, language, style and tone, which might be of significance in leading him to the truth.*

The Elizabethan Government was led by William Cecil (Lord Burghley) [PLATE 6]. He had a strongly Protestant and apocalyptic view of the need to turn England into a Protestant country. His son, Sir Robert Burghley, followed him in this position and had the same objective. They were the first to form their own version of a modern state security and intelligence department, led by the like-minded Sir Francis Walsingham (1532–90).[7]

One of its aims was to infiltrate groups of potential conspirators with its own 'agents provocateurs', in order to discredit Mary Queen of Scots – held in custody between 1567 and 1587 – and to trap her into an admission of treason. An elaborate network of Government agents was set up – including messengers, decipherers, and forgers – so that letters and other materials passing between Mary and any of her friends were intercepted and passed through Walsingham's hands, sometimes undergoing 'changes', in the form of omissions and insertions, in transit. Lingard dealt in detail with these materials, examining closely the internal evidence. As a result, his conclusions concerning such matters as Mary's involvement in the death of her husband, Darnley, in 1567, or in treason against Elizabeth in 1587, were new in his own time; but completely in line now with modern scholarship in the treatment of these matters.[8]

Lingard's account of Elizabeth [PLATE 22] may appear highly critical, only because she was raised to heights of adulation by the contemporary 'image-makers' and propagandists of Tudor government. Her uncritical acclaim and adulation received its first expression in Camden's *Annales Rerum Anglicarum et Hibernicorum Regnante Elizabethae* (1616), specially requested by Cecil, Lord Burghley, himself. The glorification and 'myth-making' of Camden's book – in which Elizabeth personified English greatness and glory – lasted up to and including most of the twentieth century. The long line of historians to whom Elizabeth could do no wrong concludes with such well-known names as Sir John Neale, A. L. Rowse and Conyers Reade. John Kenyon, in his *The History Men* (1993), acknowledges the situation and expresses surprise that 'there has not been already a bluntly revisionist biography'. Only in the late twentieth century, in works such as David Loades' *Tudor Government* (1997) and Christopher Haig's *Elizabeth I: Profiles in Power* (edition of 1998) has modern revisionism began to confirm Lingard's perception.

Lingard ascribes England's rise to power in Elizabeth's reign to the 'spirit of commercial enterprise', initiated in the reign of Mary, but fostered and developed under Elizabeth. Another factor was the successful, if unethical, foreign policy of 'sowing the seeds of dissension', fomenting the 'spirit of resistance' and aiding 'efforts of rebellion' in neighbouring countries, such as France, Spain, the Low Countries and

The Use of 'Forensic' Rules of Source Criticism

Scotland. Internal governmental policy was dictated by practical compromises between the Queen and her ministers. Her 'habitual irresolution' and 'mean-mindedness' were habitual problems for her ministers. Cecil and Walsingham played on her weaknesses, in pursuing their own agenda. She was very accomplished and brave, but also vain, irritable, authoritarian, bullying and coarse. Haughty and overbearing in Court, she had a strong populist sense of the 'common touch' outside. She wanted to be remembered as the 'virgin queen', but her behaviour forfeited 'the reputation of chastity'. The administration of justice at home was corrupt from the top. She was 'not sparing of the blood of her subjects' – though more sensitive than her ministers about it. Parliament made no significant or consistent progress in 'freedom' – perhaps the most telling comment, anticipating the researches of Professor Conrad Russell, against the old whig mythology more than 150 years later.

Lingard uses internal evidence, for example, to evaluate evidence presented against the Duke of Norfolk after the Ridolfi Plot which aimed to depose Elizabeth, with the help of Spanish aid, in 1570. Roberto Ridolfi was a somewhat mysterious Italian, resident in London. The Duke of Norfolk seems to have been dragged into the scheming; and at worst his involvement cannot now be said to have been more than 'half-hearted'.[9] The end result was that the Duke of Norfolk, a leading Catholic nobleman, was executed; whereas Ridolfi himself escaped without punishment. Lingard deals with the supposed credentials of the Duke of Norfolk, which Ridolfi carried to Philip II of Spain in 1571, adding that *'There is much to throw doubt and distrust on the authenticity of this document'*. He goes on to examine the internal evidence contained in the document:

> The astounding assertion that the duke was deputed by the majority of the English nobility to solicit from the king of Spain an invasion of the kingdom, the vapouring boast that he would join the invaders with an army of more than twenty thousand men, and the geographical errors which place Harwich in Norfolk, and Portsmouth in Sussex, must certainly be attributed to the three foreigners, the originators of the conspiracy, and real fabricators of the letter. If we may believe the subsequent confessions of Ross and Barker, the instructions for Ridolphi were devised by Ross and Ridolphi; Barker was repeatedly sent by Ross to the duke with messages, both verbal and written, and to most of them the duke, probably that he might not compromise himself, returned no other answer than the unmeaning monosyllable, <u>well</u>. The letter of credit appears to have been framed after this manner; for it reads more like a cento of scraps and patches than a continuous composition, and to have been moulded into its present shape in proportion as new intelligence was received from Barker.[10]

Lingard is able to proceed further in his consideration of the internal evidence brought to incriminate Mary Queen of Scots in the Babington

The Use of 'Forensic' Rules of Source Criticism

Plot of 1586. He draws attention to the copy of a letter from Mary to Babington, which had gone, by interception, through Walsingham's hands:

> It bears an awkward and therefore suspicious appearance, that while the language in the other points is affirmative, in this point placed in the midst of them, it should assume an interrogative form. The reader wonders how the question got there.[11]

Lingard's implication is that the incriminating question ('by what means doe the six gentlemen [intended assassins of Elizabeth] deliberate to procede?') had been added to entrap Mary.

The question concerned was the one particularly used at her trial to incriminate Mary, for the capital 'crime of imagining and compassing the death of the queen'). The Government, however, never presented the original, but only the suspect copy of the letter:

> It should be remembered that the papers exhibited to the court were only copies. No attempt was made to show what had become of the originals, or when, where, or by whom the copies had been taken. On these points the crown lawyers observed a mysterious silence.[12]

Mary denied vehemently that she had ever asked this question. She asked that her secretaries should be interrogated about it. Her request was refused. Babington himself had never been questioned on it. He had already been summarily executed. A guilty verdict based on such evidence could never have stood in a normal court of law. But Mary was found guilty of treason and executed in 1587.

THE USE OF INTERNAL EVIDENCE, HOWEVER, IS USED AS A NEUTRAL INSTRUMENT OF SOURCE CRITICISM; *not simply to discredit Government evidence. It is also used, for example, to discredit a document which would have been in favour of Mary's innocence in another matter.* Lingard refers to a document which was, by common report, a statement of the Earl of Bothwell on his death bed, asserting the innocence of Mary in the murder of Darnley, her husband, in 1567:

> That document published by Keith deserves no credit. *From internal evidence*, it is nothing more than a memorandum made by some nameless person, at least five years after the death of Bothwell, of what had been reported by a Danish merchant soon after his death.[13]

From internal evidence, this source broke several of Lingard's rules of source criticism. It was *a memory, written down several years afterwards*, of what had been *only hearsay* at the time.

The Use of 'Forensic' Rules of Source Criticism

A good example of the use of the technique of applying internal evidence is Lingard's dealing with Elizabeth's despatches, sent to Scotland, after the Massacre of St. Bartholomew (1572), intending to gain the support of Scottish Protestants. It is one of the earliest examples of the propagandist use made of the 'Black Legend' of that Massacre. Lingard writes:

> It is amusing to observe the caution with which these despatches are worded. Though the envoy is to persuade the Scottish lords that the massacre was premeditated, and a consequence of the league for the extirpation of the reformed faith, he is not ordered, but only permitted ('you may'), to say: – 1. Not that the queen knows, but 'is afraid and <u>in a manner</u> perfectly doth see it'. 2 Not that there actually exists any such league, but that 'it is said' to exist. It is plain from this document that the queen's government had no proof of the supposed league or supposed premeditation, but that they found it convenient to take both as admitted facts.

Here the internal evidence points to the truth of the matter. We now know that this league did not exist,[15] but that it was in the interest of the English Government that the Scottish Protestant lords should think that it did exist so that they would feel more dependent on the Elizabethan Government. We also know that the Massacre of St. Bartholomew was not premeditated, but a sudden action, in panic, on the part of Catherine de Medici.[16] But the story of premeditation served the same purpose of creating anxiety among the Scottish Protestant lords. This manner of intrigue was in fact characteristic of the policy of Elizabeth's Government and Lingard was the first English historian to describe its detailed application at home and abroad.[17] Detailed source criticism is necessary to get behind the statements and documents of governments in such cases where the very purpose of the administration is deceit.

Lingard also used very frequently THE TECHNIQUE OF CHECKING A SOURCE BY REFERENCE TO 'EXTERNAL' PHENOMENA, *as part of his forensic rules of source criticism.*[18] One example is found in his evaluation of the evidence in the case of the murder (1567) of Lord Darnley, husband of Mary Queen of Scots.

> In the confession of Powrie, Hay, Hepburn and Paris, *wrung from them by torture*, it is said that the powder was placed between ten and eleven at night, in the queen's bed-chamber under the king's, while she, with her attendants were with him in his own room – Laing . . . I see not what advantage could be derived from this story; yet it is difficult to believe it. Not only do the time, the distance, and the manner of conveying the powder, render it improbable; but the council, in their letter of the 10th, Mary in hers of the 12th, and the trial of Morton, prove that the house was blown up from the very foundation, so that not one stone was left upon another. Hence the real mine must have been made in the cellar . . .[19]

The Use of 'Forensic' Rules of Source Criticism

Concerning Mary, Queen of Scots' relationship with the Earl of Bothwell, Lingard observes:

> Those who represent Mary as enamoured of Bothwell attach much importance to a visit which she paid to him from Jedburgh. On the 8th (Oct. 1566) he had been wounded in the hand by an outlaw; and, if we may believe them, her love induced her that instant to take a dangerous journey to see him. But ... she allowed eight days to pass; and ... it was on the 16th that she rode from Jedburgh to Hermitage Castle, a distance of twenty English miles, and returned the same day. Her visit might be for a political purpose, as he was her lieutenant on the borders, and as she ordered a 'masse of papers' to be forwarded to him the next day – Chalmers i. 191; ...[20]

Again, concerning the date of Harold Godwinstone's detention in Normandy in 1065, we are told that:

> No writer ... has fixed the date of Harold's detention in Normandy; but we learn from Pictaviensis that the corn in Bretagne was almost ripe – Pict. 81.

So, it must have been during the late Summer of that year.[21]

With regard to the date of a papal bull of 1300, Lingard appeals again to external evidence:

> Lord Hailes says that Rymer has dated the bull erroneously in 1299 (Annals, 267). But it bears the same date, anno quinto, in Hemingford, Westminster and Fordun. From the archbishop's reply to the pope, it appears that he was twenty days on his journey to Carlisle, remained on the borders six weeks, and reached the king August 26. Of course he must have received the bull before the 27th of June; and as that is the day of the month on which it was dated, it must have been written the year before.[22]

Rowland Lee, one of the royal chaplains, was asked to celebrate Mass in a certain room in Whitehall in 1533, only to find that it was to be the occasion of the 'secret marriage' between Henry VIII and Anne Boleyn, attended by three witnesses:

> We are told that Lee, when he discovered the object for which he had been called, made some opposition; but Henry calmed his scruples with the assurance that Pope Clement had pronounced in his favour over the divorce from Catherine, and that the papal instrument was safely deposited in his closet.

Lingard adds in a footnote:

> Burnet treats this account as one of the fictions of Sanders: but it is taken from a manuscript history of the divorce presented to Queen Mary, thirty years before the work of Sanders was published ... and agrees perfectly with the attempt to keep the marriage secret for two or three months. Lee

The Use of 'Forensic' Rules of Source Criticism

was made bishop of Chester, was translated to Lichfield and Coventry, and honoured with the presidentship of Wales – Stowe, 543.[23]

The external factors here, pointing to the veracity of the account, are the accepted facts that Henry VIII wanted to keep the 'marriage' secret for a time; and that Rowland Lee was suitably rewarded afterwards for his services.[24]

For Lingard THE INTERPRETATION OF A SOURCE MUST ALWAYS BE CONSISTENT WITH THE KNOWN FACTS,[25] – *an essential prerequisite among the external factors used to verify the source*. One sub-section of this category is that THE SOURCE MUST BE MEASURED AGAINST THE KNOWN CONDUCT OF THE PEOPLE INVOLVED. The question Lingard asks is: 'Does the source's statement about someone correspond to his or her own known conduct?'.

There are many examples of a source being checked in this way. So, for example, with regard to a medieval writer's opinion of the regents in England – such as William Fitzosbern and Odo of Bayeux – appointed during William's absences:

> The previous merits of these ministers must be received on the word of their panegyrist; but their subsequent conduct does not appear to merit the confidence which was reposed in them by their sovereign.[26]

A source can be devalued in the light of what happened to others who spread the same story. Concerning the possible implication of princess Elizabeth in Wyatt's rebellion of 1554 against Mary Tudor – a problem which deceived English historians up to the present time – Lingard treats the evidence with care:

> When prisoners, to save their own lives, accuse others, their depositions are not, separately, more worthy of credit than the contrary assertions of the accused. On both sides there is the same motive for falsehood. But in the present case the charge against Elizabeth and Courtenay is confirmed by the despatches of Noailles, written in the months of December and January . . . It was rumoured that on the scaffold he [Wyatt] pronounced both the prisoners [Elizabeth and Courtenay] innocent. *This was reported by Noailles to his court; but two prisoners who had propagated the same story in the city, were put in the pillory, for spreading false intelligence.*[27]

Interestingly, the most recent historical account of this matter, by David Starkey in his *Elizabeth: Apprenticeship* (2000), says that 'modern historians', up to the present time, have been misled by too romantic a view of the princess Elizabeth; that she was a 'political player of the first rank in Mary's reign'; and that her real involvement in this plot made her a very dangerous threat to Mary Tudor.[28] Starkey's account brings the most recent research of today completely in line with Lingard's account of the subject in 1823.

Lingard had used the despatches of the French and Imperial ambassadors and a letter of Mary Tudor, among other sources, to establish the real involvement of Elizabeth in the rebellion. He still felt the need, because of the novelty of his account, to add that: 'The reader must excuse the length and frequency of these notes. They are necessary to support a narrative, which might otherwise be attributed to the imagination or the partiality of the writer.'[29] Only in 2000 did he receive support in David Starkey's *Elizabeth: Apprenticeship.*

A source is often weighed in the light of later events. Concerning an event of 1470, Lingard writes:

> The author of the Fragment is singularly unfortunate in his dates. He places this incident in the present year after Easter. Yet it is evident from authentic records, *and subsequent events, that if it happened at all, it* [the flight of Edward IV in panic], *must have happened before Lent.*[30]

Referring to the attitude of Bishop Stephen Gardiner to the princess Elizabeth in Mary Tudor's reign, Lingard refers to seemingly incriminating extracts taken from a letter of the ambassador, Renard, in 1554; but disallows them in the light of Gardiner's known and continuous protection of Elizabeth afterwards.[31]

Concerning a contemporary chronicler's statement of events in 1376, Lingard observes:

> It has been published in Archaeol. xxii. 212. I believe this statement, both because it explains the introduction of Richard of Bordeaux into parliament, *and many occurrences in the next reign.*[32]

When in 1582 Mary Queen of Scots asked her son, James, if he would accept joint kingship in Scotland, he agreed. Lingard refers to a document in the Cotton Manuscript Collection, noting:

> The captive queen fondly attributed it to the affection of the son for the mother: *the result showed that it had been drawn from him by considerations of personal interest.*[33]

One of the most interesting of these 'external' checks is that which USES THE RESULT OF ARCHAEOLOGICAL RESEARCH AND WORKS OF EXCAVATION, AS A MEANS OF CHECKING THE TRUTH OF LITERARY EVIDENCE. *Here Lingard has the opportunity of literally 'earthing' his facts in reality.* For example, Lingard (who was appointed vice-president of the British Archaeological Association), writes:

> Camden has fixed on Ashdown, Gibson prefers Assington for the scene of this battle between King Edmund and the Danes, 1016. I follow the latter. Not only does the name bear a greater resemblance to 'Assandum', but the

barrows near Ashdown which have been opened lately, show by their contents that they are not, as was supposed, of Saxon or Danish, but of Roman construction – See two very interesting letters by J. Gage, Esq. in Archaeol. vols. xxv, xxvi.[34]

Modern scholarship has agreed with Lingard in siting this important battle which made the victorious Cnut ruler of all England – except Wessex – at Assington (or Ashingdon) in Essex.[35]

Similarly, EVIDENCE PRODUCED BY LATER EXHUMATION OF BODIES *is used to substantiate or devalue literary evidence.* So, for example, Lingard states that there is no proof to substantiate the manner of Richard II's death in 1400. The story that he was killed with a battle axe is '*in reality undeserving of credit, because it was unknown in England to those whose interest it was to discover and to publish the truth*', and

> I should add, that, when Richard's tomb was opened, and the skull examined, there was no appearance of any wound, unless the opening of the suture above the os temporis might have been caused by a blow – Arch. vi. 316. The os temporis was probably concealed by the bandage when the face was exposed.[36]

Others claimed that he had been killed by starvation:

> But of this there is no proof; and the story itself, as far as regards the manner of death, had probably no other foundation than the emaciated state of the face, when it was exhibited at St. Paul's ... Much reliance has been placed on the following testimony of Archbishop Scrope ... But in my opinion this passage will bear a very different interpretation ... Most assuredly, then, Scrope had not been able to discover the manner of Richard's death.[37]

Lingard, however, asserts the probability that Richard was murdered on the order of Henry IV; and gives his reasons in terms of context, opportunity and motive:

> But how, the reader will inquire, did the misfortune prince come to his death? It is seldom that the secrets of the prison house are suffered to transpire; in the present instance we are left entirely to conjecture ... *the events immediately preceding will provoke a suspicion* that he owed the loss of his life to the order of the man who had already bereaved him of his crown. *No time could be more opportune* for the commission of such a crime. Who in England, while the heads of Richard's adherents were still mouldering on London Bridge, would venture to charge Henry with the murder? and *the death of the captive would at once relieve him* from the apprehension of the war, with which he was threatened by the king of France.[38]

Modern scholarship has come to exactly the same conclusion.[39]

Again, Lingard is able to correct Clarendon's statement that the burial

The Use of 'Forensic' Rules of Source Criticism

place of Charles I could not be discovered, by reference to a recent exhumation.

> But in 1813 it chanced the the workmen made an aperture in a vault in the choir of St. George's chapel . . . and the prince-regent ordered an investigation to ascertain the truth. One of the coffins, in conformity with the account of Herbert, was of lead, with a leaden scroll in which were cut the words 'King Charles'. In the upper lid of this an opening was made; and when the cerecloth and unctuous matter were removed, the features of the face, as far as they could be distinguished, bore a strong resemblance to the portraits of Charles I. To complete the proof, the head was found to have been separated from the trunk by some sharp instrument, which had cut through the fourth veterbra of the neck – See 'An Account of what appeared on opening the coffin of King Charles I by Sir Henry Halford, bart', 1813.[40]

A very frequently used check on source material, applied by Lingard – again reminiscent of a modern court of law – is to ASK WHETHER THE SOURCE'S STATEMENT CAN BE RECONCILED WITH THE KNOWN CHRONOLOGICAL SEQUENCE OF EVENTS. *So:*

> The French reformed writers generally ascribe the war (1562) to an affray, commonly called by them the massacre of Vassy, in which about sixty men were slain by the followers of the Duke of Guise . . . The affray happened on March 1, yet the Calvinists at Nismes begun to arm on the 19 of February at the sound of the drum. They were in the field and defeated De Flassans on March 6th – See Menard . . .[41]

Or, again:

> Camden attributed to him [Requesens] the dissolution of the English college at Douai; but Requesens died in 1576, and the college was transferred to Rheims in 1578.[42]

Perhaps the most frequently-used technique of source criticism used by Lingard is that which EXAMINES THE CHARACTER OF THE SOURCE AND THE TIME, PLACE AND CIRCUMSTANCES IN WHICH IT WAS WRITTEN, *as well as inquiring into the evidence which the source can summon for its statements. The unspoken questions which constitute the underlying assumptions of source criticism here, are: 'Is the source authentic?';*[43] *and 'On what grounds are its statements made?'.*[44]

So, a statement made by the medieval chronicler William of Newburgh (1135–98) is diminished:

> His testimony amounts only to this, that it was said that some one had said so.[45]

And an admiring modern authority has to concede that 'he [William of

The Use of 'Forensic' Rules of Source Criticism

Newburgh] liked a good story, and included several about what would now be called 'zombies'.[46]

Again: 'The reluctance of Burnet to acknowledge Mary Boleyn as one of the king's [i.e., Henry VIII's] mistresses must yield to the repeated assertions of Pole, in his private letter to Henry, written in 1535.'[47] Pole knew Henry very well and would not have brought this matter up if both had not known it to be true – especially since this letter was meant to appeal to the King's better nature.[48]

Then Lingard debars a story based on John Foxe, that Dame Eleanor, wife of the Duke of Orleans, had been persecuted as a witch in 1441, because of Bishop Beaufort's enmity towards the Duke:

> Some writers have attributed the prosecution of Dame Eleanor to Beaufort's enmity to her husband. But their assertion stands on the slightest foundation, a mere conjecture of Fox that it might be so, because the witch lived, according to Fabyan, in the neighbourhood of Winchester, of which Beaufort was bishop.[49]

Lingard corrected a groundless statement made by the historian, David Hume, by referring to the despatches of Noailles, the French ambassador, in the reign of Mary Tudor:

> I have transcribed these passages, because Hume, to account for the rejection of Courtenay [as a suitable suitor, by Mary], has given us a very romantic statement for which he could have no better authority than his own imagination.[50]

With regard to the celebrated 'Casket Letters', belonging to Mary, Queen of Scots:

> This, a most important fact in the controversy respecting the authenticity of the letters, is expressly asserted *by one who was able to judge*, the earl of Sussex.[51]

Concerning the intriguing visit of three papal envoys to visit Charles I and Archbishop Laud in 1636, Lingard dismisses the authenticity and real knowledge of the Italian historian, Mayolino Bisaccioni in his account of the *Guerre Civile*, because the letters of the three envoys show that Bisaccioni was completely ignorant of their mission. *He was not in a position to know*.[52] On the question of the Spanish Armada (1588), Lingard indicates the need to compare the English Tudor chroniclers, Camden and Stowe, with the better-placed Strada who was able to consult the Spanish original papers:

> With the narratives of our national historians should be compared that by Strada, *who had the advantage of consulting the papers of the duke of Parma* who led the Armada.[53]

The Use of 'Forensic' Rules of Source Criticism

The concern for authenticity is also apparent in the Lingard correspondence. He writes, for example, to his publisher in 1825:

> I enclose two strips of paper with facsmiles as well as I can imitate, of the writing... of which I must ascertain the authenticity. Can you procure me the opinion of some person conversant with ancient hands.[54]

And, again:

> I have enclosed the document, a facsimile of which you sent to Mr. Upcott. It is of so much importance to ascertain its value, that I have cut it out of the book, and will beg you to submit it to Mr. Upcots [sic] inspection... The document itself is of very great importance, because Carte, Hume and the advocates of Charles I, to defend the monarch, have maintained the commissions appealed to by Glamorgan have been forgeries. There is undoubtedly external evidence to the contrary: but they ask where are the originals. They have never been produced: they were not produced by Glamorgan himself. The last is false: and I can satisfy them as to the former by producing one, if not both of the originals. One, of which there can be no doubt, I keep by me: the other, of which I doubt, I have sent you. You will obtain Mr. Upcotts [sic] opinion, and that of any one else you think proper. Perhaps Mr. Ellis may be a proper man to consult... However, I will thank you to do what you can, and send me the document back again, with the opinion of those whom you consult.[55]

Mr. Upcott was a helpful employee of the 'London Institution'; and we have seen already how M. Buchon, a French expert, was employed to examine the authenticity of a manuscript in the King's Library in Paris.[56]

A basic technique, always used by Lingard, is THE TEST OF WHETHER THE SOURCE WAS IN A POSITION TO KNOW; AND WHETHER THE INDIVIDUAL IN QUESTION WAS LIKELY TO BE PREJUDICED.[57] To illustrate, we might take the following example where Lingard is dealing with the commonly-stated whig version, initiated by Burnet, that James II had personally caused the severity of punishment inflicted by Judge Jeffreys and Kirk on the defeated rebels after Monmouth's rebellion (1685). Onslow added that Jeffreys had told the doctor who attended him on his death bed, that James had ordered him to act savagely:

> But Burnet was not in England at this time; he derived his information from Dykvelt, the Dutch ambassador, a known enemy to the King; and Onslow's testimony is no better than a traditional tale received by him at the fourth hand from the original narrator. On the other side, *a witness who had the means of knowing the truth*, the earl of Mulgrave, afterwards duke of Normandy and Buckingham, assures us that James 'compassionated his enemies so much, as never to forgive Jeffreys in executing such multitudes of them in the west, contrary to his order'...[58]

The Use of 'Forensic' Rules of Source Criticism

Lingard's a footnote adds that 'Onslaw received it from Jekyl, Jekyl from Lord Somers, and Lord Somers from Dr. Scot'.[59]

Similarly, Lingard asks continually: 'WAS THE SOURCE IN A POSITION TO FORM A JUDGEMENT?'[60] *The personal character of the source is also considered;*[61] and a source's value is negated if it is based on anonymous information.[62] THE EVIDENCE OF AN EYE-WITNESS IS GIVEN GREATER WEIGHT, *other things being equal, over other sources.*[63] So in relating the account of the enforced resignation of his crown by Richard II in 1399, Lingard puts the authority of eye-witnesses above even the rolls of parliament where the latter have been influenced by Government pressure:

> Such is the account of this transaction inserted by the order of Henry [IV who replaced Richard] in the rolls of parliament; an account, the accuracy of which is liable to strong suspicion. It is difficult to believe that Richard had so much command over his feelings, as to behave with that cheerfulness which is repeatedly noticed in the record; and the assertion that he had promised to resign the crown, when he saw Northumberland in the castle of Conway, is not only *contradictory to the statement of the two eye-witnesses* but also in itself highly improbable.[64]

Again, concerning the fate of Lord Lovell, after his rebellion against Henry VII in 1487:

> On account of his disappearance several writers have supposed that he perished in the battle. But the *journal of the herald who was present* evidently proves that he escaped . . .[65]

Again:

> The altercation between Cardinal Wolsey and the Duke of Suffolk, 1529 . . . has been rejected by some writers . . . [But] it is improbable that *a writer, who was present*, should have invented or confirmed the account, if it had been false.[66]

Concerning Cardinal Wolsey's position in 1529:

> The reader may form an accurate notion of his present situation by the following extract taken from a *letter written by an eye-witness*, the Bishop of Bayonne.[67]

Concerning the execution of Anne Boleyn (1536):

> Compare Constantyne's Memoir, *who was present*, with the letter of a Portuguese gentleman who wrote soon afterwards to a friend in Lisbon . . . The Portuguese writer is certainly in error . . . he only relates the reports of the day, when he says that the council had pronounced the queen's daughter Elizabeth the child of Lord Rochford, and that the king had owned Mary Tudor for his legitimate heir.[68]

The Use of 'Forensic' Rules of Source Criticism

Much controversy had reigned over the cause of the war between the French Huguenots and the Government in France, which started in 1562. Lingard comments that Huguenot writers ascribe the war to the 'massacre' of Vassy, where sixty men were killed by the followers of the Duke of Guise:

> But ... there is every reason to believe that this affray was accidental, and provoked by the religionists themselves – See La Popelin ... and the declaration of the duke on his deathbed, preserved by Brantome, *who was present at Vassy and at his death*.[69]

In his account of the trial of the Gunpowder Plot conspirators, Lingard – in the first modern account of the episode[70] – is painstaking in his use of original papers and eye-witness accounts:

> Sir Edward Coke at the trial gave a different account of this transaction; but he made no attempt to bring forward any proof of his statement. I write from the manuscript relation of Greenway ... *who was present* ... Garnet on his trial explained it in the same manner, and his explanation is fully confirmed by the letter which he wrote to his superior in Rome on July 24, after his last conference with Catesby.[71]

In his references here, Lingard uses the original manuscript of Garnet's letter to his superior in Rome, supplied by the Jesuit archives, to correct a shortened form of the letter contained in a copy of it in the State Paper Office.[72]

Concerning Garnet's execution for participation in the Plot, Lingard comments:

> On the scaffold, according to the ambiguous language of the official account, he confessed his guilt; *but if we credit the letters of spectators*, he denied all knowledge of the plot, except by confession; and though he begged pardon of the king, he was careful to add that it was not for any participation in the treason, but for the legal offence of having concealed the general knowledge which he had acquired of some practice against the state, designed by Catesby.[73]

Lingard shows that at Garnet's trial: 'his admissions were presented to the jury stripped of those qualifications with which he had clothed them, and with which they spoke more in his favour than against him' and 'this was a forgery of evidence. *For when a qualified statement is made, the suppression of the qualification is not less a forgery, than if the whole statement had been fabricated.*[74]

As a final example of the use of eye-witness material, we may take Lingard's description of the Cromwellian massacres at Drogheda and Wexford (1649). Here he uses the account given by Thomas Wood, brother of Anthony, the Oxford diarist, who was 'at that time a subal-

The Use of 'Forensic' Rules of Source Criticism

tern, afterwards a captain in Ingoldsby's regiment'; and concludes that this account

> from the mouth of one who was an eyewitness of, probably a participator in, the horrors of that day, will enable the reader to form an adequate notion of the thirst for blood which stimulated the soldiery, and of the cruelties which they exercised on their defenceless victims.[75]

The situation in which the source was writing – time, place, and circumstance[76] – is used by Lingard as a means of evaluation. So, on the question of who made the first suggestions of Henry's divorce from Catherine of Aragon, Lingard cites different ideas put forward by various sources, including Wolsey and Henry VIII himself. Lingard chooses to believe a different source:

> But Cardinal Pole, who, writing to the king on such a subject, would hardly venture to assert what, if it were not true, Henry must have known to be false, assures us that it was first mentioned to the king by certain divines, whom Anne Boleyn sent to him for that purpose ... Pole, f. lxxxvi.[77]

Again, in considering the veracity of facts mentioned in a letter of 1582, from Mary Queen of Scots to Elizabeth, Lingard concludes:

> If we recollect that Mary's object was to propitiate the English queen, we must conclude that she would not have presumed to make such statements unless she had known that Elizabeth was conscious of their truth; and, if that was the case, we may discover in such consciousness the real reason why, during so many years, Mary could never obtain a personal interview with the English queen.[78]

The facts concerned here point to a certain insincerity, even treachery, in the conduct of Elizabeth towards Mary whom she had endeavoured, finally with success, to trap, imprison and execute.

Lingard was the first historian to deal adequately with the activities of Walsingham and his network of 'agents provocateurs' who were employed to ensnare Mary Queen of Scots [PLATE 23] in plots such as the notorious Babington Plot (1586) which led to her downfall. He uses the technique of looking at a source against its known background with great effect. So, dealing with a letter from Babington to Mary, Lingard comments:

> The reader will discover in this extraordinary document, little of that caution and disguise so natural to conspirators. It looks as if it were written for the sole purpose of drawing Mary into the plot; of seducing her to furnish evidence to be afterwards used against herself. Nor should it be forgotten that Babington's letter, whatever it originally contained, would pass through the office of Walsingham, who, instead of the original, might forward a copy so interpolated and improved by Philipps [an expert

employed by Walsingham], as to render it difficult for the queen to return an answer without betraying an approval, or at least a guilty knowledge of the proposed assassination.[79]

Lingard makes one of his rare conjectures in the accompanying footnote:

> If we score out the line 'for the despatch of the usurping conspirator' and the passage beginning 'and for the despatch of the usurper', and ending with 'tragical execution' on the supposition that they are interpolations, Babington's letter will be confined to the expected aid from the foreigners, and the safest way of carrying Mary off from Chartley.[80]

Such interpolations would mean the difference between Mary agreeing to a plan for her own escape, as opposed to a plan for the assassination of Elizabeth I.

Morgan, one of Mary's advisers, had earlier told her to have no correspondence with the conspirator, Ballard. Yet now in 1586, there was a note, supposedly from Morgan to Mary, which was going to be crucial to her conviction for treason. Lingard comments:

> Was not the draft of this note fabricated in Walsingham's office? Morgan admonished Mary to have no correspondence with Ballard, 'because he was engaged in an enterprise with which it was not meet that she should be concerned' – Murdin, 527. Would he then advise her to correspond with Babington, who was supposed to be at the very head of Ballard's enterprise?[81]

Lingard's summing up in the matter of Mary's involvement in the plot to assassinate Elizabeth is a classic of its kind:

> I do not think that the charge against the Scottish queen carries with it any great appearance of improbability. It is very possible that a woman who had suffered an unjust imprisonment for twenty years, and was daily harassed with the fear of assassination, might conceive it lawful to preserve her own life and recover her liberty by the death of her oppressor . . . But the real question is, not what she might have thought, but whether she actually gave her consent and approbation to the scheme of murder submitted to her in the name of Babington.
>
> Mary, as we have already seen, denied that 'poynts of the letters that concerned the practise against the Quene were by her written, or of her knolledg . . .'. She also affirmed upon oath that she had never been party to any design against the life of Elizabeth; and the same affirmation she repeated in the course of her prayer on the scaffold.
>
> To bring the charge home to her after her denial, it was necessary to show that the copy of her answers to Babington produced in court, was a faithful representation of the real answer which she had commissioned Curle [her secretary] to put into cipher, and forward to the conspirator. Now, without disputing the fidelity of Curle, we know that the answer passed from Curle

into the hands of Philipps at Chartley, and that it remained in the possession of Philipps and Walsingham, men actually engaged in a plot to bring Mary to the scaffold, not fewer than ten days – from the 18th to the 28th of July (1586) – before it was sent by them to Babington. Did it come out of their hands in the same state in which it came to them? Did they forward to him the original, as it was deciphered by Curle, or a transcript made by Philipps? Then what became of it afterwards? Of that we are also ignorant. At Fotheringhay Mary asked to look at the original to see whether it was written in her cipher. It was not produced; but in its place was substituted a deciphered copy. But if they had not the original, where did they procure the copy? By whom was it made? On this head again they were silent. To have given any explanation would have betrayed their secret, would have discovered, in the slang language of Philipps. 'by what way the wind came in' . . . The manoeuvres which now took place on the part of Walsingham and Philipps were so very extraordinary, that it will be worth the reader's while to follow them step by step, till we come to their conclusion at Fotheringhay.[82]

Lingard devotes an appendix of some nine closely-written pages of almost day-to-day detail to describe how, by deception and 'ingenious contrivance', Walsingham brought the legal procedure to its intended conclusion. For this, he gets behind the official proceedings to relate the manoeuvres of Walsingham and his agents behind the scenes. Lingard bases his account not only on letters which had been published in various places, but on letters from manuscript collections such as the Harleian and Egerton papers, on the public records, on 'several letters among the papers in the State Paper Office' and on the new materials contained in 'the invaluable collection of Queen Mary's letters' collected by Prince A. Labanoff.[83]

The state of modern scholarship on this matter is not further advanced than Lingard took it. There are certain facts about which we can still not be certain. But, from Lingard onwards, we know that Walsingham [PLATE 24] was the first great 'head of intelligence and security' in the history of the English nation state – just as Thomas Cromwell had earlier been the first 'head of propaganda'.[84] We know that Walsingham employed 'agents provocateurs' and agents who were experts in the arts of intercepting and interfering with letters. We know that letters between conspirators and Mary went through Walsingham's hands. And we know that he used them to bring about a successful conclusion to his long-term plan of getting rid of Mary, Queen of Scots, in the perceived interests of the state. As for Elizabeth, we know that she was left with a great sense of guilt over the matter of Mary's death; and that William Davison, a royal servant and trial commissioner, was made the scapegoat. He was blamed for getting Elizabeth to sign the death warrant; later he was fined and imprisoned in the Tower.[85]

The Use of 'Forensic' Rules of Source Criticism

In Lingard, for the first time, we see a realistic view of the nature of Elizabethan government, as opposed to the 'glorious' view which dominated English historical writing until the late twentieth century. Only at the very end of the twentieth century could a modern revisionist historian, Christopher Haigh, finally write:

> The monarchy of Elizabeth I [see PLATE 22] was founded upon illusions. She ruled by propagandist images which captivated her courtiers and seduced her subjects – images which have misled historians for four centuries.

The greatest illusion was that 'she inaugurated a golden age of national harmony and achievement'.[86] Lingard had revealed already that this was a superficial harmony, achieved by a totalitarian Government, intent on stamping its own 'mind-set' on all its citizens; and achieving this with a great deal of injustice and cruelty. Its foreign policy was based mainly on a cynical exploitation of internal difficulties in other countries.[87]

The technique of weighing the source against the background in which it was written is seen again, for example, in Lingard's treatment of a contemporary writing by the Earl of Sunderland after the downfall of James II. It was a classic instance of a universal tendency among the supporters of a defeated party. In 1689 the Earl, one of James II's ministers, published a vindication of himself, maintaining that he 'had always opposed those illegal and irritating measures which provoked the discontent of the people, and led to the expulsion of James'. But Lingard comments:

> *the circumstances in which he wrote detract from his credit and the despatches of his friend Barillon show that several of his assertions are false.*[88]

The same technique is seen to be applied with great effect in the case of Lingard's treatment of the infamous Massacre of St. Bartholomew in Paris (1572). Lingard was the first English historian to arrive at the now accepted interpretation of the Massacre. This was partly because Lingard, identifying the circumstances in which Salviati, the papal envoy, was writing, gave his despatches to Rome a central importance in interpreting all the evidence. Lingard regarded the despatches and their circumstances as the key source after considering the '*SITUATION OF THE WRITER, THE OBJECT FOR WHICH HE WROTE, AND THE TIME AND OPPORTUNITY WHICH HE POSSESSED FOR CORRECTING ANY ERROR* . . . .'.[89]

It was in regard to the same subject that Lingard used another of his rules of forensic historical criticism – *the unreliability of evidence supplied by a source looking back at events and reading history backwards* – to dismiss other evidence concerning the Massacre, which misled Lingard's

The Use of 'Forensic' Rules of Source Criticism

contemporary critic, John Allen; and was still misleading Lord Acton fifty years later.[90] This particular technique is extremely important, also, because it went to the heart of the faulty viewing system used by adherents of the whig interpretation of English history until the last part of the twentieth century. They read history backwards on the grand scale – misinterpreting evidence from the past by reading into it other knowledge which came only from hindsight. The single critical technique described above, as used by Lingard, could have corrected this faulty whig view of the past 150 years earlier, if it had come into common usage in Lingard's day.

Lingard is also *concerned with the* PSYCHOLOGICAL BACKGROUND FROM WHICH THE EVIDENCE OF A SOURCE HAS EMERGED. This was important especially when dealing with 'confession' of prisoners charged with offences against monarch or government in Tudor England. We have become more aware, in the light of modern scholarship,[91] of the difficulties presented by such 'confessions' made in an atmosphere pervaded with the notions of the 'divine right of kings' and the glorification of the state. In these circumstances a man could be made to think subjectively that he *must have been guilty* of treason against the monarch, even when objectively he had committed no crime. A modern specialist in the field has written:

> England of the sixteenth century had her state trials and her incomprehensible confessions ... those accused of treason were exposed to any form of persuasion the government cared to use.[92]

Indeed our knowledge of similar confessions produced in state trials under totalitarian regimes in twentieth-century Europe, has given a new dimension to our knowledge of the psychological as well as the physical pressures which are characteristic of such trials; and has developed our powers of critical analysis of such sources of evidence so that they are not now so 'incomprehensible' to us. Lingard, however, seems to have reached such an understanding two centuries ago.

Writing of the confession of the Earl of Essex, one of Elizabeth I's former favourites, before his execution in 1601, Lingard comments that his 'spirit ... was at last subdued by the fear of death, or the menaces of the preacher'. Essex

> sent for the lord keeper, the treasurer, the admiral and the secretary, solicited their forgiveness, and made ample avowal of every ambitious and unlawful project which had entered his mind ... His confession filled four sheets of paper; but its accuracy has been doubted; and his associates complained that he had loaded both himself and them with crimes of which neither he nor they were guilty.[93]

The Use of 'Forensic' Rules of Source Criticism

There was also the doubtful and murky case of the 'double-agent', Parry, executed in 1585 for 'treason'. His trial appeared to Lingard to have been 'a trial of skill between two experienced impostors, which should be able to entangle the other in the toils. Neville [another Government agent] succeeded':

> In the Tower he made a long confession, and wrote several letters to Elizabeth and her ministers. *To an ordinary reader they bear the marks of a distempered mind*; though perhaps those to whom they were addressed might, from their knowledge of his previous conduct, explain the contradictions with which they seem to abound.[94]

Throughout his *History*, Lingard emphasizes *the unsatisfactory nature of evidence extracted by torture in the state trials of the sixteenth century*. For example, he was the first English historian to question the guilt of the infamous Dr. Rodrigo López, Queen Elizabeth's Portuguese Jewish physician. He had been executed in 1594 for attempting, in the pay of Philip II, to poison Elizabeth. All English historians had accepted the official statement on this subject, first published in *A True Report of Sundry Horrible Conspiracies of late time detected to have . . . taken away the life of the Queenes most excellent Majestie* (1594). The text was part of the 'black legend' of Philip II as the embodiment of the national enemy[95] – the 'bogey man' of English historiography – which existed well into the twentieth century. In 1894, seventy years after Lingard, A. Dimock, in a specialized article on this subject in the *English Historical Review*, could still speak of the 'almost inconceivable baseness of Philip II and his ministers' who had been able to 'suborn a man who had been handsomely treated, and was not even "one of the faithful", to betray his trust and murder his mistress'.[96]

Lingard, alone among English historians, had not been convinced, as early as 1823, of the Government's account of this affair:

> *How far these confessions by two Government witnesses made in the Tower, and probably on the rack, are deserving of credit, may be doubted.*[97]

Lingard tried to get evidence from the Spanish state archives in Simancas, to solve the matter, but his agents 'looked in vain for Philip's counter-manifesto concerning López and the events of 1594'.[98] So Lingard could only describe his grave doubts about López's guilt, and the unsafe and unsatisfactory nature of the Government's evidence against him.[99] When the Spanish state papers were eventually published in 1899, the editor questioned the evidence brought against López and referred to a letter at Simancas which 'goes very far to explain the facts upon which his guilt was presumed'.[100] Modern historians, once again, have failed to take the

The Use of 'Forensic' Rules of Source Criticism

matter further than Lingard: 'it has been demonstrated that López was never proved guilty of the crime for which he was executed'.[101]

The corollary to Lingard's pursuit of the 'grounds' on which any source makes its statements, is *the rule of not accepting any source simply on its face value*. For example:

> We are told that . . . the pecuniary aids voted to her [Elizabeth] were few and inconsiderable . . . I know not how we are to arrive at the exact value of these grants; but they certainly exceed the average of the preceding reigns.[102]

> A foreigner, who had been ambassador in England, informs us that under Elizabeth the administration of justice was more corrupt than under her precedessors. We have no means of instituting the comparison; but we know . . .[103]

The Attorney General himself, representing the Government against Fawkes in the Gunpowder Plot Trial, is brought under Lingard's rules of evidence:

> Sir Edward Coke at the trial gave a different account of this transaction; but he made no attempt to bring any proof of his statement.[104]

Again, concerning the trial of Sir Walter Raleigh for implication in the Main Plot (1603), conducted again by Coke, Lingard is not satisfied with the standard of evidence:

> The proceedings of this trial will justify the presumption that there was something criminal in the dealing . . . but do not supply sufficient evidence that Raleigh had been guilty of treason. Such evidence was, in the opinion of James and of Beaumont, the French Ambassador, supplied by the intercepted letters of Aremberg [envoy: Spanish Netherlands]; but of the correctness of that opinion we have no opportunity of judging.[105]

Modern scholarship has got no further on this matter than the stage at which Lingard left it, D. MacCulloch concluded in 1995 that the Government, for its own purposes, linked this Main Plot (1603) 'tendentiously' with the Bye Plot of the same year, adding that: 'Official manipulation of both conspiracies remains obscure but likely'.[105]

Referring to the evidence brought by the Crown for Henry VIII against Anne Boleyn in 1536, and contrasting it with that against Catherine Howard in 1542, Lingard writes:

> The preservation of documents respecting her [Catherine's] fate enables us to estimate the value of the proofs against her; our ignorance of those

brought against Anne renders the question of <u>her</u> guilt or innocence more problematical.[106] [Lingard's underlining]

Again, Lingard's judgement has been confirmed by modern scholarship. Catherine Howard is now judged to have been guilty of adultery.[108] Anne Boleyn is regarded as having been innocent, but executed for 'reasons of state', as expressed by the will of Henry VIII and his opportunistic chief minister, Thomas Cromwell. By now Anne had failed to provide a male heir, and Henry had turned his attentions to Jane Seymour. Anne was executed in 1536 'on absurd charges, her supposed lovers having already suffered the same fate'.[109]

Another consistently-used technique is the elementary but very important *rule of* DISCOVERING WHETHER OR NOT THE SOURCE IS BIASED, SO *as to make the necessary allowances.* Thus the evidence given by an enemy or a jealous source,[110] or on the other hand by an obvious panegyrist,[111] is of limited value and has to be treated carefully. But a *favourable statement by a known adversary is of good value.*[112] So, on the question of Edward the Confessor's bequest of his kingdom to Harold of Wessex, Lingard comments:

> I am much inclined to believe this report not only on the testimony of the English writers... but because its truth is acknowledged by the enemies of Harold....[113]

An 'interested' source must be watched closely, whether its bias be religious,[114] *national,*[115] *political,*[116] *or of any other kind.*[117] For example, in the case of Thomas Becket Lingard writes:

> Thomas à Becket, a personage whom the reader will see acting for years an important part in the theatre of public affairs, and who, since his death has been alternately portrayed as a saint and hero, or as a hypocrite and traitor, according to the religious beliefs of the historians.[118]

But, again, a source might be 'interested' in favour of the truth. For example, any accusation implied in a paper written in order to propitiate the accused must be taken as good evidence of his guilt in the matter. Concerning the role of the Earl of Murray in Darnley's death, Lingard writes:

> It is difficult to doubt the sincerity of Ormiston in his confession. According to him, Bothwell declared that 'the haill lords in Craigmillar, all that wes ther with the queen' had determined on the death of Darnley... But Bothwell might exaggerate, and Murray himself maintains that he signed no bond there... I have therefore adopted the deposition of Paris: il ne veult n'ayder ne nuire... *That deposition was plainly made to propitiate*

Murray; it therefore says as little against him as was possible; and yet amounts to an acknowledgement that he was privy to the plot, and had no objection to its success.[119]

Modern scholarship accepts the association of Murray with the murder of Darnley.[120]

Again, certain people were *in a position where they would need to know and proclaim the truth for their own self-interest, if they were innocent. Silence in these cases would indicate guilt.* This approach is used, for example, in the consideration of evidence concerning the murder of King John's orphaned nephew, Arthur, in 1203.[121] Arthur had a possible claim to the throne. John [PLATE 15] saw him as a rival. Arthur was imprisoned and then disappeared. John remained silent, though he was in a position to know what had happened and he also knew that rumours were rife concerning his guilt. Lingard infers his guilt from his silence. Modern scholarship confirms that this is 'virtually certain'.[122]

The *value of the unconcerned spectator* is recognized by Lingard.[123] The corollary is that the historian must determine whether there could be a purpose behind a particular accusation,[124] or if there was any reason why the source should lie.[125]

A novel and valuable aspect of Lingard's treatment of the biased source, is that *he does not stop short before governmental materials. Lingard recognizes that the Government can be biased in its official documentation.* We are made well aware of the deficiencies of Government accounts of state trials in the sixteenth century. For example, Lord Burghley's defence of the Elizabethan Government's persecution of Catholics in his *Execution of Justice* – for so long unquestioningly accepted in English historiography[126] – is not accepted at face value by Lingard.[127]

It was an essential plank of Government propaganda after the Henrician Reformation that any allegiance, spiritual or otherwise, to an authority other than the English king was, ipso facto an act of treason. Here was a central element in the revolution that was replacing the centuries-old duality of obedience to the king in political matters and the Pope in spiritual matters. It was an essential element in changing the 'thought-mode' of English people. It was important therefore that the Government in Elizabeth's reign should present its persecution and execution of Catholics as a legitimate state action against 'traitors' and 'foreigners'. The Government's propaganda received its greatest boost from the very few individual Catholics who did get involved in plots against the Queen; for virtually all others remained loyal to the Queen as their secular ruler.[128] The role of the 'agent provocater', employed by Walsingham, was very important, therefore, to Government strategy.

Referring to the charges of treason brought against the Catholic continental seminarians and missionary priests who returned to England in

The Use of 'Forensic' Rules of Source Criticism

Elizabeth's reign to provide pastoral care to Catholics, Lingard points to the account of Camden, the most influential of the Elizabethan chroniclers who echoed the Government's line:

> Camden . . . has given an account of the seminarists, which appears to be taken from the declamatory invectives of the crown lawyers during the trial of the missionaries.[129]

The innocence of Edmund Campion and his fellow missionary priests of the charges of treason and political intrigue, brought against them by the Government in 1581, is asserted: 'The absence of proof was amply supplied by the invectives, the conjectures, and the declamations of the lawyers for the crown.'[130]

The Government's tampering with letters so as to induce guilt is demonstrated,[131] and government accounts of certain episodes are checked against other less partial accounts.[132] Lingard's *critical rule is that 'implicit faith' cannot be given to the documents published by the Government in Elizabeth's reign*.[133] It was a long time after Lingard that modern Elizabeth historians came to the same conclusion, concerning Campion's innocence and the essential injustice of his trial.

Lingard indicates *a number of types of source which are of little value*. Rumour or reports of the day were not good evidence of fact.[134] Similarly, hearsay,[135] conjecture[136] or unconfirmed charges[137] should be given little or no weight as evidence. A source's estimation of its own value,[138] a man's statement about himself,[139] or the statement of a man accusing another to save himself,[140] are obviously unsafe as evidence. Eloquence and zeal are of little value in a source.[141]

Having built up his narrative, Lingard is concerned to indicate the precise value of the evidence supporting it. So we get a careful statement of what is fact and what is conjecture,[142] what is certain and what is uncertain,[143] and what is known as opposed to that which is only probable.[144] Sometimes the statement made in the text is qualified by a footnote which tells us more exactly the nature of the evidence behind it.[145] For example, Lingard's definition of a 'forgery' is any omission or addition to a document calculated to deceive. Referring to 'forged' despatches during Elizabeth's reign, he explains:

> I think I may call it a forgery. Leicester had written to Hatton a letter which the ministers determined to suppress, as it was more calculated to irritate than to appease the queen. Afterwards, finding it necessary to gain time, 'they [the ministers] conferred of the letter again, and blotting out some things, which they thought would be offensive, and mending some other parts as they thought best', they presented it to her – Hardwicke Papers, 300.[146]

The Use of 'Forensic' Rules of Source Criticism

Again, describing the trial of Anne Boleyn [PLATE 20], Lingard writes: 'Anne according to the testimony or the fiction of a foreign poet, instantly burst into the following exclamation.' He proceeds to elucidate in a footnote:

> It is extraordinary that we have no credible account of the behaviour of this unfortunate woman on her trial. There can be no doubt that she would maintain her innocence, and therefore I have admitted into the text that exclamation, which is generally attributed to her. It comes to us, however, on very questionable authority, that of Meteren, the historian of the Netherlands, who says that he transcribed it from some verses in the Platt-Deutsch language, by Crispin, lord of Milherve, a Dutch gentleman present at the trial.[147]

A further development of Lingards's concern to indicate the precise value of the evidence supporting his narrative, is his stating why a source should not ordinarily be given much value or credence, but why, on a particular occasion, some other consideration operates to give it a greater value. We have seen how Lingard would have devalued the evidence of fellow conspirators (now prisoners) concerning the involvement of Elizabeth and Courtenay in Wyatt's Rebellion (1554) against Mary Tudor.[148] However, there was *confirmatory evidence from the papers and despatches of both the French and Imperial ambassadors.* These 'were written in cipher, the key to which Noailles thought would not be discovered – Noailles . . . He was, however, mistaken – Renard MS . . .'.[149]

The above episode was the result of Lingard's successful pursuit of the Renard despatches (during Mary Tudor's reign) kept at the Besançon archives in France. He was able to send his publisher, Mawman, something interesting to insert in the notice for the *History*, in a letter of 1823:

> By comparing the printed despatches of Noailles the French ambassador at the accession of Mary, with the manuscript despatches of Renard the imperial ambassador at the same period the writer has been enabled to lay before his readers a correct account of the intrigues which led to the marriage of the queen with Philip of Spain, and of the origin, the objects, and the progress of the insurrection under Wyat . . . [Elizabeth] assented to the project [the Rebellion], and . . . , if she escaped the punishment of a traitor, it was through the intervention of Gardiner; who maintained that her offence did not come within the operation of the statute, because she had not committed any overt act of treason.[150]

In Lingard's judgement the evidence implicating Elizabeth was such as to leave no doubt of her involvement in the conspiracy. Modern scholarship, until very recently, has left the matter as something unproven – 'no evidence could be found' – but Starkey's study in 2000 confirms Lingard's account.[151]

Another example is when Lingard notes that Lord Grey, a former companion of the Duke of Monmouth, began to make disclosures in 1685, implicating Lord Brandon in the Rye House Plot of 1683:[152]

> There might be reason to doubt the accuracy of his statements for his moral character did not stand very high... and he would naturally be tempted to merit the royal favour by removing the blame from his own shoulders to those of his accomplices: yet his testimony must have been substantially correct, since it was not only not publicly called into question after the revolution, but he himself was created by King William earl of Tankerville, and appointed lord privy seal and first lord of the Admiralty. James II was satisfied with his narrative.[153]

Again, Lingard writes of an event in 1673:

> There is, however, in Burnet's narrative, so much unquestionably false, that it is difficult to judge what may be probably true. But his account of Shaftesbury's speech is confirmed by the lord-keeper Guildford...[154]

And concerning Clarendon's account of Lord Digby's character in 1641, we find Lingard's comment: 'Clarendon was an adversary, but this assertion seems to be fully supported by the facts.'[155]

Also, *a source might seem to be true according to one criterion and yet be unworthy of acceptance when weighed against another*:

> This story, which from its minuteness of detail might be thought to have some foundation in fact, was believed on the continent; *but is in reality undeserving of credit, because it was unknown in England to those whose interest it was to discover the truth.*[156]

In all these examples we see the source passing one test of source criticism but failing another, or failing one test yet gaining sufficient marks, as it were, on the other tests to be judged worthy of credit. The examples cited above provide a good illustration of Lingard's technique used throughout his *History*. They also reveal the very 'open' manner in which he places his findings before the reader, so that the latter can know the process by which the narrative has been built up and the evidence on which it rests.

In dealing with conflicting and polemical secondary sources – the works of previous historians belonging to different parties – Lingard will often summarize the attitudes of both sides[157] before making his own judgement, based on a critical examination of the original sources. So, concerning the Earl of Murray, regent in Scotland during Elizabeth's reign:

The Use of 'Forensic' Rules of Source Criticism

> Murray has been described by the writers of one party, as an honest and patriotic nobleman, by those of the other, as one of the most selfish, designing and unprincipled of men. I will merely remark as something extraordinary, that almost every charge made against him by the advocates of Mary is confirmed by the contemporary memoir of Bothwell, though of the existence of that memoir they must have been ignorant.[158]

In the light of modern scholarship, Murray is associated with the murder of both Rizzio and Darnley.[159]

Concerning the execution of the Catholic missionary priest Edmund Campion [PLATE 26] in 1582, Lingard remarks in a footnote:

> Between the torturings he had been several times called to dispute on religion . . . Camden says that he hardly supported his reputation . . . ; the Catholic writers boast of his success, and appeal to the conversions by which the conferences were followed . . . Two of the audience were committed to prison, because they said that Campion 'was discreet and learned, and disputed very well . . .'.[160]

We shall see Lingard's own judgement on the Campion case below.[161] He concludes his revisionist account[162] of Elizabeth's reign:

> The historians who celebrate the golden days of Elizabeth, have described with a glowing pencil the happiness of the people under her sway. To them might be opposed the dismal picture of national misery, drawn by the Catholic writers of the same period. Both have taken too contracted a view of the subject.[163]

Summing up his treatment of the persecution of Protestants under Mary Tudor, Lingard writes:

> The reformed writers have described, in glowing colours, the sufferings, and sought to multiply the number, of the victims; while the Catholics have maintained that the reader should distrust the exaggerations of men heated with enthusiasm and exasperated by oppression; and from the catalogue of the martyrs should be expunged the names of all who were condemned as felons or traitors, or who died peaceably in their beds, or who survived the publication of their martyrdom, or who would for their heterodoxy have been sent to the stake by the reformed prelates themselves, had they been in possession of the power. Yet these deductions will take but little from the infamy of the measure. After every allowance, it will be found that, in the space of four years, almost two hundred persons perished in the flames for religious opinion; a number, at the contemplation of which the mind is struck with horror, and learns to bless the legislation of a more tolerant age, in which dissent from established forms, though in some countries still punished with civil disabilities, is nowhere liable to the penalties of death.[164]

The Use of 'Forensic' Rules of Source Criticism

Another example is his dealing with the infamous 'Irish Massacre' of 1641 – a favourite subject of anti-Catholic propaganda in England for over three centuries.¹⁶⁵ Lingard draws his conclusions:

> By degrees the war in Ulster had assumed the most ferocious appearance. The natives, looking on the planters as intruders and robbers, had stripped them of their property, and chased them away from their homes, and in some instances had taken their lives. On the other hand, the military, acting by the orders of the council, executed, where they had the power, martial law on the insurgents, laying waste the country, and slaying the fugitives without distinction or mercy. One act of violence was constantly retaliated by another; the thirst for revenge was reciprocally excited and gratified; and men on both sides learned to indulge in murder without remorse, even with feelings of triumph. It has been usual for writers to present to their readers only one half of the picture, to paint the atrocities of the natives, and to conceal those of their opponents; but barbarities too revolting to stain these pages are equally recorded of both; and, if among the one there were monsters who thirsted for the blood of their victims, there were among the others those who had long been accustomed to deem the life of a mere Irishman beneath their notice.¹⁶⁶

Indeed Lingard goes beyond the actions of the two sides, to lay the main blame on those who had created the conditions of gross injustice and exploitation which had produced the conflict.¹⁶⁷ Lingard's account of the Irish rebellion was the first modern interpretation, giving a balanced view which was to be repeated by modern English historians in the twentieth century.¹⁶⁸

Again, describing the celebrated 'massacre' of the Protestant Vaudois in Piedmont (1657), about which Milton had written his famous sonnet¹⁶⁹ in defence of the Protestant cause, Lingard sought the balanced view for the first time in English writing:

> to the ravages of the military in Angrogna and Lucerna, are opposed the massacres of the Catholics in Perousa, and San Martino. In favour of the Vaudois may be consulted Léger, Histoire Générale des Eglises Evangeliques &c (he was a principal instigator of these troubles); Stouppe, Collection of the several papers sent to his highness, &c, London, 1655; Sabaudiensis in Reformatam Religionem Persecutionis Brevis Narratio, Londini 1655; Morland, 326–384, and the papers in Thurloe ... Against them – A Short and Faithful Account of the late Commotions, &c, with some reflections on Mr. Stouppe's Collected Papers, 1655; Morland ...; Siri ... and Thurloe ....¹⁷⁰

Lingard's understanding of the mentality involved in controversy is revealed in another remark concerning a theological conflict in James II's reign, between Catholic and Anglican theologians:

The Use of 'Forensic' Rules of Source Criticism

> The contest was carried on with equal spirit by both parties during the reign of James, both claiming the victory of course; *for it is seldom that in such controversies men take the trouble to study the real argument of their adversaries; they generally confine their reading to the works published on their own side.*[171]

As a final example of Lingard's approach of seeking the balance between conflicting parties with regard to historical facts, we may consider his conclusions on the 'deprivations' following the Hampton Court Conference, 1604, when the new Government under the first Stuart king had attempted to bring puritan-minded clergy into line with the Anglican state church:

> But while they [Puritan writers] make the deprived clergy amount to three hundred individuals, their adversaries reduce the number to fifty, exaggerate the obstinacy and unreasonableness of the sufferers, and claim for the prelates the praise of moderation and forbearance. The representations of both are probably too highly coloured. It must have been that on such an occasion many cases of individual hardship, perhaps some of unjustifiable rigour, would occur; yet it will remain a difficult task to show on what ground men could expect to retain their livings while they refused to submit to the doctrine or to conform to the discipline of that church by which they were employed.[172]

The examples cited above reflect Lingard's genuinely-held and often-stated belief that the historian must stand outside party or religious interests and make comments from the viewpoint of an 'unconcerned spectator'. This is the reason why his pursuit of historical truth can so often be correlated with the processes of forensic evidence and rules of evidence as is pursued in a modern court of law.

Readers will know how in our own time legal decisions made in the past half century, have been overturned by courts of appeal, on re-examination of the evidence outside the excitement and emotions of the contemporary context in which the facts were first presented. In the light of this experience, we can appreciate more fully, the comments made by Lingard about the qualities needed by the historian in pursuit of the truth about the past. He writes:

> the same object will often appear in a very dissimilar light to the spectator who views it calmly from a distance, and to the man who acts under the influence of public excitement, and with a judgement swayed by the views and prejudices of party.[173]

Indeed, in a statement of his position which he takes to be axiomatic for all historians, Lingard asserted his belief in the possibility of achieving objective truth about what happened in the past[172] – without for a moment underestimating the many difficulties, technical and personal, that need to be overcome. His statement stands as a noble expression of a belief in and pursuit of objectivity in historical writing. It sets a high standard at which to aim, for all historians; otherwise

> [the historian] will be continually tempted to make an unfair use of the privilege of the historian; he will sacrifice the interests of truth to the interests of party, national, or religious, or political. His narrative may still be brilliant, attractive, picturesque; but the pictures which he paints will derive their colouring from the jaundiced eye of the artist himself, and will therefore bear no very faithful resemblance to the realities of life and fact.[174]

In demonstrating Lingard's workmanship, I hope to have shown that he carried out his aim in practise to the best of his considerable ability. As a result he achieved an unsurpassed measure of reliability in his account of the English past. I know of no serious matter in which a later court of appeal, in terms of modern scholarship, has overturned a historical judgement or major historical interpretation made by Lingard nearly two centuries ago; and I know of no other English historian of whom this can be said.

CHAPTER VIII
The Application of Lingard's Rules of Source Criticism to Some Celebrated Historical Problems

'Thus as I have learned of them that much knew and little cause to lie.'
Sir Thomas More

In his Preliminary Notice to his last edition of the *History* (1849), Lingard remarked:

> Few persons are indeed aware how many statements may be found in most modern histories, which, though generally credited, have no foundation in fact, but are admitted at once, because they have long been repeated by writer after writer without scruple or refutation.[1]

He was referring to one of the great obstacles to the advancement of historical understanding between the sixteenth and twentieth centuries – the repetition by popular historians of the story found in the books of their predecessors, without any attempt at further research.

One result of Lingard's determination to write from original sources is that his conclusions were often very different from ideas which had been fashionable for centuries. He was liberating English historiography from generations of repetitive writing. It is not surprising, therefore, to hear from Lord Macaulay the criticism that Lingard's 'great fundamental rule of judging seems to be that the popular opinion cannot possibly be correct'.[2]

In this same Preliminary Notice to the final edition of the *History*, Lingard felt it necessary to refer in particular to three topics in which his treatment of the subject had been 'received by popular writers of the day with bursts of indignation, and contradicted by them with sneers of contempt'. He was alluding to:

> the irreverent manner in which I had spoken of the Scottish hero, Sir

William Wallace, to the unfair character – so it was deemed – which I had drawn of Archbishop Cranmer, and to the cause to which I attributed the massacre at Paris on the feast of St. Bartholomew.[3]

Before we begin looking at some test cases of new findings discovered by Lingard, as a result of applying his range of source criticism, it will be useful to notice very briefly the three historical judgements which caused so much popular indignation in Lingard's own day.

William Wallace (?–1305) has lived – and still lives – in the popular mind as a great leader of Scottish patriotic resistance against the English. This is an image or myth from the past which has detached itself from reality and acquired a 'life' of its own in the popular imagination. Wallace in fact had become a 'folk' hero. Such a phenomenon frequently inspires great popular feeling and sentimental support – in this case among Scottish people living in England and all over the world, as well as in Scotland. Who would dare to throw the corrective light of reality on this subject?

Lingard was not in the least sentimental; which does not mean that he was not full of human feeling. Sentimentality – as opposed to a genuine expression of 'the intelligence of the feelings' – was an obstruction to the truth. As a historian he could do no other, as he saw it, than approach the subject with the same aim which inspired all his historical work. He was interested only in pursuing and discovering the historical truth. He was always willing to be surprised by the evidence; but in this case, he found nothing to substantiate the popular myth about Wallace. Lingard argued that there was no evidence to show that Wallace had performed any great service to his country between his loss of the battle of Falkirk (1298) and his death on the scaffold in England, by command of Edward I, in 1305. It was his execution which created the myth:

> That death still appears to me to have been the apotheosis to which he was indebted for the worship afterwards paid to his memory in Scotland . . . ;

> It may perhaps offend the national partiality of some among my readers, but I greatly suspect that Wallace owes his celebrity as much to his execution as to his exploits.[4]

Unpopular though this judgement seems to have been in his own day, the verdict of modern scholarship completely supports it. The latest comments on the subject at the end of the second millennium are that it is not easy 'to explain his emergence as a Scottish leader in 1297'; that he 'unwisely' entered the battle of Falkirk, incurring a disastrous defeat, after which support for him waned in Scotland. The rest of his life was lived in 'relative obscurity' until he was captured and unjustly executed, in an extremely barbarous manner, for treason, in 1305. But:

The Application of Source Criticism

From that day Wallace has been regarded as one of the greatest heroes in Scottish national history.[5]

His most recent and very sympathetic biographer, James Mackay, writes in *William Wallace* (2000):

> In life he had had a brief moment of power and glory, followed by seven years in the political wilderness, discredited but never quite defeated. Wallace in adversity became a folk hero ... His death, rather than any achievement in life, ensured him immortality.[6]

Lingard's treatment of this topic reminds us that *he regarded sentimentality as a dangerous enemy to truth and the good of mankind*. Lingard's judgement forms in a real sense one of his most important criteria for the proper approach to source criticism. It was another example of the way in which he broke free from the modes of contemporary culture. Sentimentality was a feature of the Romantic Movement which was affecting all aspects of England's cultural life at this period – manifesting itself, for example, in the historical writing of Lingard's contemporaries, Robert Southey and Sharon Turner.[7] But Lingard was completely unaffected by the movement; as he had been equally unaffected by the earlier cultural movement known as the 'Enlightenment', with its emphasis on the supremacy of human rationality. Lingard's life span crossed the artificial division normally ascribed to these two movements in English life and culture. Romanticism, among historians as well as poets, in the early nineteenth century – emphasizing the romantic, mystical, pietistic and nationalist elements – was a reaction against the extremely rationalistic approach of the 'Enlightenment' in the eighteenth century. Part of Lingard's greatness was that he retained a consistent balance between the claims of reason and faith in his personal outlook and approach during a lifetime when the prevailing modes of culture swung from one extreme to another. In this sense, too, he rose above the pressures of his own time, to reach the higher level of a more timeless approach to historical objectivity in the science of source criticism. Even Ranke, the greatest German exponent of scientific history, failed to draw clearly the lines between the restricted discipline of historical writing and the other legitimate and wider realms of theological and mystical thinking. Ranke's failure affected his work as a 'scientific' historian.[8] Lingard, whose training in theology made him better qualified in the field, significantly had the ability to make a clear distinction between the two areas of human endeavour, which made him superior in his work of historical source criticism.[9]

Lingard – whatever his private views on the matter and in contrast to Ranke as a historian makes no attempt to attribute any historical events to a providential agency;[10] Lingard wrote, quite sceptically qua historian, about the 'heavenly voices' of Joan of Arc, suggesting other possible rational explanations; but he was not dogmatic on the subject.[11] The *Oxford and Cambridge Review* had to concede in 1846 that Lingard was 'as free from the perils of metaphysical flights . . . as he is uninfluenced by a religious or political bias'.[12] His objectivity in politics is demonstrated by the fact that one modern writer, T. P. Peardon, has described him as 'mildly Whig' and another, D. F. Shea, as a Tory 'at heart'.[13] The distinguished Cambridge historian, G. P. Gooch, praised Lingard's objectivity in religious matters by writing that his *History* 'gave no indication that the author was a Catholic priest and few of his readers would have guessed it'.[14]

The second topic which aroused great indignation against Lingard was much nearer the heart of English people themselves. He dared to criticize some of the actions of Archbishop Thomas Cranmer [PLATE 21], the first Archbishop of Canterbury in the new regime established by Henry VIII. One critic had already pointed out that Church and State were now so closely intertwined that 'whatever is calumny on the former, must be calumny on the latter'.[15]

Lingard's first criticism of Cranmer's actions related to the way in which he took a public oath of obedience to the Pope in order to become Archbishop in 1534, while making a 'private' statement to a few chosen witnesses that he was making his oath with reservations. His intent was to support Henry VIII in the matter of the Divorce and in his aim to make himself 'supreme head' of the Church of England. Cranmer knew that he was not going to obey the Pope even as he was taking the oath of obedience. Lingard stated that this was an act of duplicity:

> I will only observe that oaths cease to offer any security if their meaning may be qualified by previous protestations made without the knowledge of the party who is principally interested.[16]

The other 'outrageous' observation of Lingard was that Cranmer – who was to be burnt himself in Mary Tudor's reign after trying to save himself by a recantation, the failure of which caused him to reassert his real beliefs – had himself taken a leading part in the burning of Protestant heretics, such as Joan of Kent, in 1550. Also he had tried to bring Catholics to the same fate by his proposed 'Reform of Ecclesiastical Laws' in 1552, which were meant to identify the adherents of the ancient faith, representing all English people up to 1534, as 'heretics'.[17]

Such statements concerning Cranmer were met with horrified opposition in Lingard's day; but the advent of modern scholarship has supported him completely in them. Diarmaid MacCulloch, in his authoritative study of *Thomas Cranmer* (1996), writes that his taking of the public oath of

The Application of Source Criticism

obedience to the Pope, while making private reservations which would nullify it, represented 'a most dubious manoeuvre'. It was 'a procedure which can reflect no credit on him at all'.[18]

Similarly, MacCulloch accepts, with Lingard, as opposed to the 'tender-hearted admirers of Cranmer' who had argued the opposite 'since the time of John Strype (1643–1737)', that Cranmer persuaded or 'bullied' the unwilling young Edward VI into 'doing his duty to burn his first heretic, one Joan Bocher in 1550'. There is no doubt that Cranmer's proposed new code of canon law, the *Reformatio Legum Ecclesiasticarum* of 1552, attempted to bring all Catholics under the same punishment for heresy.[19]

On the third of the topics which seemed to have aroused most indignation against Lingard's *History* – his completely new account of the Massacre of St. Bartholomew – European scholarship has accepted Lingard's account since the 1880s, as we have seen above. It is now accepted that this infamous event was an opportunistic and criminal act caused by the panic and fear of Catherine de Medici – afraid for her own safety – in Paris (1572), not the result of a long-planned design by the Pope and the King of Spain, in conjunction with Catherine.[20]

✻ ✻ ✻

Lingard's acute ability as a historical 'detective' derives from the professional methodology of source criticism with which he approached and evaluated the original sources (or 'witnesses'). In this he is a perfect model not only for historians, but for all aspiring legal or criminal investigators.

The 'Wars of the Roses' in the fifteenth century, between the Houses of Lancaster and York, occurred in a particularly turbulent period in English history when the abilities of the 'forensic' historian are needed to a very high degree in order to get at the truth behind some very murky happenings. A modern specialist historian of this period, Professor R. Griffiths, wrote in 1998:

> A civil war like the 'Wars of the Roses' places peculiar and formidable historiographical difficulties in the path of the historian: the written statements of contemporaries on the subject of kings and their achievements are almost inevitably distorted by partisan considerations, private fears, or personal obsequiousness.[21]

It will be useful, as exemplars of the effectiveness of Lingard's professional approach in matters of historical evidence, to observe his treatment of two episodes from this period, which are famous or infamous in the annals of historical 'mysteries'. Both are sufficiently indicative of the turbulent nature of English politics at this period; and both demand an exceptionally sure and perceptive handling of conflicting evidence.

The Death of King Henry VI in 1471: Murder or Natural Causes?

The Lancastrian king had a peculiarly chequered career, reigning from 1422 to1461, then deposed by Edward IV (Yorkist), only to be restored to the throne in 1470 (after Edward's flight to Holland); and deposed again in April 1471, after Edward's return and triumphant march into London, prepared for by his younger brother, Richard of Gloucester.

Henry [PLATE 18] died in the Tower in 1471. The dilemma for historians was whether he was murdered or died a natural death. Among the many conflicting sources, there were two most salient elements central to the investigation. Lingard showed his exceptional ability in seeing 'the wood for the trees' in keeping these two elements firmly in sight. One was the question of motive; the other a matter of chronology and timing.

With regard to motive, Lingard, following one of his basic rules, was determined to establish the correct sequence of events and dates leading to the death of Henry. In April 1471, Richard of Gloucester [PLATE 19] had won the battle of Tewkesbury against the Lancastrian forces and afterwards executed the Duke of Somerset, son of Henry VI:

> There now remained but one person whose life could give uneasiness to Edward. As long as the son lived to claim the crown of his father, the blood of Henry VI was not worth shedding; but now that the young prince was no more, to remove the old king was to remove the last temptation from his adherents, whose attachment to their ancient sovereign appeared to grow with the decline of his fortunes.[22]

On Tuesday, 21 May, the triumphant Edward IV entered London, and on the following day, the dead body of Henry VI was shown to the public at St. Paul's Cathedral.

Lingard argued from this sequence of events that there was an obvious and strong political motive for the murder of Henry. Gloucester had already slain Henry's son earlier in the month, immediately after the battle of Tewkesbury. Gloucester was also known to have been at the Tower during the time of Henry's death.

Lingard observes:

> To satisfy the credulous, it was reported, as had been formerly reported of Richard II, that he [Henry VI] died of grief. But though Edward might silence the tongues, he could not control the thoughts or the pens of his subjects; and the writers who lived under the next dynasty not only proclaimed the murder, but attributed the black deed to the advice, if not to the dagger, of the youngest of the royal brothers, Richard, Duke of Gloucester.[23]

Lingard quotes the contemporary Croyland chronicler on this point, but notes that an opposite account was given by another contemporary chronicler, Fleetwood (Harleian MSS. 543) who was in the service of Edward IV and who provided the official line that Henry had died of 'pure displeasure and melancholy'.[24] Lingard discards this second account, because:

> It detracts, however, from his [Fleetwood's] credit, that he appears in other instances to have suppressed or disguised facts which bore hard on the character of his patron [Edward IV], particularly Edward's perjury at York, and the murder of the prince after the battle of Tewesbury.[25]

David Hume [PLATE 8], in his celebrated and highly influential *History of England* (1754–62), underrated the political motive behind the murder:

> It is pretended, and was generally believed that the duke of Gloucester killed him, but the universal odium which that prince has incurred, induced perhaps the notion to aggravate his crimes without any sufficient authority.[26]

Subsequent historians followed Hume whose *History* was the dominant account of English history for the next century.[27]

The chief argument used by those who wished to exonerate Edward IV and his brother, Richard, was that Henry had not died on the 21st of May as the Croyland chronicler stated, but much later. So, they argued, there was no obvious and immediate sequitur between Edward's entering London and the death of the imprisoned Henry.

By Lingard's own day, this argument had been buttressed, seemingly, by some antiquarian research into the state records. Edmund Malone, a well-known Irish judge and antiquarian, to whom Edmund Burke had dedicated his famous *Reflections on the French Revolution* (1790), stated:

> it appears on the face of the public accounts allowed in the Exchequer for the maintenance of Henry VI and his numerous attendants in the Tower, that he lived till the twelfth of June, twenty-two days after the time assigned for his pretended assassination.[28]

On the basis of Malone's findings, the Scottish historian Malcolm Laing, at the beginning of the nineteenth century, acquitted Richard of the murder of Henry, 'on the ground that he did not die at the time assigned [by the chronicler], but much later'.[29] Lingard's contemporary, Sharon Turner, in his *History of England from the Norman Conquest to 1500* (1814–23), repeated the same view, based on the same evidence.

In 1819 Lingard showed that his contemporaries and predecessors had misinterpreted and misunderstood a vital part of the detailed evidence concerning the sequence of dates. He referred in 1819 to Thomas Rymer's massive, twenty-two volume collection of state documents, the *Foedera, Conventiones, et Acta Publica, ab 1101* (1704–35), in dealing with the Exchequer accounts on this matter concerning the payment of monies for Henry VI's subsistence in the Tower:

> These accounts are to be found in Rym. xi. 712. But they afford no proof that Henry lived till the 12th of June. The latest date of any particular charge is that of William Sayer for the maintenance of Henry and ten guards, for a fortnight, beginning the 11th of May, and of course ending on the day on which the king is said to have been buried.[30]

Lingard then explains how the errors had arisen. The antiquarian, Malone, followed by the historians, had mistaken the day of the payment of certain monies by the Exchequer, for the day on which they had been *incurred*. They

> had taken the day of the month on which the accounts were allowed at the Exchequer, for the day on which the expenses ceased; which is so far from being the case that it even belongs to a different year, 1472, and not 1471; as appears from the next two accounts, which, though allowed on the 24th of June, refer to expenses in September and October of 1471 – See them in Rym. xi. 713, 174.[31]

It revealed the dangers involved when even a court judge and antiquarian tried to interpret evidence which needed the attention of a 'professional' historian.

Lingard had really now settled the matter beyond reasonable doubt though later historians still tended to skirt around the matter. Keith Feiling, for example, in his *History of England* (1959), wrote of Henry VI: 'How he had died no one can tell, though Edward's youngest brother, Richard of Gloucester, was supposed to know.'[32]

Indeed, Richard III has become one of the most controversial of English kings. Partly in reaction to Shakespeare's very critical description of him, there has arisen in recent times the *Richard III Society* whose members admire Richard and try to exonerate him. But in the first authoritative and specialist account of the period, E. F. Jacob wrote in his *The Fifteenth Century, 1399–1485* (1961):

> The King [Edward IV] entered the capital on 21 May, 1471. On that Tuesday night Henry VI was put to death in the Tower by Edward's order.[33]

And finally, in the extremely detailed and definitive *The Reign of King Henry VI*, by R. A. Griffiths, published in 1981, we come back to the decisive matter of the strength of political motive, together with the circumstantial evidence of time, place and opportunity – as Lingard had emphasized in 1819. Griffiths concludes:

> There can be no reasonable doubt that he [Henry] died violently, despite the claims or Yorkist propaganda, or even that his death was authorized by the king [Edward IV] to remove once and for all now that Prince Edward was dead any possibility of a Lancastrian coup similar to the one that had troubled Edward IV in the previous year.[34]

In 1995, Professor John Gillingham states categorically:

> The killing of his only child [Prince Edward], at the battle of Tewkesbury sealed Henry's fate. He was now the last obvious representative of the Lancastrian dynasty, and Edward judged that he could no longer allow him to live: Henry VI was murdered on 21 April 1471.[35]

The position achieved by modern scholarship at the beginning of the twenty-first century, on the death of Henry VI, is exactly that achieved by Lingard nearly two centuries earlier, against contemporary opposition. He had established the historical truth by the application of the rules of source criticism which he had created for this purpose; particularly, in this case, by pursuing the 'source of the source' (used by Malone) and showing that it had been misinterpreted by other historians.

The Deaths of the Princes in the Tower, 1483

The second case taken from the period known as the 'Wars of the Roses' is that of the deaths in the Tower of London of the two young nephews of Richard III in 1483. Richard III [see PLATE 19] was that same Duke of Gloucester, and youngest brother of Edward IV, who had been implicated in the murder of Henry VI. On the death of Edward IV in 1483, Richard became protector for the twelve-year-old Edward V (son of his brother, Edward IV) and of his younger brother Richard. Richard had the two boys declared illegitimate and imprisoned in the Tower. Richard was then proclaimed king in June 1483; and the two young princes disappeared from the Tower, never to be seen again.

From the time of these events there has been considerable controversy as to whether or not Richard III was responsible for the deaths of his young nephews. On the one hand, there was the memorable description of the villainous Richard in Shakespeare's *Richard III*, which occupied an important place in the English theatre and in the public mind. On the other hand, there has always been opposition to this view, illustrated by the

The Application of Source Criticism

modern appearance of the *Society of Richard III*, dedicated to clearing his name.

Lingard examined all the evidence and arguments, and came to the conclusion that two sources were the most reliable. One source was the *Croyland Chronicle*. Lingard wrote:

> It would be difficult to name a writer more deserving of credit than the Croyland historian, *who composed his narrative in the month of April following the death of Richard*.[37]

The chronicler *was in a position to know and had proved himself in other matters to have been a reliable source.*

The other source was Sir Thomas More's *Richard III* (1513). More had been five years old when the princes died in the Tower; *but he received much of his information from Cardinal Morton* (1420–1500) who had served during the reigns of Henry VI and Edward IV, before becoming chief minister to Henry VII, Archbishop of Canterbury in 1486 and chancellor in 1487. More's information on Richard III was later used by the Tudor chroniclers, Grafton, Stow, Hall and Holinshed. Shakespeare, in turn, had based his facts on the chroniclers, especially Holinshed. More, an eminently truthful man himself, was therefore indirectly a source for Shakespeare's highly influential play which did more than anything else to create the popular image of Richard III.

In stating his reason for basing his account of the princes' murder on the *Croyland Chronicle* and Thomas More's description, Lingard uses another of his rules of source criticism (*external evidence*), pointing out that:

> *The same conviction appears to have been common to all those persons who were the most interested in ascertaining the truth*, including the duke of Buckingham who now had to find another contender to support against Richard, Elizabeth, widow of Edward IV who now feared for the lives of her own daughters, Rouse who died in 1491 who openly asserted that 'the princes were slain, but so privately that few knew in what manner' and Andre, 'the contemporary historiographer of Henry VII', who 'says that Richard ordered the princes to be put to the sword (ferro feriri jussit)' – MS. Domit. A. XVIII.[38]

Sir Thomas More,

> who wrote soon after, in 1513, not only asserts that they were murdered, but gives the particulars of the murder from the confession of the assassins themselves given during the next reign.[39]

Lingard then applies an important element of '*external*' source criticism: '*It furnishes a strong presumption in favour of More's narrative, that all*

The Application of Source Criticism

the persons mentioned by him as implicated in the murder, became objects of the king's bounty'. He traces the research in some detail:

> To Greene, the messenger, was given the office of receiver of the lordships of the Isle of Wight and of Porchester Castle; and the numerous grants of money and land, and lucrative offices to Tyrrel and Brackenbury may be seen in the notes by Strype to Buck's history, in Kennet, i. 551, 552. Nor were the more obscure agents, the actual murderers, Dighton and Forest, neglected by the gratitude of their patron. The first was made bailiff for life of the manor of Aiton in Staffordshire . . . ; and, as Forest lived but a few months in possession of the office given to him in Barnard Castle, an annuity of five marks was settled on his widow and son . . . This coincidence must appear very extraordinary, if we suppose More's account to be fabulous.[40]

Again, More's account, from the murderers' own admission, states that the princes were buried at the foot of the stairs. Lingard *draws on some archaelogical evidence to support this*:

> In July, 1674, in consequence of an order to clear the White Tower from all contiguous buildings, as the workmen were 'digging down the stairs which led from the king's lodgings to the chapel in the said Tower, about ten feet in the ground, were found the bones of two striplings in (as it seemed) a wooden chest, which upon the survey were found proportionable to the ages of the two brothers, viz. about thirteen and eleven years'. On inquiry it was concluded that they were the bones of the murdered princes, and in consequence, after they had been sifted from the rubbish, they were honourably interred in the chapel of Henry VII in Westminster – Sanford, 427, 429.[41]

Here was 'strong confirmation of the murder; since we know of no other two boys who perished in the Tower'.[42]

Thomas More said that *his information was not 'hearsay', but based on reliable evidence, from witnesses who had been in a position to know and had no reason for lying*:

> But I shall rehears you the dolorous end of those babes, not after every way that I have heard, but after that way I have heard by such men and by such means as methinketh it were hard but it should be true . . . *Thus as I have learned of them that much knew and little cause had to lie,* were these two noble princes privily slain.[43]

More's is just the sort of evidence which fitted Lingard's own rules of source criticism.[44]

Lingard proceeds to deal with the various arguments with which previous historians had said that More's account could not have been true and that Richard could not have planned and accomplished the deaths of the two princes. Thomas Carte, in his *The History of England* (1747–55),

The Application of Source Criticism

Horace Walpole, in his *Historic Doubts* (1767) and Malcolm Laing in his *History of Scotland* (1800–4) all argued that it was impossible for Richard to have been involved because of the time limits set by his itinerary or 'progress' around England during the crucial time mentioned by Thomas More. Lingard observes:

> Now it must be acknowledged that, if the limits assigned to the progress of Richard by his advocates be correct, it is impossible to crowd within so short a space all the facts mentioned by More. But are these limits correct? ... is it certain that he was at Westminster on the 31st of August? *for on the accuracy of that date depends all the reasoning of the king's advocates.* The only proof of it is, that two such instruments are to be found in Rymer, dated August 31; ... But such instruments prove nothing more than that the chancellor was at Westminster. The king might have been at the distance of three hundred miles. They were said to be issued teste rege because they were issued from his high court of Chancery. Thus we know that at the death of Edward IV, on the 9th of April, 1483, his son Edward V was at Ludlow, and did not reach London before the 4th of May following. And yet on the 23rd of April, eleven days before he came to Westminster, thirty three writs were published in his name, dated at Westminster teste rege – Rym. xii. 79 ... Hence it is evident that the writers in question on which Carte, Walpole and Laing rest their principal argument, prove nothing as to the presence or absence of Richard on the day on which they are dated.[45]

Lingard goes on to show from the *Croyland Chronicle* that Richard was in fact in the neighbourhood of York on that date and that this chronicler's account of his 'progress' agrees with that given by Thomas More.[46]

Dealing with Walpole's other argument, Lingard comments:

> Walpole (pp. 70, 71) transcribes a passage from the roll of parliament of 1484, to prove that Edward V was alive when that parliament was sitting and consequently could not have been put to death during Richard's progress to York. But if he had paid more attention to the roll, he would have found that he was copying from the petition presented to the protector at Baynard's Castle, and that the passage in question proved only that Edward was alive at the time when his uncle usurped the throne – See Rot. Parl. vi. 241.[47]

Then Lingard comes to the evidence exonerating Richard, supplied by T. P. Bailey in his *History of the Tower* (1803). Bailey had found some warrants for the delivery of clothing and the payment of provisions for the use of 'the lord bastard, given under our signature at Westminster the ix day of March, anno secundo, p. 353'. Bailey had supposed that this 'lord bastard' was one of the young princes who was therefore still alive eighteen months after their supposed death. Lingard goes to the

The Application of Source Criticism

original source of this supposition, in Thomas Rymer's great collection of state documents:

> There can be no doubt that the lord bastard mentioned in the warrants was Richard's own son, John of Gloucester, whom he made two days later governor of Calais for life, reserving to himself the exercise of the office till the boy should come of age – Rym. xii. 265.[48]

Finally, Lingard meets the argument for exonerating Richard supplied by the celebrated Francis Bacon in his *The History of the Reign of King Henry the Seventh*, published in 1622. Bacon had said that, soon after the imposter Perkin Warbeck asserted that he was one of the young princes and claimed a right to the throne in the reign of Henry VII, the two actual murderers of the princes, Tyrrel and Dighton, were imprisoned in the Tower and were said to have admitted their crime to Henry VII. Yet, wrote Bacon, Henry made no use of their supposed 'confession' to prove that Warbeck was an imposter.

Lingard, again used the published state documents *to establish the correct sequence of events*:

> Now, if it were true that Henry examined these persons at the time of Perkin's appearance, and yet did not use their evidence to prove that he [Warbeck] was not the duke of York, the omission would certainly justify a suspicion that they did not acknowledge the murder. The real fact is, that they were examined only a short time before the execution of Tyrrel, as Bacon himself says; but that execution did not take place, as he supposes, soon after the appearance of Perkin, but at the distance of ten years, in 1502, for having favoured the escape of the earl of Suffolk – Rot. Parl. vi. 545. Of course Henry could not employ their confession in any of his declarations against Perkin, which were published long before. This is also plain from Sir Thomas More's history, who wrote a few years afterwards. 'Very truth it is, and well known, that at such time as Sir James Tyrrel was in the Tower for treason committed against King Henry VII, both Dighton and he were examined, and confessed in manner above written' – More. 68.[49]

Lingard, in another appendix, sets out the arguments in detail which convinced him, as opposed again to Carte, Walpole and Laing, that Perkin Warbeck was an imposter:

> The consideration of these circumstances has left no doubt in my mind that Warbeck was an imposter.[50]

In dealing with a subject on which there was a mass of conflicting evidence, Lingard had identified two sources – the contemporary Croyland chronicler and the later *History of Richard III* (1513) by Thomas More – which, apart from the public records, were the most authentic (reliable) when judged by his methods of source criticism.[51] It will be of interest, therefore, to look at the judgement of these sources supplied by modern scholarship.

One modern specialist, C. Ross, describes the *Croyland Chronicle* as 'the most important single source for the reign of Richard III as a whole, and indeed, also for the entire second decade of Edward IV's reign'.[52] Another authority, Professor R. Griffiths, comments in 1998 on the same source: 'there is no disputing that the author was a highly-placed, intelligent and informed eye-witness of most of the events and personalities he describes.'[53]

With regard to Sir Thomas More's *History of Richard III*, the author of the most recent study of the murder of the princes in the tower, A. Weir, describes it as 'rich in compelling eye-witness detail – which itself argues its reliability'. It is written by a man of 'integrity' and 'based on first-hand information'.[55]

We know that much of More's creative work, such as *Utopia* (1516), is in the tradition of 'rhetoric', with a strong use of the devices of irony and drama. However, More's extraordinary concern for the truth is as renowned as his integrity as a lawyer. In the light of careful discernment which is always needed when reading his work, it seems clear that, within the context of making a judgement on the innocence or guilt of a real person who died when More himself was seven, and taking into account More's first-hand knowledge of the subject from Cardinal Morton, we can rely completely on More's account of this subject as a first-class source with extraordinary accuracy of factual detail, based on first-hand information. It certainly satisfied two of Lingard's criteria on the part of any source – eye witness or first-hand knowledge and integrity of character (see PLATE 4).

The state of scholarship on these matters at the end of the twentieth century exactly reflects Lingard's own conclusions in 1819: that the young princes were murdered in the Tower, that Richard III was responsible for the deed; and that Perkin Warbeck was a complete imposter. A Weir concludes her own study in 1997: 'given all the evidence ... then only one man can have been responsible for their deaths: Richard III'.[56]

K. Duckrey writes in 1997 that their deaths were 'probably ordered' by him 'before mid-September 1483'.[57] Professor John Gillingham added in 1995 that Perkin Warbeck followed 'a career of impersonation' including that of 'Richard, the younger Prince in the Tower'.[58] But no one has set out the evidence in terms of source criticism better than, or even as well as, Lingard did two centuries ago. A whole range of his techniques of source criticism was brought to bear on the Tower deaths, to ensure a successful resolution of the problems involved.

The other feature which emerges clearly from Lingard's correction of contemporary and earlier writers is his obvious superiority in the skills of interpreting original sources. He emerges as a professional historian, at least as well equipped as any modern professional scholar to deal with the intricacies and pitfalls of source interpretation. In comparison, his predecessors and contemporaries appear as amateur historians, making the most basic mistakes in their attempts to use sources for their own purposes, dipping occasionally into original materials but evidently lacking the skills needed to interpret them properly. It places Lingard in perspective as a man whose professional skills show him to be in an entirely different class from his predecessors and contemporaries. Of no other historian could it be said so realistically that he was in a class of his own.

The Origins of the Bayeux Tapestry

Lingard's critical skills are well demonstrated in the way in which he deals with physical evidence from the medieval period – for example, the celebrated *Bayeux Tapestry* [PLATE 16]. There had been a long tradition that the tapestry was the work of Queen Matilda, wife of William the Conqueror. This was believed in Lingard's time and he made a penetrating critique of the tapestry to demonstrate that 'it is difficult to conceive on what ground it is so confidently and pertinaciously attributed to the queen of William'.[59]

He sets out the necessary tests required when dealing with a traditionary belief of this sort, before it could even be accepted as 'probable':

> To make it even probable that this tapestry was, as is often affirmed, the work of the Conqueror's queen Matilda, or a gift from her to the church of Bayeux, it is necessary to show that there exists some historical testimony, or, in the absence of both of these, something in the character of the tapestry itself, which may serve to connect it with the name of that princess.[60]

Having set out the framework of source criticism on the subject, Lingard deals systematically with each criterion in turn. He begins by pointing out that it 'is admitted on all hands' that 'there is *no historical testimony* which bears in any way on this question'. Also, there is *no* 'ancient tradition', as distinguished from contemporary popular beliefs:

> It may be at present the popular belief at Bayeux; but it is not an ancient tradition; it cannot be traced further back than the year 1730, when it is first mentioned by Lancelot and Montfaucon. We are acquainted with earlier writers who have described the city of Bayeux, its cathedral and

curiosities; but not one of them have ever noticed this supposed tradition. It was probably the conjecture of some antiquary, which was at first gratefully accepted, and has since been carefully preserved by the inhabitants.[61]

Lingard describes two old inventories of articles belonging to the church at Bayeux, one made in 1369, the other in 1476. These inventories mentioned the names of the donors of all the articles but not the donor of the Tapestry:

> Most assuredly, if there had then existed at Bayeux any popular belief respecting the original of the tapestry, they would have mentioned it in the same manner ... *Their silence then is a satisfactory proof* that the tradition to which appeal is now made, had no existence in the middle of the fifteen century.[62]

Thirdly, Lingard comes to *consideration of the 'internal' evidence in the Tapestry itself*. There is 'absolutely nothing' in the Tapestry itself, he concludes, to 'induce a belief that it was the work or the gift of Matilda'. She is not represented in the superscriptions or the drawings:

> There were many compartments into which she might with propriety have been introduced; but she seems to have been as much forgotten by the artist as if he had never heard of her existence.[63]

Again, *the nature of the materials used* do not suggest a royal benefactor:

> It is of the most homely materials, of ordinary canvas worked with worsted of different tints, which serve only to depict the forms of the objects and not to imitate their natural colours. There is in it no embroidery of gold, none of silver, none of silk, nothing worthy of the rank or the munificence of the supposed donor.[64]

Then, he asks, by whom and for what was it likely to have been created? The great disproportion between the breadth of the tapestry (about 19 inches) and its length (226 feet) indicates that it was 'originally intended to decorate some building of considerable extent'. What building?:

> Plainly the church of Bayeux; for there we find it centuries ago, annually decorating on certain festivals the whole circuit of the nave, its measurement being then, as it still is, the same with that circuit.[65]

Then, there is much *internal evidence* to show that it was designed 'also to commemorate the share which the men of Bayeux bore in the conquest of England'. Only two of the more powerful men accompanying the Conqueror are depicted and named, and that only once: 'but the attention of the spectator is directed in the same manner to Odo, the bishop of Bayeux, in three separate compartments'. Again, three of the individuals are 'equally distinguished in compartments 11, 49, 62' – Turold, Vital and Wadard, 'as if they were of higher importance in the estimation of the donor or artist than the most illustrious barons and chieftains in the army'. Who were they? These names cannot be found in the history books: 'They were unknown to William of Poitou, and Orderic and Wace'.

Then Lingard plays his 'trump card', turning to evidence from an unimpeachable source. Lingard's move is not surprising when we consider his constant rule of source criticism: *go to the original and the most credible source – to the 'fountain-head' rather than the 'troubled stream'* – for answers to your historical queries. The Domesday Book is regarded by today's scholars as 'a fundamental source for all types of historical enquiry';[66] 'It is the most remarkable statistical document in European history.'[67] Its making was contemporaneous with the making of the Bayeux Tapestry. Lingard *brought together these two primary sources* to solve the problem of the three obscure men highlighted so inexplicably on the Bayeux Tapestry, but not noticed in any of the accounts of contemporary chroniclers. From this *collation of evidence*, he finds the answer to the problem.

> But open the record of Domesday, and there you meet with them in almost the first page, three men of Bayeux, all homagers of Bishop Odo, all rewarded by him with lands in England for their services. Ralph, the son of *Turold* – the father was probably dead when the survey was made – appears in possession of nine different properties in Kent (Domesd. i., 7, 8, 9), Vital of three (ibid. 7, 10) and Wadard – the hic est Wadard of the tapestry – of more than thirty in the counties of Kent, Surrey, Dorset, Warwick and Lincoln, besides six burgage messuages in Dover (ibid., 6, 7, 10, 32, 77, 155, 238, 342).

Lingard concludes:

> What right could these obscure retainers of the bishop of Bayeux have to be depicted and designated by name in preference to the most noble and celebrated of William's associates? I would rather believe that the tapestry originated in the personal vanity of some of these men, or of their descendants, than that Matilda would so highly distinguish them in work designed by her to commemorate the conquest of England by the arms of her husband.[68]

Lingard's investigation reveals the insights derived from his skilful use of a variety of sources, applying to them the range of critical techniques which he employed throughout his *History*.

As late as 1994 we were told that: 'Although its manufacture is traditionally associated with Queen Matilda, it may have been commissioned by Odo bishop of Bayeux.'[69] But in 1997 Dr. S. D. Lloyd updated the most recent modern scholarship on the subject:

> Internal evidence indicates that the tapestry was produced for Bishop Odo of Bayeux... It is now generally accepted that it was made in England... probably in Kent, of which Odo was earl.[70]

Lingard had reached these conclusions some two centuries earlier, in an account which is still the best survey of the evidence on the subject.

The Casket Letters (1567)

A famous 'mystery' in English historiography has always existed around the subject of the 'Casket Letters'. The subject relates to the uncovering by the Elizabethan Government in 1567 of eight letters between Mary Queen of Scots [PLATE 23] and the Earl of Bothwell in a silver casket belonging to Bothwell. Bothwell was the instigator of the plan to murder Darnley, Mary's husband, and he later married the widowed Mary. The letters were used by the English Government at the York-Westminster Conference (1568-9) to incriminate Mary in the murder of Darnley. They seemed to prove that she had been involved in the murder plot.

In English historiography there was a long tradition, initiated in the sixteenth century, of viewing English history through the eyes of the English Government.[71] The bias had always been to glorify Elizabeth I at the expense of Mary Queen of Scots; and to justify the later execution of Mary in 1587, at the hands of the Elizabethan Government. The casket letters were regularly used to prove Mary's guilt in Darnley's murder and so to blacken her character. This was the line taken before Lingard by his predecessors such as William Tytler (1711-92) in his *Inquiry concerning Mary Queen of Scots*; William Robertson in his detailed *History of Scotland during the Reigns of Queen Mary and James the Sixth* (1759); David Hume in his famous and very popular *History of England* (1754-61); and Malcolm Laing in his *History of Scotland* (1800-1804).

Lingard exposed the 'copies' of the Casket Letters for the first time in the historiography of the subject, to *a rigorous, detailed critique, based on external and internal evidence*. The originals had 'disappeared' in 1584. But in fact, as Lingard notes, Mary and her advisers had been denied any sight of the originals from the beginning, even though Mary had specifically asked to see them.[72]

Lingard observes, *from internal evidence*, that the letters mention only Bothwell and Mary herself. They so carefully exclude any reference to Maitland and Morton, who are known to have been involved: 'as if they

The Application of Source Criticism

had been written by the murderers themselves'. Indeed the names of these two men are not mentioned at all, until *after* the Conference of 1567–8: 'All this wears the appearance of fraud'.[73]

Secondly, when first introduced the casket seems to have contained only the letters. Additional material (a sequence of 'sonnets' and two contracts of Mary's later marriage to Bothwell) appeared only when the evidence was laid before the English commissioners. Lingard asks: 'How came the contracts and sonnets to be then suppressed, if they existed at all?'[74]

Thirdly, the letters had initially been described as 'written and *subscribed*' by Mary. Later this was altered to '"written halelie" (wholly) with her own hand'. The word 'subscribed' is omitted and the word 'halelie' (wholly) added. Lingard comments: 'This alteration furnishes another ground of suspicion'.[75]

Fourthly, there is, says Lingard, '*a strong chronological contradiction*'. He explains:

> The two first letters are said to have been written on the 23rd and 24th of January, and to have been answered from Edinburgh by Bothwell on the 24th and 25th. The last answer was written by him after dinner. Now, if we believe Murray's diary, Bothwell left Edinburgh to go into Liddlesdale on the night of the 24th, and returned only on the 28th. Here is evidently a contradiction.[76]

Fifthly, *based on external evidence*:

> Mary is represented as writing two of the letters, one on a very trifling subject, on the two nights that she remained at the house of Kirk-o'field. This almost exceeds belief. Bothwell had just left her; he was gone no further than his lodgings in Holyrood House; he would be in her company in the morning; and yet the queen, instead of retiring to rest, sits up to write to him letters of no consequence, and sends a servant after midnight to awaken him out of his sleep, and deliver them into his hands.[77]

Sixthly: 'If Mary wrote the letters at all, it would be in the French'. We know, however, that the extant letters are 'translations'. This is because the original letters were translated into Latin, and then translated again back into the present French copies: 'There is little probability, therefore, that the original French letters will ever be laid before the public.' Only one – the least important – has been discovered in the State Paper Office. The others have disappeared. Mary herself instructed her advisers:

> In case they allege they have any writings of mine, which may infer presumption against me in this case, you shall desire the principals (originals) to be produced, and that I myself have inspection thereof, and make answer

thereto. For ye shall affirm in my name, I neve writ any thing concerning that matter to any creature; and, if any such writings be, they are false and feigned, forged and invented by themselves, only to my dishonour and slander . . .[78]

Lingard's conclusion is that:

For my own part I have little doubt that the letters were for the most part written by Mary. But, in this hypothesis, two questions will arise, to which her adversaries will not be able to give satisfactory answers. 1. To whom were they written? Those in the casket were exhibited without any address. For aught we know, they might be written to different persons. Two of them appear to me to have been letters sent by her long before to Darnley. 2. Were they originally written, as they afterwards appeared? It was easy to collect several of the queen's letters, to omit some passages, alter others, insert hints here and there, and by describing them as written to Bothwell, and on particular occasions, to give to them a character of criminality, which they did not originally possess. This appears to me to have been the meaning of the queen's lords in their instructions, September 12, 1568, where they say, that 'in the writings produced in parliament there was no plain mention made, by which her highness might be convicted, albeit it were her own hand writ, *as it was not*; and also the same was culled by themselves in some principal and substantious clauses . . .[79] [Lingard's italics]

Lingard adds that the one original copy discovered in the State Paper Office:

is one of the least important, No. IV., but much more intelligible than any of the translations, and of a nature to make us regret the loss of the others.[80]

Again the present state of scholarship of this matter, at the beginning of the twenty-first century, has been taken no further than Lingard's account, and arrives at the same conclusion. In 1997, Dr. R. A. Mason summarized the issue of the 'Casket letters':

The authenticity of the material cannot now be certainly established . . . However, surviving copies suggest that, while not outright forgeries, the material was clumsily doctored by Mary's opponents at the York-Westminster conference in 1568–69.[81]

We know that Lingard's view on forgery was rather different. To him, any document which had been interfered with for a deliberate attempt to deceive was just as much a forgery as a completely forged document.[82]

The Trial of Edmund Campion (1581) – the Issues Involved

Lingard broke new ground in his treatment of the reign of Elizabeth I because he refused to look at matters simply from the viewpoint of the Queen and her Government, which had been the standpoint of English historians from the sixteenth century up to the end of the twentieth century. Moreover, he refused to take up the conventional mode of looking at history backwards and making judgements about sixteenth-century history in the light of later happenings. Rather, he placed himself in the position of the actual participants at the time; for they were obviously the products of their own past, rather than the future.

A final example of Lingard's willingness to challenge the Elizabeth Government's official version of events in the second half of the sixteenth century is concerned with his treatment of Cecil, Lord Burghley's *The Execution of Justice in England for maintenance of public and Christian peace against certeine stirrers of sedition* (1583) [see PLATE 6]. Cecil's was the classic statement of Government propaganda: that the persecution of Catholics and priests in particular was a necessary defence of the State against political traitors. His book was the real source of the line taken by historians writing in England up to and including the twentieth century. Lord Burghley's interpretation of the Catholic persecution has been one of the most enduring pieces of sixteenth-century Government propaganda. Historians such as A. F. Pollard (*History of England from the Accession of Edward VI to the Death of Elizabeth, 1547–1603*, 1910); E. Conyers Read, *Mr. Secretary Walsingham and the policy of Queen Elizabeth*, 1925); J. B. Black (*The Reign of Elizabeth*, 1936); J. E. Neale (*Queen Elizabeth*, 1953) and *Elizabeth I and her Parliaments*, 1953); and A. L. Rowse (*The England of Elizabeth*, 1950), all took Cecil, lord Burghley's framework of thought for granted and proceeded from there. In other words, English historians have taken the viewpoint of the Elizabethan Government and seen things through its eyes, because it was this viewpoint which seemed to be leading to the future.[83] That view was one of the most unthinkingly-accepted of the old legacies of whig historiography.

Lingard was the first historian writing in England who looked critically at the propaganda element of Government policy. *He changed the viewing mechanism, so to speak. He was looking at the scene in Elizabethan England from the truly historical perspective of what had gone before, rather than what came afterwards.* It had been an essential part of the mind-set of all English people for more than a thousand years, that they, as Catholics, owed political allegiance to their monarch and spiritual allegiance to the Pope. The greatest revolution in English history occurred when the Henrician and Elizabethan Governments set out to change this mind-set and replace it with a completely new way of looking at things. The new way was to make all English people understand that they now owed total loyalty and allegiance, in things spiritual as well as political, to one authority – the English monarch. Anyone who contracted out of this undertaking was a traitor, fully or potentially. The campaign was to become so successful that eventually English people no longer understood how anything different could have been the case; and this, of course, was the new assumption of thought which underpinned the writing of later English historians, looking back at this period.

But this fundamental change in the way people thought had not been accomplished until well into Elizabeth's reign. The Government campaign of propaganda and persecution, meant to achieve this end, reached its peak with the trial of the Jesuit missionary priest Edmund Campion in 1581. As with the earlier trial of Thomas More in 1535, the Campion trial crystallized in dramatic fashion the clash between the major points of difference involved in the changing assumptions of thought between the old and the new.

Edmund Campion [PLATE 26] and twelve other priests were tried for treason in 1581. Their mission had been simply to serve the pastoral needs of Catholics in England. They were not interested in politics. Lingard quotes Campion, speaking in his own defence, at his trial:

> The self-same articles ... were required of me by the commissioners, but I was much more urged to the point of supremacy [the Act of Supremacy], and to further supposals, than I could think of. I said, indeed, they were bloody questions, and very pharisaical, undermining my life; whereunto I answered as Christ did to the dilemma; Give unto Caesar that is due to Caesar, and to God that to God belongeth! I acknowledge her majesty both *de facto et de jure* to be queen. I confessed an obedience due to the crown, as to my temporal head and primate. This I said then, this I say now. If, then, I failed in aught, I am now ready to supply it. What would you more? I willingly pay to her majesty which is hers; yet I must pay to God what is His. Then, as for excommunicating her majesty, it was exacted of me, admitting that excommunication were of effect, and that the pope had sufficient authority so to do, whether then I thought myself discharged of my allegiance or no? I said this was a dangerous question, and they demanded this demanded my blood. But I never admitted any such matter; neither ought I to be wrested with any such suppositions. What then say they, because I would not answer flatly to that I could not, forsooth I sought corners; mine answers were aloof. Well, since once more it must needs be answered, I say generally, that these matters be merely spiritual points of doctrine, and disputable in the schools; no part of mine indictment, not to be given in evidence and unfit to be discussed at the King's Bench. To conclude, they are no matters of fact; they be not in the trial of the country; the jury ought not to take notice of them; for although I doubt not but they

The application of Source Criticism

are very discreet men, and trained up in great use and experience of controversies and debates, pertinent to their callings, yet they are laymen, they are unfit judges to decide so deep a question.[84]

Lingard points out that by this statement in court, Campion

contradicts the account published by government; that when he was asked 'whether he did, at that present, acknowledge her majesty to be a true and lawful queen, or a pretended queen, and deprived, and in possession of the crown only *de facto*, he answered that question depended on the fact of Pius V., whereof he was not judge, and therefore refused further to answer'.[85]

And secondly, that it

shows that the real question between the government and the prisoners was not that they denied the queen's right, and strove to withdraw her subjects from their allegiance . . . but whether, in certain hypothetical cases, the pope possessed the power to depose princes.[86]

The defendants declared that

whatsoever might be pretended, their religion was their only offence; and, in proof of the assertion, remarked that liberty had been previously offered to each individual among them, provided he would conform to the established church.[87]

Lingard concludes that

The report of their trial must convince every reasonable man of their innocence. Campian, with his usual ability and eloquence, vindicated the missionaries from the charge of disloyalty, and showed that not an atom of evidence had been adduced to connect himself and his companions with any attempt against the life or the safety of the queen. But the public mind had been prepared to believe in the existence of the conspiracy by a succession of arrests, sermons and proclamations; the absence of proof was amply supplied by the invectives, the conjectures and the declamations of the lawyers for the crown; and the jury, after an hour's deliberation, returned a verdict of guilty against all the prisoners.[88]

He adds that, *from external evidence*:

Even their principal accuser afterwards vindicated their innocence, and, in excuse for his own falsehood, alleged the terror that seized him when he was led to the foot of the rack and saw himself surrounded with the instruments of torture.[89]

Lingard supplies all the evidence, including letters written later by the informer, Nichols, to show that the latter had been enlisted as an agent by the Government. He was not, however,

The Application of Source Criticism

> produced at the trial ... soon afterwards he recalled his charges against the missionaries, and crossed the sea to France ... and confessed that all he had said or done proceeded from fear of the rack.[90]

In 1997 a modern scholar, Dr. A. S. Hargreaves, summed up the state of modern scholarship on the question of Campion's trial:

> Captured at Lyford (Berks.) through a servant's treachery, and taken to the Tower, his refusal to recant led to torture on the rack, but he remained steadfast. Trumped-up charges of conspiracy to overthrow the queen, and an unjustly conducted prosecution, brought conviction of treason and hanging at Tyburn.

And in 2001, F. Edwards comments on the 'morass of the mid-1580's':

> the plots of those years, like those of the Ridolfi season, do not stand up to close scrutiny as bona fide plots engineered by papists or sympathisers.[91]

The *Eikon Basilike* (1649)

As a final example of Lingard's critical approach to historical materials in his treatment of certain famous or infamous subjects, we may take the case of the *Eikon Basilike* [PLATE 27, and p. 195], or *The Portraiture of his Sacred Majesty in his Solitude and Sufferings*. This book was supposedly written by Charles I, containing his private religious and political meditations during the time leading up to his execution in 1649.

It quickly became a best-seller, setting up the image of Charles as a martyr for Kingship and the Anglican cause. It has been described recently as 'arguably the most influential new book in 17th-century English politics'.[92] Nearly fifty editions were called for within a year. However, after the Restoration of the monarchy in 1660, a Dr. Gauden, who had been chaplain to Charles I, came forward privately to claim the authorship. The new Government procured his silence by conferring on him the bishopric of Exeter; and later, the richer bishopric of Worcester. After Gaudon's death, his claim became known and led to much controversy between Gauden's friends and the admirers of Charles I.

In Lingard's day, a certain Dr. Wordsworth had published a four-hundred page book entitled: *Who Wrote Eikon Basilike?* in which, in Lingard's words, he had:

> collected with patient industry every particle of evidence which can bear upon the subject; and after a most minute and laborious investigation, has concluded by adjudging the work to the king, and pronouncing the bishop an impudent imposter.[93]

The *Eikon Basilike* (1649). See the caption to PLATE 27 for full details of the 'King's Book' on 'Royal Image', which purported to be Charles's own devotions and meditations on religion and politics before his death.

Nevertheless Lingard disagreed. He said that in spite of Dr. Wordsworth's extraordinary industry and detailed work: 'My incredulity is not subdued.'[94]

Once again, by applying his rules of source criticism, Lingard is able to see 'the wood for the trees'. Firstly *there is the* EVIDENCE OF ORIGINAL AND AUTHENTIC SOURCES. Lingard refers to the letters of Gauden himself, written to the earl of Clarendon and published in the *Clarendon papers*; and other letters from him to the earl of Bristol. *Clarendon, in particular, was in a position to know and to acknowledge the truth*. Lingard remarks:

> These letters have so firmly established Gauden's claim, that, whoever denied it must be prepared to pronounce that prelate an imposter, to believe that bishops Morley and Duppa gave false evidence in his favour, and to explain how it happened, that those, the most interested to maintain the right of the king, namely Charles II, his brother the duke of York, and the two earls of Clarendon and Bristol, yielded to the deception.[95]

Here, again, we find Lingard's rule of STRESSING THE GREATER AUTHORITY OF EVIDENCE GIVEN BY PEOPLE WHO HAD NO INTEREST WHATSOEVER IN ACCEPTING THE FACTS, *if they were not true. On the contrary, they were people – the king's supporters – who would have denied them if they could have done so.*

Secondly, Lingard looks critically at *the 'internal' evidence*:

> There is much in the Eikon Basilike itself which forbids me to believe that Charles was the real author, though the latter, whoever he were, may have occasionally consulted and copied the royal papers.[96]

Lingard finally concludes that:

> the claim of Gauden appears too firmly established to be shaken by the imperfect and conjectural improbabilities which have hitherto been produced against it.[97]

And in 1995 the present state of scholarship on this subject has been summarized succinctly by MacCulloch with the statement that the *Eikon Basilike*: 'was supposedly written by Charles' but was in fact 'probably mostly composed by his chaplain John Gauden'.[98]

In all these examples one sees the application of those techniques of source criticism described in previous chapters. These techniques are applied to different sets and types of sources, so as to evaluate and prioritize, in a way which finally leads to a clear judgement on the subject in hand. In these cases and in many others, Lingard was challenging the accepted view of his predecessors and contemporaries. He came to a historical judgement which anticipates the present state of scholarship after another two centuries of progress in the accumulation of source materials and the development of modern research facilities in our universities and institutes. It is not clear to me that any modern historian, with all the added advantages of modern developments, has improved on, or even equalled, Lingard's techniques of source criticism; or emulated the extraordinary level of reliability which he reached in his historical judgements and interpretations; and all this while bearing in mind that modern historians usually specialize in comparatively narrow periods of history. Lingard achieved this level of scholarship in his work over the whole history of England up to 1688–9, making important and innovative contributions in detailed analysis and in re-shaping our understanding of whole sections of our history in all its different periods. Lingard's achievement is unparalleled.

Apart from the application of 'scientific' source criticism to his materials for the first time in English historical writing, I became aware during my research on Lingard of quite another element discernible in his work. His historical antennae – his intuitive skills – came into play, to 'sense', as it were, that there was something wrong with a document or with its interpretation; that things in it did not feel right. Here we enter, I think, the area of intuitive judgement which is discernible in the work of the very best exponents of any profession. It is based partly on human experience, common sense, profound knowledge of human nature and professional insight – together with a higher level quality which we might call wisdom.

Chapter IX
Lingard's Place in English Historiography

> 'By any objective measure, Lingard's achievement was colossal.'
> Norman Davies

John Lingard [PLATE 10] has been hardly known in England. The present volume has the ambitious aim, therefore, of demonstrating objectively that there are strong grounds for regarding him as the greatest English historian of the second millennium.

Lingard was the first English historian to consciously and persistently base his work on original sources. He stated his aim:

> My object is truth; and in the pursuit of truth I have made it a religious duty to consult the original historians [sources]. Who would draw from the troubled stream, when he may drink at the fountain head.[1]

He not only said this. He actually did it. His approach was new to English historiography. It enabled him to cut through centuries of repetitive writing in history and to look at the whole in a completely new light. No other English historian has ever attempted to write the whole *History of England* from original materials. Secondly, Lingard was the first English historian to consciously oppose the anglo-centric approach adopted by all previous English historians and all his successors up to the end of the twentieth century. He considered it the historian's duty:

> to contrast foreign with native authorities, to hold the balance between them with an equal hand, and, forgetting that he is an Englishman, to judge impartially as a citizen of the world.[2]

Lingard was possibly the best-equipped of all English historians in his knowledge of European languages. He was proficient in Latin, Greek, Hebrew, Anglo-Saxon, French, Italian and Spanish; he also knew some German, which he started to learn in the 1830s. His determination to write as a 'citizen of the world' was an astonishing breakthrough in historical thinking in England. Moreover, he put what he preached into practice. His method was not really taken up again by historians writing about England until the last decade or so of the twentieth century. Historians of today are still struggling with its implications. Lingard sought in continental archives for original materials which would place English history in a wider European perspective. He achieved insights and perspectives 150 years ago – as, for example, in his treatment of the medieval period, the Reformation and the 'Glorious Revolution' of 1688–9 – which anticipated 'new' findings by the 'revisionist' school of historians in the late twentieth century. The whole of English history was reshaped within this new perspective.

Thirdly, the whole of his work was based on a substructure of informed and scientific source criticism, the like of which had never been seen in England before and was never to be repeated on the scale with which Lingard applied it. In the last analysis, it was this foundation that made Lingard's work so remarkably durable and extraordinarily unscathed by the advances of modern scholarship.

Advances in technical history and source criticism were taking place on the European continent during Lingard's time, particularly in Germany. The conventional view has been that no such advances took place in England, though Lord Acton had interested himself in the latter part of the nineteenth century in what was happening on the Continent. Sir Herbert Butterfield – the outstanding name in the history of historiography in England in the twentieth century – still accepted this conventional view in his *Man On His Past* (1955). Butterfield's book was the published version of his Wiles lectures, given at Queen's University Belfast, in November 1954. This view has lasted until now, because there was no ostensible published reason for thinking differently.

Nobody in England has known that there existed an English historian well suited to stand with the greatest of the Continentals in the field of scientific historiography. Lingard, like Bede nearly a millennium before him, lived in comparative isolation, but both had minds which ranged far and wide across European scholarship. Lingard sought information from the archives of France, Italy (including Rome and the Vatican), Spain, Malta, Portugal and Germany, long before these archives had been opened to foreign scholars. The full story of Lingard's Continental work has yet to be published, though there is a general survey of it in *The English Nation*.[3]

Lingard's scientific source criticism has had to be 'unearthed' by detailed research. It was a matter of getting behind the deceptively simple form of his narrative, couched in the classical style, to the substructure of scientific source criticism which underlies it. The unique significance of his contribution to British and European historiography has not been properly understood until now. Like Bede's work so long before, Lingard's scholarship has an important place in the story of European as well as British historiography.

Lingard can also be said to have produced, for the first time, the conditions necessary for the advancement of historical writing as an independent discipline, with its own identifiable requirements in terms of personal qualities, technical aptitude and abilities. He broke the mould of English historical writing within which historians regarded history as a branch of philosophy or 'high literature'. Long before anyone else in England, he established the ground rules for the modern study of history as it exists in the research departments of our modern universities.

* * *

Lingard's 'colossal achievement' was huge in size as well as quality. If a modern professional historian, through research, manages to produce a new insight into one part of one period of English history, his or her achievement is rightly highly praised in academic circles – as was the work of Sir J. E. Neale, for example, in *The Elizabethan House of Commons* (1949), or of Sir G. R. Elton in the *The Tudor Revolution in Government* (1953). Lingard's methods of research on original materials and his new insights, however, informed his work, in ten large volumes, on the whole history of England from the coming of the Romans up to 1688. His *History* was not the kind of valuable survey often written by modern historians, based mainly on the research work of others, but informed by personal insights and judgements. Lingard relied on his own special research throughout, working on all the available printed original sources, and seeking manuscript evidence at home and abroad, long before Ranke in Germany realized that the latter constituted essential evidence.

The combination of detailed research, carried out over the whole sweep of English history, combined two elements which are usually regarded as essential to the status of a 'great' historian. Lingard's detailed scholarship was impeccable; and he was able at the same time to cover a large theme, moving continuously over a significant historical time-span of nearly two millennia. He achieved this by using a style which, in its economy of language and clarity of expression, could be regarded now as a classical example of the best vehicle of meaning for the writing of history.[4]

So why has Lingard not been appreciated until now?

The power and national popularity of the 'Great Myth' of the English past,[4] built up over four centuries, was so great and so influential in informing English attitudes, that any deviation from it could not be properly accepted by the English academic or cultural Establishment. Lord Macaulay, perhaps the most influential English historian of the nineteenth century, wrote dismissively at the time that Lingard's 'great fundamental rule of judging seems to be that the popular opinion cannot possibly be correct';[5] and two other contemporary historians, Henry Hallam and Thomas Keightley combined to spurn Lingard's critical reappraisal of the past, with the confident remark that 'we must abandon all faith in public fame if it is really unfounded'.[6]

The assumptions of thought about the English past remained largely invulnerable as long as the English nation seemed to be ruling the world – when the British Empire covered so much of the earth, and when England's wealth and power was unparalleled. It seems that it was not until these conditions changed – as they did by the end of the twentieth century – that it was possible for a voice like Lingard's to be heard properly and his message taken seriously; but by then his work had been forgotten. Only in 1999 was it possible for a major English historian to write that 'By any objective measure, Lingard's achievement was colossal'.[7] I doubt very much whether it would have been possible to publish my own work, entitled *The English Nation: The Great Myth* (1999), at the time – in the 1950s – when most of the original research was done. I recognize now that it needed the changed political conditions of the last fifty years of the twentieth century, as well as the persistent advances in scholarship over this time,[8] to have made my main conclusions sufficiently acceptable to be taken seriously.

Similarly, it is only now in 2001 that the present study of Lingard's unprecedented technical scholarship in terms of source criticism could be published, although the main research and conclusions were completed in 1956. It needed the critical acclaim given to the chapter on Lingard in *The English Nation: The Great Myth* (1st edition, 1999),[9] for the claims made for him in the present volume to be taken sufficiently seriously to be considered. It also required, of course, a sufficiently open-minded publisher.

I believe that the present study provides the final evidence needed to establish objectively for Lingard the status of the greatest historian of England in the second millennium. His creation, in isolation, of the critical rules of scientific source criticism on which he based his account of the English past was an unparalleled as well as unacknowledged achievement in English historiography. It represented the greatest advance forward in historical writing since the Venerable Bede's *Historia Ecclesiastica Gentis Amylorum* in 731. It was certainly the power base for his *History*, and alongside his other extraordinary achievements, I see no other English historian to rival him.

There is no mystery now about the fact that the few historians who had 'dipped' into Lingard's work for one reason or another have commented on his uncanny reliability in his statement of facts, judgements and interpretations. The Cambridge scholar A. W. Ward wrote in 1916:

> there has never been a more vigilant recorder of the facts than Lingard, or one whom criticism was less successful in convicting of unfounded statements.[10]

I know of no other historian of whom it could have been said by a later fellow historian and keen critic of people's weaknesses, that Lingard 'has never been found wrong' (Lord Acton).[11] I also know of no other historian who has anticipated in such detail and over such a wide area, the radically advanced work of 'revisionist' historians, a century and a half later. It is Lingard's technical scholarship, completed at a time when the modern convention has been to attribute such an achievement only to continental scholars such as Ranke in Germany, which finally clinches the argument about Lingard's status.

The preceding chapters have shown that Lingard's view of historical writing was one that brought it into the modern world of professional scholarship – where the historian is seen as pursuing an independent discipline with its own rules of inquiry. David Hume, whose *History of England* (1754–62) was the dominant force in English historiography for a century, regarded history very much as a branch of philosophy.[12] Lord Macaulay, whose *History of England* (1849–61) superseded Hume's work as the most popular influence for the next century, saw history as a branch of fine literature.[13] F. W. Maitland, whose greatest works were *The History of English Law before the Time of Edward I* (1895) and *Domesday Book and Beyond* (1897), was the next English historian after Lingard to regard history as an independent discipline with its own rules of procedure;[14] and Maitland, consequently, is now regarded as 'arguably the greatest of all historians of medieval England'.[15] But Maitland's work was written nearly eighty years after Lingard's *History of England* and was concerned with only one aspect – the legal and constitutional – of one period (the medieval) of English history.

We now usually evaluate the work of historians, according to the standards of their own times. Because Lingard achieved 'modern' standards of source criticism in his own day, other historians of that period, such as Macaulay, can now be judged properly against these standards. Indeed Lingard himself judged the value of the work of his contemporaries against them.

In Lingard's eyes, Macaulay [PLATE 13] was not a proper historian at all; and others, too, fell below the required standard of historical scholarship. These verdicts are to be found in Lingard's private correspondence. He writes not from any sense of animosity, but simply states as a matter of fact that they have no idea of source criticism or the proper use of sources. He writes to a critic who wanted him to include some of Hume's stories about Oliver Cromwell: 'I will give Hume's stories about Ol. Cromwell, if I find any authority for them.'[16] Then, towards the end of his life, he writes to a friend concerning Macaulay's *History* which was just appearing: 'It will not do. Macaulay does not write history';[17] and again, in 1850, a year before his death, Lingard, now aged seventy-nine, writes:

> His [Macaulay's] account of Charles [Charles II's] sunday before his death is, I remember, beautiful. Of the kings company and trifling on such a day he tells many stories, not one of which is established on any authority, though not one of them is absolutely improbable....[18]

When the *Rambler* journal praised Macaulay's use of sources, Lingard wrote to his friend, Walker, in 1849:

> Did the *Rambler* ever examine and weigh these authorities? Does he know anything of them besides the names at the foot of the page. I can tell him that generally among them is one or two that are not deserving of the least notice, mere libels published on broad sheets, as was the custom then, and now mentioned as authority, because he had no other for something that he has introduced into his own narrative.[19]

When Sir Charles Firth wrote his *A Commentary on Macaulay's History of England* (1983), he made precisely the same criticism of Macaulay's work:

> He does not weigh the value of the evidence he employs with sufficient care, if he is judged by the standard of today.[20]

Another modern admirer of Macaulay, Sir Hugh Trevor-Roper, calls him 'unquestionably the greatest of the whig historians', but has to concede that 'a great gulf separated Macaulay from the new German pioneers of historical method and criticism'.[21] We can now add that Macaulay was severely lacking in this respect, even when judged by the best standards which had been established already in England in his own day. Nevertheless Macaulay's *History* has still been regarded throughout the twentieth century as a 'great' historical work. It was as late as 1997 that P. Ghosh published a scholarly article which stated for the first time since Lingard, that Macaulay's enduring status could no longer rest on his work as a historian, but must reside in his undoubted brilliance as an essayist.[22]

Lingard also expressed his private views on other contemporary historians, measuring them against the high criteria which he had set himself. He writes confidentially in a letter to a friend, concerning Miss Agnes Strickland who wrote the *Lives of the Queens of England*:

> The greatest of Miss Strickland's peccadilos is that she cares not for authority. Any anecdote which will please the readers has sufficient authority for her. She gives it as an indisputed fact.[23]

Then there is an interesting letter concerning Robert Southey's *Book of the Church* (1824):

> I have hastily looked through Mr. Southey's 'Church' and think it will add little to his reputation as a historian. It has plainly been written for a purpose to please the high-church party: it was therefore unnecessary to be at the trouble of much research: he has consulted party writers before him, and selected from them what he thought would be most pleasing to those whose approbation he sought. He may talk of having sufficient authority for his statements in his collections: but I suspect that, had he given these authorities, they would have proved to be not original documents, but statements made by persons heated with controversy, and stimulated by prejudice. In his reigns of Henry, Edward and Mary he has done little more than make a compendium of Fox, and has related without the least semblance of a doubt as to their accuracy the hearsay stories collected by that writer.[24]

The above estimate of Southey's book has been confirmed by a modern authority.[25]

Concerning a contemporary *Life of Augustine*, written by a High-church Anglican, repeating the old legend of an early British Church, established directly from the East by one of the early apostles, Lingard writes to a friend in 1844:

> I have been reading the life of St. Augustine by the Puseyite – very pretty, very imaginative, and very fabulous. He gives us every fable about St. Peter, St. Paul, Aristobulus &c &c in Britain. His canon is not you are to prove the facts, but to believe them, if they are not disproved.[26]

Interestingly, Lingard did make a public statement, indirectly, about Thomas Carlyle (1795–1881), who produced an edition of Cromwell's letters and speeches in 1845. In his 'Preliminary Notice' to the last edition of *History*, Lingard notes: 'these documents are well worth the serious attention of the historical student'. But he is careful to add:

> I mean the letters and speeches themselves, not the running commentary with which the editor has accompanied them, in language most glowing and oracular. In every edition of this work [his own *History*] I have allotted to Cromwell that share of praise which I thought, and still think, his due, – a much larger share than he has received from many other writers; but I feel no disposition to fall down before the idol, and worship him at the command of his panegyrist.[27]

Carlyle, a much admired and brilliant essayist and writer, was fascinated with German history and culture. He is now regarded as a man who, in such celebrated works and 'brilliant imaginative accounts'[28] as his *French Revolution* (1837), the edition of *Oliver Cromwell's Letters and Speeches* (1845) and the huge tome on *Frederick the Great* (1858–65), did in fact come to 'worship' the 'heroes' of extraordinary strength who could provide the answer to all society's ills.[29] Indeed Sir John Seeley, who later

(1869–95) 'deserves every credit for rescuing history as a discipline at Cambridge',[30] remarked of Macaulay and Carlyle, that they both 'may be expected to be remembered some day as representing an extraordinary aberration in the English mind, an extraordinary misconception of the nature of history'.[31] Lingard, working in isolation, had obviously come to the same conclusion much earlier.

It is obvious, then, that Lingard was well aware of the absence of true historical scholarship in the English historiography of his own time. Yet he never engaged in heated controversy. He simply expressed his views about contemporary historians, with the one exception of Carlyle, in private letters to his friends. Nevertheless his judgements are extraordinarily accurate in every respect, as we can now see clearly after a century and a half of advancing scholarship.

Moreover, we can now also see that every one of the particular historical interpretations about which he himself was criticized by his contemporaries such as Macaulay and Henry Hallam, has been decided in Lingard's favour in the light of the most recent scholarship.[32] Lingard himself was always satisfied to leave matters to the future. 'Time and experience must decide between us',[33] seems to have been his answer to all attacks.

Lingard's qualities, like those of most modern historians, are not so obvious or so immediately attractive as the 'high-literature' skills of Macaulay and Carlyle. The latter have an immediate appeal to the senses. Macaulay stated his intention to write history in order to 'produce something which shall for a few days supersede the latest fashionable novel on the tables of young ladies'[34] and he was highly successful in this. Lingard, on the contrary, needs to be studied closely. His work demands an intellectual response. He is always the professional craftsman rather than the entertaining artist, because he believed historical writing to be about the pursuit of historical truth.

Lingard provides an interesting subject for the modern student. He appears as one who was 'born before his time'. His work was not properly understood or appreciated by his own generation, nor indeed by succeeding generations, until the present day. No historian now reads Gibbon, Hume, Macaulay or Carlyle in order to discover the truth about the periods to which they devoted their historical work; though they might indeed survive as books to be read in courses of English literature or culture. Scholarship, in the modern sense, was not their domain. Lingard, however, could be included on any university list of required reading, not only for his enduring level of scholarly excellence, but as a role model for all aspiring young historians in the use of source criticism and other basic tools of the profession.

The lack of a close study of Lingard's mastery of the techniques of source criticism, together with the fact that he was not telling people what they wanted to hear in England in the nineteenth and most of the twentieth centuries, has meant that he has remained in comparative obscurity in England until now. He lacked the popular appeal of more celebrated literary exponents of historical writing who wrote in a brilliant literary style and represented, by and large, the thinking and the assumptions of thought of their own day. The prestige of Hume, Macaulay, Gibbon and Carlyle was immense during the last three centuries. Indeed it was the very brilliance of their literary style which was one factor in the survival of the 'Great Myth' of the English past.

Lingard was more widely acclaimed and honoured on the international scene – on the European Continent and in the United States – than in Britain. His *History* was translated into French in 1826; and the University of Paris, by an Arrête Special, ordered that a copy be made available in every college library in France, and copies be given as prizes to students. He was proposed, together with Ranke, as a foreign member of the French Academy in 1838. The *History* was translated into Italian in 1826; and it was very popular in the Vatican, where both Pius VII and Leo XII esteemed Lingard highly. Pope Pius VII conferred the unusually high honour of a triple doctorate on him. It was widely held that Pope Leo XII had Lingard in mind when he announced the creation of a cardinal *in petto* (not yet publicly announced) to

> a man of great talents and scholarship, whose writings drawn from the original sources, *ex nativis fontibus*, had delighted Europe.[35]

But Lingard made it plain that he would not want it, because it would take him away from Hornby and his work. Rather amusingly, he wrote to his publisher that 'such an appointment in the present circumstances would be very inexpedient' and he was relieved that the Pope seemed 'aware of the impropriety of interfering with my literary engagements'.[36]

In 1827 the *History* was translated into German. The universities of Munich and Berlin, together with the celebrated historian Dr. Döllinger, acclaimed it. The last edition was published in Boston in 1851, and the American journals greeted it warmly. For example, the *Eclectic Magazine* of New York wrote:

> too much praise cannot be awarded it ... unquestionably, the very best, ... the most impartial ... fullest, and the completest history of England.

While the New York *International Monthly* described Lingard as 'one of the most distinguished historians of the time'.[37]

The conclusion from this study is that Lingard is certainly one of the most important and significant figures in the history of historical writing in England. Indeed, from the premiss that historical writing is an independent discipline, concerned essentially with discovering and expressing the truth about what happened in the past, I would say that there are two 'great' historians who stand as 'sign-posts' in the history of English historiography. One is the Venerable Bede. His *Ecclesiastical History of the English People* (731) belongs, as we have seen, 'to the small class of books which transcend all but the most fundamental conditions of time and place'; and 'in regard to all the normal substance of history his work can be judged as strictly as any historical writing of any time'. The Preface to this great work 'reads like the introduction to a modern work of scholarship'; in short, 'he had reached the conception of history'[38]. There was a huge gap of over a millennium before another English historian appeared, of whose *History of England*, the self-same comments could be made. It is hardly too much, then, to claim for John Lingard, the title of the 'greatest' English historian of the second millennium, as Bede was of the first.

Epilogue:
'Hic caestus artemque repono'

Lingard died peacefully at the Presbytery in Hornby, where he had lived and worked for forty years and of which he once said, 'here, everything, every place is endeared to me'. He died at the age of eighty, on 17 July 1851 and was buried at Ushaw College where he had lived and taught as a young man. Having completed his final edition of his great work in 1849, he wrote, concluding the Preface:

> a long and painful malady, joined with the infirmities of age ... has admonished me to bid a final adieu to those studies with which I have been so long familiar ... I now take my leave of the public, and – to borrow the words of the retiring veteran in Virgil–
>
> *'Hic caestus artemque repono'*
>
> (Here I lay down the tools of my profession)

A close friend describes this last edition as the last literary effort of 'his great and powerful mind', though he survived another two years:

> suffering intensely from an accumulation of maladies; but always cheerful, always resigned, always manifesting that vigour of intellect, that playfulness of thought, that kind, considerate, gentle disposition, which had endeared him through life to all who had possessed the happiness of his acquaintance.[1]

Another friend writes, three weeks before his death, saying that Lingard's mind was still 'alive to a joke' and he seems to have retained his good humour to the end.[2]

* * *

I visited Hornby in September 2001. After a long journey from South Wales, I stayed at the *Royal Kings Arms Hotel* in Lancaster, one of those enchantingly ancient English cities with Roman and Saxon as well as medieval ancestry and remains. Lancaster takes its name from the Roman camp (*castrum*) situated on the river Lune at this point. The following day

Epilogue: 'Hic Caestus Artemque Repono'

after visiting the attractive, parkland campus of Lancaster University (for a conference on Lingard), I set out along the lovely valley of the river Lune which rises among the fells of the Pennines and flows down through Lancaster to the Irish Sea. Hornby lies in this valley, about eight miles from Lancaster, and it was here that I came to my destination.

I visited the old presbytery with other members of the North-West Catholic History Society, by kind invitation of Canon Nicholas McArdle, the present occupant. I first went to visit the small chapel which Lingard had built himself, with money derived from the sale of his *History*. The remainder of this money was given to provide bursaries for students to attend Ushaw College. The chapel formed the focal point for Catholic worship in the village. I walked in the spacious garden and looked at the oak tree, planted by Lingard, and at the long pathway winding down to a stream which runs into the Lune. He loved to walk along here as a daily routine, a path on which he said his 'office' (the daily prayers which all priests have to say). I had a leisurely look around the fine old presbytery, built by the generosity of Mrs. Anne Fenwick in 1762, examining the books, and other personal possessions of Lingard which are maintained in a room now designated as a kind of Lingardian 'museum'. I looked with special interest at the quill which Lingard had last used for his work; comparison with the easy advantages of my own word-processor made me wonder even more at his achievements. The whole ethos of the village, the church and the house is still very peaceful. I felt almost as if I had taken a step back in time.

Lastly I called into the Anglican church across the road, where Lingard's friend, 'Mr. Proctor' served. There on the wall was a tablet to commemorate Lingard the Catholic priest, set up by his Anglican friends, I wondered if there was another example of this anywhere. It had the final line:

'Quis desiderio sit – Modus tam caro capitis?'

(What limits should be set to grief, for so dearly esteemed a person?)

My experience at Hornby confirmed a new aspect of Lingard which I discovered recently. It was not only in the field of historical writing that he was creative in breaking new ground. As a parish priest in this small village, he anticipated very modern developments in the world-wide Catholic Church, which we associate now with the Second Vatican Council (1962–5). His views on liturgical reform (including more active participation by the laity);[3] on Catholic relationships with the non-Catholic world; on the rights and status of general councils, of bishops, priests and laity, of governments and of non-Catholics[4] – indeed of all human beings. All these ideas had to wait for full and explicit expression over a hundred years later in the dynamic documents of Vatican II.[5]

Epilogue: '*Hic caestus artemque repono*'

As Thomas More had represented in his thinking the 'development'[6] of the Church itself in the new world of the Renaissance, so did John Lingard (and Cardinal Newman, later) herald the next great stage of 'development' in the Church of the new Millennium. In my mind Lingard stands alongside Thomas More (PLATE 4) and Cardinal Newman as the outstanding Catholic thinkers in England in the last four centuries. These individuals made, in their different fields, seminal contributions to the development of the universal Church as well as to the life and values of English culture.

I said my farewell and thanks to Canon McArdle for his gracious welcome and left Hornby, setting out for Lancaster and the M6 motorway which I could not help visualizing as two steps back into the more clamorous nature of the modern world. Among my reflections as I motored down the Lune valley was the hope that I could get my book published in time to commemorate the 150th anniversary of the death of someone of such stature, and to give him the recognition which he deserves as a great Englishman who was also a great 'citizen of the world'.[7] This would not, I think, matter much to him; but is very important for us, as we find our way in the new world of this third millennium, seeking guidance, if we are wise, from the best minds and values of the past.

APPENDIX I

The Development of Lingard's History *through the Various Editions*

The first edition of Lingard's *History* appeared between 1819 and 1830. Five editions were published during his lifetime but there were only two major revisions of the work. These occurred in the fourth edition (1837–8) and the last edition (1849).

I conducted a detailed survey of the ways in which the *History* developed through the editions. I used Lingard's volume on the reign of Elizabeth I as the main period of detailed study for an examination of the way in which the increasing availability of original sources during the intervening periods affected his *History*; and also of the way in which the *History* developed in its style of presentation during these years.

Immediately apparent is the change in 'audience-reaction' between the editions. The first edition was awaited with great suspicion and unease by its English audience. It was published at the start of the decade leading to Catholic emancipation (1829) which was regarded by many as a grave threat to Church and State in England. It provoked some immediate responses, such as Southey's *Book of the Church* (1824), Soames' *History of the Reformation* (1826) and Turner's *History of England* (1829), together with a great deal of opposing pamphlet literature.

The high feelings of that decade diminished somewhat after 1830, with the recognition of the accomplished fact of Catholic emancipation. Also, it is fair to say that the balanced scholarship and calm tone of Lingard's *History* had helped to reduce fears and anxiety. In his first edition of the *History*, for example, Lingard mentioned that the Catholics were still being unjustly accused of starting the Great Fire of London in 1666. This charge, he demonstrated, was without any foundation and 'no vestige of proof could ever be discovered'.[1] It simply exemplified the scaremongering which accompanied anti-Catholic prejudice. Yet though the charge could not stand even in its own day, the false accusation had been left for all to see. Lingard wrote in his first edition:

Appendix 1

> Subsequently . . . on the Monument erected to perpetuate this calamitous event, it was, and long stood, recorded, that 'The burning of this Protestant city was begun and carried on by the treachery and malice of the popish faction, in order to the effecting of their horrid plot for the extirpating of the Protestant religion and English liberties and to introduce popery and heresy.'[2]

In the later editions of the *History*, Lingard adds an interesting comment:

> Since, however, the first publication of this work, the passage mentioned in the text, with the following line in the Latin inscription: 'Sed furor papisticus, qui tam dira patravit, nondum restinguitur' – was erased, by order of the city on 6th Dec. 1830'.[3]

Lingard's last two volumes of his first edition, covering the period 1660–89 had appeared earlier in that same year (1830).

Lingard himself was becoming more confident. In a letter to Edmund Price, editor of *Dolman*'s magazine, in 1847, he says:

> I see that you quote my Quarto edition. I am sorry. that was the first edition. I had then to acquire credit among Protestants, & was therefore extremely cautious – & I believe in that respect, successful . . . this made me much bolder in the 12vo. edition, in which I introduced much respecting the penal laws, which I had withheld in the former.[4]

It is certainly true that Lingard's *History* contains much more material in the later editions. In the first place, he spent a great deal of time making sure that he was acquainted with all the publications of original materials which appeared in between the editions of his own work. He also continued his researches far and wide in the pursuit of original materials in England and abroad, which were still in manuscript form. All relevant materials were used to strengthen and sometimes to change his text in the light of new knowledge. When we consider that he was doing all this for the whole of English history, from the coming of the Romans up to 1689, we can visualize the immensity of the task which he set himself.

The picture which emerges is that of a perfectionist who had given himself a life's task of first writing the *History* and then spending the next thirty years making sure that it was made as accurate and reliable as possible, in the light of increasing knowledge from new original materials.

The attempt to eradicate error was a constant preoccupation of Lingard, as it emerges from his correspondence. In 1826 he writes to his friend, Tierney:

> That numerous errors must occur in a voluminous work like mine is evident,

& I shall always feel grateful to any of my friends, who may point them out, that they may be correct in a future edition.[5]

In 1830, he writes to another friend, Husenbeth:

> I am going to review the whole of my historical work, and to make such correction etc. as I may think proper. Should you have remarked any errors, I shall esteem it a favour, if you would mark them out to me.[6]

In 1839, just after the publication of the final volumes of his fourth edition, he writes to Tate:

> Your friend is correct about the blunder . . . It is of importance and must be corrected in an erratum at the end of the last volume and in the plate itself for copies that may be taken off hereafter.[7]

Preparing for his final edition, he writes to Walker in 1846: 'If you are acquainted with any errata, errors etc. . . . let me know.'[8] Criticisms are invited and in two letters to Walker in 1845 we find: 'Thanks for your criticisms, I shall adopt some of them';[9] and 'A thousand thanks to you for your criticisms'.[10]

Apart from any errors that might creep into the manuscript itself, there were all the other possibilities of error arising from slips happening between the writing of the work and its publication. There are various instances recorded in the correspondence of printer's errors,[11] especially in the matter of dates, the accuracy of which was so important to Lingard. He writes in 1849, in his own 78th year, to Walker:

> I am equally convinced with you of the value of dates, and frequently base my narrative upon them. Yet of nothing is so little reliance to be placed in a printed book. More mistakes are made in them by the printers than in anything else, and such mistakes most frequently escape detection. I am aware that there are many such mistakes in the new edition. I have however, cursorily mentioned it.[12]

He refers in one letter to the time taken up by correcting printer's errors.[13] Even after the printing stage things are not perfectly safe, for there are still the hazards of the binder and we hear in the correspondence of 'a blunder of the binder'.[14] Lingard's concern about all this is sufficiently apparent. He writes in 1849:

> Now all my anxiety is about this. I greatly fear some mistake about the insertion of alterations in their proper places, & think that the safest way would be to send me a revise of it.[15]

APPENDIX I

There is a letter of Lingard, written a year before his death, in which we find an amusing reaction towards the publication of his last edition. It is another remarkable example of Lingard's striving for scholarly perfection to the very end:

> A very box arrived including my ten vols. of the new edition, with a note stating that they were the first copy sent out. On examination two things occurred to enrage me. Some body had changed the spelling of cestus in the preface... I wrote a warm letter to Dolman [publisher], and spent two days (they are short now) running from house to house borrowing dictionaries and Virgils to see if any good authority could be found for the spelling of caestus – The first day I found none: all had cestus – the second I found that Adams in his dictionary of high repute in the high school in Edinburgh spells it caestus. This pacified me: as I found that I could allege his authority in my defence. Yesterday Dolman told me that he had been to the printing office, to inquire the reason: that the foreman shewd him the Delphine and another edition, which they keep there to consult and Aynsworths Dictionary – all of which have caestus – and therefore thinking it probable that I had made a mistake, he took it upon himself to change it...

Then, concerning a second mistake, Lingard proceeds:

> All I have now time to say is that I ordered the text to be changed, and on looking for it in the new edition found that no notice had been taken of the correction. I wrote to Dolman. His answer pacified me. He will do all he can now. In the copies already sent out, it is too late: but in those still to be sent out he will cancel a leaf at the end of the vol, or the last volume – and reprint afresh its contents with the addition of the correction, stating that it had been omitted by mistake. This will do.[16]

The garguantan task of reading all the findings of new and original scholarship covering the whole history of England, is a major theme in Lingard's life. He writes to Tate in 1835 while preparing his fourth edition:

> My employment therefore is at present to read over the whole of the work and to make corrections as I proceed. And a laborious task it is; for since I began to write the different parliamentary commissions have published above one hundred vols: of the deeds, letters, charters &c. These also I have to read, sometimes for hours together without meeting with anything of moment.[17]

He is too busy about this period, with his revision, even to wish to be interrupted by a visit from the famous German scholar, Dr. Döllinger, who had been highly impressed with Lingard's *History*.[18] Again, preparing for his last edition, he writes in 1846:

APPENDIX I

> I am seriously employed in preparing for my new edition. To be ready if anything new turns up respecting St. Thos. of Canterbury, I have got Dr. Giles's new publication of all the lives of him written at the time, and of the letters... I have also received from Tierney the late vols. of the archaeologia to see if there be anything new there. Also other books.[19]

Lingard is equally zealous in his pursuit of any new manuscript sources in between editions. Preparing for his treatment of Elizabeth's reign for the fourth edition, for example, Lingard writes:

> I, of course desirous to make this, the last edition that I shall ever see [sic], as perfect as possible, am employed in revising the whole of it. I am now in the reign of Elizabeth, and could therefore wish to know what was the result of Mr. Leigh's mind after the research which he made in London, and the comparison there of his documents with others. I could also wish to know whether he would be willing to allow me the inspection of his documents, or copies of them, or at least would inform me on what points they may contradict any part of my statement.[20]

These letters in the possession of Mr. Leigh related to the Babington Plot (1586) and threw much new light on the part played by Walsingham and his agents during this episode. They included letters belonging to Cecil, Lord Burghley and letters written by some of Walsingham's agents, which are used in the fourth edition of Lingard's *History*. He recognizes his use of them:

> I should state that for my acquaintance with this letter, and with several others which follow, I am indebted to the kindness of Will. Leigh, esq. who with extraordinary zeal and research has made a large collection of valuable and inedited [unpublished] documents, illustrative of the secret history of this transaction.[21]

There are other endless examples of Lingard's pursuit of any new materials – published or manuscript – which became available between the various editions of his *History*.[22]

Finally, the Lingard correspondence throws valuable light on the personality behind the evolving *History* – an aspect of the scholarly pursuit of truth which should never be neglected. It is in the letters of the later period, the 1840s, that we see vividly portrayed the struggle of a great scholar fighting to retain his powers of critical acumen and rigorous scholarship in the face of advancing age and infirmity [PLATE 11]. Lingard's eyesight was beginning to fail in 1840, and he writes in his 'matter of fact' manner:

> one of them, the right, is evidently growing more and more clouded every day, & the best I can do is to take care of the other one.[22]

Appendix 1

He writes in 1840: 'But my memory grows very treacherous with respect to papers';[24] and in 1844: 'My memory is so treacherous that I may be mistaken . . .',[25] as he tries to remember from where he had obtained certain information.

We must not forget either his pastoral and religious duties, which always come first for the parish priest. In 1847, Lingard writes to Mrs. Lomax in a letter which reveals much of the daily life routine – his daily contact with the timeless quality of the spiritual life, his daily attention to the basic and practical needs of his own and other people's lives, and his sense of humour with it all:

> You suppose me occupied with the revision of my history. Not so. I cannot get more than two or three half hours in a week. My office [the daily Mass and private period of prayer required of the priest], sick calls [attending to his sick and dying parishioners] (I have more lately than ever before), my own maladies, the newspapers, letters and calls from people popping in and not popping out again, and blindness in the evening hardly leaves me any time.[26]

I am convinced that many of his great qualities as historian stemmed from this constant contact with the ultimate realities of life around him. He did not live in an 'ivory tower' of an academic or any other sort.

By 1849, things are getting worse

> I feel that I am worked out. The brain has been taxed too severely. One hour's application is now followed by exhaustion during the rest of the day.

Adding a typically humorous shaft directed at himself:

> if the application last for an hour; for frequently before half of the hour is over I find myself asleep & am fully aware that if I write in such a state my readers will soon be asleep too.[27]

Lingard suffered in old age from an extremely painful enlarged prostate. Modern historians have modern medicine as well as modern historical resources, for which to be thankful. Old age is, in a special sense, a precious time for historians. For this is a time when (hopefully!) they can reflect on the past with that experience and knowledge of life which are essential ingredients in the making of more balanced historical judgements and interpretations of the human condition in times past as well as present. Lingard spent the last decade of his life, bringing all these powers to bear on a final revision of his great *History* – knowing that this would be his last. His fight against pain and illness, without any of the helps which modern medicine can offer, becomes even more impressive and inspiring in these circumstances. What never failed him up to the last, was

Appendix 1

the balance of mind and sense of humour which were, again, so much part of his character as a man as well, inevitably, as a historian. They are indeed personal qualities without which it would be impossible to achieve real greatness.

In the Summer of 1848, he writes to a friend:

> In great pain, less blood than yesterday . . . My doctor is to come every evening and operate, to sleep here, operate again in the morning and go back. Addio.[28]

Again, in 1849, we hear: 'The moment I sit down to study and compose, that moment I fall asleep'.[29] There are little incidental and poignant comments:

> Who was Grant of Rome? – I cannot conceive – I have had a second fall on the floor, by slipping off my chair. A bump on the hip: that is all. But I am so liable to fall I must take care of my poor brain. There, it is time for letters to go to post.[30]

He good-humouredly chides a friend who has been suggesting further work for him:

> Now, My Dear Fellow, for you, in your turn. I am inclined to be angry with you. You seem to think that I have all along been telling you lies about my ailments. You cut out for me as much, as if I were still fervidus juvente, Consule Planco. I can assure you that it is no easy matter to write history or prefaces, when you are 79 years old, every moment feeling acute pain, or thinking how you may prevent it or mitigate it the next moment, without memory, or hardly any other faculty in working order, and in a state both of decrepitude and lassitude. Last week I was very ill indeed and lost a great part of it.[31]

In a letter of the same year, 1849, he writes:

> Thus my days go. This is now gone. I am no longer fit for anything. This is the third letter of the day. You talk as if I had several hours every day. I give as much as I can to study: but some thirty years hence you will find that in your best hours pain, and the apprehension of pain, and the thought of contriving against pain & other things of that kind, will leave you but few minutes in wh. [sic] you will be fit for composition. On saturday I sent my first chapter of the reign of James to the printer. I have lengthened it so, that instead of two I shall have three chapters, and have been obliged to transfer the end of the first about Scotland and Ireland to the beginning of [sic] second chapter this morning: but I have not time. I was rather unfortunate this morning in drawing the water out of the bladder: and have been continually reminded of it by pain, and continually contriving in thought, how to

APPENDIX I

do better about 12 o clock. How think you am I to undertake a new work, such as a review of Mac: [Macaulay] in these circumstances.
Well: never mind. We must do as well as we can.
Thine in aevum
For ever and for aye . . .[32]

Incredibly, the 1840s was a period of great activity for Lingard. His last, fifth edition, of the *History* was published in 1849; he had worked astonishingly hard, making a thorough revision of it, keeping abreast with all the new original materials which had appeared since the previous edition. Taking the year 1848 – he was now seventy-eight – we find him writing in February, with his inevitable humour breaking through:

> I am busy: for I have had a visit from the devil – Don't start – I mean the printer's devil. He wants copy. They have run me down; but I have sent him a shillings worth of copy by post, and must get ready as quickly as I can a shillings worth more.[33]

In August, he writes:

> I have just received notice to send the 10th vol. of the small edition to the printer, before the end of the week. I have therefore scarcely a moment to write in.[34]

And in October, we hear:

> They have lately worked me like a coach here, requiring from me almost three vols. by Christmas. I have attended so to that business that I am quite bewildered.[35]

Even as late as 1850 we find him chasing around eagerly to correct errors in the final edition.[36]

It is only when seen against these difficulties of old age [PLATE 11] and his medical condition that we can fully appreciate the personal qualities of courage, determination, perseverance and good humour in Lingard which made such a scale of revision possible. Greatness is never simply a matter of fine scholarship and historical acumen.

Turning now to the *History* itself, a detailed examination of the different editions shows immediately the extent of substantial development in the light of new and original materials which had become available. Indeed, as we have seen,[37] Lingard's prefaces are written very much in the manner

Appendix 1

of a modern professional historian, listing the new and important sources which have become available since the last edition. This has an immediate effect on the text itself. Interestingly, for example, Lingard himself, on a very few occasions, had been obliged to follow previous writers when there had been no original materials available. He was eager on these occasions to admit his mistakes in detail and rewrite in the light of these original materials now that they were available. On the subject of diplomatic proceedings in Rome at the time of Elizabeth's accession, for example, Lingard in his first and fourth editions, had written:

> Carne, the resident ambassador at Rome, was ordered to acquaint the pontiff that she [Elizabeth] had succeeded to her sister, and had determined to offer no violence to the consciences of her subjects, whatever might be their religious creed.

It had been maintained consistently in English historiography that the Pope had ignored Elizabeth's proffer of friendship at this stage. Lingard had written:

> It was the misfortune of Pope Paul, who had passed his 80th year, that he adopted opinions with credulity, and maintained them with the pertinacity of old age. His ear had been preoccupied with the diligence of the French ambassador who suggested that to admit the succession of Elizabeth would ...[38]

All this was changed in the last edition:

> The whole of this narrative is undoubtedly a fiction, invented, it is probable, by the enemies of the pontiff, to throw on him the blame of the subsequent rupture between England and Rome. Carne was, indeed, still in that city; but his commission had expired at the death of Mary; he could make no official communication without instructions from the new sovereign. According to the ordinary course, he ought to have been revoked, or accredited again to the pontiff. But no more notice was taken of him by the ministers, than they could have done had they been ignorant of his existence. The only information which he obtained of English transactions was derived from the reports of the day. Wearied with the anomalous and painful situation in which he stood, he most earnestly requested to be recalled, and at last succeeded in his request, but not till more than three months after the queen had ascended the throne. It is plain that Carne made no notification to [Pope] Paul; and if any one else had been employed for that purpose, some trace of his appointment and his name might be discovered in our national or in foreign documents and historians.[39]

Lingard's explains this narrative change in the footnote:

APPENDIX I

> In former editions I followed the stream of writers on this subject; the researches of the late Mr. Howard of Corby Castle have convinced me that all are in error. This appears from Carne's letter of Decemb. 31 to Cecil (State Paper Office, Bundle no. 4, Rome and Italian states); and an original letter in Cotton MS. Nero, B. vi. p. 9. His letter of recall was dated Feb. 9, and received by him March 10. The same appears also from a Mandamus to Carne from the cardinal secretary of state enclosed in the last letter, stating that huc usque Carne had no appointment but from Queen Mary.[40]

Again, in the last edition, Lingard changes his account of an episode in Anglo-Scottish history. In 1572 the English Government had sent Killegrew 'to procure the death of the Scottish queen by the hands of her own subjects'.[41] Lingard had written that 'the regent Marr was not a character to pander to the jealousies or resentments of the English queen';[42] but recent research had convinced him otherwise. In the sixth edition of 1849 he writes:

> Recent discoveries have, however, proved that, if at the first he [Earl of Marr] affected to look upon the project as attended with difficulty and peril, he afterwards entered into it most cordially, and sought to drive a profitable bargain with Elizabeth . . . he required that she should take the young James under protection . . . that an English army of two or three thousand men should conduct the captive queen across the borders . . . that the arrears of pay due to the Scottish forces should be discharged by the queen of England. On these terms he was willing to engage that Mary Stuart should not live four hours after she should arrive in Scotland.[43]

A footnote explains:

> These particulars have been discovered by Mr. Tytler in the official correspondence, partly in the State Paper Office, and partly in the British Museum – Tytler, vii. 313, 384. It appears to me that the queen's consent to this project was extorted from her by the representations of Burghley and Leicester. She was plainly ashamed of it. She told them and Killegrew, that, as they were the only persons privy to it, if it ever became known, they should answer for having betrayed the secret.[44]

Another example, revealing Lingard's scrupulous respect for the exact truth, is an instance when Lingard had described secret but overheard conversations in the Tower between Garnet and Oldcorne, who had been imprisoned after the Gunpowder Plot (1605). Lingard tells us in a footnote to the last edition:

> In former editions I stated, on the authority of Gerard and Greenway, that Garnet to a question from Oldcorne, replied . . . If he ever used these words,

Appendix 1

it must have been in the first meeting, the report of which is lost. There is no mention of them in the reports of the other four published by Mr. Jardine.[45]

The reference here is to Jardine's *Criminal Trials* (1845) which included many original materials published for the first time. Lingard's information from Gerard and Greenway was contained in his original manuscript accounts, sent to him from the Jesuit archives.[46]

Again, having given several examples in earlier editions to show that medieval instruments issued in the king's name, 'teste rege', from the high court of Chancery, did not mean that the King himself was in that place at that particular time, Lingard adds in a footnote to the last edition:

> In former editions I referred to another instance from the reign of Richard II. But Mr. Duffus Hardy (Introduc. to Close Rolls, xv) has shown that Rymer, on whose authority I relied, had mistaken the real date.[47]

By the nature of things, three centuries of domination by Protestant writers meant that most headway in terms of scholarly advance would now favour a Catholic interpretation of many episodes; but Lingard also applied his critical techniques to episodes where this was not the case. A final example of this type of development is when Lingard is seen to be determinedly unwilling to allow any abuse of historical truth, even when it would have supported his own theological position. Indeed, he brought the complete battery of his rules of source criticism to bear on the issue detailed below, as he would have done on any matter of historical truth.

In his last edition, Lingard gave a much fuller treatment of the transfer of ecclesiastical authority from the Catholic episcopacy to the Anglican, in 1559 at the accession of Elizabeth. The sixteen Catholic bishops from Mary's reign all refused to take the oath to the new act of Supremacy, making Elizabeth head of the Church. A story arose that the new bench of Anglican bishops had 'derived its existence from the mummery said to have been practised at the Nag's Head a nearby tavern, by the jocular Bishop Scorey'.[48] Lingard roundly refutes this scandalous story, pointing out the official registration of the new archbishop's appointment in the *Archbishop's Register*, supported by a document from the State Paper Office and:

> another in a contemporary hand (often supposed to be the original notarial instrument from which the entry was made in the register), still in the library of Corpus Christi College, Cambridge, to which it was left a legacy, with other papers by the archbishop Matthew Parker himself. A facsimile of this instrument was published by the Cambridge Antiquarian Society in 1841.

Appendix 1

The proponents of the 'Nag's Head' story claimed that this document was not authentic, claiming it to be a forgery. Lingard replies:

> But there was nothing to countenance such a supposition. The most experienced eye could not discover in the entry itself, or the form of the characters, or the colour of the ink, the slightest vestige of imposture.[49]

Also, if *external confirmation* were wanting:

> there was the archbishop's diary or journal, a parchment roll, in which he had been accustomed to enter the principal events of his life, and in which, under the date of the 17th of December, ann 1559, is found – Consecratus sum in archiepiscopum Cantuarien'; and:

Another confirmation, to which no objection can be reasonably opposed, occurs in the Zurich letters, in which we find Sampson informing Peter Martyr on the 6th of January 1560, that Dr. Parker had been consecrated archbishop of Canterbury during the preceding month.[50]

Here we see Lingard bringing all his critical powers of source criticism, with regard to the *authenticity* and the *authority* of a source, to show that Parker did actually receive a form of consecration in 1559 as the new archbishop.

Similarly Lingard deals with the controversy as to whether William Barlow – one of the four consecrating bishops from the reigns of Henry VIII and Edward VI – had ever in fact been consecrated himself:

> Now it happened most vexatiously that no record of his [Barlow's] consecration was known to exist. Though searches were repeatedly made in every likely repository, no trace of it could be found, nor I believe, has any allusion or reference to it been discovered to the present day in any ancient writer or document. Still the absence of proof is no proof of non-consecration. No man has ever disputed the consecration of Gardiner of Winchester; yet he was made bishop whilst on a mission abroad, and his consecration is involved in as much darkness as that of Barlow. When, therefore, we find Barlow during ten years, the remainder of Henry's reign, constantly associated as a brother with the other consecrated bishops, discharging with them all the duties, both spiritual and secular, of a consecrated bishop, summoned equally with them to parliament and convocation, taking his seat among them according to his seniority, and voting on all subjects as one of them, it seems most unreasonable to suppose, without direct proof, that he had never received the sacred rite, without which, according to the laws of both church and state, he could not have become a member of the episcopal body.[51]

Here is Lingard, this time using the qualities of reason and common sense

Appendix 1

– also important elements in source criticism – to refute those who argued that Parker had never gone through a form of consecration; and this, though Lingard believed for other reasons,[52] that the transfer of spiritual authority from the Marian episcopate to Elizabethan, was invalid.

In the later editions of the *History* there is another form of development, indicating Lingard's more confident approach. He introduces comment and general observations to clothe what had been a bare statement of facts in the previous editions. For example, in the later editions, we find Lingard being more confident and expansive enough to make the general observation:

> It has been the uniform practice, wherever the Reformation penetrated, to reward the services of its lay abettors out of the possessions of the church.[53]

Again, when narrating the religious conflicts in Scotland and the treatment of Mary Queen of Scots by the Elizabethan Government at the Treaty of Edinburgh (1560), Lingard felt able in the fourth edition of the *History*, to observe:

> The right of intervention, even in its most liberal acceptance, can never authorise one prince to intrigue clandestinely with the subjects of another, and to induce them, by the offer of assistance, to rebel against their sovereign at a time when he has bound himself by oath to live in perfect amity with that sovereign, and to refuse any kind of aid, secretly or openly, to his enemies.[54]

There are in fact several such observations made in the later editions about the 'utter contempt' of Elizabeth and her Government for 'the maxims and forms' of justice, both in the workings of the English courts and in the realm of international politics.[55]

The *History* also develops through the various editions in maturity of workmanship. We find numerous examples of a fuller and more literary presentation of something that was short and abrupt in an earlier edition, a replacement of short, 'snappy' phrases by a more continuous narrative.[56] Much of this fuller presentation derives of course from the addition of new source materials. There are, however, also illustrations added to confirm previous statements in earlier editions;[57] qualifications added to statements that were previously unqualified;[58] and statements which are considered at greater length than they were hitherto.[59]

We see, too, the attempt to draw together strings which had been left hanging loose in previous editions – unanswered questions and gaps in knowledge are remedied,[60] and precise and clear statements replace what had previously been vague and imprecise.[61] There are instances of critical evaluations added in later editions to sources and statements made earlier.[62] We have examples of footnotes being built up through the three editions as new source material becomes available;[63] and additional explanatory comments in the notes.[64]

A greater emphasis is sometimes given in later editions to points already made previously;[65] and sometimes people merely mentioned previously become much more substantial figures in later editions. The character of Gifford, for example, a leading Government agent in the web of intrigue surrounding the Babington Plot, becomes much more substantial in the later editions – bringing out the type of character (usually a lapsed or disaffected or ambitious Catholic), coming from a certain background, which the Government was fond of using as agents or 'agents provocateur' in Elizabeth's reign. They are usually people who disappear quickly from the scene of English history – sometimes slipping away to the Continent – as soon as their role is completed.[66] There are innumerable instances of new references being added to those used in previous editions, taken from the new original sources which had become available in manuscript or print form.

To illustrate the way in which new materials from foreign archives were incorporated in the later editions, it will be useful to take a few examples. Before 1830 the archives abroad were completely closed to English scholars, though Lingard had managed to get information, as we have seen, by indirect ways and unusual procedures.[67] After 1830, however, there began to appear, sporadically, some publications or archival papers by men who were in control of foreign archives. Lingard eagerly sought and made use of any such publications, which were used in his later editions. In 1832 there appeared the *Apuntamiantos para la historia de Felipe II . . . y la reina l'Inglaterra*, collected and published by Don Tomás González, the official in charge at the Spanish State Archives at Simancas. González had already helped Lingard's 'agents' to get information unofficially, which had been used to good effect in Lingard's first edition of his volume on Elizabeth's reign, in 1823. The publication of the *Apuntamiantos* in 1832 enabled Lingard to reinforce and sometimes revise his earlier, 'unofficial' use of the Simancas documents in his own later editions of his *History*.[68]

The publication of the French and Spanish despatches and the *Lettres de Marie* formed the basis of much of the additional material in Lingard's last edition of the history of Elizabeth's reign. So, for example, the seizure of the Spanish treasure fleet in 1568 is given 245 words in the 1823 edition, 342 in the 1839 edition, and 834 in the last edition. The seizure was a powerful act of aggression, threatening the life blood of the Spanish king's empire in Europe. The money from the colonies was needed to finance the government of Philip's widespread European kingdoms. The covert English support of the opposition to Philip in the Netherlands and

Appendix 1

to the French monarchy in France were also acts of aggression. An additional footnote in the fourth edition tells us:

> From the despatches of the French and Spanish ambassadors, it appears that they made innumerable complaints to the queen [Elizabeth] of the aid given to the insurgents in France and the Netherlands. Sometimes she had recourse to evasions; sometimes she justified her conduct by fairly alleging the supposed league for the extirpation of protestantism. But when she was called for proof of the existence of such a league, she could only conjecture ... They assured her that it was a fiction, devised and employed to alarm her, and her protestant subjects. See Fénelon...[69]

Again, the account of the Babington Plot and the various manoeuvres of Walsingham and his agents to entrap Mary Queen of Scots and cause her downfall and execution in 1587, increases from 1,570 words in the fourth edition to 2,250 in the last.

When the Spanish Armada eventually set sail against England in 1588, Lingard was able to give the first balanced account of the event in English historiography, using Spanish documents from Simancas as well as English sources. Lingard allows himself a personal note of admiration for 'that contempt of danger and that spirit of enterprise which had long been characteristic of the British sailor' and in the final outcome 'the Spaniards had learned to respect the courage and power of their enemy'.[70] He also recorded the fact of the important part played by English Catholics in the war against Spain[71] in an expression of loyalty and allegiance to their own country in political matters.

In all my extremely detailed examinations of Lingard's use of sources, I found just two possible lapses on his part from the extremely high standard of scholarship which he had set himself. Neither is a clear-cut case. Each is surrounded with some sense of mystery (recalling Marc Bloch's remark about the appearance and disappearance of archival documents[72]) and each is connected with Lingard's use of the Simancas documents. He generally used the information from Spain very carefully, wherever possible in conjunction with other authoritative documents.[73]

The first matter represents, in any case, only Lingard's stated 'suspicion' as he quite fairly put it, which he quickly withdrew in the next edition of his *History*. In 1569 Philip II suddenly insisted that Elizabeth should recall her ambassador, Mann, from Spain and replace him. Lingard asked his friends, Cameron and Sherburne at the seminary in Valladolid, to try to find out from the archives what lay behind this event. Cameron visited the Archives and wrote back to say that the Elizabethan

Appendix 1

'cabinet' had tried, through Mann, to engage Don Carlos, Philip's disaffected son, to assassinate his father. Sherburne, however, having visited Simancas himself, had questioned the circumstances: 'This fact does not appear in the archives.'[74] What seems clear from the Simancas correspondence is that Cameron did not see the documents himself, but was given information by: 'The Gentleman in whose custody they are,' who

> declined entering into further details because any communication of the kind is strictly prohibited, and for the same reason he cannot give a copy of the extracts he has made.[75]

Sherburne then took a 'ride westwards' and did better: 'I . . . have *read a great part of* the extracts from the original documents'. He could not find the evidence on Don Carlos; but then he had not read all the extracts.

Very unusually, Lingard, he expressed a 'suspicion' in a footnote to his first edition (1823):

> I suspect there was another and more important reason for the recall of Mann. It was at the time of the incarceration of the unfortunate Don Carlos, the son of Philip, whose real history will not be known till the Spanish government shall have allowed the publication of the records in Simancas. From them it will appear, that the prince was charged not only with a design to murder his father, but also with having entered in to a treasonable negociation [sic] with the English cabinet. In such circumstances it will not appear surprising, if Mann became an object of jealousy to Philip.[76]

But when in 1832 González published his collection of Simancas documents and again there was no evidence to substantiate it, Lingard abandoned his earlier 'suspicion' and replaced the earlier footnote, with another in his next edition:

> according to González, he [Mann] had called the king [Philip] a papist and hypocrite, had foretold the triumph of the insurgents in the Netherlands and had suffered his servants to behave with disrespect in a church at the elevation of the host – Memorias, 328. Philip complained of him to Elizabeth (April 6) as 'no ambassador, but a pertubator of the peace'. She recalled him in June.[77]

Lingard previously had expressed a 'suspicion' which the evidence before him – taken as a whole – did not warrant. The custodian in the archives had said the evidence was there. Lingard believed that it would be found. He did not pretend that there was evidence for it, only that he suspected it. Also, we know that there was a history of materials being lost from these archives, ever since they had been moved to Paris in 1812 and returned again after Napoleon lost Spain in 1813; nor was this the end of

Appendix 1

it.⁷⁸ Nevertheless, for Lingard, writing of his 'suspicion' was surprising. He was not used to having even his 'suspicions' uncorroborated.

The second case of a fall from perfection in Lingard's scholarship is again to do with the Simancas archives, that in the first edition of 1823, Lingard wrote that he had

> joined much important information from the archives of Simancas in Spain, where Philip II deposited all the dispatches which he received from his ambassadors in the different courts of Christendom.

And that from this, and other sources, he had:

> derived much information . . . which in a great measure has hitherto been withheld from the knowledge of the English reader of history.⁷⁹

In fact we now know that the two agents generally conveyed the meaning of the documents which they actually saw and copied, correctly – as can be demonstrated by comparing their work with the same materials published officially later in the century.⁸⁰

In 1823 Sherburne reported from Simancas that one despatch, from the ambassador Quadra to Philip II in 1561, stated that:

> so current is the rumour that Eliz. *lives* with Robert Dudley, that in one of the audiences which I had of the Queen she took upon herself to treat on this matter with me, & showed me la disposicion de su camera y alcoba.⁸¹

An account of the above despatch was also given later by Tomás González in his later publication, *Apuntamientos para la historia* de Felipe II . . . *y la reina d'Anglaterra* (1832), which was used by Lingard in his fourth edition. But the document has never appeared since. We are reminded that Conyers Read, a modern bibliographer, warns us that González's publication 'contains notes and transcripts of dispatches now lost';⁸² and there is other evidence of information which Lingard received from Simancas, but which never appeared again in official publications of the Simancas documents in Spain.⁸³

There ensues a mystery which may never be solved. In a letter of 1823, Cameron told Lingard that there existed at Simancas certain correspondence between Philip II and Elizabeth's 'Camerera Mayor' [private maid of the bed-chamber] who 'communicated the secrets of the court to him, & among other things Eliz.'s criminal intrigues with the Earl of Leicester (called in the corresp: Lord Robert)'.⁸⁴ And if this correspondence was ever published 'it will show the virgin queen in her true colours'.⁸⁵ Cameron had obviously not been able to see the correspondence because he was not able to give the maid's name:

Appendix 1

> The Camerera mayor I take to be the first lady of honor, her name is in the correspondence, but they did not tell it me because they did not know how to pronounce it.[86]

Sherburne then went to Simancas to try to discover her name, but he, too, failed.[87]

Lingard was still pursuing these letters in 1832, in preparation for his next edition, but no trace of them could be found. The agent, Sherburne, concluded that they might have been lost when sections of the Simancas archives had been removed to Paris by Napoleon's order. Was this correspondence the invention of an over-fertile imagination in the mind of a Simancas official; or, were the letters lost, leaving only a memory of their contents in the minds of people who had seen them years before?

Lingard mentions in an appendix to his last edition, information from the Simancas documents, giving the detailed story of Arthur Dudley, who later claimed that he was the child of Elizabeth and Dudley. The document was later published in 1899 in the *Calendar of State Papers: Simancas IV. Elizabeth 1587–1603*;[88] but no mention of the evidence of the 'Camerera mayor' has appeared among the Simancas papers.

Lingard's fault was to mention, as part of a footnote, the existence at Simancas of 'several letters from an English lady ... describing in strong colours the dissolute manners of Elizabeth and her court',[89] by which he presumably meant the letters of the above-mentioned 'Camerera mayor'. Here again, be seems on the face of it to have fallen from his usually impeccable standards of scholarship. These letters, as we have seen, were never published from Simancas.

It seems, however, that Lingard's instinct – that such evidence existed – was right after all. For in 2000 David Starkey produced the most recent account of Elizabeth[90] and gives evidence from a Catherine Ashley, 'chief gentlewoman of her [Elizabeth's] privy chamber, her most intimate personal attendant' – surely the aforementioned 'Camerera mayor' – that 'something serious was afoot' between Elizabeth and Dudley. The chief gentlewoman had previously given evidence against the loose behaviour of the princess Elizabeth with her uncle Thomas Seymour.[91] On this much later occasion, after Elizabeth had become queen, the same senior Lady, responsible for the care of Elizabeth, had become hysterical and remonstrated strongly with Elizabeth about the damage to her reputation, being caused by her flagrant behaviour with Robert Dudley, Earl of Leicester in 1561.

Starkey, an admirer of Elizabeth and her achievements, tells us that as a girl princess she had been abused by her uncle, Thomas Seymour. He suggests that from then on she had possibly become a 'sort of abuser' in turn. All her chosen suitors resembled Seymour and all of them were finally abandoned.[92] We also know from Starkey that the 'Camerera

Appendix 1

Mayor', Lady Catherine Ashley, had been holding the same position of responsibility for the personal care of Elizabeth during the reign of Mary Tudor and would have had the opportunity of getting to know her husband, Philip of Spain. It was to Philip that her letters concerning Elizabeth's misdemeanours were sent, according to Lingard's information from Spain.

As Marc Bloch reminded us,[93] there are often intriguing reasons behind the appearance and disappearance of documents in and from archives. Archives often have a fascinating story of their own to tell. Sometimes, however, they remain obdurately silent.

Perhaps Sherburne, Lingard's agent in Spain, had the last word on this particular subject, when he wrote to Lingard in 1832, recalling his conversation with Don Tomás González, who had worked in the archives at Simancas from at least 1815 after the confusion caused by 'the depradation of the French invader, subsequent neglect, and the partial return of the papers which followed the peace'.[94] Sherburne wrote:

> When I visited Simancas I recollect Dn Tomás saying 'that bundel has furnished my materials, pointing to the papers on a particular shelf'. This was in 1823. When the extracts [for Don Tomás's published collection in 1832] were made I know not, but about 1812 king Joseph [Napoleon's brother, made King of Spain by Napoleon in 1808] ordered most of the papers to France, and altho' they were retaken at Vittoria [sic: at Vitoria, 1813, Wellington defeated Napoleon, ending the latter's rule over Spain], it is no way improbable that some may be missing.[95]

Appendix 2
Lingard's System of Reference and Quotation

I examined Lingard's references and quotations by tracing them back to their original sources and comparing the finished narrative with the documents on which the source in question was based. Again I took his detailed treatment of the reign of Elizabeth I as the testing ground for this systematic inquiry. Two main conclusions emerged. The first and most important result was the manifest fidelity with which Lingard used his sources. Indeed the whole range of critical techniques described in earlier chapters was used to ensure the reliability of his interpretation of the sources. I did not find a single case of Lingard's distorting or reporting falsely the meaning of any source; or of his making a mistake in conveying its meaning. We can compare this with the results of the only previous such investigation of which I have knowledge. Gilbert Burnet's *History of the Reformation* (1679–1715) was still regarded in Lingard's day as one of the 'Standard ecclesiastical authorities'.[1] It contained a 'Collection of Records', inserted successfully to give a semblance of authority to his main narrative.[2] Even today, he has been accredited with 'being conscious of the need for accuracy' and 'having a nineteenth-century reverence for archive or record material'.[3]

Burnet's *History* was examined in detail by Thomas Smith in 1705. The scholarly Smith, who composed the first proper catalogue of the Cottonian collection of original documents, compared Burnet's work with the originals in that collection. He concluded that there 'is little or no credit to be given to Dr. Burnet's Collections: he and his Scotch Amanuensis having been guilty of shameful omission and perversions in numerous instances'.[3] Then in 1865 Nicholas Pococke edited in detail the last edition of the same *History* and performed the same check against the original documents. He reported 'numerous and important blunders', and apart from printing errors and slips of that sort:

> about ten thousand downright mistakes made in the original folios . . . which have appeared in every subsequent edition down to the present day.[4]

APPENDIX 2

My own researches revealed that Burnet was totally disrespectful of all medieval documents;[5] and quite prepared to deliberately falsify a document of the Reformation period in order to give it a different (indeed opposite) meaning which he required to get from it.[6] The contrast between Burnet's and Lingard's attitude towards documents could not be greater.

The work of the medievalist, non-juror scholars, such as Thomas Hearne and Henry Wharton at the turn of the seventeenth century, had already set high standards for the editing of original documents.[6] With Lingard, however, we see the beginning of the same respect for the accuracy of original documents among narrative historians, which was to be a feature of modern historical scholarship. Burnet can be shown to have had little fidelity towards sources, in writing his narrative history. For Lingard it was essential to 'earth' his narrative in the accuracy of the sources. Herein lies the beginning of the modern type of narrative history in England.

The second general conclusion derived from this investigation reveals the sense in which Lingard was after all, and in spite of his great pioneering work in many fields of historical investigation, inevitably a man of his own time in certain subsidiary matters. For his standards in the use of the quotation mark were quite different from that of the modern professional historian at the beginning of the twenty-first century.

His aim in writing *History of England* was to discover and express the truth about the English past; but he also wanted to make his work as cohesive, self-sufficient and understandable as possible for the general intelligent reader. He had a different method, therefore, of dealing with quotations in his main narrative, from his treatment of them in the more detailed realm of technical source criticism – as for example, in some of his appendices.[7]

In his technical appendices he is meticulous in quoting sources in their exactly original form.[8] When, in his main narrative, however, he used a quotation from a source couched in old English, he did not hesitate to modernize the language so as to make it more easily understood by his readers.[9] When he quotes a long passage which would be too unwieldy to quote in full in a general history, he just paraphrases it, taking the most important points and stringing them together as one quotation.[10] He will sometimes for the sake of convenience join together in a paraphrase, points made in the same context in the source but taken from separate passages.[11] Two sentences from a source are pushed into one and the punctuation likewise altered to suit the needs of compression.[12] To enable a quotation to stand on its own, or to save referring back to an event or person indicated in the quotation by a pronoun, he will insert the relevant noun and so make the quotation self-explanatory.[13] Unimportant or irrelevant words may be omitted from the quotation.[14]

Slight differences in the detail of punctuation and spelling are intro-

Appendix 2

duced to make the meaning clear, even when the language of the quotation has not been modernized.[15] Tense and person are sometimes switched about in a quotation – the past tense and the third person replacing the present and first respectively.[16] Indirect speech may be turned into direct speech.[17] Roman numerals may be changed into Arabic form.[18] The coded form of names in secret letters is replaced by the names themselves so as to make the extracts coherent to the reader.[19] The words of a foreign document may be translated into English, obviously for the benefit of the reader.[20]

I took great care to make completely sure that none of these expedients were designed to misrepresent the source or deceive the reader; and this indeed was the case. Truth is never sacrificed to the strategies of making the narrative more meaningful and clear to the reader. There was not one occasion where there was an attempt to deceive in any way. Indeed, if properly explained beforehand, all of these expedients would be quite acceptable. But Lingard does all this without the least warning. It is an assumption of thought which he would have shared with everyone else at the time, that there is nothing wrong about this.

Modern professional standards in these matters are designed to make sure that there is no perversion of the evidence, intentional or unintentional. Lingard's techniques of source criticism, together with his self-conscious determination to control any prejudices within himself, were designed to achieve the same aim – of establishing the truth. Everything was made subordinate to this.[21] It would not have occurred to him to misrepresent a source.

Lingard's technical writing, when he will turn evidence around, beneath the penetrating light of his battery of source criticisms, takes place mainly in lengthy footnotes and in the detailed appendices of his *History*; here the attention to detailed exactness in the use of original sources is made manifest. The appendices and footnotes form the substructure of his work. The finished textual narrative is written in a simple classical style – the clearest possible and most durable vehicle of meaning. It is at this level that the quotations are subject to quite arbitrary changes in order to help the reader. He or she is encouraged always, however, to 'go through' into the 'workshop', so to speak, of unprecedented footnotes and appendices, to look further and learn more.

The innocent character of what we would regard as faulty methods of quoting sources is evident, too, from its general use. The deliberate misrepresenter's technique is perfect, apart from the occasions when he or she wishes to misrepresent; but Lingard's faults in this respect are a perfectly obvious part of his approach to narrative writing, which belonged to an accepted mode of writing at this earlier stage of modern historiography.

When we turn to Lingard's reference system, I can report the discovery of a number of detailed mistakes which occurred in spite of Lingard's efforts to be meticulous. There are some incorrect references,[22] many of them being obviously printer's errors.[23] The search for references which had been incorrectly numbered was the most irksome part of my task. I soon discovered simple but useful rules of approach, such as: 'if not p. 333 as stated, try pages 3 and 33'.[24] I was able in the end to trace the references back to their sources on almost all occasions.

Many of these faults must be ascribed to errors which occurred during the various stages between the writing of the *History* and its publication. The picture is that of a perfectionist struggling in conditions which were by no means conducive to perfection. There are so many slips possible between the writing of the work and its publication, apart from the errors which might creep into the manuscript itself. We find him writing to request the printers to make an exact rendering of a document and to adopt the exact punctuation.[25] There are various instances recorded in the Lingard correspondence of printer's errors, especially in the matter of dates. Lingard believed in their primary importance. He knew that the fifth would be his last edition and he was determined to make it as accurate as possible. It was, then, a matter of the utmost frustration for him when thing still went wrong.[26]

Lingard himself is probably more at fault in those cases when references are not exact enough. There are some instances when the most important references to support a particular statement lie not so much on the page quoted, but on a page a little before or after. On very few occasions – I can quote only two[27] – there were no reference numbers at all for some undiscoverable reason, but I was still able to trace both of them.

I traced five actual errors in Lingard's use of sources.[28] These included a mistaken date, a mistaken period of time, a mistaken amount of money and a mistake of detail in a purely descriptive passage. All these errors were slight and not significant. There was no possibility involved in these mistakes of a misuse of a source for an ulterior motive. They were the result of human error.

The last word on the subject is probably given by Lingard himself, when he wrote: 'That numerous errors must occur in a voluminous work like mine is evident',[29] a statement with which anyone with experience of historical writing will readily agree. The wonder is that Lingard's mistakes were so few and that his accuracy in detail was so great.

APPENDIX 3
Lingard as Literary Artist and Scientific Historian

Lingard's characteristic form of writing was the clear, classical style – the perfect vehicle for expressing historical truths which are not simply ephemeral in nature. I have argued that the 'great' historian, like the great scientist or great poet, must be able to have contributed significantly towards a body of truth. For the scientist, this will mean the sum of knowledge about the way in which the world and its various elements work. For the poet, it means an expression of the truth about human feelings and perceptions – the opposite, incidentally, of sentimental expressionism. For the historian, this truth resides in the core of knowledge which comes to be accepted among a range of scholars as the truth about what happened in the past. Lingard's style, like that of the Venerable Bede – the 'great' English historian of the first millennium – is very disciplined. It is timeless in its readability and therefore best suited for its purpose. That is not to say, however, that Lingard was lacking in the powers of more imaginative writing which characterized and often predominated, for example, in the work of Macaulay.

Sometimes, in dealing with certain subjects which are concerned not precisely with his central political narrative, but which deal more with the 'common feelings of humanity', Lingard reveals extraordinary powers of descriptive writing. But even on these occasions, he – unlike Macaulay[1] – never gives his imaginative power licence to free itself from the world of factual reality. His historical writing is always contained within the framework of reality. It is always 'earthed' to facts and figures, derived from reliable or authoritative sources. To show exactly what I mean, I will take his treatment of a subject which occurred in the penultimate volume of the first edition of his *History*. It was published in 1829, ten years after the appearance of the first volume; and already the success of his earlier volumes had given him the confidence to express himself more freely. I will take his description of the Great Plague of 1665–6 to reveal a surprising ability at vivid description, powerful suggestion and masterly handling of literary devices in order to recreate the atmosphere of that time:

Appendix 3

In the depth of the last winter two or three isolated cases of plague had occurred in the outskirts of the metropolis... it could not be concealed that the number of deaths... was progressively on the advance. In this state of suspense, alternately agitated by their hopes and fears, men looked to the result with the most intense anxiety; and at length, about the end of May, under the influence of a warmer sun, and with the aid of a close and stagnant atmosphere, the evil burst forth in all its terrors. From the centre of St. Giles's the infection spread with rapidity over the adjacent parishes threatening the court at Whitehall, and, in defiance of every precaution, stole its way into the city. A general panic ensued. The nobility and the gentry were the first to flee; the royal family followed; and then all, who valued their personal safety more than the consideration of home and interest, prepared to imitate the example... In the daytime officers were always on the watch to withdraw from public view the bodies of those who expired in the streets; during the night, the tinkling of a bell, accompanied with the glare of links, announced the approach of the pest-cart, making its round to receive the victims of the last twenty-four hours... The disease generally manifested itself by the usual febrile symptoms of shivering, nausea, headache and delirium... till a sudden faintness came on, the maculae, the fatal 'tokens' appeared on his breast... On the third or fourth day, buboes or carbuncles arose... The sufferings of the patients often threw them into paroxysms of phrensy. They burst the bands by which they were confined to their beds; they precipitated themselves from the windows; they ran naked into the street, and plunged into the river. Men of the strongest minds were lost in amazement, when they contemplated this scene of woe and desolation; the weak and the credulous became the dupes of their own fears and imaginations... numbers assembled at different cemeteries to behold the ghosts of the dead walk round the pits... To add to their terror came the fanatics, who felt themselves inspired to act the part of prophets. One of these, in a state of nudity, walked through the city, bearing on his head a pan of burning coals, and denouncing the judgements of God on its sinful inhabitants; another assuming the character of Jonah, proclaimed aloud as he passed 'Yet forty days, and London shall be destroyed'; and a third might be met, sometimes by day, sometimes by night, advancing with a hurried step, and exclaiming with a deep sepulchral voice, 'Oh the great and dreadful God!'

During the months of July and August the weather was sultry, the heat more and more oppressive... London presented a wide and heartrending scene of misery and desolation. Rows of houses stood tenantless and open to the winds; others, in almost equal numbers, exhibited the red cross flaming on the doors. The chief thoroughfares, so lately trodden by the feet of thousands, were overgrown with grass. The few individuals who ventured abroad walked in the middle, and when they met, declined on opposite sides, to avoid the contact of each other. But if the solitude and stillness of the streets impressed the mind with awe, there was something yet more appalling in the sounds which occasionally burst upon the ear. At one moment were heard the ravings of delirium, or the wail of woe, from the infected dwelling; at another, the merry song, or the loud and careless

Appendix 3

laugh issuing from the wassailers at the tavern, or the inmates of the brothel. Men became so familiarized with the form, that they steeled their feelings against the terrors of death. They waited each for his turn with the resignation of the Christian, or the indifference of the stoic. Some devoted themselves to exercises of piety; others sought relief in the riot of dissipation, and the recklessness of despair.

September came; the heat of the atmosphere began to abate; but contrary to expectation, the mortality increased. Formerly a hope of recovery might be indulged; now infection was the certain harbinger of death, which followed generally in the course of three days, often within the space of twenty-four hours . . . in the following week more than ten thousand victims, a number hitherto unknown, sank under the augmented violence of the disease. Yet even now, when hope had yielded to despair their deliverance was at hand. The high winds, which usually accompany the autumnal equinox, cooled and purified the air; the fever, though equally contagious, assumed a less malignant form, and its ravages were necessarily more confined, from the diminution of the population on which it had hitherto fed . . . Though more than one hundred thousand individuals are said to have perished, yet in a short time the chasm in the population was no longer discernible. The plague continued, indeed, to linger in particular spots, but its terrors were forgotten or despised; and the street, so recently abandoned by the inhabitants, were again thronged with multitudes in the eager pursuit of profit, or pleasure, or crime.[2]

The above extracts from Lingard's description might be sufficient to indicate its quality. The *Edinburgh Review* of 1831 remarked:

The latter [the Plague] has never been noticed by any historian in more than few lines. Dr. Lingard has made good use of his materials, and may fairly challenge comparison with the well-known account of the plague at Athens by Thucydides.[3]

Unlike Macaulay's literary descriptions, however, Lingard's account of the Plague is 'earthed' by continual reference to a range of sources of different types, which he is careful to analyse for their reliability. First, there are the sources of first class quality on this subject, such as Statutes of the Realm and the Lords Journals;[4] together with the Rugge manuscript collection,[5] and the contemporary diaries of Evelyn and Pepys.[6]

Secondly there were the contemporary but unreliable weekly bills published in London, enumerating the dead lists:

The weekly returns of the dead for these months of July and August were, 1,006, 1,268, 2,785, 3,014, 4,030, 5,312, 5,568, 7,496. I take no notice of the distinction made by the bills between those who died of the plague, and those who died of other diseases, because I conceive no reliance can by placed on it.[7]

Appendix 3

> The number returned on Sep. 12th was 8,297. but it was generally acknowledged that the bills were very incorrect, and seldom gave more than two-thirds of the real number.[8]

Contemporary newspapers are used.[9] Lingard's view of them was that: 'Though not of great authority, yet I conceive they might be very useful with respect to the march of events.'[10] Interestingly and in contrast, Macaulay used newspapers as a major source in his *History of England*.[11]

Finally, Lingard made some careful use of Daniel Defoe's *Journal of the Plague Year* (1722):

> Though De Foe, for dramatic effect, wrote as an eye-witness, which he could not be, yet his narrative, as to the substance of the facts, is confirmed by all the other authorities.[12]

A modern authority comments that Defoe's work 'embodied information from various sources including official documents'.[13]

Similarly, Lingard makes some critical use of the contemporary Earl of Clarendon's *Life* (only published in complete form in 1827):

> Clarendon, with his usual inaccuracy, makes the number of dead, according to the weekly bills, to amount to 160,000, which, he says, ought, in the opinion of well-informed persons, to be doubled. Clarendon, 326. The number of burials according to the bills, was only 97,306 – Table prefixed to Loimologia. If we add one-third for omissions, the amount will be about 130,000, but from these must be deducted the deaths from other causes than the plague. *In the tables themselves the deaths from the plague in this year 1665 are 68,596; in 1666, they are 1,196; in 1667, they fall to thirty five, to fourteen in 1668, and after that seldom reach to half-a-dozen.*[14]

In 1995 a modern Oxford scholar, J. Innes, stated that 'In London, 70,000 deaths were reported – perhaps 15 per cent of its population';[15] and in 1997, another scholar, Dr. J. Boulton, stated that 'The last "Great Plague" in London in 1665 . . . killed about 56,000 people'.[16]

The Plague episode reflects very well the way in which Lingard, even in his rare moments of eloquent artistic description, retains always that 'feet-on-the-ground' approach – earthing the literary description to historical facts as deduced from his methodology of source criticism – which is surely the hallmark of the true historian, as opposed to the literary artist.[17] As a historian, he was well aware of the primary need to tell the truth about what happened in the past, as opposed to an undisciplined play on emotional feelings, imagination and sensitivities of his readers.

APPENDIX 4
Lingard on St. Dunstan and the Tenth-Century Reforms

One of the main characteristics of post-Reformation popular historiography, as opposed to the work of antiquarian and non-juring scholarship in the seventeenth century, was a complete contempt for the medieval world – often extended back into the Anglo-Saxon age – which was considered not worth studying.[1] To look at a few of Lingard's exact contemporaries, we find Sharon Turner describing the medieval Church in 1829:

> Avarice was their character, from the highest to the lowest, and they were never satisfied. Luxury, profligacy, incest, gluttony, and every species of flagitiousness and abomination, were in practice among them, and the fountain of all this depravity was the Roman court. Their ignorance equalled their vices.[2]

Speaking of the Reformation and Renaissance period, he says:

> The change was the more striking to the imagination from the comparative darkness and destitution of the middle ages which had preceded.[3]

Henry Hallam had no idea of the value of the Anglo-Saxon sources, especially Bede. He could hardly conceive of any worthwhile learning in the 'Dark Ages'[4] and cannot understand the respectful attitude adopted towards these early writers by the French historians. He wishes it 'to be understood that I pretend hardly any direct acquaintance with these writers'; and refers to 'the annals of barbarians so unworthy of remembrance'.[5] This is reminiscent of Gilbert Burnet's boast in the seventeenth century, that he would rather dig in mines than read the writings of medieval people.[6]

Here, then, is the general approach of English historians of the time – that the Reformation had brought England out of the 'Dark Ages' into the 'light' of its great progress to the position of a world power. It was a framework which dominated historical writing in England until well into the twentieth century. It is against this sort of background that we may understand the contemporary reaction to Lingard's treatment of certain themes from the 'Dark Ages'; and it is instructive to look at the way in which a modern and authoritative scholar deals with the same matters.

The *Edinburgh Review* of 1825 attacked a statement made by Lingard earlier, in his *Anglo-Saxon Church* (1806), expressing exactly the incredulity and scorn with which Lingard's writing was greeted by many of his contemporary audience, when it stated:

> After a learned, and to us, an original disquisition on <u>double</u> monasteries, a singular institution, where a convent of monks or canons was annexed to a nunnery, and subjected to the spiritual government of its abbess, Dr. Lingard tells us, that 'during the two first centuries after the conversion of our ancestors, the principal monasteries were established on this plan; nor are we certain that there existed any others of a different description. They were held in the highest estimation; the most distinguished of the Saxon female saints, and many of the most eminent prelates, were educated in them; so edifying was the deportment of the greatest part of these communities. The monastery of Coldingham <u>alone</u> forms an exception . . . *The hardihood of this assertion excites, we must confess, our admiration . . . We shall not prosecute further. Enough has been said to show that the virgins of Coldingham were not the <u>only</u> exception from the general purity of manners and strictness of conduct attributed by Dr. Lingard to our Anglo-Saxon nuns.*[7]

Turning to one of our most eminent Anglo-Saxon scholars in the twentieth century, we find Sir Frank Stenton writing on just this matter in 1950:

> Already before the age of Bede the idea that men and women might be associated in the religious life had created a number of double monasteries which were eminent in learning as well as devotion . . . The double monastery was obviously a normal feature of the earliest English monasticism, and, indeed, it is doubtful whether any houses for women only were ever founded in this period . . . The strictness with which these relations were controlled can be safely inferred from the good repute of these houses. Only one of them – Coldingham, isolated above the seas in the far north of Bernicia – is known to have given grounds for scandal.[8]

One of the aims of Protestant historiography was to find justification for post-Reformation events in pre-Reformation history. So the monks of the tenth century must be castigated in order to justify their later explusion in 1536:

> Anglo-Saxon ecclesiastical history stamps the Benedictines as intruders and their expulsion as an act of justice.[9]

APPENDIX 4

Similarly precedents were sought in pre-Reformation England, for clerical marriages,[10] attacks on 'images',[11] and attacks on the doctrine of transubstantiation.[12] Everything in fact must be made to show that 'the present ecclesiastical estate of England is the lineal successor and lawful representative of the ancient church'[13] – which in fact never existed as they depicted it.

One of the most unpopular periods in all this was the tenth century, with its monastic reform movement; St. Dunstan, its initiator, was a particular target. Soames declared that: 'Dunstan's establishments were nurseries of fanaticism';[14] and 'many of them reared their heads amidst a considerable mass of individual suffering, and greatly to the disapprobation of a numerous party'.[15] The whole thing in fact was an 'ill-advised innovation'.[16]

Dunstan was attacked by Soames for bringing the unwilling King Edwy to the council of his nobles in 955.[17] Post-Reformation historiography made good propagandist use, from the time of the Tudors onwards, of any pre-Reformation event which seemed to show the Church interfering with the rights and status of English kingship. Lingard observed:

> By the language of modern prejudice the share which Dunstan bore in this transaction has been described as an attempt to subdue the spirit of the king, and a daring insult to the royal authority; but let the reader advert to the manners of the age, and he will not be surprised, if the witan resented the abrupt departure of the king, or their messengers treated with little ceremony by the women who had drawn him away.[18]

Stenton deals with this affair in 1950:

> According to Dunstan's earliest biographer the king left the solemn feast which followed his anointing in order to amuse himself with a noble woman and her daughter, each of whom was trying to entice him into marriage. The absence of the king on such an occasion was an insult to the whole English artistocracy and to avoid serious trouble Dunstan and his kinsman, the bishop of Lichfield, were sent in search of him.[19]

Again, Lingard's contemporaries blamed the revolt of Mercia against King Edwy in 957 variously on the machinations of Dunstan who was 'panting for revenge', on the monks of Mercia who 'preached up the duty of revolt', or on the 'political influence' of Archbishop Odo.[20] Lingard commented in 1823:

> To account for the revolution which transferred the sceptre of Mercia from the hands of Edwy to those of Edgar, modern writers have set aside the authority of the original historians, and supplied its place with conjectures of their own ... But not one of these fictions can bear the test of inquiry

Appendix 4

> ... If Edwy forfeited the crown to Mercia, it was owing to his own lawless and oppressive conduct, which was not confined to a few monks, but extended to his grandmother, his kindred, the friends of his late uncle, and the principal thanes of his kingdom.[20]

Stenton's observation in 1950 is:

> It was probably through mere irresponsibility that within two years of his accession Eadwig lost the greater part of his kingdom. There is no trace of any particularist feeling behind this revolution ... Dunstan's earliest biographer attributes the rejection of Eadwig by the northern peoples to his [Eadwig's] folly in choosing young advisers as thoughtless as himself. The probability is that in the society of his West Saxon friends, he fell completely out of touch with the local aristocracy of remoter parts.[21]

On the tenth-century reform movement itself, the contemporary attitude in Lingard's day was one of censure and deprecation. It represented an important stage in the development from the 'ancient church' to the 'dreaded medieval Church'. Lingard described, however, the great merits of Dunstan (909–88), to whose zeal the great abbeys of Glastonbury and Abingdon owed their rejuvenation and success; who, as Abbot, led the great movement for reform of the Benedictine Order; and as Archbishop of Canterbury, appointed by Pope John XII, was a great ecclesiastical reformer, aided by King Edgar (944–75). Dunstan had been inspired by the reforms of the monastic order and its churches on the Continent, which he had seen while in exile in Flanders.[22] Lingard states:

> The Danish invasion had both relaxed the sinews of ecclesiastical discipline, and dissolved the greater number of the monastic and clerical establishments.

But as the result of the work of Dunstan and his 'two active co-operators, the bishops Oswald and Ethelwold', these 'dissolved' monasteries 'rose from their ashes' and recovered their life and strength. At the start of Edgar's reign the Benedictine 'order was nearly extinct', but nearly fifty abbeys were strongly established during it.[22]

Turning now to Stenton, we find him concluding a lengthy chapter on the subject:

> There can, in fact, be no question that the Benedictine reformation of the tenth century brought fresh vitality to the whole of the English church. But its significance is misunderstood if it is dismissed as one of the many movements which have merely influenced a generation and then passed into history. It opened a new phase of English culture, and contributed to the distinctive quality of medieval English civilisation.[23]

APPENDIX 4

The great medievalist, M. D. Knowles, Regius Professor at Cambridge, wrote of Dunstan in 1962:

> this great and eminently holy man . . . sympathetic, receptive nature . . . unshakable strength . . . wisdom and statesmanship which enabled him to be the counsellor and friend of successive kings and one of the creators of a united England, the gift of artistic creation of the highest order . . . the mature sanctity which in his later years transcended and superseded all his other activities, a figure of singular attractiveness.

Knowles tells us that the great work of Dunstan, abbot and later Archbishop (of Canterbury) – assisted by his fellow abbots and bishops, Ethelwold and Oswald – restored to England in the tenth century the full life and culture of monasticism and the Church after so much had been destroyed by the Viking invasions. Indeed 'they called the dead to life; they created a great and flourishing system upon vacant soil'.[24] The contribution of the much earlier monks, Bede, Boniface, Aidan and Wilfrid and the later contribution by Anselm and Lanfranc in the monasticism of the Norman period, have been recognized; but the importance of the tenth-century reformers has been neglected. Knowles comments that 'They and their work . . . have failed to receive due recognition in modern times'.[25]

Yet Lingard was giving the work of Dunstan and his helpers full recognition more than a century before Knowles, the greatest of our monastic historians, was writing his magisterial *The Monastic Order in England* (1949). Knowles himself – a man who weighed his words very carefully – once told me, when we met at Peterhouse, of his respect for Lingard's work in his own specialist field of monastic history. Here is yet another example of the way in which Lingard's original insights were illuminating the history of England in yet another period. In fact Lingard used the same original sources – such as Bridferth's contemporary *Life of St. Dunstan*, Wulfstan's *Life of St. Ethelwold*, the Anglo-Saxon Chronicle, Henry Wharton's great collection of documents in his *Anglia Sacra* (1691) and other extant manuscript sources – which were to be used more than a century later by Sir Frank Stenton and Dom David Knowles.

Very significantly, Lingard also brings to these sources his usual range of critical techniques, which ensured that his interpretation of events is in line with the findings of the most modern scholarship. So, for example, he insists that contemporary Anglo-Saxon accounts must be given greater weight than the more familiar accounts written later, after the Conquest.[26] Two contemporary and reliable authorities are invoked to point out a mistake made by the formidable scholar Henry Wharton in his *Anglia Sacra*:

> MS. Cleop. 79. Osb. 109. Wharton (Ang. Sac. ii. 197, not.) infers from the words of Osbern (p. 110), that Dunstan possessed Rochester Bishopric with

Appendix 4

Canterbury. This is a mistake. Osbern says the contrary. So also does Eadmer, 214.[27]

And Lingard warns us about weaknesses in the post-Conquest authorities, caused by their failure to exercise proper source criticism on their own documents:

> These later Anglo-Norman historians ... who wrote from documents, which on their own showing were far from authentic.[28]

Then, dealing with a 'fable' of later historians – that Dunstan had been motivated on one occasion 'by a supernatural voice from a crucifix, saying: Make no change. Your former decision was right'" – Lingard comments:

> I mention this fable, because it occupies a prominent place in most modern histories, but is not to be found in any Anglo-Saxon writer ... We are indebted for it to writers after the Conquest.[29]

Again, Lingard comments, with dry humour, on an occasion when the floor seems to have fallen through at a certain meeting, leaving only Dunstan 'secure in his seat above'; that Dunstan, 'if we may believe modern writers, had the impudence to fabricate a miracle in defence of the monks'. Lingard proceeds to divest the event of 'its modern embellishments' which are 'unknown to any ancient historian'; and then reduces the whole affair to something which is amenable to rational explanation.[30]

Sir Herbert Butterfield [PLATE 12] said that 'the recovery and exposition of the medieval world' in the nineteenth century is still perhaps 'the greatest achievement of historical understanding' in the history of historical writing.[31] John Lingard made the first and most important contribution to such understanding in English historiography. First, he introduced a much wider European framework, within which English history was seen in a new perspective; secondly, he applied the rules of 'scientific' source criticism to the documents and writings of the Anglo-Saxon and medieval periods.

So, for example, the nature and character of the Church in England during these periods, were changed from a narrowly insular, erastian and nationalistic interpretation imposed by post-Reformation historians, to the more veridical picture of the Catholic or 'universal' Church, centred in Rome, of which the Church in England formed part, as did the Church in other European countries.[32] Similarly, his treatment of the feudal system before the Norman Conquest (48 pages) and afterwards (24 pages), all based on original and tested sources, made it obvious that feudal institutions were common to European countries. In fact they were

Appendix 4

brought to England from the Continent, both before and after the Conquest.[33] Again, Lingard demonstrates in an important section (15 pages) that the international Canon law formed a centrally important part of English life in the medieval period, alongside the less sophisticated and less rationally structured Common Law.[34]

Lingard's seminal ideas – stated very simply and undramatically – within these sections of analysis of medieval institutions in England, were later to bear fruit in the hands of F. W. Maitland, and later still in those of Z. N. Brooke.[35] These individuals changed the way in which academic historians in the twentieth century came to view the medieval past in all its aspects.

The new historical framework and perspective which Lingard established enabled him to provide the first modern treatment of more detailed episodes, such as the controversy of King John with the Papacy, and the Statutes of Provisors and Praemunire.[36] It was to be well over a century later that modern and specialist medieval scholars came to rediscover Lingard's interpretation of these and other episodes. So, too, Lingard was able to provide the first modern understanding of the Anglo-Saxon Church[37] and of the character and nature of such topics as St. Dunstan and the tenth-century reform movement, described above.

Lingard's assessment of the importance of Dunstan and the reform movement of the tenth century, which affected the whole of English life, is just one example of very many instances in the whole history of England, where Lingard saw and described the importance and significance of events and movements in the past, which were completely lost on, or misinterpreted by, his predecessors and contemporaries – including in many cases, his successors in the twentieth century. The standard of source criticism which he brought to bear on the original documents for all periods of English history was not to be replicated until the specialist work of the mid and late twentieth century. No historian of the whole history of England has ever come near replicating the standard of Lingard's original research and enduring scholarship over such an extended period.

Notes

Preface

1 His aim was 'to contrast foreign with native authorities, to hold the balance between them with an equal hand, and, forgetting that he is an Englishman, to judge impartially as a citizen of the world', J. Lingard, *History of England* (4th edn, 1837–8), Preface, vi.
2 E. Jones, *The English Nation: The Great Myth* (Sutton, 2nd edn, 2000).
3 N. Davies, *The Isles* (Macmillan, 1999), p. 519.
4 Lingard to unknown person, 10 December 1820, Ushaw MS, 'Lingard Transcripts', B.11.
5 See E. Jones, MA Thesis, 'A Study of John Lingard's Historical Work, with special reference to his treatment of the reign of Elizabeth I', 1956, University College of Swansea, Library.
6 Sir Herbert Butterfield and Sir Lewis Namier were described by Professor John Vincent in 1995 as the two greatest historians of the twentieth century in England. J. Vincent, *An Intelligent Person's Guide to History* (London, 1995), pp. 48–62. Cf. 'The work of Sir Herbert Butterfield was one of the major influences upon the architecture of English historiography in the years immediately before and after the Second World War', J. Derry, *The Historian at Work*, ed. J. Cannon (George Allen & Unwin, 1980), p. 171.
7 H. Butterfield, *George III and the Historians* (1957), p. 119.
8 See E. Jones, Ph.D. Thesis, 'English Historical Writing on the English Reformation, 1680–1730' (1958), Cambridge University Library.
9 Sir H. Butterfield to E. Jones, 28 September 1967 (in the author's possession).
10 J. Lingard, *History of England* (4th edn, 1837), Preface, p. vi.
11 See Jones, *The English Nation*, pp. 31–60, 70–8.
12 The highly successful propagandist, Joseph Goebbels, claimed the 'Hitler myth' as his greatest achievement; but it could not restore morale once Germany began to fail in the War from 1943. Cf. Nicholas Reeves, *The Power of Film Propaganda in Myth and Reality* (London and New York: Cassell, 1999).
13 Jones, *The English Nation*, p. 21.
14 'Rich quotations from Lingard's correspondence as well as his works fully support Jones's claim that Lingard deserves to be better known as the forerunner of revisionist history', Professor Kevin Sharpe, *Times Literary Supplement*, 28 August 1998, p. 12. Cf. 'Jones provides a fascinating and powerful account of John Lingard, and convincingly demonstrates the ways in which Lingard prefigures modern "revisionist" history', Professor Glen

Burgess, *Reviews in History* (http://www.history.ac.uk/ihr/reviews/2glenn). The chapter 'on Lingard is particularly notable, and one wishes that he had published it years ago', Professor Patrick Collinson, Regius Professor of Modern History, Cambridge University, jacket cover of Jones, *The English Nation* (1st edn, 1998).

15 Davies, *The Isles*, p. 388.
16 Ibid., Introduction, p. xxiii.
17 Ibid., *The Isles*, p. 519.
18 See Jones, *The English Nation*, pp. 23, 152, 219, 229.
19 Cf. Lingard, *The History and Antiquities of the Anglo-Saxon Church* (3rd edn, 1845), Preface, p. vii.
20 See Jones, *The English Nation*, pp. 179–94.
21 Ibid., *The English Nation*, p. 519.
22 F. W. Maitland's motive in pursuing historical research was so 'that mankind should believe what is true, and reject what is false' (quoted in D. Andrew Penny, *The Historical Journal*, 40(1), March, 1997, p. 123. For Lingard's attitude in the same matter, see Jones, *The English Nation* pp. 176–7.
23 See Jones, 'English Historical Writing on the English Reformation, 1680–1730', Ph.D. Thesis, ff. 115–30.
24 Jones, *The English Nation*, pp. 179–80.
25 'In 1681 Mabillon's *De Re Diplomatica libri vi* was published, which founded the science of diplomatics and palaeography, and remains to this day a classic of its kind', J. W. Thompson, *A History of Historical Writing* (New York, 1942), ii, p. 11.
26 See Thompson, *A History of Historical Writing*, p. 23.
27 See J. P. Chinnici, *The English Catholic Enlightenment: John Lingard and the Cisalpine Movement, 1780–1850* (Patmos Press, 1980), pp. 6–11. Cf. Rev. Dr. P. Phillips, 'Lingard's Historical Background', *A Catholic of the Enlightenment: Essays in Lingard's Work and Times*, ed. J. A. Hilton (Wigan: North West Catholic History Society, 1999), pp. 21, 23.
28 H. Butterfield, *Man On His Past* (Cambridge University Press, 1955), pp. 36, 40, 57.
29 P. Phillips, 'John Lingard and the *Anglo-Saxon Church*', *Recusant History* (October 1996), Vol. 23, no. 2, pp. 180–1.
30 History only became in independent discipline in terms of an Honours Graduate Course at Oxford in 1872 and at Cambridge in 1875. CF. J. Kenyon, *The History Men* (Weidenfeld and Nicolson, 2nd edn., 1993), p. 150.
31 Jones, *The English Nation*, p. 173.
32 Ibid., pp. 171–2.
33 For his views on the responsibility of being a historian, see below, p. 33–4.
34 Butterfield, *Man On His Past*, pp. 182, 191, 199
35 Ibid., pp. 179, 183 n2, 198.
36 See below, pp. 41–4, 47–9
37 Butterfield, *Man On His Past*, Preface, p. xv.
38 Lord Acton, Cambridge University Library MS, Add. 4863, fol. 171.
39 Butterfield, *Man On His Past*, p. 191.

Introduction: The Background to Lingard's Work

1. See Thomas Cahill, *The Gifts of the Jews* (Lion, 1999).
2. See P. Hazard, *La Crise De La Conscience Européenne, 1680–1730* (Paris, 1935), i, chapters II and V. Cf. J. W. Thompson, *History of Historical Writing* (New York, 1942), iii, 51–7. Cf. A. Momigliano. 'Ancient History and the Antiquarian', *Warburg Institute Journal*, iii (1950), pp. 286–313.
3. E. Jones, 'English Historical Writing on the English Reformation, 1680–1730', Ph.D. Thesis, ff. 115–129. It was a modern-type Mabillon, Pere Grosjean (a scholar in the Bollandist section of the Jesuit Order) – reacting against another form of nihilism – who was brought from his scholarly work on the *Acta Sanctorum*, by the French Resistance, to break the Nazi Code of communication in the early 1940s.
4. M. Bloch, *The Historian's Craft*, trans. P. Putnum (Manchester University Press, 1954), p. 133.
5. A. Momigliano, 'Ancient History and the Antiquarian', p. 313.
6. Cf. Mabillon: 'Piety and truth must never be considered as separable, for honest and genuine piety will never come into conflict with the truth', quoted by M. D. Knowles, *Journal of Ecclesiastical History*, 10 (1959), p. 169.
7. A. Momigliano, 'Ancient History and the Antiquarian', p. 303.
8. C. Cheney, 'Introduction', *English Historical Scholarship in the 16th and 17th Centuries*, ed. L. Fox (Oxford University Press, 1956), p. 5.
9. See E. Jones, 'English Historical Writing on the English Reformation, 1680–1730', Ph.D. Thesis, ff. 22–43, 93–110.
10. See ibid., ff. 115–30.
11. W. Nicolson to R. Thoresby, 17 July 1699, *Letters Addressed to Ralph Thoresby*, ed. W. T. Lancaster (Leeds, 1912), p. 75.
12. Jones, *The English Nation*, pp. 82, 88, 89, 118.
13. Quoting a source at third hand, T. Hearne to R. Thoresby, 7 January 1707, *Letters of Eminent Man Addressed to Ralph Thoresby* (1832), ii, 89.
14. *Life of Alfred the Great by J. Spelman*, ed. T. Hearne (1709), 133 n3.
15. T. Hearne to Anstis, 16 May 1721, British Musuem Library MS, Stowe, 749, f. 156.
16. T. Hearne to Anstis, 11 December 1718, British Museum Library MS, Stowe, 749, f. 60.
17. T. Hearne to Charlett, 19 September 1715, Bodleian Library (Oxford) MS, 'Hearne's Diary', no. 58, ff. 11–12.
18. D. C. Douglas, *English Scholars* (Jonathan Cape, 1939), pp. 143, 234, 240. Cf. E. Jones, 'English Historical Writing on the English Reformation, 1680–1730', Ph.D. Thesis, ff. 231–62.
19. See E. Jones, 'English Historical Writing on the English Reformation, 1680–1730', Ph.D. Thesis, ff. 235–6. Cf. Jones, *The English Nation*, pp. 83–4.
20. J. W. Thompson, *The English Nation*, p. 23.
21. See E. Jones, 'English Historical Writing on the English Reformation, 1680–1730', Ph.D. Thesis, ff. 231–63.
22. Jones, *The English Nation*, p. 83.
23. Anon. *Impartial Memorials of the Life and Writings of Thomas Hearne, by several Hands* (London, 1736), frontispiece.

24 'Hearne's Catalogue', Bodleian Library MS, English Miscellaneous e. 49.
25 Concluding remarks of the *Impartial Memorials*.
26 See P. Phillips, 'John Lingard and the Anglo Saxon Church', *Recusant History*, 23 (2), October 1996, pp. 181, 186.
27 Lingard to Gradwell, 28 June 1821. Ushaw MS, Lingard Transcripts B.11.
28 D. C. Douglas, *English Scholars*, pp. 176, 185, 186. See below, pp. 38, 231, 242, 287.
29 Jones, *The English Nation*, p. 180.
30 Ibid., p. 43.
31 See J. A. Hilton, *A Reasonable Service: Two Essays on Lingard* (Wigan, 1998), p. 15. Cf. J. P. Chinicci, *English Catholic Enlightenment*, p. 109; and T. P. Peardon, *Transition in English Historical Writing*, p. 277.
32 H. Trevor-Roper, *Lord Macaulay. The History of England* (Penguin Classics, 1979), Introduction, p. 7. Cf. E. Jones, *The English Nation*, pp. 152–3, 218–20.
33 Butterfield, *Man On His Past*, p. 53.
34 D. Hume, *Enquiry Concerning Human Understanding*, ed. L. A. Selby-Biggs (2nd edn, 1902), p. 83, para. 65.
35 D. Hume, *History of England* (1826 edition, Preface).
36 D. Hume, *A History of England, Incorporating the Corrections and Researches of Recent Historians* (London: John Murray, 1860), p. 15.
37 Jones, *The English Nation*, pp. 195–7.
38 J. Lingard, *History of England*, i, p. 52, note 3.
39 Ibid., i, 92, note 1.
40 J. Kenyon, *The History Men*, p. 6.
41 See below, pp. 17–17, 54–5, 118–18, 121, 123, 133, 138, 238.
42 F. M. Stenton, *Anglo-Saxon England* (Oxford: Clarendon Press, 2nd edn, 1946), pp. 186–7.
43 Ibid.
44 D. Bates, *The Companion to British History*, ed. J. Gardiner and Neil Wenborn (Collins & Brown, 1995), p. 72.
45 A. E. Redgate, *The Oxford Companion to British History*, ed. John Cannon (Oxford University Press, 1997), p. 91.
46 J. Lingard, *History of England*, i, 132.
47 Cf. E. Jones, *The English Nation*, pp. 23, 218–19.
48 C. Firth, *A Commentary on Macaulay's History of England* (Macmillan, 1938), p. 275.
49 *The Complete Works of Lord Macaulay*, ed. Lady Trevelyan (G. Putnum & Sons, 1898), vol. ix, 119.
50 H. Trevor-Roper, *Lord Macaulay, The History of England*, Introduction, p. 36.
51 See J. Kenyon, *The History Men*, p. 77.
52 C. Firth, *A Commentary on Macaulay's History of England*, pp. 28–9, 65.
53 *Macaulay's Critical and Historical Essays*, ed. G. M. Trevelyan (1903), ii, 38.
54 Cf. G. N. Clarke, *The Later Stuarts* (Clarendon Press, 1949), pp. 69–70; M. Ashley, *England in the Seventeenth Century* (Penguin, 1952), p. 129; T. Munck, *Seventeenth Century Europe* (Macmillan, 1993), p. 115.
55 J. Lingard, *History of England*, Preface, pp. xvii–xviii.

56 Lingard to Walker, 19 May 1836, Ushaw MS, A.1., a.3.
57 Lingard to Mrs. T. Lomax. 1 March 1850, *The Letters of Dr. John Lingard to Mrs. Thomas Lomax (1835–51)*, ed. J. Trappes-Lomax (Catholic Record Society, 2000), letter xc, p. 155.
58 Lingard to Coulston, 11 December 1848, Ushaw MS, 'Lingard to Others, 1815–21'.
59 See above, p. 11.
60 P. Ghosh, 'Macaulay and the Heritage of the Enlightenment', *The English Historical Review*, cxii, no. 47, April 1997, p. 395.
61 Professor Norman Davies, author of *The Isles* (1999).
62 See Jones, *The English Nation*, p. 273, note 13.
63 Ibid., pp. 148, 238, 252.
64 J. Lingard, *The History and Antiquities of the Anglo-Saxon Church* (Newcastle, 1806), i, preface vi.
65 Lingard to Kirk, 18 December 1819, Ushaw MS, 'Lingard Transcripts', B11.
66 Lingard to Kirk, 25 November 1820, Ushaw MS, ibid.
67 Lingard to ?, 10 December 1820, Ushaw MS, ibid.
68 J. Mabillon, quoted by M. D. Knowles, 'Jean Mabillon', *Journal of Ecclesiastical History*, 10 (1959), p. 169.
69 J. A. Cannon, *The Oxford Companion to British History*, ed. John Cannon (Oxford University Press, 1997), p. 609.
70 C. N. L. Brooke, Foreword to Z. N. Brooke, *The English Church and the Papacy* (Cambridge University Press, new edn, 1989), p. xiii.
71 D. Englander, *The Companion to British History* (1995), p. 493.
72 See above, p. xvi, Preface, note 22.
73 Lingard to Price, 13 February 1847, Ushaw MS, 'Lingard Transcripts', B10, f. 363.
74 Lingard to Walker, 25 May 1846, Ushaw MS, 'Lingard to Walker, 1846–50', A.3, f. 24.
75 See below, pp. 45, 47–8.
76 See *Edinburgh Review*, lxxxiii (April 1825), pp. 3, 4, 6, 7.
77 J. Black and D. MacCaill, *Studying History* (Macmillan, 2nd edn, 2000), p. 50.
78 J. A. Hilton, *Catholic Englishmen*, edited by J. A. Hilton (The North West Catholic History Society, Wigan, 1984), p. 39.
79 J. P. Chinnici, *The English Catholic Enlightenment: John Lingard and the Cisalpine Movement 1780–1850*, pp. 134–5.
80 J. A. Hilton, *Catholic Englishmen*, p. 37.
81 Ibid., p. 39.

Chapter I An Invitation to the Historian's Workshop

1 See *English Historical Review*, LXVI (1951), p. 455.
2 M. A. Tierney, 'Memoir of the Rev. Dr. Lingard', prefixed to Lingard's *History of England*, pp. xxxi–xxxii. Cf. 'Mrs. Lingard's Narrative', printed by F. Fletcher in *Lingard Society Papers* (20 October 1924). Cf. E. Bonney and M. Haile, *The Life and Letters of John Lingard 1771–1851* (1911), p. 17.

3 Tierney, 'Memoir of the Rev. Dr. Lingard', pp. xxxiii–xxxiv.
4 T. P. Peardon, *The Transition in English Historical Writing, 1760–1830* (New York, 1933), p. 277. Cf. P. Phillips, 'John Lingard and the Anglo-Saxon Church', *Recusant History* (October 1996), pp. 181–7. By now, too, Lingard was reading widely and voraciously. Cf. his Journal for 1800: 'Gibbon read and compared with Fleury, Froissart, Villani, Muratori . . . Read life of Clement XIV in French by Curraciolo and jottings on various other subjects such as the wars of the Turks against the Venetians or the character of Philip II of Spain', quoted in E. Bonney and M. Haile, *The Life and Letters of John Lingard 1771–1851* (1911), pp. 74–5.
5 Tierney, 'Memoir of the Rev. Dr. Lingard', pp. xxxiii–xxxiv.
6 Lingard to Rev. F. Trappes, 20 July 1841, *Letters of Dr. J. Lingard to Mrs. T. Lomax* (2000), letter 11, p. 218.
7 *Letters of Lingard to Mrs. Lomax*, p. 9.
8 Sydney Smith (1771–1845), Anglican wit and clergyman, whose enlightened views brought him into conflict with abuses such as slavery, transportation, Game laws and inhuman treatment of prisoners. He was against the main Anglican opinion of his day, in being an advocate of Catholic emancipation. See H. Pearson, *The Smith of Smiths* (1934); *Twelve Miles from a Lemon. Selected Writings and Sayings of Sydney Smith*, compiled by N. Taylor and H. Hankinson (Lutterworth Press, 1996).
9 Sydney Smith, *The Works of the Rev. Sydney Smith* (3rd edn, 1845), iii, 296. Cf. ii, 2323–3; iii, 49-5-, 275 n*, 276, 283, 284, 2912, 293, 325–6, 336–7, 347, 365–70.
10 Ibid., ii, 232–3, 293.
11 See Jones, *The English Nation*, p. 195.
12 *Westminster Review*, vii (1827), p. 187.
13 *Edinburgh Review*, xlii (1825), p. 30.
14 *Edinburgh Review*, liii (1831), pp. 18–19.
15 'To catch a Priest either tripping or napping is a great gratification to a large & various section of *our hommes de lettres*', Dr. William Shepherd a Unitarian minister to Lingard. Ushaw MS (undated), 'Gillow Transcript – Correspondence of Rev. John Lingard – Miscellaneous', f. 10.
16 Dr. Kipling to Lingard (undated). Ushaw MS, 'Gillow Transcripts – Correspondence of Rev. John Lingard – Miscellaneous', f. 28.
17 Lingard to Gradwell, 20 February 1822. Ushaw MS, 'Copies of the letters of Dr. Lingard from the archives of the English College, Rome, 1812–24', 'Lingard Transcripts', B.11.
18 The history of this historiography contains the 'Great Myth', described in Jones, *The English Nation: The Great Myth*.
19 Lingard to Kirk, 18 December 1819. Ushaw MS, 'Lingard Transcripts', B.11.
20 Lingard to Oliver, 9 October 1840. Ushaw MS. 'Gillow Transcripts. Letters between the Rev. Dr. Lingard and the Rev. G. Oliver', 11, Code o, letter 32.
21 Lingard to Mawman, 15 July 1823. Ushaw MS, 'Lingard to Mawman 1818–27', B.3, letter 16, 15 July 1823.
22 Lingard to Oliver, 11 August 1827. Ushaw MS, 'Gillow Transcripts – Correspondence between Lingard and Oliver', Code o, f. 3.
23 See David Mathew, *Catholicism in England* (2nd edn, 1948), pp. 69–70. The subject concerns Fr. Garnet and the Gunpowder Plot.

24 See Jones, *The English Nation*, pp. 131–8, 203.
25 Lingard to Coulston (undated). Ushaw MS, 'Lingard to Various Others, 1815–21'.
26 J. Lingard, *History*, iv, 592.
27 Ibid., iv, 592–6.
28 Ibid.
29 Ibid., 419, note 1.
30 Ibid., i, 359–60 and 360,note 1.
31 F. Stenton, *Anglo-Saxon England* (2nd edn, 1950), p. 460.
32 Lingard, *History*, v, 367.
33 R. H. Tawney, *Religion and the Rise of Capitalism* (Penguin, 1948), pp. 148–9, 304–5.
34 Lingard, *History* (4th edn, 1837), i, Preface, p. ix.
35 Lingard to Mawman, 17 June 1825. Ushaw MS, 'Lingard to Mawman, 1818–27', B.3, M.39.
36 See examples in Lingard, *History*, iii, 27 n2, 329 n1, 378 n1; v, 26 n2, 359 n2, 493 n2; vi, 130 n1, 379, 691, note O; viii, 264 n2, 415 n1.
37 See examples in Lingard, *History*, iii, 426 n1; vi, 515 n2, 645 n2; viii, 85 n1; ix, 112 n1.
38 See examples in Lingard, *History* ii, 400 n4; iii, 441 n1; iv, 434 n3, 505 n2; v, 207 n1, 334 n2; vi, 415 n2; vii, 300 n1.
39 For example, Lingard, *History*, viii, 27–8 n3, 146 n1, 147 n1.
40 For example, Lingard, *History*, iv, 79–80; vi, 140–1; vii, 528.
41 Ibid., iv, 79–80.
42 Ibid., vi, 140–1.
43 Ibid., vii, 528.
44 Ibid., viii, 469–70, n1.
45 Ibid., ix, 426.
46 For example, Lingard, *History*, v, 68; vi, 490, 595, 600 n3; viii, 424 n1, 608 n2; ix, 202 n2, 303–4 n2.
47 For example, Lingard, *History*, iii, 321; iv, 125–6 n4, 161–2, 169; v, 77–8; vi, 306, 310, 353, 362–3 n2, 386 n2, 409 n1, 407, 576–7 n2, 587–8.
48 Ibid., vi, 416 n2.
49 Ibid., vi, 140–1.
50 Ibid., v, 413–14 n2; viii, 469–70 n1; x, 27 n1.
51 Ibid., vi, 649 n1; vii, 227 n2.
52 Ibid., iii, 412; vi, 418 n4; vii, 59, 63 n1, 261 n2.
53 Ibid., ii, 571 n2; iv, 333 n1; v, 151 n1, 381 n2.
54 Ibid., viii, 387 n2.
55 Ibid.
56 See P. R. Ghosh, *The English Historical Review*, c xii, no. 47 (1997), p. 395.
57 C. Firth, *A Commentary on Macaulay's History of England* (Macmillan, 1938), pp. 53–5.
58 C. Firth, *A Commentary on Macaulay's History of England*, p. 65.
59 Lingard, *History* (1st edn, 1825), vi, Preface, pp. v–vi.
60 Lingard to Gradwell (n.d.), Ushaw MS, 'Copies of the letters of Dr. Lingard from the archives of the English College, Rome, under Correspondence and Rescripts 1824–25, Lingard Transcripts', B.11.

61 *Westminster Review*, vii (1827), p. 188.
62 See above, p. 14.
63 Ibid.
64 The *Scientist* (15 August 1997) reports that in this age of 'postmodernism', when sceptics are denying the existence of objective truth, Religious and Scientific writers are united in a common stand, insisting that there is a real and objective truth to be discovered.
65 *English Historical Review*, June 1999, vol. xciv, no. 457, pp. 806–7.
66 Ibid.
67 See Jones, *The English Nation*, pp. 145–8.
68 H. Butterfield, *The Whig Interpretation of History* (Bell, 1931).
69 Lingard, *History*, i, 437.
70 Ibid., iv, 225.
71 Ibid., iii, 212.
72 Ibid., vii, 153.
73 Ibid., vii, 537. Cf. 'In Macaulay's work all the heroes are Whigs and all the villains are Tories. It was done out of justification for Britain; for Protestantism; for Parliament; and for the great British institutions and traditions', J. B. Black and D. M. MacCaill, *Studying History*, pp. 44–5.
74 C. Russell, *Unrevolutionary England* (Hambledon Press, 1990), Introduction, pp. ix–x.
75 Ibid.
76 Ibid.
77 See above, p. xii.
78 Jones, *The English Nation*, p. xvii. It is this approach which informs the work of many modern practising historians. It lies behind all the important advances in historical research and writing. It is an essential part of the activity of being a historian.
79 Lingard, *History*, i, Preface, xiii–xiv.
80 See above, pp. 33–4.
81 G. P. Gooch, *History and Historians in the Nineteenth Century* (2nd edn, 1952), p. 273.
82 Jones, *The English Nation*, p. 178.
83 Marc Bloch, *The Historian's Craft*, trans. P. Putnum (Manchester University Press edition, 1954), p. 71.
84 For the development of historical criticism at Göttingen, see H. Butterfield, *Man on his Past* (Cambridge University Press, 1955), pp. 51–62.
85 Lingard to Mrs. Lomax, 13 March 1836, *Letters of Lingard to Mrs. Lomax* (2000), p. 55.
86 Lingard to Mrs. Lomax, 3 October, 1848, *Letters to Lomax*, p. 141.
87 Cf. H. Butterfield, *Man On His Past*, Preface, pp. xiv–xv.

Chapter II The Historiography of the Massacre of St. Bartholomew

1 A. Layman, *Papal Pretensions or The Right of the Church of Rome to Power in Great Britain* (1826), p. 19.

NOTES TO PP. 39–45

2. Lord Acton, Cambridge University Library MS, Add. 4863, fol. 171.
3. Cf. Butterfield, *Man On His Past*, p. 178.
4. Lingard, *History* (1st edn, 1823), v, 646.
5. See Butterfield, *Man On His Past*, pp. 192–3. By 1913, 'the old idea of a long period of treachery would seem to have been put out of court for ever', ibid., pp. 197–8.
6. Cf. P. Hughes, *Dublin Review*, vol. 167 (1920), p. 274. Cf. 'Lord Acton had the reputation of being the greatest man of learning in England in the closing decades of the nineteenth century', H. Butterfield, *Man On His Past*, p. 62.
7. Ibid., *Man On His Past*, pp. 193–4.
8. Ibid., pp. 190–1.
9. Ibid., p. 191.
10. Ibid., p. 185.
11. Ibid., p. 187.
12. 'Ranke, the recognised leader of the continental school', H. Butterfield, *Man On His Past*, p. 86.
13. H. Butterfield, *Man On His Past*, p. 179.
14. 'having reasoned himself early out of all belief, he spent the rest of his life trying to lead others to the same conclusion, or to laugh them into scepticism ... He [Allen] was in fact a genuine bigot in materialism', W. H. Torrens, *Memoirs of ... Viscount Melbourne* (1878), p. 100.
15. Butler to Lingard, 17 October 1826, Ushaw MS, 'Lingard's Letters and C. Butler's (transcripts)'.
16. J. Allen, *Edinburgh Review*, xliv (1826), p. 94.
17. J. Lingard, *A Vindication of Certain Passages in the Fourth and Fifth Volumes of the History of England* (London: Mawman, 1826), p. 3.
18. Lingard, *Vindication*, p. 9.
19. Ibid., p. 20.
20. H. Butterfield, *Man On His Past*, pp. 189, 191.
21. Lingard, *Vindication*, pp. 21–2, cf. D. Shea, *The English Ranke*, p. 42.
22. Lingard, *Vindication*, p. 48.
23. Ibid.
24. Ibid., pp. 10–11, cf. D. Shea, *The English Ranke*, p. 43.
25. For Napoleon's scheme for bringing all the European archives to Paris, see *Calendar of State Papers*, i (1862), ed. G. A. Bergenroth. Cf. Acton, Cambridge University Library MS, 4863, fol. 417–18.
26. This started about the year 1860, when 'it was the overthrow of governments which led to the opening of archives', H. Buttefield, *Man On His Past*, p. 79. There had been some collections of documents, published by custodians of the archives, from 1830 onwards. Cf. below, p. 224.
27. Mostyn to Lingard, Versaille, 23 October 1826, Ushaw MS, 'Lingard Correspondence F–M 1805–48'.
28. Lingard, *Vindication*, p. 69.
29. Lingard to Mawman, 1 August 1836, Ushaw MS, 'Lingard to Mawman, 1818–27', B.3, letter M.49.
30. Cf. E. Jones, *The English Nation*, pp. 145–8.
31. For example, Sir Maurice Powicke. Cf. E. Jones, *The English Nation*, p. 146.
32. Gradwell to Lingard, Monte Porzio near Rome, 23 September 1826, Ushaw

MS, 'Lingard Transcripts and Gradwell Correspondence', A.4, ff. 118–19.
33 Lingard to Gradwell, 17 October 1831, Ushaw MS, ibid.
34 Lingard to Wiseman, 29 October 1838, Ushaw MS, 'Lingard to Various Others, 1815–51'.
35 Lingard, *History*, vi, 685.
36 H. Butterfield, *Man On His Past*, pp. 179, 183.
37 Ibid., p. xv.
38 Ibid., p. 186.
39 Ibid., p. 179.
40 See below, p. 48.
41 *Macaulay's Critical and Historical Essays*, ed. G. M. Trevelyan (1903), ii, p. 38.
42 See above, p. 45.
43 See above, p. 45.
44 Acton once claimed that Ranke lacked perspective. Cf. Butterfield, *Man On His Past*, pp. 86–7. Both Acton and Ranke failed to see 'the importance of establishing the individual roles, the personal relationships, and the internal and external setting of events in the years before August 1572, if the evidence is to be properly interpreted', ibid., p. 193.
45 See above, pp. 41, 43–4.
46 See above, p. xx.
47 Lingard, *History*, vi, 687.
48 Ibid., vi, 696–87.
49 See Butterfield, *Man On His Past*, pp. 193, 198–9. It was from the 1880s that it became apparent to the scholarly world that there was no real case for premeditation. Ibid.
50 Interestingly, these were early criticisms of Ranke by Lord Acton. See Butterfield, *Man On His Past*, pp. 86–7.
51 Quoted by Butterfield, ibid.
52 See below, p. 140. Cf. E. Jones, *The English Nation*, p. 170.
53 See below, pp. 208, 217–18, 243. Cf. Jones, *The English Nation*, p. 173.
54 'Le rire est avant tout, une correction', Henri Bergson (1859–41), a French philosopher who won the Nobel Prize for Literature in 1928. In his *Creative Evolution* (1907), he tried to show that all progress and evolution are produced by the 'élan vital' or life force.

Chapter III The Collation of Sources and Lingard's Use of Public Records as a Tool of Source Criticism

1 C. Sharp to Lingard, 6 May 1837. Ushaw MS, 'Lingard Correspondence N-Y Miscellaneous 1806–51', B.2.
2 Lingard to Kirk, June 1821, Ushaw MS, 'Lingard Transcripts', File B.11.
3 Lingard to Kirk, 26 March 1822. Ushaw MS, ibid., File B.11.
4 Quoted in J. W. Thompson, *History of Historical Writing* (New York, 1942), ii, 45.
5 Cf. above, pp. 8–9.
6 Cf. Lingard to Walker, 6 May 1850, Ushaw MS, 'Lingard to Walker

1850–51', Folder 7; Lingard to Coulston, 11 July 1848, Ushaw MS. 'Lingard to Various Others 1815–51'; Lingard to Gradwell, 3 June 1819, Ushaw MS, 'Copies of the letters of Dr. Lingard from the archives of the English College, Rome, 1812–24', B.11.

7   Lingard, *History*, x, 176–7 n1.
8   Ibid., viii, 187 n1.
9   Ibid., viii, 178 n1.
10 Ibid., viii, 388 n2.
11 Ibid., viii, 389 n1.
12 Ibid., viii, 164 n1.
13 Cf. Lingard, *History*, vi, 313 n1; 507 n1; 511 n1; viii, 377 n2.
14 Cf. Lingard, *History*, i, 234 and note 2; iii, 413; iv, 239 n1; v, 181 n1; vi, 148 n3, 120 n1, 132 n1, 415 n3, 419 n1, 645–6 n2; vii, 75 n1, 510 n1; viii, 520 n1; x, 176–7 n1; 156 n1.
15 Cf. Lingard, *History*, v, 275 n2; vi, 714 Note CC.
16 Cf. Lingard, *History*, v, 396 n1; vi, 147 n2, 220 n2.
17 Cf. Lingard, *History*, vi, 518; vii, 279–80, 428 n2; ix, 37; x, 351 n1.
18 Cf. Lingard, *History*, v, 114 n1; vi, 689 n0, 438 n1, 461 n1; vii, 78 n1, 81 n2, 145 n1; ix, 218 n1; x, 53 n1.
19 Cf. Lingard, *History*, v, 396 n1, 400 n1, 505 n1, 448 n2; vi, 235 n2.
20 Cf. below pp. 125–7.
21 See above, p. xii.
22 Cf. below, p. 91
23 See E. Jones, *The English Nation*, pp. 184–94.
24 Lingard, *History*, i, 134 n1, 334 n1, 351 n1, 328 n1, 318 n1, 319 n1, 296 n1, 280 n1, 280 n2, 270 n1, et al.
25 Cf. E. Jones, *The English Nation*, pp. 103–4.
26 Cf. ibid., p. 45.
27 Lingard, *History*, i, 134 n1.
28 See E. Jones, *The English Nation*, pp. 196–7.
29 See above, p. 54; below, pp. 133–4, 242.
30 See below, pp. 57–8. Cf. E. Jones, *The English Nation*, pp. 136–8.
31 See E. Jones, *The English Nation*, pp. 131–8.
32 Lingard, *History*, ii, 626.
33 C. R. Cheney, 'The Alleged Deposition of King John', *Studies in Mediaeval History Presented to F. M. Powicke*, ed. R. W. Hunt, W. A. Pantin and R. W. Southern (Oxford, 1948), p. 116.
34 Ibid.
35 Lingard, *History*, ii, 626.
36 Ibid., ii, 331–2.
37 Jones to Lingard, 4 December 1833, Ushaw MS, 'Lingard Transcripts', B.10, f. 199.
38 C. R. Cheney, 'The Alleged Deposition of King John'; F. M. Puwicke, *Stephen Langton* (Oxford, 1928), p. 79; M. D. Knowles, 'The Canterbury Elections of 1205–6', *The English Historical Review* liii (1938), p. 211.
39 Ibid., ii, 396 n1; III, 201 ni.
40 Ibid., ii, 376 n1.
41 Ibid., iii, 300 n1, 326 n3.

42 Ibid., iii, 329 n1.
43 Ibid., iii, 481 n1.
44 Ibid., iii, 444.
45 Ibid., iii, 360 n3.
46 See J. Kenyon, *The History Men*, pp. 241, 245–6.
47 Lingard, *History*, iii, 223–5.
48 Ibid., iii, 222.
49 See, for example, G. M. Trevelyan, *History of England* (Longman Green, 1947), pp. xix-xx, 179.
50 See *Edinburgh Review*, lxxxiii (April 1825), Ushaw MS 3, 4, 6, 7. Lingard is here criticized for the lack of 'purple' passages in which whig historians were want to enthuse over the continuous growth of 'English freedom'. Again, he is attacked for lacking any of those 'philosophising' passages, which the English public had come to accept in historical works. This meant that he was 'thus certainly falling short of the first rank among historians', *Edinburgh Review*, liii, no. cv (1831), p. 18.
51 See E. Jones, *The English Nation*, pp. 218–47.
52 See J. Kenyon, *The English Nation*, pp. 245–6.
53 See above, p. xii.
54 Ibid.
55 Lord Acton (1834–1902) and Dr. G. P. Gooch (1873–1968), both eminent Cambridge historians, were pioneers in England in the study of the history of historiography. See H. Butterfield, *Man On His Past*, p. 22. Cf. J. D. Fair, *Harold Temperely* (Associated University Presses, 1992), p. 11.
56 See below, p. 121–2.
57 E. Jones, *The English Nation*, pp. 42–4.
58 See the works of such contemporary writers as Sharon Turner, Henry Soames, Thomas Keightley and Henry Hallam. Ibid.
59 Cf. E. Jones, *The English Nation*, pp. 52–9.
60 Cf. E. Jones, *The English Nation*, pp. 70–8.
61 See E. Jones, *The English Nation*, p. 70.
62 For example, Lingard's contemporary, Henry Soames, in his *History of the Reformation of the Church of England* (1826), Preface viii–ix.
63 Sir Francis Palgrave, *History of Normandy and England* (1851), Preface, pp. xlv, xlvi, xlii.
64 For example, Burnet's propagandist *History of the Reformation* (1679) was 'commissioned' by leaders of the Established Church as a counter to the recent French edition of Nicholas Sander's *De Origine ac Progressu Schismatis Anglicani*, which had been first been published in exile at Cologne in 1585. The leaders of the 'whig' or 'Country' party also 'commissioned' it as an anti-Popish weapon to wield against the prospect of a future Catholic king in the shape of James, Duke of York. This was part of the 'Exclusion Crisis'. See E. Jones, 'English Historical Writing on the English Reformation, 1680–1730', Ph.D. Thesis, ff. 17–20.
65 Lingard, *History*, iv, 92 n2.
66 Ibid., v, 128 n1.
67 Ibid., v, 312 n1.
68 Ibid., v, 210–11 n2.

69 Ibid., v, 275 n2.
70 Ibid., v, 402, n2.
71 Lingard's critical techniques are used impartially, dealing objectively with evidence on any side of a religious or political issue. For example, see below pp. 65, 144, 221–2.
72 Lingard, *History*, v, 495 n2.
73 Ibid., v, 443 n1.
74 Ibid., iv, 384 n2.
75 Ibid., vi, 144 n1.
76 Ibid., vi, 119 n1.
77 Ibid., vii, 442 n2.
78 Ibid., viii, 577 n2.
79 Ibid., x, 400 n1.
80 Ibid., x, 400 n2.
81 Ibid., x, 110 n2.
82 Ibid., x, 143 n2.
83 Ibid., x, 179 n2.
84 Ibid., vii, 488 n1.
85 Ibid., viii, 46 n1.
86 Ibid., vii, 73 n1.
87 Ibid., viii, 252 n1.
88 Ibid., ix, 33 n2.
89 Ibid., ix, 101–2 n2.
90 Ibid., x, 244 n2.
91 Ibid., v, 275 n2.
92 Lingard to Mawman, 1 May 1822, Ushaw MS, 'Lingard to Mawman 1818–27', File B.3, letter M.8.
93 Lingard to Mawman, 12 March 1827, Ushaw MS. Ibid., letter M.61.
94 Lingard to Tate, 17 January 1849, Ushaw MS, 'Lingard to Tate ii', File B.4, letter T.127.
95 Lingard to Walker, 22 March 1850, Ushaw MS, 'Lingard to Walker 1850–51', Folder 7.
96 One of the extraordinary pamphlets, describing the alleged cruelty and depravity of the Irish rebels, was *The Rebels Turkish Tyranny*, which spoke in the wildest and most inflammatory terms, to incite the English public. See G. Davies, *The Earlier Stuarts 1603–60* (Oxford University Press, 1937), pp. 114–15. Davies also mentions the 'popular stories' circulated about the atrocious conduct of the Irish priests during the rising – another 'black legend' disproved by Lingard's appeal to the official records, Lingard, *History*, vii, 558–9. The exceptional Sydney Smith berated his contemporaries for believing and spreading such stories: 'You have got hold, I perceive, of all the vulgar English stories . . . and seriously believe that every Catholic beggar . . . is only waiting for better times to cut the throat of the Protestant possessor and get drunk in the hall of his ancestors, *The Works of the Rev. Sydney Smith* (3rd edn, 1845), iii, 347.
97 Lingard, *History*, vii, 554–5.
98 Ibid., vii, 557.
99 Ibid., 558.

100 Ibid.
101 Ibid.
102 Ibid.
103 Ibid.
104 Lingard to Gradwell (n.d.), Ushaw MS, 'Lingard Transcripts', B.11.
105 Ibid.
106 T. Keightley, *The History of England* (1839), ii, 529.
107 G. M. Trevelyan, *England Under the Stuarts* (Oxford, 1925), pp. 218-19.
108 G. Davies, *The Earlier Stuarts* (Oxford: Clarendon Press, 1937), pp. 114-15.
109 J. Morrill, *The Oxford Illustrated History of Tudor and Stuart Britain*, ed. J. Morrill (Oxford University Press, 1996), pp. 339-40.
110 M. P. Maxwell, *The Outbreak of the Irish Rebellion of 1641* (Gill & Macmillan, 1994), p. 259.
111 See below, p. 97.
112 See below, Chapter IV.
113 See below, pp. 136-9.
114 See above, p. xiv.
115 See below, p. 203.
116 Cf. below, p. 87; cf. above, p. 69.

Chapter IV The Role of Private Sources and their Use as a Tool of Source Criticism

1 Lingard, *History* (4th edn, 1837), i, Preface, v-vi.
2 Mr. Leigh had discovered these papers in the attic of his ancestral home in Bardon. He never published them, but they were published in 1909 as *The Bardon Papers*, ed. Conyers Read (Camden Society 3rd, series, 17). Cf. *The Letters of Dr. John Lingard to Mrs. Thomas Lomax (1835-51)*, ed. J. Trappes-Lomax (Catholic Records Society, 2000), p. 186 n196.
3 Ibid.
4 See E. Jones, *The English Nation*, pp. 180-1.
5 Lingard to Sewell, 7 December 1821, Ushaw MS, 'Lingard Correspondence from the Archives of the English Province S.J.', ff. 1-2.
6 S. M. Toyne, 'Guy Fawkes and the Gunpowder Plot', *History Today* (November 1951), p. 16. Cf. A. Fraser, *The Gunpowder Plot* (Weidenfeld & Nicolson, 1996). Fraser used Lingard's *History* as a reference book.
7 Lingard, *History*, vii, 37 n2.
8 Lingard, *History*, viii, 503. The Treaty, written in French, was reprinted from Lingard in *English Historical Documents*, ed. D. C. Douglas, vol. vii, 1660-1714, ed. A. Browning (Eyre and Spottiswoode, 1967), pp. 745-6.
9 Cf. M. Ashley, *England in the Seventeenth Century* (Pelican, 1952), p. 130. Cf. *The Companion to British History*, ed. G. Gardiner and N. Wenborn (Collins and Brown, 1995), p. 245.
10 See E. Jones, *The English Nation*, pp. 181, 307 n111.
11 Lingard to Oliver, 11 August 1827, Ushaw MS, 'Correspondence between Lingard and Oliver', code o, 1. Transcript letter 3.
12 Ibid.

13 E. Jones, *The English Nation*, pp. 184–94.
14 Ibid., 186.
15 Lingard to Gradwell, 3 June 1819, Ushaw MS, 'Copies of the letters of Dr. Lingard from the archives of the English College Rome', Lingard Transcripts, B.11.
16 Lingard to Gradwell, 19 October 1821, Ushaw MS, ibid.
17 Lingard to Gradwell, 3 June 1819, Ushaw MS, ibid.
18 Lingard to Walker, 24 August 1846, Ushaw MS, 'Lingard to Walker 1846–50', A.3, letter f. 31.
19 G. R. Elton, *The Tudor Revolution in Government* (Cambridge, 1953).
20 See E. Jones, *The English Nation*, pp. 32–8.
21 E. Jones, *The English Nation. The Great Myth*.
22 B. H. G. Wormald, 'The Historiography of the English Reformation', *Historical Studies: Papers read before the Second Irish Conference of Historians*, 1958, p. 56; but cf. below, pp. 109–12.
23 Lingard, *History*, iv, 532–3 n3. Cf. iv, 479 n3, 492 n3.
24 See, for example, the 'long and confidential despatch' from Wolsey to Henry, iv, 585. See also Lingard, *History*, iv, 473 n1, 484 n2, 486 n1, 487 n1, 488 n1, 489 n1, n2, n3, 491 n1, 492 n1, 493 n1, 494 n1, n3, 496 n4, 502 n1, 506 n1, 510 n1, 511 n1, 512 n1, 513 n1, 514 n1, 415 n1, 522 n1, 523 n1, 529 n1, n2, 530 n1, n2, 531 n1, n2.
25 Lingard, *History*, iv, 595. See also iv, 446–7 n3, 475 n1, 476–7 n4, 480 n2, 502 n1, 545 n1, 548 n1, 489 n2, 551 n2, 552–3 n2, 554 n2, 556 n1, 557 n1, 558 n1, 559 n2, 563 n1, 593.
26 Ibid., *History*, iv, 384 n1.
27 Ibid., iv, 383–4.
28 Cf. Lingard, *History*, iv, 557–8; vi, 51–2, 142–3, 148–9. Cf. E. Jones, *The English Nation*, p. 206.
29 Cf. D. Loades, *The Reign of Mary Tudor* (Longman, 2nd edn, 1995), p. x.
30 Ibid. Cf. J. Guy, *The Oxford Illustrated History of Tudors and Stuarts*, ed. J. Morrill (Oxford University Press, 1996), p. 23.
31 Lingard, *History*, vi, v, 462.
32 Ibid., v, 530 n1, 531. See E. Jones, *The English Nation*, p. 207.
33 Lingard to Gradwell, 5 June 1819, Ushaw MS, 'Copies . . . from the archives of the English College, Rome, 181–24', Lingard Transcripts, B.11.
34 J. Guy, *The History of Tudors and Stuarts*, p. 23.
35 The story of Lingard's contact with the archive at Besançon can be followed in the correspondence between Lingard and Bishop Poynter in the Ushaw MSS., File B.11 for 1823.
36 Lingard to Mawman, 10 May 1823, Ushaw MS.
37 Lingard, *History*, v, 404 n1.
38 Ibid., v, 461 n3.
39 Burnet used this 'threat' with great effect in the seventeenth century, to scare Protestant landowners, see E. Jones, *The English Nation*, p. 76.
40 Lingard, *History*, v, 495 n1.
41 E. Jones, *The English Nation*, pp. 41–8.
42 Ibid., *The English Nation*, p. 32.
43 See below, pp. 84, 159–60. Cf. L. Baldwin Smith. 'English Treason Trials and

Confessions in the Sixteenth Century', *Journals of the History of Ideas* (1954), xv, no. 4, pp. 471–2; also Smith, *Treason in Tudor England, Politics and Paranoia* (Jonathan Cape, 1986).

44 Camden. Buchanan, Knox and Conn are all corrected in the light of private letters and papers. See Lingard, *History*, vi, 119 n2, 138 n3, 253 n1, 422 n1, 416 n1, 463 n1, 597 n2.
45 Lingard, History, vi, 431 n2.
46 Ibid., vi, 353 n2.
47 Lingard, *History*, vi, 445 n1.
48 Ibid., vi, 652 n1, 652 n2.
49 Ibid., vi, 45 n3.
50 Ibid., vi, 111 n1.
51 Ibid., vi, 492 n1.
52 Ibid., vi, 540 n2.
53 Ibid., vi, 406–7.
54 Ibid., vi, 406–16.
55 Ibid., vi, 408–10.
56 Cf. Elizabeth's 'utter contempt for the maxims and forms ordinarily observed in courts of justice', Lingard, *History*, vi, 704.
57 Lingard, *History*, vii, 81–2 and 82 note i.
58 Ibid., vii, 259 n2.
59 Ibid., vii, 423 n2.
60 Ibid., viii, 16.
61 Lingard to Mawman, 3 November 1825, Ushaw MS, 'Lingard to Mawman', B.3, letter m.41.
62 Lingard, *History*, viii, 137.
63 Milton's 'apocalyptic fervour' was aroused and expressed in his sonnet 'On the Late massacre in Piedmont' (1655).
64 Lingard, *History*, viii, 470 n1.
65 Ibid., viii, 470.
66 See above, p. 27.
67 Cf. above, p. 48.
68 Lingard, *History*, ix, 318 n1.
69 Sir William Temple (1628–99). Diplomat and author. His reputation as a writer rests on his essays, cf. *The Oxford Companion to British History*, ed. J. Cannon (Oxford University Press, 1997), p. 913. His secretary was Jonathan Swift, who later satirized Temple's style in *The Battle of the Books*. Ibid.
70 See E. Jones, *The English Nation*, pp. 218–19.
71 Ibid., p. 229.
72 *Macaulay's Critical and Historical Essays*, ed. G. M. Trevelyan (1903), ii, 38.
73 G. M. Trevelyan, *History of England* (Longman, Green & Co., 3rd edn, 1945), p. 457.
74 G. N. Clarke, *The Later Stuarts* (Clarendon Press, 1949), pp. 69–70.
75 M. Ashley, *England in the Seventeenth Century* (Penguin, 1952), p. 129.
76 T. Munck, *Seventeenth Century Europe* (Macmillan, 1993), p. 374.
77 Lingard, *History*, ix, 159–60 n1.
78 Ibid.

79 See E. Jones, *The English Nation*, 'Lingard's Placing of English History within a European Context', pp. 184–94.
80 Lingard, *History*, ix, 159–69 n1.
81 Cf. E. Jones, *The English Nation*, p. 245.
82 Cf. E. Jones, *The English Nation*, pp. 70–8.
83 See E. Jones, *The English Nation*, pp. 245–7.
84 G. M. Trevelyan, *History of England* (3rd edn, new impression, 1947), pp. 375, 377, 379, 472, 511, 615.
85 J. Black, *A History of the British Isles* (Macmillan, 1996), p. 157.
86 J. Spurr, *History Today*, 17(3), March 1997, p. 53.
87 Lingard, *History*, x, 321. See this whole chapter.
88 Ibid., *History*, i, Preliminary Notice, pp. xi–xiii.
89 Lingard to Coulston, 11 December 1848, Ushaw MS, 'Lingard to Various Others, 1815–51'. Cf. 'But how did I get Mazure's papers. Through an intimate friend Mm. de St Victor. He purchased them for me of [sic] Miss Mazure on the death of her father', Lingard to Mrs. Lomax, 1 March, 1850, *Letters of Lingard to Lomax* (2000), p. 155. Cf. 'In the following pages, whenever I annex the date of the letter, the reader will understand that I refer to the unpublished letters [despatches of Barillon]. The same may be observed of the references to the despatches of D'Avaux and Bonrepaus', Lingard, *History*, x, 119 n2. Barillon was Louis XIV's ambassador in England during the reign of Charles II and James II. This episode forms part of the story of Lingard's contacts with the French archives. Similarly, he commissioned a friend to work on the 'MSS. de Bethune, Bibliothèque De Roi' in Paris, concerning 'Henry VIII's connexion with Anne Boleyn'; and enrolled the services of an expert, M. Buchon, to prove the authenticity of a manuscript concerning Richard II's captivity against the opposition of the critic, John Allen (the same Allen who later to attacked Lingard's account of the Massacre of St. Bartholomew); and then a whole range of 'agents', including the Archbishop of Besançon, were 'commissioned' to help in the unearthing of the despatches of the Imperial ambassador, Renard (during Mary Tudor's reign), which had been deposited in the library at Besançon. Also Mr. Charles Browne sent valuable information and offered his services at any time for research work in the archives of Paris or Versailles. Another 'agent' assisted later, in the 1840s, in showing that the manuscript in Paris mentioned by Agnes Strickland (author of *Lives of the Queens of England*) was a hoax – 'The MS est une chimère'. For details of Lingard's pursuit of information from foreign archives in France, Spain, Italy, Portugal, Germany and Malta, – some very helpful, some fruitless – see E. Jones, 'A Study of John Lingard's Historical Work, with special reference to his treatment of the reign of Elizabeth I', MA Thesis, ff. 59–97.
90 Lingard, *History*, x, 286–7.
91 Ibid., ix, 253–4 and note 1.
92 Cf. Lingard, *History*, x, 315 n1, 318 n1, 323 n1, 323 n2, 324 n2, 325 n1, 326 n1, 327 n1, 330 n2, 333 n1, 335 n1, 336 n1, 337 n1, 338 n1, 339 n1, 339 n2, 340 n1, 341 n2, 344 n2, 345 n1, 347 n1, 348 n1, 349 n3, 351 n1, 351 n1, 353 n1 et al.

93 Lingard, *History*, x, 315.
94 Ibid., x, 320.
95 Ibid., x, 321.
96 Ibid., x, 324.
97 Ibid., x, 330.
98 Ibid., x, 332–3.
99 Ibid., 333 n1.
100 Ibid., x, 334.
101 Ibid., x, 343.
102 For example, Lingard, *History*, x, 185, 200, 202–5, 207, 209, 214, 220, 221–2, 249, 250, 252, 255, 257, 260, 263, 294, 296, 297, 303, 307.
103 Ibid., x, 375.
104 Ibid., x, 376.
105 Ibid., x, 381.
106 See E. Jones, *The English Nation*, pp. 3–42.
107 Ibid., pp. 70–8. Cf. T. Claydon, *William III and the Godly Revolution* (Cambridge University Press, 1995).
108 For example, see Lingard, *History*, x, 318–26, 332–3.
109 J. Callow, *The Making of James II* (Sutton, 2000), p. 11.
110 Ibid.
111 See H. Butterfield, *Man On His Past*, p. 85.
112 Acton manuscript card, Cambridge University Library MS, Add. 120. Cf. Butterfield, ibid.
113 H. Butterfield, *Man On His Past*, p. 85.
114 'Acton passionately believed that his role was not only to assess the work of men and nations but to pass moral judgement upon them. In fact his view of the historian's function was ridiculously high-flown', J. Kenyon, *The History Men*, p. 137.
115 Regius Professor of Modern History, Dom David Knowles, *The Historian and Character*, inaugural lecture delivered at Cambridge, 17th November 1954 (Cambridge University Press, 1955), p.13.

Chapter V The Great Step Forward: Pursuit of the 'Source of the Source'

1 See above, p. 5.
2 Cf. H. Butterfield, *Man On His Past*, p. 79.
3 See E. Jones, *The English Nation*, pp. 152–7, 229.
4 Ibid., pp. 219, 229.
5 See above, p. 37.
6 Cf. H. Butterfield, 'The Göttingen Achievement', *Man On His Past*, p. 61.
7 Cf. E. Jones, *The English Nation*, p. 216.
8 Cf. D. F. Shea, *The English Ranke: John Lingard* (Humanities Press, New York, 1969), pp. 95, 99.
9 Cf. E. Jones, *The English Nation*, p. 194.
10 Ibid.
11 Ibid., 188–92.

12 Lingard to unknown person (no date), Ushaw Correspondence of Lingard – Miscellaneous' (transcript).
13 Lingard to Gradwell, 18 February 1821, Ushaw MS, 'Copies . . . from the archives of the English College, Rome, 1812–14', Lingard Transcripts' B.11.
14 Ibid.
15 Lingard to Gradwell, 3 June, Ushaw MS, ibid.
16 Lingard to Gradwell, 17 May 1820, Ushaw MS, ibid.
17 Ibid.
18 Gradwell to Lingard, 1 August 1818, Ushaw MS, 'Lingard Transcripts and Gradwell Correspondence', A.4, f. 1.
19 Lingard to Mawman, 1 September 1822, Ushaw MS, 'Lingard to Mawman 1818–27', B.3, letter m.10.
20 Three friends were commissioned for the task in 1822 – Dr. Poynter, Mr. Tuite and Mr. Langan who actually transcribed the documents containing the information which Lingard required. The Archbishop of Besançon was also enrolled as a 'willing helper'. Dr. Poynter paid the expenses involved in the commission. See Lingard's correspondence with Dr. Poynter in the summer and autumn of 1822 and the spring and summer of 1823, in Ushaw MSS., 'Lingard to Poynter – Transcripts', B.11.
21 Lingard to Poynter, 29 October 1822, 'Lingard Transcripts', B.11.
22 Lingard to Mawman, 1 September 1822, 'Lingard to Mawman 1818–17', B.3, letter m.10.
23 T. M. Langan to Lingard, Paris, 7 February 1823, Ushaw MS, 'Lingard Correspondence, F–M, 1805–48'.
24 Lingard to Walker, Good Friday, 1844, Ushaw MS, 'Lingard to Walker 1840–9', Folder 6.
25 See E. Jones, *The English Nation*, pp. 137, 201–2.
26 Lingard, *History*, ii, 626.
27 Cf. E. Jones, *The English Nation*, 201–2.
28 *King John: New Interpretations*, ed. S. D. Church (Boydell Press, 1999), pp. 289, 315, cf. E. Jones, *The English Nation*, pp. 131–8.
29 Lingard, *History*, ii, 393–4 n4. Cf. below, p. 264 n91.
30 Ibid., i, 470 n1.
31 Ibid., iii, 189 n1.
32 Ibid., i, 470 n1.
33 Ibid., vi, 51 n1, 108–9 n2, 111 n2.
34 Ibid., vii, 376 n1.
35 Ibid., vii, 281 n1.
36 Ibid., viii, 146 n1.
37 Ibid., viii, 192–3 n2.
38 See E. Jones, *The English Nation*, 180–1.
36 The Treaty was kept secretly in the Clifford archives until 1830 when Lord Clifford 'permitted me to publish it from the original in his possession', Lingard, *History*, ix, 503.
39 Cf. M. Ashley, *England in the Seventeenth Century* (Pelican, 1952), p. 130. Cf. *The Companion to British History*, ed. J. Gardiner and N. Wenborn (Collins & Brown, 1995), p. 245.
40 See E. Jones, *The English Nation*, p. 180.

41 Lingard, *History*, ix, 183–4 n1.
42 Ibid., x, 212 n1.
43 Ibid., x, 293–4 n2.
44 Ibid., ix, 322 n1.
45 Ibid., ix, 393 n1.
46 Ibid., i, 233–4 and note 2.
47 Ibid., ii, 304 n3.
48 Ibid., v, 108 n1.
49 Ibid., vi, 512 n1.
50 Ibid., i, 405 n1.
51 F. W. Maitland, *The Constitutional History of England* (Cambridge University Press, 1961), p. 8.
52 Lingard, *History*, i, 234 n2.
53 Ibid., iv, 503 n2.
54 B. H. G. Wormald, 'Historiography of the Reformation', *Historical Studies: Papers read before the Second Irish Conference of Historians* (London, 1958), p. 56.
55 Lingard, *History*, iv, 328–9 n2.
56 Gerónimo de Zurita (1512–80) was patiently zealous 'in the search and use of manuscripts' and a founder of 'critical scholarship in Spain'. Juan de Mariana (1532–1624) had 'modern views of contemporary affairs', R. B. Merriman, *The Rise of the Spanish Empire* (1925), iv, 482–3.
57 Alexander Cameron to Thomas Sherburne, Valladolid, 5 May 1820 (re-addressed and forwarded to Lingard, 29 May 1820), Ushaw MS, 'Lingard Correspondence F–M, 1805–48'.
58 Cameron to Sherburne, Valladolid, 20 May 1820, Ushaw MS. Ibid.
59 Ibid.
60 Lingard, *History*, iv, 335 n2.
61 Lingard to Tierney, 13 April 1831, Ushaw MS, 'Lingard Transcripts', File B.10, ff. 183–4.
62 Lingard to Tierney, 7 October 1836, Ushaw MS, 'Lingard Transcripts, B.10, ff. 229–30.
63 Lingard to Tierney, 7 October 1836, Ushaw MS, 'Lingard Transcripts', B.10, ff. 221–2.
64 Lingard to Tierney, 4 April 1837, Ushaw MS, ibid. f. 232.
65 Lingard to Tierney, 7 October 1836, ibid. Cf. E. Jones, 'A Study of John Lingard's Historical Work', MA Thesis, f. 31.
66 Lingard, *History*, iv, 478 n1.
67 Ibid., iv, 477–8.
68 Ibid., iv, 477 n1.
69 Ibid., iv, 477 n2.
70 Ibid., iv, 479 n3. Cf. J. Scarisbrick, *Henry VIII* (Eyre and Spottiswoode, 1968), pp. 148–9.
71 Ibid., iv, 476–7.
72 J. Cannon, *The Oxford Companion to British History* (Oxford University Press, 1997), p. 36.
73 Lingard, History, vi, 353 n2.
74 Cf. J. R. Jones, *The Oxford Companion to British History*, p. 263.

75 Lingard to Walker, 18 March 1850, Ushaw MS, 'Lingard to Walker 1850–51', Folder 7.
76 Cf. Lingard to Coulston, 11 July 1848, Ushaw MS, 'Lingard to Various Others 1815–51'; Lingard to Tierney, 27 May 1848, Ushaw MS, 'Lingard Transcripts', B.10, f. 309; Lingard to Oliver, 1 September, 1848, Ushaw MS, 'Correspondence Lingard and Oliver', code O (transcripts), iii, letter 59.
77 Lingard to Walker, 29 January 1849, Ushaw MS, 'Lingard to Walker 1846–50', A.3.
78 See D. MacCulloch, *The Companion to British History*, p. 212.
79 J. R. Jones, *The Oxford Companion to British History*, p. 263.
80 Lingard, *History*, iv, 541 n1.
81 Ibid., v, 7 n1.
82 Ibid., vi, 378 n1.
83 Ibid., vi, 103 n1.
84 Ibid., v, 438 n1.
85 Ibid., vii, 29 n1.
86 S. M. Toyne, 'Guy Fawkes and the Gunpowder Plot', *History Today* (November 1951), p. 16.
87 Fr. Gerard had escaped to the Continent and written a manuscript account of the happenings in England in 1604–5. Lingard was sent this account from the Jesuit archives in Rome.
88 Lingard, *History*, vii, 547 (Appendix).
89 Ibid., 547–8.
90 Ibid.
91 Ibid. For other examples of Lingard's noticing defects in translations, copies, printed editions etc., when compared with the complete documents in their original form, see Lingard, *History*, vi, 417 n2, 109 n1; vi, 8 n1, 359 n1, 378 n1, 704 n1, 108–9 n2, 110–11 n2, 616 n2; vii, 241 n2; viii, 403 n1; x, 127–8 n1. An example of Lingard's concern with impartial accuracy is when, knowing that Garnet was innocent, he still reports some subterfuges in Gerard's manuscript account (in the latter's attempt to help Garnet escape). This was revealed when Lingard compared the copy of Garnet's letter in the manuscript account with the original in the State Paper Office (*History*, vii, 542–3). Lingard writes: 'I have been severely blamed, & called an enemy of the Jesuit order for it, by some of their friends. But the fact is, I could not be silent ... My researches in the State Paper Office were the cause of the paper being found', *Lingard to Lomax*, p. 73.
92 Lingard to Fr. Sewall, 18 April 1822, Ushaw MS, 'Lingard Transcripts', B.11, f. 7.
93 Ibid.
94 See above, p. 7.
95 Lingard to Mawman, May 1825, Ushaw MS, 'Lingard to Mawman, 1818–27', B.3, m.35.
96 Lingard, *History*, viii, 650.
97 Ibid., x, 351 n1.
98 See below, pp. 133–4.
99 The story may well have derived its origin from the fabled account of the British past in Geoffrey of Monmouth's *History of the Kings of Britain*

(1139), supposedly based on a 'very ancient book in the British tongue'. It named Lucius Brutus, great-grandson of Aeneas of Troy, as the mythical founder of Britain. This fantastical account was a best-seller in its day.
100 See E. Jones, *The English Nation*, pp. 195–7. Cf. G. Williams, 'Some Protestant Views of Early British Church History', *History*, xxxviii (1953).
101 Lingard, *Anglo-Saxon Church* (3rd edn, London 1845), p. 4.
102 Lingard, *History*, i, 153.
103 Ibid., i, 54 and note 1.
104 Ibid., i, 54 n2.
105 Ibid., i, 51–3, including footnotes.
106 See H. Butterfield, *Man On His Past*, p. 147.
107 Lingard to Wiseman, 20 August 1837?, Ushaw MS, Lingard to Others 1815–51.
108 Lingard to Walker, 11 January 1836, Ushaw MS, 'Lingard to Walker', AS1, a.23.
109 Holmes to Lingard (no date), from the British Museum Library, Ushaw MS, 'Lingard Correspondence N–Y, Miscellaneous 1806–51', B.2.
110 Lingard to Mrs. Lomax, 8 & 9 January 1837, *Lingard to Lomax*, 73–3.
111 Lingard, *History*, vi, 704 note S.
112 See above, p. 44.
113 Cf. H. Butterfield, *Man On His Past*, p. 58.
114 Ibid., p. 53 n2. Cf. 'the *Decline and Fall* . . . seems out of line with the techniques and aspirations of today's professional historians . . . the exquisite artistry of his imagination . . . Gibbon sought above all to be a philosophical historian . . . in a manner matched only, if at all, by Hume. Nor was it Gibbon's aim to achieve . . . a kind of scientific objectivity . . . In some ways, Gibbon's priorities for the historian were very much those of his age . . . He was fascinated by history as the creation of the historian's mind and . . . its capacity to enlighten, entertain, interest and instruct', Roy Porter: *Gibbon: Making History* (Phoenix Giants, 1988), pp. 159–64.
115 See H. Butterfield, *Man On His Past*, p. 79.
116 Ibid., pp. 90–1.
117 See above, pp. 118–20.
118 See above, pp. 41, 47, 48, 49–50.
119 See above, p. 61.

Chapter VI A Critical Apparatus for Prioritizing the Authority of Sources

1 Lingard, *History*, i, 230 n1.
2 J. Gillingham, *The Companion to British History*, ed. J. Gardiner and N. Wenborn (Collins and Brown, 1995), p. 812.
3 Lingard, *History*, ix, 356 n1.
4 G. N. Clarke, *The Later Stuarts, 1660–1714* (Oxford University Press, 1949 reprint), p. 410.
5 Lingard, *History*, vii, 508 n1.
6 Ibid., *History*, x, 85 n2.

7 Cf. E. Jones, *The English Nation*, p. 20.
8 Lingard, *History*, iv, 284.
9 Ibid., *History*, x, 244 n2. Cf. x, 237 n2.
10 E. Jones, *The English Nation*, p. 186.
11 Lingard, *History*, iv, 540 n1.
12 E. Cameron, *The Oxford Companion to British History*, ed. J. Cannon (Oxford University Press, 1997), p. 999.
13 Lingard, *History*, vi, 213 n1.
14 Cf. Lingard, *History*, vi, 190–1 n2.
15 Lingard, *History*, v, 507 n2.
16 Ibid., v, 457 n1.
17 Ibid., vi, 198–9 n1.
18 Ibid., i, Preface, p. xi.
19 Cf. D. Starkey, *Elizabeth: Apprenticeship* (Chatto and Windus, 2000), pp. 68–9, 76, 314–15.
20 Lingard, *History*, vii, 280 n1.
21 Ibid.
22 Ibid., x, 130–1.
23 Ibid.
24 Cf. E. Jones, *The English Nation*, pp. 219–20.
25 G. N. Clarke, *The Later Stuarts*, pp. 69–70.
26 Cf. E. Jones, *The English Nation*, p. 220.
27 Lingard, *History*, vi, 60–1 n2.
28 Ibid., vi, 410 and 410.
29 Ibid., vii, 43–4 n2.
30 Ibid., ii, 304.
31 Ibid., ii, 303.
32 S. D. Lloyd, *The Oxford Companion to British History*, p. 535. Cf. Lingard's view, see above, pp. 55–6
33 Lingard, *History*, vi, 312 n1.
34 Ibid., vi, 636 n2.
35 S. Alford, *The Oxford Companion to British History*, p. 965.
36 Lingard, *History*, vi, 495 n1.
37 A. S. Hargreaves, *The Oxford Companion to British History*, p. 459.
38 Lingard, *History*, iv, 328–9 n1.
39 Ibid., ii, 478–9.
40 Ibid., ix, 224 n1.
41 J. Innes, *The Companion to British History*, ed. Gardiner & Wenborn, p. 115. Cf. *Oxford Companion to English Literature*, ed. M. Drabble (Oxford University Press, 5th edn, 1985), p. 148.
42 Lingard, *History*, viii, 535 n1 and 328 n1.
43 Ibid., viii, 192–3 n2.
44 D. MacCulloch, *The Companion to British History*, p. 399.
45 R. B. Merriman, *The Rise of the Spanish Empire* (1925), iv, 482–8.
46 Lingard, *History*, iv, 486 n1.
47 Lingard, *History*, ii, 478–9.
48 R. Vaughan, *Matthew Paris* (Cambridge University Press, 1958), p. 263.
49 See E. Jones, *The English Nation*, pp. 200–2.

50 Lingard, *History*, ii, 617 n1.
51 Ibid., ii, iii, 300 n1, 326 n3. Cf. a modern view of Froissart: 'His style is vivid and he is intensely readable, although, sometimes his information has the value of high-class gossip. J. Gillingham, *The Companion to British History*, p. 325.
52 Ibid., i, 230 n1.
53 Ibid., ii, 35 n1.
54 Ibid., ii, 172.
55 Ibid., ii, 172 n2.
56 J. A. Cannon, *The Oxford Companion to British History*, p. 412.
57 *The New Companion to the Literature of Wales*, ed. Meic Stephens (University of Wales Press, Cardiff, 1998), p. 264.
58 Lingard, *History of the Anglo-Saxon Church* (1845 edn), i, Note B pp. 357–62.
59 *The Oxford Companion to English Literature*, ed. M. Drabble, p. 392. *Dictionary of British History*, ed. J. P. Kenyon (Wordsworth Editions, 1994), p. 152. Cf. D. Bates, 'an important, if exceedingly obscure, record of the period of the English invasions of the 5th and 6th centuries', *The Companion to British History*, ed. Gardiner & Wenborn, p. 339.
60 J. Kenyon, *The History Men* (Weidenfeld and Nicolson, 2nd edn, 1993), p. 6.
61 Lingard, *History*, i, 132.
62 See above, p. 10.
63 Lingard, *History*, iii, 454.
64 Ibid., iii, 532.
65 J. Gillingham, *The Companion to British History*, p. 377. Cf. Felipe Fernández Armesto expressed the modern, revisionist view, questioning the reputation of Henry V, in 'Kings in Waiting', BBC 2, 13 October 2001.
66 L. Rollason, *The Oxford Companion to British History*, p. 468.
67 Lingard, *History*, iii, 531.
68 Ibid., iii, 531–2 n1.
69 Ibid., x, 296 n1.
70 Ibid., iv, 476–7 n1. Cf. below, p. 203.
71 Ibid.
72 Lingard to Walker, 22 December 1846, Ushaw MS, 'Lingard to Walker 1846–50', A.3, letter g.22.
73 John Strype (1643–1737) published useful collections of original papers; but wrote from the viewpoint of the Establishment which he wished to serve; and his scholarship was poor and inaccurate. Cf. R. O'Day, *The Debate on The English Reformation* (Methuen, 1985), pp. 47–52.
74 See H. Soames, *History of the Reformation of the Church of England* (1826), Preface pp. v–ix.
75 See S. Turner, *The History of the Reigns of Edward VI, Mary and Elizabeth* (1829), iii, Book 2, pp. 500–1, notes 11–16; p. 502, notes 18, 19, 20; pp. 458–9, notes 26, 27, 28; p. 498, notes 8 and 9; pp. 455–6, note 20; p. 481 note 57; pp. 476–7 note 46; et al.
76 H. Hallam considered 'the annals of barbarians so unworthy of remembrance', *View of the State of Europe During the Middle Ages* (1829 edn), ii, 2.

77 H. Hallam, *View of the State of Europe During the Middle Ages* (1819 edn), p. 335 n*.
78 'Indeed I am not at all out of Countenance to own that I have not much studied those Authors of the mediaeval period . . . If anyone that has more Patience than I, can think it worth while to search into that *Rubbish*, let him . . . To dig in Mines were not to me a more ingrateful imployment. I am contented to take these things from second hand, and am no more out of Countentance to own this . . .' G. Burnet, *Letter . . . To The Lord Bishop of Coventry and Litchfield* (1693), pp. 15–16.
79 For example: 'I lately met with an advertisement of the publication of stories etc translated from Wendover and Matt. Paris – and from the animus of the advertisement I concluded that it was a collection of tales of the incontinence of priests and monks to be found in these authors (for it appears that the monastic writers were fond of telling such stories to the prejudice of the clergy, and the clerical writers repaid them by similar stories of Monks)' Lingard to Walker, 23 October 1849, Ushaw MS, 'Lingard to Walker 1840-9', Folder 6. Cf. Lingard: 'These statements of the chroniclers may, after all, have no other foundation than the unauthenticated scandal of the day', *History*, ii, 176 n1.
80 H. Soames, *Elizabethan Religious History* (1839, p. 209 and note 1.
81 See E. Jones, *The English Nation*, pp. 137–8, 201–3.
82 Ibid.
83 H. Hallam, *View of the State of Europe in the Middle Ages* (1819 edn), iii, 348–50 n*.
84 Ibid., iii, 15 n*, 41 n*.
85 Ibid., iii, 4 n*, 98 n*, 61 n*.
86 H. Hallam, *Constitutional History of England* (1827), pp. 73
87 Ibid., 68 note, 73 n*, 105 note, 147 n+, 176 n*. He was, however, often opposed to Lingard. Cf. his *Constitutional History* pp. 34, 113 n+, 139 n*.

Chapter VII The Use of 'Forensic' Rules of Source Criticism

1 E. Bonney and M. Haile, *The Life and Letters of John Lingard 1771–1851* (1911), p. 17. Lord Henry Brougham, Lord Chancellor (1830–33), was one of the group of friends who presented Lingard with the Lonsdale portrait of himself. I owe this information to Rev. Dr. Peter Phillips.
2 See collection of letters: 'Lingard to Poynter', Ushaw MS.
3 Cardinal Wiseman, *Recollection of the last Four Popes* (1859), 208.
4 J. B. Black, *The Reign of Elizabeth* (Oxford: Clarendon Press, 1936), Preface, p. vi.
5 J. Kenyon, *The History Men*, p. 217.
6 Lingard, *History*, i, pp. xiii–xiv.
7 'The two Cecils [William, 1520–98; Robert, 1563–1612] dominating the two monarchs [Elizabeth I and James I] with subtlety and discretion, pursued with skill, intelligence and determination the policy of turning England into a Protestant country', F. Edwards, *Recusant History* (May, 2001), Vol. 25, no. 3, p. 377. Sir Francis Walsingham (1532–90). Cambridge-educated, with

early and strong Protestant/Puritan sympathies and legal training, he became principal royal *Secretary* to Elizabeth in 1573. He had travelled abroad during the reign of Edward VI and Mary Tudor. Extremely able, he was anxiously 'watchful against Catholic plots' and wanted a European coalition of Protestant powers. He established a network of agents for security and information at home and abroad. See, MacCulloch, *The Companion to British History*, 786 and S. Alford, *The Oxford Companion to British History*, 965. His epitaph could be one of his lines: 'there is less danger in fearing too much than too little', S. Alford, ibid.

8   See below, pp. 157, 190
9   D. MacCulloch, *The Companion to British History*, p. 654. Cf. 'the reasonable if not quite inevitable conclusion is that Thomas Howard [4th duke of Norfolk] and Mary [Queen of Scots] were both unjustly convicted of complicity. The real plot was contrived by Cecil to get rid of a rival and a threat to his master plan for the new England', F. Edwards, *Recusant History* (May, 2001), Vol. 25, no. 3, p. 378.
10 Lingard, *History*, vi, 257.
11 Ibid., vi, 439 n2.
12 Ibid., iv, 439.
13 Ibid., vi, 439 n2.
14 Ibid., *History*, 283 n1.
15 Cf. J. B. Black, *The Reign of Elizabeth* pp. 126, 128 n1; cf. H. Butterfield, *Man On His Past*, pp. 193, 198.
16 Ibid.
17 Lingard, *History*, vi, 650. For further examples of the effective use of 'internal' evidence, see Lingard, *History*, i, 421 n1; ii, 352 n2; iii, 430 n1, 440 n1; iv, 220–1 n1, 254 n1, 317 n1, 576; vi, 352 n1, 414, 626 n1; viii, 84–5 n1, 137; ix, 170 n1, 329–30 n2; x, 272 n1, 271.
18 For examples of this see Lingard, *History*, i, 354 n4; ii, 562 n1; v, 3 n1, 244 n2, 465 n1; vi, 133 n1, 139 n3, 143–4 n3, 144 n3, 431, 516 n2; viii, 517 n1; x, 176–7 n1, 177.
19 Ibid., vi, 139 n3.
20 Ibid., vi, 133 n1.
21 Ibid., i, 354 n4.
22 Ibid., ii, 562 n1.
23 Ibid., v, 3 and n1.
24 'Lee was made bishop of Chester, was translated to Lichfield and Coventry, and honoured with the presidentship of Wales-Stowe, 453' Ibid.
25 See Lingard, *History*, iv, 296 n2, 284 n2; v, 360 n1; vi, 168 n1; vii, 491 n1; x, 242 n1.
26 Lingard, *History*, i, 440. For other examples, see ibid., v, 464, 480; vi, 162 n1, 193, 194 n1, 442; x, 205 n1, 243.
27 Ibid., v, 434 n2.
28 'The preparation of arms and provisions which she made for the purpose of rebelling with the others, and of maintaining herself in strength in a house (Donnington) to which she sent the supplies . . . Modern historians have failed to give it due weight because they miscalculated Elizabeth's position. It is so romantic, is it not, to see her as a "weak woman", vulnerable and

defenceless? The fact that Elizabeth used these words herself when she entered the Tower should put us on our guard', D. Starkey, *Elizabeth: Apprenticeship* (Chatto & Windus, 2000), pp. 143–4. Starkey says that D. Loades, in his *Two Tudor Conspiracies* (Cambridge, 1965), 'consistently underplays' Elizabeth's involvement'; and that she was a 'political player of the first rank in Mary's reign', p. 326. This had been Lingard's judgement in 1821.

29 Lingard, *History*, v, 419 n1.
30 Ibid, iv, 172 n1.
31 Ibid., v, 438 n1. Cf. above, pp. 114–15.
32 Ibid., iii, 201 n3.
33 Ibid., vi, 357.
34 Ibid., i, 302 n1.
35 D. Bates, *The Companion to British History*, p. 269.
36 Lingard, *History*, iii, 413 n1.
37 Ibid., iii, 413 and note 2.
38 Ibid., iii, 412–13.
39 Cf. N. Saul, *Richard II* (Yale University Press, 1997), p. 425; It was 'Henry IV's decision to have him [Richard II] murdered', J. Gillingham, *Companion to British History*, p. 652.
40 Lingard, *History*, viii, 240–1 n1.
41 Ibid., vi, 74–5.
42 Ibid., vi, 295 n2.
43 See Lingard, *History*, iv, 316 n1; v, 109 n1; 182 n1, 257, 381 n1, 675–6, 681 Note J; vii, 227 n1; x, 274 n1.
44 For examples, see Lingard, *History*, ii, 127 n1, 376 n1; iii, 189 n1, 457 n2; iv, 57 n3, 76 n2, 79–80, 158 n1, 332, 367–8 n1, 384 n2, 426 n2, 473 n1, 477 n1; v, 5 n1, 70 n1, 74 n1, 109 n1, 118 n2, 128 n1, 174 n1, 393 n1, 441 n2, 464; vi, 92 n1, 92 n1, 110–11 n2, 119 n2, 122 n1, 162 n1, 167–8 n2, 331 n1, 357 n3, 490, 512 n1; vii, 48–9 n1, 62 n1, 65 n1, 279–80, 428 n2, 500–1 n3, 512 n2, 554 Note I; viii, 208 n1; ix, 127 n1, 312 n1; x, 296 n1, 304 n2, 351 n1.
45 Lingard, *History*, ii, 127 n1.
46 J. Gillingham, *Companion to British History*, p. 813.
47 Lingard, *History*, iv, 475 n1.
48 Ibid., iv, 480 n2.
49 Ibid., iv, 76 n2.
50 Ibid., v, 393 n1.
51 Ibid., vi, 182 n1. The 'fact' was that 'Murray knew that his charge against Mary would be met with a similar charge against his associates, and that her proofs were better able to bear investigation than his'. Ibid.
52 Ibid., *History*, vii, 376 n2.
53 Ibid., vi, 512 n1.
54 Lingard to Mawman, 1825 (no date), Ushaw MS, 'Lingard to Mawman 1818–27', B.3, letter m.30.
55 Lingard to Mawman, April or May 1825, ibid., letter m.32.
56 See below, p. 261, note 89.
57 See Lingard, *History*, i, 439; iv, 158 n1, 272 n1; vi, 541–2 n1, 308 n1, 352

n1, 626 n1, 647 n1, 697 Note M; vii, 37 n2, 65 n1, 485 n1; viii, 10, 328 n1, 634; ix, 77 n1, 318 n1; x, 104–5 n2, 184, 341 n1.
58 Ibid., x, 184.
59 Ibid., x, 184 n2.
60 For examples, see Lingard, *History*, iv, 158 n1; vi, 182; n1, 651 n1, viii, 177–8; x, 243–4.
61 For examples, see Lingard, *History*, iv, 426 n2; viii, 636; x, 27, 194.
62 For examples, see Lingard, *History*, vi, 164 n1, 352 n1, 420.
63 For examples, see Lingard, *History*, ii, 266 n1, 405 n1; iii, 394; iv, 187, 272 n1, 282 n1, 528 n1, 533 n2; v, 77 n1, 118 n2; vi, 74 n1, 193, 321, 533 n2; v, 77 n1, 118 n2; vi, 74 n1, 193, 321, 469 n1, 647 n1, 648, 713 Note BB; vii, 48–9 n1, 55 n1, 81; viii, 635.
64 Lingard, *History*, iii, 394.
65 Ibid., iv, 282 n1.
66 Ibid., iv, 528 n1.
67 Ibid., iv, 533 n2.
68 Ibid., v, 77 n1.
69 Ibid., vi, 74 n1.
70 S. M. Toyne, 'Guy Fawkes and the Gunpowder Plot', *History Today* (November 1951).
71 Lingard, *History*, vii, 55 n1.
72 Ibid., vii, 540–1.
73 Ibid., vii, 81.
74 'I will only add that implicit faith is not to be given to the documents published by the government', Lingard, *History*, vii, 549. For a masterly and critical survey of the evidence, based on authentic materials, showing the manoeuvres of the Government to indict Garnet of treasonable involvement in the Gunpowder Plot, see Lingard's appendices, *History*, vii, 540–50. Cf. F. Edwards observations in 2001 on the Gunpowder Plot in notes 93 and 106 below.
75 Lingard, *History*, viii, 635.
76 For examples, see Lingard, *History*, iv, 480 n2; vi, 358–9 n1, 414, 626 n1, 687 Note M; vii, 280 n1; x, 415 Note D.
77 Lingard, *History*, iv, 480 n2.
78 Ibid., vi, 358–9 n2.
79 Ibid., vi, 414.
80 Ibid., vi, 415 n1.
81 Ibid., vi, 415 n2.
82 Ibid., vi, 696–7.
83 Ibid., Appendix S, pp. 696–704.
84 See E. Jones, 'Building the Official Version', *The English Nation*, Chapter I, pp. 31–60.
85 See the Government's treatment of Davison, Lingard, *History*, vi, 457–74.
86 C. Haigh, *Elizabeth I. Profiles in Power* (2nd edn, Longman, 1998), 10.
87 See E. Jones, *The English Nation*, pp. 207–10. For cultural 'achievements' see ibid., pp. 42–9, 51–4. Cf. P. McGrath and J. Rowe, 'The Imprisonment of Catholics for Religion Under Elizabeth I', *Recusant History* (October 1991), Vol. 20, no. 4; cf. P. Williams, *Later Tudors*, pp. 467–8.

88 Lingard, *History*, x, Note D, p. 415.
89 Ibid., vi, 687 Note M.
90 Action, MS card, Cambridge University Library MS, Add. 4863, f. 415.
91 See L. Baldwin Smith, 'English Trials and Confessions in the Sixteenth Century', *Journal of the History of Ideas* (1954), xv, no. 4. Cf. L. Baldwin Smith, *Treason in Tudor England. Politics and Paranoia* (Jonathan Cape, 1986).
92 L. Baldwin Smith, *Journal of The History of Ideas* (1954), xv, 4, pp. 471–2.
93 Lingard, *History*, vi, 619–19. F. Edwards argues that 'Events of 1601, including the eclispse of Essex, were part of Sir Robert Cecil's long-term plan in master minding the Gunpowder Plot, *Recusant History* (May, 2001), Vol. 25, no. 3, p. 409.
94 Ibid., vi, 380.
95 The legend of Philip II as a 'monster of iniquity' was created originally by William the Silent in his *Apologia*. It can be seen in Robert Watson's *History of the Reign of Phillip II* (1777); and through influential works of English historiography in the nineteenth century as J. A. Froude. *History of England* (1856–70), J. L. Motley, *Rise of the Dutch Republic* (1855) and W. H. Prescott, *History of the Reign of Philip II* (Boston, 1855–58). Sharon Turner, Lingard's contemporary, described Philip as 'the vindictive arm of the Papacy' and 'the relentless enemy of every patriotic Englishman', S. Turner, *The History of the Reigns of Edward the Sixth, Mary and Elizabeth* (2nd edn 1829), iv, 141 n1. Lingard was the first English historian to give a more balanced view of Philip, based partly on documents from the Simancas archives, E. Jones, *The English Nation*, p. 191.
96 A. Dimock, 'The Conspiracy of Dr. López', *English Historical Review*, ix (1894), p. 470. Dimock referred to W. H. Prescott for his account of Philip II's 'ethics'.
97 Lingard, *History* (1st edn, 1823), v, 535.
98 Sherburne to Lingard, 28 February 1823, Ushaw MS, 'Miscellaneous, 1806–51', 11.
99 Lingard, *History* (1st edn, 1823), v, 535.
100 *Calendar of State Papers: Simancas IV. Elizabeth 1587–1603*, ed. M. A. S. Hume (1899), Introduction, p. liii.
101 R. B. Merriman, *The Rise of the Spanish Empire*, iv, 558–9.
102 Lingard, *History*, vi, 664.
103 Ibid., vi, 661. In *The English Nation* (p. 209) I inadvertently ascribed this view to Lingard, rather than to the 'foreign ambassador', and take this opportunity to correct it.
104 Lingard, *History*, vii, 55 n1.
105 Ibid., vii, 21 n1.
106 D. MacCulloch, *The Companion to British History* (1995), p. 493. F. Edwards, however, in 2001, says that the Main and Bye plots 'which helped to discredit the secular clergy' were 'Further important stages along the way' to producing Sir Robert Cecil's 'master piece in the gunpowder plot', *Recusant History* (May, 2001), Vol. 25, no. 3, p. 409.
107 Lingard, *History*, v, 158 n1.
108 D. MacCulloch, *The Companion to British History*, p. 136.

NOTES TO PP. 162–4

109 Ibid., p. 32.
110 For example, Lingard, *History*, iii, 44; iv, 383, 451, 540 n1; vii, 48–9 n1; ix, 37, 137, 426; x, 243.
111 See Lingard, *History*, i, 440; ii, 53.
112 Lingard, *History*, i, 359 n2; ix, 218 n1.
113 Ibid., i, 359 n2.
114 For example, Lingard, *History*, ii, 108; v, 481–2, 485–6; vi, 664.
115 For example, Lingard, History, i, 75–6, 82, 358–9, 374, 457; ii, 45, 166; iii, 527 n1; v, 305 n1.
116 For example, Lingard, *History*, viii, 12 n1, 542 n1; x, 80 n1, 244 n2.
117 For example, Lingard, *History*, i, 439; ii, 127, 172; v, 360–1 n2, 496; vi, 30 n1, 357; vii, 37 n2, 278, 280 n1, 201; viii, 459 n1; x, 72–3 n2, 130.
118 Lingard, *History*, vi, 140–1.
119 Ibid., vi, 136–7 n3.
120 D. MacCullock, *The Companion to British History* (1995), p. 719.
121 Lingard, *History*, ii, 303.
122 'If the manner of his death could have borne investigation, John for his own honour would have made it public. His silence proves that the young prince was murdered', Lingard, *History*, ii, 303. Modern scholarship now agrees that John's guilt in this matter is 'virtually certain'. Dr. S. L. Lloyd, *The Oxford Companion to British History*, p. 535.
123 For examples, see Lingard, *History*, i, 439; vi, 184, 236; vii, 278; viii, 415 n1.
124 See, for example, Lingard, *History*, iv, 532 n2; v, 98, 108, 432 n2; vi, 150 n1, 687 Note M; vii, 48 n1; ix, 81 n1; x, 243.
125 See, for example, Lingard, *History*, vi, 162 n1. This concerns a charge of treachery towards Mary Queen of Scots by the Archbishop of St. Andrews (leader of the Hamiltons), in 1567: 'On what authority then is he now charged . . . ? Upon hearsay only . . . told so by . . . two of Mary's bitterest foes, and told so at a moment when it was necessary to raise doubts of the sincerity or the Hamiltons in the mind of Elizabeth . . .', ibid.
126 For example, Henry Soames refers to this tract as having 'the plain solid character to be expected from such a paternity', *Elizabethan Religious History* (1827), p. 309.
127 See below, pp. 191–4.
128 See P. Hughes, *The Reformation in England* (Hollis & Carter, 1954), iii, 366.
129 Lingard, *History*, vi, 331.
130 Ibid., vi, 341.
131 Ibid., vi, 378 n1.
132 For example, Lingard, *History*, vi, 714 Note CC; vii, 78 n1.
133 Lingard, *History*, vii, 549.
134 For examples, see Lingard, *History*, ii, 376 n1; v, 77 n1; vi, 302, 648, 649 n1, 518; vii, 500–1 n3; viii, 542 n1; ix, 154 n2; x, 69, 244 n2, 306 n1, 306.
135 For example, Lingard, *History*, ii, 189 n1; vi, 162 n1, 270; ix, 132.
136 For example, Lingard, *History*, iv, 76 n2, 82 n1, 260; v, 464; vi, 235 n2, 352 n1, 393, 676; vii, 63 n1, viii, 21 n1, 108 n1; ix, 132; x, 412.
137 For example, Lingard, *History*, vi, 518; vii, 279–80, 428 n2; ix, 37; x, 351 n1.

138 Lingard, *History*, viii, 328 n1.
139 For example, Lingard, *History*, vi, 522, 517–18; vii, 227 n2; viii, 398.
140 Lingard, *History*, vii, 13.
141 Ibid., v, 367.
142 For example, Lingard, *History*, i, 353, 380–1; vi, 416 n2; vii, 500–1 n3; viii, 187 n1.
143 For example, Lingard, *History*, vi, 138 n2, 474, 661, 663; vii, 450 n1, 481.
144 For example, Lingard, *History*, iv, 71 n2, 80; vi, 274, 420, 488; vii, 500–1 n3; viii, 238.
145 For example, Lingard, *History*, vi, 38 n1, 402 n1, 416 n2, 530 n1; vii, 227 n2; viii, 542 n1, 554 n2; x, 52 n1.
146 Lingard, *History*, vi, 402 n2.
147 Ibid., v, 70 n1. Cf. iv, 57 n3; vii, 37 n2.
148 See above, p. 147.
149 Lingard, *History*, v, 436 n2.
150 'Lingard to Mawman, 10 May 1823, Ushaw MS, 'Lingard to Mawman, 1818–27', B.3, letter m.18.
151 'Princess Elizabeth was sent to the Tower under suspicion of complicity, but no evidence against her could be found', J. Cannon, *Oxford Companion to British History* (1997), p. 625. But D. Starkey updates this in 2000, by showing the serious involvement of Elizabeth in the Rebellion in *Elizabeth: Apprenticeship* (2000), p. 144.
152 A failed plot to kill Charles II and James, Duke of York, as they travelled past Rye House in Hertfordshire, on their way to London from the Newmarket races.
153 Lingard, *History*, x, 194.
154 Ibid., ix, 224 n1.
155 Ibid., vii, 491 n1.
156 Ibid., x, 194.
157 For examples, see Lingard, *History*, v, 482, 485–6; vi, 145–6, 148–9, 220 n2, 286–7 n5, 339 n1, 664, 695 Note Q; vii, 36–7, 75 n2, 510 n1, 527–8; viii, 469–70 n1, 104 n2; ix, 426; x, 226.
158 Lingard, *History*, vi, 220 n2.
159 D. MacCulloch, *Companion to British History*, p. 719.
160 Lingard, *History*, vi, 339 n1. Cf. F. Edwards in 2001 refers to the 'sham propaganda exercise of Edmund Campion's debates in the Tower'. *Rucusant History* (May, 2001), Vol. 25, no. 3, p. 377.
161 A. S. Hargreaves, *The Oxford Companion to British History*, p. 159.
162 See E. Jones, *The English Nation*, pp. 207–10.
163 Lingard, *History*, vi, 664.
164 Ibid., v, 485–6.
165 Cf. E. Jones, *The English Nation*, pp. 220–2.
166 Lingard, *History*, vii, 527–8.
167 Ibid., vii, 558.
168 See E. Jones, *The English Nation*, pp. 207–10.
169 This sonnet, 'Avenge O Lord they slaughter'd Saints', was an impassioned expression of Protestant feelings. Cf. Lingard's treatment of this subject, above, pp. 27, 86.

170 Lingard, *History*, viii, 469–70 n1.
171 Ibid., x, 226. This refers to a dispute between Anglican and Catholic theologians in England at this time in James II's reign.
172 Ibid., vii, 36–7. This refers to the dispute between Anglican and Puritan representatives after the Hampton Court conference (1604).
173 Ibid., ix, 495.
174 Ibid., i, xiv.

Chapter VIII The Application of Lingard's Rules of Source Criticism to Some Celebrated Historical Problems

1 Lingard, *History*, i, xvi.
2 See above, p. 87.
3 Lingard, *History*, i, xiv–xv.
4 Ibid., i, xv; and ii, 572–3.
5 See B. Webster, *Oxford Companion to British History* (1997), pp. 962–3; and D. Bates, *Companion to British History* (1995), p. 785.
6 J. Mackay, *William Wallace* (Mainstream Publishing, 2000), p. 267.
7 Southey was also one of the 'Lake poets' of the Romantic movement, See E. Jones, *The English Nation*, pp. 163–55. For Turner, see E. Jones, *The English Nation*, pp. 160–3. Cf. Lingard's comment, when Turner complimented him on his *Anglo-Saxon Church* (1806): 'It was very unexpected & very kind of him. He added as a present his poems on Richard III, just published. But only think – he is 77, and has just published a poem. I am only 75, but I should think myself in my second childhood if I were to publish a poem', Lingard to Mrs. Lomax, 4 June, 1845, *Letters to Lomax* (2000), p. 133.
8 See E. Jones, *The English Nation*, p. 224; cf. Ranke's view of Providence which seems to act 'at marginal points or by remote control', Butterfield, *Man On His Past*, p. 140. Cf. 'The truth is that technical history is a limited and mundane realm of description and explanation . . . achieved by a disciplined use of tangible evidence . . . When the events have been laid out by the technical historian, they can be taken over by the Catholic or Protestant or atheist – they are equally available for Whig or Tory', ibid., p. 139. This would have been Lingard's view as well.
9 See above, Chapter II.
10 See E. Jones, *The English Nation*, p. 172.
11 Lingard, *History*, iv, 27.
12 *The Oxford and Cambridge Review* (1846), ii, p. 38.
13 T. P. Peardon, *The Transition in English Historical Writing*, p. 279; and D. Shea, *The English Ranke*, p. 35. Cf. Lingard wrote of himself: 'I persuade myself that no writer has hitherto set down to the task more free from political prepossession than myself', Lingard to Mawman, 8 July 1824, Ushaw MS, Lingard to Mawman, 1818–27, File B.3, letter M.21.
14 G. P. Gooch, *History and Historians*, p. 284.
15 See above, p. 22.
16 Lingard, *History*, v, pp. 7–8.

17 Ibid., v, 322–3, 347–8, 463.
18 See D. MacCulloch, *Thomas Cranmer* (Yale University Press, 1996), pp. 88–9.
19 See D. MacCulloch, *Thomas Cranmer*, pp. 476, 440, 557. Cf. F. W. Maitland, *Roman Canon Law in the Church of England* (1896), p. 178; cf. P. Hughes, *The Reformation in England* (Hollis and Carter, 1954), ii, 131–2.
20 See above, Chapter II.
21 R. Griffiths, *The Reign of Henry VI* (Sutton, 1998), p. 2.
22 Lingard, *History*, 190–1.
23 Ibid., 191.
24 Ibid., 191–2 n2.
25 Ibid.
26 D. Hume, *A History of England, Incorporating the Corrections and Researches of Recent Historians* (John Murray, London 1860), p. 225.
27 See E. Jones, *The English Nation*, pp. 152–6.
28 E. Malone, *Shakespeare's Works*, ed. E. Malone (London, 1804), xi, 653.
29 M. Laing, *History of Scotland* (1800–4), xii, 393.
30 Lingard, *History*, iv, 192 n2.
31 Ibid.
32 K. Feiling, *A History of England* (Macmillan, 1959), p. 310.
33 E. F. Jacob, *The Fifteenth Century* (Oxford Clarendon Press, 1961), p. 569.
34 R. A. Griffiths, *The Reign of Henry VI* (Sutton, 1998), p. 892.
35 J. Gillingham, *Companion to British History*, pp. 377–8.
36 Cf. 'Richard is one of England's most controversial figures, immortalized as evil personified by Shakespeare, sanctified by a society dedicated to clearing his name', A. J. Pollard, *The Oxford Companion to British History*, p. 805.
37 Lingard, *History*, iv, 576, Note C, appendix.
38 Ibid.
39 Ibid., iv, p. 577.
40 Ibid., iv, pp. 577–8.
41 Ibid., iv, p. 577.
42 Ibid.
43 Quoted by Lingard, *History*, iv, 578. Cf. Thomas More: 'I personally learned this ... long ago by trustworthy report'. More shared Lingard's approach to source criticism, stating that 'people's suspicions and conjectures' supply 'a route which occasionally leads to the truth but more often away from it', T. More, 'History of Richard III' in the *Complete Works of St. Thomas More*, Vol. 15, ed. D. Kinney (Yale University Press, 1986), p. 327.
44 Cf. below, p. 196.
45 Lingard, *History*, iv, 578–9.
46 Ibid., 580.
47 Ibid. Cf. H. Walpole, *Historic Doubts on the Life and Reign of King Richard the Third*, ed. J. Dodsley, London, 1768 (Facsimile reprint, Wakefield, E. P. Publishing, Towota, New Jersey, Bowman & Littlefield, 1974), p. 7. Walpole states that Richard 'deserves to be entirely acquitted of it', p. 7.
48 Lingard, *History*, iv, 580.
49 Ibid., iv, 581.
50 Ibid., iv, 584.

51 See above, p. 180.
52 C. Ross, *Richard III* (Yale University Press, 1999), pp. lvii–lx.
53 R. Griffiths, *Reign of Henry VI*, p. xiv.
54 A. Weir, *The Princes in the Tower* (Pimlico, 1997), p. 8.
55 Ibid., pp. 9–10. Cf. C. Ross, *Richard III*, p. 5.
56 A. Weir, *The Princes in the Tower*, p. 25.
57 K. Duckrey, *Richard III. A Source Book* (Sutton, 1997), p. xxxviii.
58 J. Gillingham, *Companion to British History*, p. 787. Cf. C. Cheeseman and J. Williams, *Rebels, Pretenders & Imposters* (British Museum Press, 2000), pp. 90–4.
59 Lingard, *History*, i, 548.
60 Ibid., i, 547.
61 Ibid. Cf. Hume had written simply that 'According to tradition, it was worked by Matilda, the wife of William the Conquerer', *A History of England* (J. Murray, 1860), p. 69 n*.
62 Ibid., i, 548.
63 Ibid.
64 Ibid.
65 Ibid.
66 D. R. Bates, *Oxford Companion to British History*, p. 300.
67 J. Gillingham, *The Companion to British History*, p. 242.
68 Lingard, *History*, i, 549.
69 *Dictionary of British History*, ed. J. Kenyon (Wordsworth edn), p. 34.
70 Dr. S. D. Lloyd, *Oxford Companion to British History*, p. 87.
71 Lingard, *History*, vi, 190–3.
72 Ibid., vi, 684, Note J.
73 Ibid., vi, 681.
74 Ibid., vi, 681.
75 Ibid., vi, 682.
76 Ibid., vi, 682.
77 Ibid., vi, 682–3.
78 Ibid., vi, 683–4.
79 Ibid., 683.
80 Ibid.
81 R. A. Mason, *Oxford Companion to British History*, p. 173.
82 See above, p. 154.
83 Cf. 'Indeed in Neale the present is always before our eyes as we consider the past, and he is much more of a Whig historian than many who are branded as such', J. Kenyon, *The History Men* (1993), p. 218.
84 Lingard, *History*, vi, 690–1.
86 Ibid.
86 Ibid.
87 Ibid., vi, 340–1.
88 Ibid.
89 Ibid., vi, 342–3.
90 Ibid., vi, 343 n1.
91 S. Hargreaves, *Oxford Companion to British History* (1997), p. 159; and F. Edwards, *Recusant History* (May, 2001), Vol. 25, no. 3, p. 379.

92 D. MacCulloch, *Companion to British History* (1995), p. 278.
93 Lingard, *History*, viii, 633.
94 Ibid.
95 Ibid.
96 Ibid.
97 Ibid.
98 MacCulloch, *Companion to British History*, pp. 277–8.

Chapter IX Lingard's Place in English Historiography

1 Lingard, *The History and Antiquities of the Anglo-Saxon Church* (3rd edn, 1845), Preface, p. vii.
2 Lingard, *History of England* (4th edn, 1837), Preface, p. vi.
3 See E. Jones, *The English Nation: The Great Myth*, pp. 184–94. For a fuller account, see E. Jones, 'A Study of John Lingard's Historical Work', MA Thesis, ff. 59–97.
4 See above, pp. 13, 15–16.
5 *Macaulay's Criticism and History Essays*, ed. G. M. Trevelyan (1903), ii, 30.
6 T. Keightley, *The History of England* (1839), ii, 529.
7 N. Davies, *The Isles: A History* (Macmillan, 1999), p. 519.
8 See E. Jones, *The English Nation*, pp. 238–47.
9 See above, p. xv, note 14.
10 A. W. Ward, *The Cambridge History of English Literature*, xiv (1916), p. 54.
11 Quoted by P. Hughes, *Dublin Review* vol. 167 (1920), p. 274. Cf. 'Lingard's *History of England* has been of more use to us than anything that has since been written; it was so far superior to the books that preceded it . . . The impartiality of scientific research is our surest ally if we adopt it', Lord Acton, *The Rambler* (New series, xi, 1859), p. 85.
12 See above, pp. 8–9.
13 Ibid.
14 F. W. Maitland, like Lingard, saw historical writing as a pursuit of the truth about the past. See above, p. xvi, note 22.
15 Dr. D. Englander, *Companion to British History* (1995), p. 493.
16 Lingard to Walker, 15 April, 1847, Ushaw MS, 'Lingard to Walker', A.3, g.11.
17 Lingard to Coulston, 11 December 1848, Ushaw MS, 'Lingard to Various Others, 1815–51'.
18 Lingard to Walker, 2 April 1850, Ushaw MS, 'Lingard to Walker', folder 7.
19 Lingard to Walker, 8 February 1849, Ushaw MS, 'Lingard to Walker', A.3, j.5.
20 C. Firth, *A Commentary on Macaulay's History of England*, p. 36.
21 H. Trevor-Roper, *Macaulay's History of England*, p. 36.
22 P. Ghosh, *English Historical Review*, cxii, no. 446, April, 1997, p. 395.
23 Lingard to Walker, 16 November 1843, Ushaw MS, 'Lingard to Walker', A.2, d.34.
24 Lingard to Mawman, 14 February 1824, Ushaw MS, 'Letters to Mawman', B.3, m.22.

25 T. P. Peardon, *Transition in English Historical Writing*, pp. 240–3.
26 Lingard to Walker, 18 June 1844, 'Lingard to Walker', Folder 6.
27 Lingard, *History*, Preliminary Notice, p. xi. Cf. *Lingard to Lomax*, p. 139.
28 Dr. N. Phillipson, *Oxford Companion to British History* (1997), p. 168.
29 Dr. D. Englander, *Companion to British History* (1995), p. 132.
30 J. Kenyon, *The History Men* (1993), p. 177.
31 D. Wormell, *Sir John Seeley and the Uses of History* (Cambridge, 1980), p. 126. Seeley considered that neither Macaulay nor Carlyle were primarily interested in historical truth; both were 'bent upon producing an effect, upon interesting and thrilling the reader', ibid. Cf. J. Kenyon, *The History Men* (1993), pp. 178–9. Carlyle achieved great fame in his own day; his lectures on *Heroes, Hero Worship and the Heroic in History* (1814) were delivered to 'glittering and fashionable audiences', *Oxford Companion to English Literature* (1994 reprint), p. 171; but his reptuation as a historian has waned in the twentieth century, ibid.
32 See above, pp. 67–9, 87–9.
33 See above, p. 14.
34 See above, p. 11.
35 See Tierney, 'Memoir', Lingard's *History*, xl–xlii. Cf. D. Shea, *The English Ranke*, pp. 72–4. Lingard usually made light about the 'Cardinalate in Petto'; but see *Lingard to Lomax* (2000), pp. 8, 10, 171, note 23. At any rate Lingard made it clear that he did not want it; nor did he want to stay in Rome. Tierney, 'Memoir', Lingard's *History*, xlii. Leo XII presented Lingard with a gold medal (1825) which 'etiquette then generally confined to cardinals and princes'. Leo in 1826 said that he reserved a cardinalate 'in petto' for 'a man of great talents, an accomplished scholar, whose writings, drawn *ex authenticus fontibus*, had not only rendered great service to religion, but had delighted and astonished Europe', ibid.
36 Lingard to Mawman, 20 January 1827 (?) Ushaw MS, 'Lingard to Mawman 1818–27', B.3, letter M.60.
37 D. Shea, *The English Ranke*, pp. 73–4.
38 See above, p. 10.

Epilogue: *'Hic caestus artemque repono'*

1 M. A. Tierney, 'Memoir of Dr. Lingard', *Lingard's History*, i, pp. xlv–xlvi.
2 Mrs. T. Lomax to unknown person, 27 June 1851 quoted in M. A. Tierney, 'Memoir of the Rev. Dr. Lingard', p. xlvi. Cf. the last letter written by Lingard, known to me, was on 14 March 1851 to Mrs. Lomax: 'February was the month of my birthday [5th February]. It nearly proved the epoch of my deathday . . . I was in such a state that I had little doubt that I was on the brink of eternity. However God has spared me once more . . . in spite of a medical warning I yesterday ventured to write a long letter and the consequence was such intolerable pain in the head and spine too, that I begun to think that the consequence with which I had been threatened by the doctors, the paralysis of the brain, was taking place. Today I have rallied again, and mention all this to account to you for my apparent neglect of your kind letter',

Lingard to Mrs. T. Lomax, 14 March, 1851, *Letters to Lomax*, letter xcix, p. 164.
3 E. J. A. Riley, 'Lingard as Liturgist', *A Catholic of the Enlightenment* (1999), ed. J. A. Hilton, pp. 33–48.
4 J. A. Hilton, 'The Cisalpines', *Catholic Englishment*, ed. J. A. Hamilton, pp. 18–19.
5 For a convenient summary, see *Outlines of the 16 Documents: Vatican II*, prepared by V. M. Heffernan (Fowler Wright Books, 1968).
6 'Development' here is in the sense conveyed by J. H. Newman in *An Essay on the Development of Christian Doctrine* (1895). In the 'organic' life of the Church, deeper meanings, implications and insights can be drawn in an 'evolutionary' process, from the original doctrines, but these later developments cannot contradict original and essential doctrines.
7 See above, p. xii.

Appendix 1 The Development of Lingard's *History* through the Various Editions

1 Lingard, *History*, ix, 132.
2 Ibid., 132 n2. Lingard records the execution of a Frenchman who had 'confessed' to starting the fire, observing – after referring the reader to the judicial examination of the prisoner in Howell's *State Trials* – that the man was 'clearly insane'. Ibid. A modern scholar, G. N. Clarke, writes of 'the judicial murder of a miserable Frenchman who persisted . . . in an insane confession, that he had started the Roman Catholic plot', *The Later Stuarts*, p. 64.
3 Lingard, *History*, ix, 132 n2.
4 Lingard to Price, 13 February 1847, Ushaw MS, 'Lingard Transcripts', B.10, f. 363.
5 Lingard to Tierney, 2 September 1826, Ushaw MS, 'Lingard Transcripts', A.4, f. 125.
6 Lingard to Husenbeth, 24 December 1830, Ushaw MS, 'Lingard Transcripts', B.11, f. 7.
7 Lingard to Tate, 9 January 1839, Ushaw MS, 'Lingard to Tate', B.4. T.18.
8 Lingard to Walker, 14 May 1846, Ushaw MS, 'Lingard to Walker', A.3, f. 22.
9 Lingard to Walker, 25 May 1846, Ushaw MS, ibid., letter f. 24.
10 Lingard to Walker, 7 September 1846, Ushaw MS, ibid., letter f. 32.
11 Cf. Lingard to Tierney, 2 September 1826, Ushaw MS, 'Lingard Transcripts', A.4, f. 125.
12 Lingard to Walker, 31 July 1849, Ushaw MS, Folder 6.
13 Lingard to Walker (no date), Ushaw MS, 'Lingard to Walker', A.1, a.17.
14 Lingard to Walker, 18 March 1850, 'Lingard to Walker 1850–51', Folder 7.
15 Lingard to Price, 1849 (no more precise date), Ushaw MS, 'Lingard Transcripts', B.10, f. 38.
16 Lingard to Walker, 12 January 1850, Ushaw MS, 'Lingard to Walker', Folder 7.
17 Lingard to Tate, June 1835, Ushaw MS, 'Lingard to Tate', B.4, T.6.

18 Lingard to Tate, 1836, Ushaw MS, letter T.11. Cf. Lingard to Tate, 1838, Ushaw MS, letter T.13.
19 Lingard to Walker, 14 May 1846, Ushaw MS, 'Lingard to Walker', A.3, letter f. 17.
20 Lingard to Oliver, 9 November 1836, Ushaw MS, 'Correspondence between the Rev. Dr. Lingard and the Rev. G. Oliver' (transcript), I. code O, letter 16.
21 Lingard, *History* (4th edn, 1838), viii, 206 note. Cf. viii, 219 n*.
22 For example, Lingard, to Tierney, 17 October 1831, Ushaw MS, 'Lingard Transcripts and Gradwell Correspondence', A4; cf. Lingard to Gradwell, 21 September 1831, Ushaw MS, 'Lingard Transcripts and Gradwell Correspondence', A4; Lingard to Walker, 24 August 1846, Ushaw MS, 'Lingard Transcripts and Gradwell Correspondence', B11; Lingard to Wiseman, 15 March 1839, Ushaw MS, 'Lingard to Various Others 1815–51'; Lingard to Wiseman, 29 October 1838, Ushaw MS, 'Lingard to Various Others 1815–51'.
23 Lingard to Tierney, 11 March 1840, Ushaw MS, 'Lingard Transcripts', B.10, f. 262.
24 Ibid.
25 Lingard to Tate, 30 May 1844, Ushaw MS, 'Lingard to Tate', B.4, letter T.58.
26 Lingard to Mrs. T. Lomax, 24 April 1847. *Letters to Lomax*, p. 137.
27 Lingard to Price (no date), probably end of 1849, Ushaw MS, 'Lingard Transcripts', B.10, f. 392.
28 Lingard to Mrs. T. Lomax, 23 or 24 July, 1848, *Lomax Letters*, p. 139.
29 Lingard to Walker, 31 July 1849, Ushaw MS, 'Lingard to Walker', Folder 6 marked '1840–49'.
30 Lingard to Walker, 18 October 1850, Ushaw MS, 'Lingard to Walker, 1846–50', A.3, letter j.27.
31 Lingard to Walker, 23 May 1849, Ushaw MS, letter j.22.
32 Lingard to Walker, 5 February 1849, Ushaw MS, letter j.4.
33 Lingard to Walker, 19 February 1848, Ushaw MS, letter h.6.
34 Lingard to Walker, 30 August 1848, Ushaw MS, letter h.25.
35 Lingard to Walker, 29 October 1848, Ushaw MS, letter h.32.
36 See above, p. 214.
37 See E. Jones, *The English Nation*, pp. 182–3.
38 Lingard, *History* (1st edn, 1823), v, 146.
39 Lingard, *History*, vi, 5–6.
40 Ibid., vi, 6 n1.
41 Lingard, *History* (1st edn, 1823), v, 337.
42 Ibid., v, 337, and 4th edn (1838), viii, 100.
43 Lingard, *History*, vi, 284.
44 Ibid., vi, 285 n1.
45 Ibid., vii, 75 n1.
46 See E. Jones, *The English Nation*, p. 180.
47 Lingard, *History*, iv, 579 n1.
48 Ibid., vi, 671.
49 Ibid.
50 Ibid.
51 Ibid.

52 Lingard, *History*, vii, 672. Lingard's refutation of the 'Nag's Head scandal' was brought up in 1859 by a Mr. Alfred T. Lee who argued in *Notes and Queries* (2nd Series, vii, 1859, p. 50) that Barlow was in fact consecrated. The evidence was sufficient to 'convince any candid and unprejudiced mind. That they did convince the great Roman Catholic historian, Lingard, should be sufficient to end the controversy. It will perhaps be best to give his own words . . .' A Mr. F. C. H. answered, that 'Those who are so proud of Lingard's opinion must be reminded that, after all, he never admitted the validity of Anglican orders . . . he never believed that the consecration of Parker was valid after all . . .' (ibid., 202).
53 Lingard, *History*. Cf. 1st edn, v, 156, with the 4th edn, vii, 263.
54 Lingard, *History*, cf. 1st edn, v, 184, with 4th edn, vii, 293.
55 Lingard, *History*, cf. 1st edn, viii, 440, with last edn, vi, 704. Also Cf. 1st edn, v, 494 n28 with 4th edn, viii, 276 n+.
56 For example, Lingard, *History*, cf. 1st edn, v, 432–3 with 4th edn, viii, 197; 1st edn, v, 436 with 4th edn, viii, 200–1; 1st edn, v, 341 with 4th edn, viii, 163–4; 1st edn, v, 287 with 4th edn, viii, 41.
57 For example, Lingard, *History*. Cf. 1st edn v, 622 n85 with 4th edn, viii, 408 n*; 1st edn, v, 623 with 4th edn, viii, 409 n*.
58 For example, Lingard, *History*, cf. 1st edn, 240 n87 with 4th edn, vii, 360 n*.
59 For example, Lingard, *History*, cf. 1st edn, v, 359 n94 with 4th edn, viii, 125 n*; 1st edn, v, 574 with 4th edn, viii, 357.
60 For example, Lingard, *History*, cf. 1st edn, v, 287 with 4th edn, viii, 42 n*.
61 For example, Lingard, *History*, cf. 1st edn v, 327 with last edn vi, 270 n1; 1st edn v, 612 with 4th edn, viii, 397.
62 For example, Lingard, *History*. Cf. 1st edn, v, 292 n71 with 4th edn, viii, 48 n*; 1st edn, v, 228 n62 with 4th edn, vii, 347 n*; 1st edn, v, 277 n60 with 4th edn, vii, 346 n*.
63 For example, Lingard, *History*. Cf. 1st edn, v, 216 n35 with 4th edn, vi, 329 n+ and with last edn vi, 99 n2; 1st edn v, 285 n55 with 4th edn, viii, 39 n* and with last edn, vi, 199–200 n2; 1st edn, v, 506 with 4th edn, viii, 288 n* and with last edn, vi, 519 n1.
64 For example, Lingard, *History*, cf. 1st edn, v, 246 n100 with 4th edn, vii, 366 n+.
65 For example, Lingard, *History*, cf. 1st edn, v, 257 with 4th edn, viii, 5–6.
66 Lingard, *History*, cf. 4th edn, viii, 201 with last edition, vi, 407–8. Gifford was from an ancient Catholic family in Staffordshire. Educated abroad by the Jesuits, he was somehow inveigled into the secret service of Walsingham under the assumed name of Nicholas Cornelius. He became an 'agent provocateur' in the Babington Plot. Cf. The 'false witness' who incriminated Edmund Campion and then fled to the Continent, where he retracted his evidence, given, he said, under fear of the rack, Lingard, *History*, vi, 343 n1.
67 See below, pp. 205–8; also E. Jones, *The English Nation*, pp. 184–94; and E. Jones, 'John Lingard and the Simancas Archives', *The Historical Journal*, x, 1 (1967).
68 Ibid.
69 Lingard, *History*, vi, 235 n2.

70 Ibid., *History*, vi, p. 511.
71 Ibid., *History*, vi, 505.
72 See above, p. 37.
73 To illustrate the general accuracy with which Lingard received and conveyed the information from the Simancas Archives, compare the information in a letter from Sherburne of 26 November 1832 to Lingard (Ushaw MS, Lingard Correspondence N–Y 1806–51, 11), with Lingard's published account of the documents in *History* (4th edn, 1837–8, viii, note x, p. 458 – Appendix); and also with the Simancas documents published much later in *Calendar of State Papers: Simancas IV. Elizabeth 1587–1603*, ed. M. A. S. Hume (1899), pp. 101–6.
74 Sherburne to Lingard, 19 February 1823, Valladolid, Ushaw MS, Lingard Correspondence N–Y Miscellaneous 1806–51, 11.
75 Ibid. Sherburne was copying the information from Cameron's visit, but added some comments of his own, such as the one mentioned above, note 73.
76 Lingard, *History*, (1st edn, 1823), v, 304 n90.
77 Lingard, *History* (4th edn, 1838), viii, 62 n*.
78 See below, p. 229.
79 Lingard to Mawman, 10 May 1823, Ushaw MS, 'Lingard to Mawman 1818–27', letter m.18.
80 See above, note 73.
81 Sherburne to Lingard, Valladolid, 28 February 1823, Ushaw MS, 'Lingard Correspondence F–M 1806–51', 11.
82 Conyers Reade, *Bibliography of British History – Tudor Period* (2nd edn, Oxford, 1959), no. 874, p. 73. González's account is as follows: 'The rumours that Elizabeth now indulged in the most intimate intercourse with Leicester became so brim, that in one of the audiences with De Cuadra she tried to exculpate herself, showing him the arrangement of her private apartments...' T. González, *Documents from Simancas Relating to The Reign of Elizabeth (1558–1568)* first published in Spanish, 1832, edited and translated by Spencer Hall, 1865, p. 70.
83 See above, note 78.
84 Sherburne to Lingard, Valladolid, 23 February 1823, Ushaw MS, 'Lingard Correspondence 1806–51', 11. Sherburne is here transcribing Cameron's notes for Lingard.
85 Cameron to Sherburne, 10 January 1823, Valladolid (forwarded to Lingard by Sherburne), Ushaw MS, 'Lingard Correspondence, 1805–48. Cf. 'it [the correspondence] exhibits a shocking picture of Elizabeth's lewdness, total want of principle, & readiness to comit [sic] every crime', ibid.
86 Sherburne to Lingard, 19 February 1823 (Sherburne is transcribing Cameron's notes for Lingard), Ushaw MS, 'Lingard Correspondence 1806–51'.
87 'I could not meet with the name of the Camerera mayor, but am promised it shall be found for the next post', ibid; but here Sherburne is writing on his own part.
88 *Calendar of State Papers – Simancas IV 1587–1603*, edited by M. A. S. Hume (1899), p. 106.
89 Lingard, *History*, vi, 659–60 n1. Lingard had actually been able to quote

from existing Simancas despatches, de Quadra's statement that 'Under the pretext that Dudley's apartment in a lower storey of the palace was unwholesome, she removed him to another, contiguous to her own chamber – 'una habitacion alta junto a su camera, pretestando que la que tenia era mal sana'. In September of the same year these rumours derived additional credit from the change in the queen's appearance: 'La reigna (a lo que entiendo) se hace hydropica, y comienza ya a hincharse notablemente ... lo que se parece es que anda discarda y flaca en extremo, y con un color de muerta ... que la marquesa di Noramton y milady Coban tengan a la reyna por pelegrosa y hydropica, no hay duda', ibid.

90 See D. Starkey, *Elizabeth: Apprenticeship* (Chatto & Windus, 2000), pp. 68–9, 76, 314–15.
91 Ibid.
92 Ibid.
93 See above, p. 37.
94 See E. Jones, 'John Lingard and the Simancas Archives', *Historical Journal*, x, 1 (1967), p. 72.
95 Sherburne to Lingard, 26 November 1932, Ushaw MS, 'Lingard Correspondence N–Y Miscellaneous 1806–51', 11.

Appendix 2 Lingard's System of Reference and Quotation

1 F. Palgrave, *The History of Normandy and England* (1851), Preface, pp. xlv–xlvi.
2 See E. Jones, *The English Nation*, pp. 76–7.
3 J. Kenyon, *The History Men*, 2nd edn (Weidenfeld & Nicolson, 1993), p. 38.
4 T. Smith to T. Hearne, 31 December 1705, *Letters Written by Eminent Persons in the Seventeenth and Eighteenth Centuries*, ed. J. Walker, 1813, i, 143.
5 G. Burnet, *The History of the Reformation of the Church of England*, ed. N. Pocock (1865), Editor's Preface, p. 67.
6 Cf. E. Jones, *The English Nation*, pp. 77–8.
7 Ibid.
8 For example, Lingard, *History*, vi, Note C, pp. 668–73; Notes J and K, pp. 681–4; Note S, pp. 696–704; vii, Note B, pp. 540–1; Note C, pp. 541–4; Note D, pp. 544–50; Note I, pp. 554–9.
9 Lingard, *History*, vi, 91 n2, 210–11, 388.
10 Ibid., vi, 194, 240 n2, 378 n1, 388, 415 n2, 506 n1, 532 n1, 415 n2.
11 Ibid., vi, 50–1 n2, 429.
12 Ibid., vi, 58 n1.
13 Ibid., vi, 40–1 n3, 89 n2, 250 n2, 168–269 n2.
14 Ibid., vi, 46 n1, 52–3 n1, 100 n4.
15 Ibid., vi, 503 n1, 538 n1, 660 n2.
16 Ibid., vi, 289 n1, 306, 347 n1.
17 Ibid., vi, 522 n1.
18 Ibid., vi, 211, 503 n1, 530 n1.
19 Ibid., vi, 576–7 n2.

20 Ibid., vi, 47.
   [All these examples in notes 8 to 20 show only where these instances occur, not how the discrepancy occurs. They are the result of having pursued the reference to its source and thus discovering the discrepancy. To show how the discrepancy occurs would necessitate the over-complicated procedure of quoting the source itself alongside Lingard's version of it, in each instance.]
21 See above, pp. 14–15.
22 Lingard, *History*, vi, 440 n2, 573 n1, 655 n2.
23 Ibid., vi, 172 n1, 183 n3.
24 Ibid., vi, 172 n1.
25 Lingard to Mawman, May 1825, Ushaw MS, 'Lingard to Mawman, 1818–1827', B.3, letter m.35.
26 See above, p. 214.
27 Ibid., *History*, vi, 633 n1, 646 n1.
28 Ibid., vi, 38 n2, 434 n1, 633 n2, 647 n1, 658 n1.
29 Lingard to Tierney, 2 September 1826, Ushaw MS, 'Lingard Transcripts and Gradwell Correspondence', A.4, f. 125.

Appendix 3 Lingard as Literary Artist and Scientific Historian

1 See above, p. 11.
2 Lingard, *History*, ix, 107–14.
3 *Edinburgh Review*, liii (1831), p. 18.
4 Lingard, *History*, ix, 109 notes 1 and 2.
5 Ibid., ix, 110 n1; 114 n3.
6 Ibid., ix, 224 n2.
7 Ibid., ix, 112 n1.
8 Ibid., ix, 113 n3.
9 Ibid., ix, 114 n2.
10 Lingard to Mawman (his publisher), end of 1825 (no date), Ushaw MS, 'Lingard to Mawman 1818–27', B.3, letter m.47.
11 'One of the characteristics of the *History* [Macaulay's] is the extent to which Macaulay uses contemporary newspapers', C. Firth, *A Commentary on Macaulay's History of England*, p. 81.
12 Lingard, *History*, ix, 110 n1.
13 *The Oxford Companion to English Literature*, ed. M. Drabble (Oxford University Press, 5th edn, 1994), p. 769.
14 Lingard, *History*, ix, 114 n2.
15 J. Innes, *The Companion to British History*, p. 352.
16 J. Boulton, *The Oxford Companion to British History*, p. 352.
17 See above, pp. 15–16.

Appendix 4 Lingard on St. Dunstan and the Tenth-Century Reforms

1 See E. Jones, *The English Nation*, pp. 152–3.
2 S. Turner, *History of England* (1814–23), Introduction.

3 Ibid.
4 H. Hallam, *View of the State of Europe during the Middle Ages* (1829), ii, p. 2.
5 H. Hallam, *View of the State of Europe during the Middle Ages* (1829), ii, p. 2; iii, 334–5 and 335 n*.
6 See above, p. 269, note 78.
7 *Edinburgh Review*, xlii (1825), p. 18.
8 F. Stenton, *Anglo-Saxon England* (ed. 1950), p. 161.
9 H. Soames, *Anglo-Saxon Church* (1835 edn), Preface p. xxix.
10 Soames, *Anglo Saxon Church*, pp. xxviii–xxix and p. 196.
11 Ibid., Preface, p. xxxii.
12 Ibid., p. xxxi.
13 Ibid., p. xxxii.
14 Ibid., p. 185.
15 Ibid., p. 196.
16 Ibid., p. 208.
17 Ibid., pp. 184–5.
18 Lingard, *History*, i, 255.
19 Stenton, *Anglo Saxon England*, pp. 360–1.
20 Lingard, *History*, i, 258.
21 Ibid.
22 Lingard, *History*, i, 267.
23 Stenton, *Anglo Saxon England*, p. 451.
24 D. Knowles, *Saints and Scholars* (Cambridge University Press, 1962), pp. 20, 22.
25 Ibid., 22. Cf. D. Knowles, writing on St. Dunstan and the tenth century Reform movement in *The Monastic Order in England* (Cambridge Unversity Press, 1949 edn), pp. 31–56, 472–3, 552–3, 680–1.
26 '... MS. Cleop. p. 76. This writer was a contemporary ... nor does the contrary appear from the Abingdon Charters', Lingard, *History*, i, 255 n2.
27 'MS. Cleop. 79. Osb. 109. Wharton (Ang. Sac. ii. 197 ...) infers ... This is a mistake. Osbern says the contrary. So also does Eadmer, 214', Lingard, *History*, i, 261 n1.
28 Lingard, *History*, i, 269 n1.
29 Ibid., i, 274 n1.
30 Ibid., i, 275
31 H. Butterfield, *Man On His Past*, p. 33.
32 E. Jones, *The English Nation*, p. 147.
33 Lingard, *History*, i, chapter 7; ii, pp. 208–25.
34 Ibid., ii, 119–34.a
35 Cf. F. W. Maitland, *Roman Canon Law in the Church of England* (1898) and Z. N. Brooke, *The English Church and the Papacy* (Cambridge, 1931).
36 See E. Jones, *The English Nation*, pp. 195–205.
37 Ibid.

Manuscript Sources

I have made extensive use of footnotes, which act as a 'running bibliography', so that a further bibliographical section would, I believe, be superfluous. But it will no doubt be useful for some readers if I include here a list of the main manuscript sources related to the research behind this study; many of the sources below are referred to in the text and notes.

1 Ushaw College Library (near Durham)

Here there exists the best collection of the letters and papers of John Lingard. I have made use, especially, of the following:

File A.1 is marked 'Lingard to Canon Walker of Scarborough, April 1, 1837– Dec. 28, 1841). These are originals.
File A.2 continues this correspondence from 1 January 1842 to 26 December 1845. Thes are originals.
File A.3 continues this correspondence from 2 January 1846 to 18 October 1850. These are originals.
File A.4 is marked 'Lingard Transcripts and Gradwell Correspondence'. These are transcripts.
File Ab is marked 'Lingard to Mewsham 1837–50'. These are originals.
File B.3 marked 'Lingard to Mawman 1818–27'. These are originals.
File B.4 is marked 'Lingard to Tate'. These are originals.
File B.10, is marked 'Lingard Transcripts'.
File B.11 is marked 'Lingard Transcripts'. Includes a section of transcripts from the archives of the English Jesuit Province. Also, letters to Husenbeth.
File marked 'Lingard to Various Others 1815–51'. Originals.
File marked 'Lingard Correspondence F-M 1805–48'. Originals.
File marked 'Lingard Correspondence N-Y 1806–51'. Originals.
Folder 6 is marked 'Lingard to Rev. Canon Walker of Scarborough, June 1840–Dec. 1849'. Originals.
Folder 7 is marked 'Lingard to Walker Jan. 12, 1850–April 25 1851'. Originals.
Folder 8 contains miscellaneous letters.
Folder marked 'Wiseman Papers, 772–833'. Originals.

Manuscript Sources

The books of transcripts are kept apart from the files and folders, in a special part of the library. They were presented to the College by Joseph Gillow and are sometimes referred to as the 'Gillow Transcripts'.

Three books are marked 'Correspondence between the Rev'd Dr. Lingard and The Rev'd G. Oliver' – Code letter O.

Other books are marked 'Lingard's letters and C. Butler's'; 'Correspondence of Rev. John Lingard – Miscellaneous'; 'The Rev. J. Lingard's Journal on a tour to Rome and Naples in the summer of 1817'.

There is also a notebook marked: 'Lingard Notes. W. W. St. Peter's Lancaster'.

2 Cambridge University Library

Add. = Additional Manuscripts

Add. 4022 (Some Remarks upon Bishop Burnet's *History of his own Times* by William Sherwin, 1725).
Add. 4479 (Sir Henry Ellis: Observations upon Saxon Literature, 1810).
Add. 4481 (Sir Henry Ellis: Notes on Anglo-Saxon Scholars).
Add. 4863 (box of slips of papers in Lord Acton's own hand).
Add. 9418 Certificate of Triple Doctorate (Theology, Canon and Civil Law) conferred on John Lingard by Pope Pius VII.
Baker, Thomas (Marginal notes on his copy of G. Burnet's *History of the Reformation*).
Baker Collection. Vol. 27, Mm. 1, 38; Vol. Mm. 1, 39; Vol. 29, Mm. 1, 40; Vol. 30, Mm. 1, 41; Vol. 31, Mm. 1, 42; Vol. 32, Mm. 1, 43; Vol. 33, Mm. 1, 44; Vol. 34, Mm. 1, 45; Vol. 35, Mm. 1, 46; Vol. 36, Mm. 1, 47; Vol. 37, Mm. 1, 48; Vol. 38, Mm. 1, 49; Vol. 39, Mm. 1, 50; Vol. 42, Mm. 1, 53; Vols. A, B, C.
Baumgarten papers: 8 (vols. of Strype Correspondence); 9 (Strype Correspondence, Baker Papers part I); 10 (Strype Correspondence, Baker Papers, part II).
Dd. 3. 12 (Original letters of Sir Henry Spelman II).
Dd. 3. 64 (Folio book of Original Letters written during the seventeenth century).
Dd. 8. 52 (Thomas Barlow, Bishop of Lincoln, Queen's College, Oxford, Paper MS. volume of 43 pages on 'The English Historians' dated 30 October, 1656).
Mm. 2. 25 (ff. 166–173 – materials on the Dissolution of Religious Houses).
Mm. vi. 49 (Collection of Letters bound in a folio volume: 'The Correspondence of the Rev. John Strype, 1679–1721').

3 St. John's College Library, Cambridge

'Life of Baker' – Collections, 54.0.
Letter – Thomas Baker to Hon. John Anstis, Garter Principal King of Arms, 15 July 1700.
Photograph of a letter – Gilbert Burnet to Thomas Baker, Windsor Castle, 23 July 1700.

Manuscript Sources

(These two letters, in individual envelopes, are among other letters deposited in cardboard boxes. The classmark of the boxes is W.1, and the letters are indexed under authors.)

4 Corpus Christi College Library, Cambridge

MS. 102, f. 271. 'Cogitationes Lutheri de Sacramento, *Scriptae manu propria*' (Thoughts of Luther on the Sacrament – in his own hand).

5 The Bodleian Library, Oxford

Add. D. 18 (Burnet's History of My Own Time – Autograph I).
Ballard 3 (92 Original Letters Wake to Charlett).
Ballard 5 (including letters from Gibson to Charlett).
Ballard 15 (Strype to Charlett – letters).
Ballard 18 (Browne Willis to Charlett – letters).
Ballard 41 (194 Original letters from Thomas Hearne, William Brome and Thomas Rawlinson, to George Ballard).
Eng. Hist. D. 1 (Non-jurors' Papers – transcripts).
Eng. misc. c. 75 (Thomas Hearne's letters).
Eng. misc. c. 88 (Hearne's letters to Constable &c. transcripts).
Eng. misc. e. 49 (Hearne's Catalogue of his Library).
Eng. Th: c. 22 (Dr. Geo: Hickes: Reply to Vindication of Bishop of St. Asaph's Sermons).
Hearne's Diaries (vols. 5, 44, 48, 52, 56, 58, 61, 63, 71, 72, 102, 104, 106, 112, 114, 115, 122, 124, 142, 174).
Ms. Musaeo 107 (Sir Henry Spelman's 'Original of the Law Terms').
Rawlinson B. 180 (Hearne's Prefaces).
Rawlinson B. 263 (Collections given to Hearne by Browne Willis).
Rawlinson B. 264 (Willis's Mitred Abbies, with some corrections by Hearne).
Rawlinson D. 1002 (Life of Thomas Hearne).
Rawlinson D. 1166 (Transcripts of Hearne's letters).
Rawlinson J. folio 8. Rawlinson's Collections for Cambridge Writers.
Rawlinson Letters 8 (letters to Hearne).
Rawlinson Letters 22 (Thomas Baker to Hearne – 93 letters).
Rawlinson Letters 23 (177 letters Baker to Hearne).
Rawlinson Lettes 26 (including letters from George Hearne to his son, Thomas).
Rawlinson Letters 27A (including letters from Browne Willis to Hearne).
Rawlinson Letters 39 (Mostly transcripts of Hearne's letters, including some originals).
Rawlinson Letters 89 (including a letter from Spelman to Ussher).
Rawlinson Letters 107 (including letters from Thomas Baker to Rawlinson).
Rawlinson Letters 110 (Drafts of letters from Hearne).
Smith, 5, 9, 14, 16 (including letters exchanged between Dom Jean Mabillon and Edward Barnard).
Smith 47 (including letters from Thomas Baker to Smith).

Manuscript Sources

Smith 127 (Smith's letters to Hearne).
Willis 35 (Miscellaneous Collections For the Province of York).
Willis 37 (Collections for the Cathedral & Diocese of St. David).
Willis 38 (Collections for Cathedrals and Dioceses).
Willis 39 (Collections for the Cathedral & Diocese of Lincoln).
Willis 44 (Collections relating to English Monasteries).
Willis 45 (Collections for the Cathedrals and Dioceses of Ely, Oxford & Peterborough).
Willis 49 (Notes of Leases of Abbey & Crown Lands: Temp. R. Eliz).
Willis 76 (Collections for the Cathedrals & Dioceses of Ely, Oxford, Bristol & Peterborough).

6 British Museum Library, London

Add. 56820, 5829, 5832, 5833, 5840, 5941, 5845, 5853, 5860 (Cole Collections).
Add. 6209 (Letters of Learned Men to Professor Ward – ff. 59–60, Baker to Ward).
Add. 22596 (Huddesford's Lives of A. Wood, Hearne and Lister).
Add. 25384 (Letters of Sir Henry Spelman, 1611–1683).
Add. 34599 (Sir Henry Spelman's Correspondence I – 1600–1633).
Add. 34600 (Sir Henry Spelman's Correspondence II – 1634–1640).
Add. 20763, folio 70 (a letter of John Lingard).
Hargrave 15932 (Autographs connected with Oxfordshire – f. 2 Thomas Tanner to Browne Willis).
Hargrave 15935 (Original letters of Browne Willis to Ducarel).
Harley 3777 (Letters: Baker to H. Wanley).
Harley 3780 (Letter to H. Wanley, 1692–1725, vol. iv).
Harley 7048 (Thomas Baker's Collections, vol. xxi).
Lansdowne 1024 (Bishop Kennett's Collections, vol. xxi).
Sloane 1008 (Dr. E. Borlase – Irish Rebellion Papers – 1608–1682, ff. 291, 295, letters of Burnet).
Sloane 1710 (ff. 219, 221, 223 – Burnet's letters).
Sloane 2251 (Letters and Papers of F. Glisson – f. 19, on R. Brady).
Sloane 3299 (Original Letters, Warrants etc. – f. 150, Burnet).
Sloane 4042 (Original Letters to Sir Hans Sloane, vol. vii).
Sloane 4043 (Original Letters to Sir Hans Sloane, vol. ix).
Sloane 4044 (Original Letters to Sir Hans Sloane, vol. ix).
Sloane 4045 (Original Letters to Sir Hans Sloane, vol. x).

7 National Library of Wales, Aberystwyth

MS. 3815C William Floyd's notes on various historians (including John Lingard, Hume and Carte).

Index

Abingdon Abbey, 241
Abingdon Charters, 287
Acta Sanctorum, 2, 247n3
Acton, Lord (1834–1902), ix, xix, xv, xx,
    39, 41, 47–9, 70, 96–7, 159, 199,
    202, 254, 256, 262, 279
Adam of Usk (c.1352–1430), 135
Aeneas of Troy, 266
'Agents Provocateurs', 82, 142, 155, 163,
    193, 224, 283
Agincourt, Battle of (1415), 134
Aidan, Bishop (d. 651), 242
Aix-La-Chapelle, Treaty of (1668), 87
Alcuin (735–804), 133, 138
Aldred, Archbishop of York, 24
Alexander II, Pope, 24
Allen John, xix, 41, 42–5, 159, 253, 261
Alva, Duke of, 39, 49, 43–4
American historians, 90
American Journals, 206
Andre (historiographer of Henry VII),
    180
Andrea, xxiii
Andrews, Bishop of Chichester, 115
Anglican Church/Theologians/Bishops, x,
    110, 168–9, 174, 194, 204, 209,
    222–3, 276
Anglo-centric, x, xii, xiv, 33, 54, 78–9,
    88, 90, 96, 108, 131, 198
  Irish relations, 70
  Norman, 242–3
  Saxon Chronicle, 54–5, 242
  Anglo Saxon Church, ix, 6, 7, 19, 239,
    244
  Saxon dooms, 106
  Saxon England, 25, 118, 133–4, 138,
    198
  Saxon Judicature, 107
  Saxon Language and Literature, 4, 7,
    17, 138, 198
  Saxon Period, 7, 17, 33, 54, 238, 243
  Saxon scholars/scholarship, 4, 10, 239,
    243
  Saxon songs, 123
  Saxon sources, 19, 138, 238, 242
  Scottish history, 220
Angrogna, 168
Anselm, St. (c.1033–1109), 242
Anti-Catholic prejudice, 74–5
Appeals, Act Against (1533), 112
*Apuntamientos para la historia de Felipe
    II* (1832), 227
Arabic numerals, 232
Archaeology/*Archaelogica*, 12, 148–9,
    181, 215
Archbishop's Register, 221
Archives, European, xvi, 75, 98–9, 100,
    121, 229
  French, x, xiv, 54, 75, 199, 261
  German, 75, 199, 261
  Italian, x, xiv, 54, 75, 199
  Maltese, xiv, 54, 75, 199, 261
  Portuguese, xiv, 54, 75, 199
  Spanish, x, xiv, 54, 75, 160, 199,
    225–7, 229, 261, 273
  Vatican, 54, 74, 75, 199
Archivium del Sant Officio di Roma, 201
Aremberg (Spanish envoy), 161
Aristobolus, 204
Aristocracy, English, 240–1
Arles, Council of (314), 9, 118
Armada, Spanish (1588), 106
Army, 53
Arrête Special, 200
Art, 16
Artefacts, 3
Arthur of Brittany, 128–9, 163
Arthur, Prince, 77
Ascension, Feast of, 102
Ashdown, Battle of (871), 148–9
Ashley, Lady Catherine, 228–9
Ashley, Maurice, 87

INDEX

Asserius (Asser, d. c.909; *Vita Elfridi Regis*), 138
Assington (Ashingdon), Battle of (1016), 148–9
Attainder, Acts of, 124
Atheist, 276
Athelstan, King (895–939), 123
Athens, 236
Aurelius, Roman Emperor, 118
Australia, xxii

Babington, Anthony, 144, 155–7
Babington Plot (1586), 83, 119, 127, 143–4, 155, 215, 224–5, 283
Babour (Chronicler), 132
Bacon, Sir Francis (1561–1626), 183
Bailey, T. P., 182
Ballads, 106
Ballard, John, 156
Barberini Archives (Rome), 12
Barillon (French ambassador), 52, 92–3, 117, 127, 158, 261
Barker (Ridolfi conspirator), 143
Barlow, William, Bishop, 115, 283
Barnard Castle, 181
Barnard, Edward, 290
Barrows, 149
Barthes, Roland (post-modernist), 30
Bates, Professor D., 10, 268
Bath, Bishop of, 77
Bayeux Tapestry, 25, 185–8
Bayle, Pierre B. (1647–1706), 2, 30
Baynard's Castle, 187
Bayonne, Meeting at (1565), 39, 40, 44
Bayonne, Bishop of, 78, 153
Beaufort, Bishop, 151
Beaumont (Fr. ambassador), 161
Becket, St. Thomas (c. 1120–70), 162, 215
Bede, Venerable (673), ix, 10, 16, 17, 54, 55, 117–18, 121, 123, 133, 138, 199, 201, 207, 234, 238, 242
Belfast, 199
Belgium, x, xx, 2
Benedict (Chronicler), 128
Benedictines, 2, 97, 135, 239, 241
Bergson, Henri (1859–1941), 50, 254
Berlin University, 206
Bernicia (Kingdom of), 239
Besançon, Archbishop of, 261, 263
Besançon Archives MSS., 80, 101, 165, 259, 261
Bethune MSS., 83, 261
Biancini (Italian historian), 101
Bibliothèque de Rois (Paris), 261

Bisacciano, Mayolino (Italian historian), 104, 151
Black, Professor Jeremy (*History of the British Isles*, 1996), 90
Black, J. B. (*The Reign of Elizabeth*, 1936), 90
'Black Legend', 39, 40–1, 145, 160, 257
Blackwood's Journal, 29
Blair, Tony, 70
Bloch, Marc (*The Historian's Craft*, trans. 1954), 2, 37, 225, 229
Bocher, Joan, 175
Boleyn, Anne (1507–36), 75, 77, 101, 107, 109, 111–12, 135, 136, 146, 153, 155, 161, 165, 261
Boleyn, Mary, 77, 111, 151
Boleyn, Sir Thomas, 111
Bolland, John, 2
Bollandist scholars, 2–3, 99, 261
Bonelli, Cardinal, 41, 43, 48
Boniface, St. (c.675–754), 242
Bonrepaus (French ambassador), 92, 261
'Book of Martyrs' (1563), 62, 65
Borlase, Dr. E. (1608–82 Irish Rebellion Papers), 291
Boston, 206
Bothwell, Earl of (c.1535–78), 144, 146, 162, 188, 190
Boulton, Dr. J., 237
Brandon, Lord, 166
Bretagne, 146
Bridferth (Contemporary *Life of St. Dunstan*), 242
Brienne MSS., 78
Bristol, Earl of, 196
Britain, 9, 74, 133, 204, 252
Britain, Roman, 133, 204
British Archaeological Association, 13
  Bishops, 118
  Catholics, 14
  Church, 21, 204
  Constitution, 22
  Early history, 118
  Empire, 136, 201
  History, 96
  Historians, 118
  Historical tradition, xi
  Historiography, ix, x, 15, 199
  Institutions, 252
  Museum Library, 74, 220, 266
  Sailors, 225
  Spirit, 61
  Tradition, 252
  Uniqueness, 90
Britons, 9

Index

Brompton, 128
Buccleugh MSS., 52
Buchanan (Chronicler), 81, 260
Buchon, M., 152, 261
Buckingham, Duke of, 129
Buckingham, Earl of, 93-4
Bunzl, Martin, 30
Buoncampani Papers, 46
Burgess, Professor Glen, 245
Burgh, Hubert de, 58
Burghley, Lord William (1520-98), 126-7, 129, 142-3, 163, 191, 215, 220, 269
Burghley State Papers, 62, 81
Burke, Edmund (1729-97), 46, 177
Burnet, Gilbert (1643-1715), xiv, 62-4, 54, 71, 89, 90, 92, 93-4, 96, 106, 130, 137-9, 146, 151-2, 166, 230-1, 238, 256, 269
Burton, 83
Butler, Dom Alban, xviii
Butler, Mr. (of Burton Constable), 73
Butler, Sir Pierce, 111-12
Butterfield, Sir H. (1900-79), ix, x, xiii, xix, 47-8, 96-7, 199, 243, 245
Bye Plot (1603), 161, 273

'Cabal', 73-4
'Caesar', 192
Calendar of State Papers, Simancas, 228
Calvinists, 45, 150
Camp, Roman (castrum), 208
Cambridge Antiquarian Society, 221
  Scholars, 15, 205
  University, xx, 97, 99, 136, 146, 269
  University Library, xx, xxii, 50, 96
Cambrensis, Giraldus (Gerald of Wales, d. c.1220), 132
Camden, William (1551-1623), ix, 81, 83, 142, 148, 150-1, 164, 167, 260
'Camerera Mayor', 227, 228-9
Cameron, Alexander, 225-7
Campeggio, Cardinal Lorenzo, 75-7
Campion, St. Edmund (1540-81), 164, 167, 191-4, 175, 183
Can, Mr. (priest), 22
Cannon, Professor J., 112
Canon Law, 112, 244
Canterbury, 55, 215
Capacini, Mgr., 46
'Cardinalate in Petto', 280
Carlisle, 140
Carlos, Don (s. Philip II), 226
Carlyle, Thomas (1795-1851), ix, 204-5, 280

Carne, Sir Edward, 219-20
Carte, Thomas (*History of England*, 1747-55), 152, 181-3
'Casket Letters', 151, 188-90
Catesby, Robert, 84, 154
Catherine de Medici (1519-89), 39-40, 43, 46-7, 49, 126, 145, 175
Catherine of Aragon (1485-1536), 77, 107-9, 112, 146, 155
Catherine Howard (1520-42), 161-2
Catholic Bishops, 50, 140, 221
  Church, 1, 7, 9, 30, 69, 209-10
  Emancipation (1829), 20-1, 39, 50, 67, 211, 250
  Enlightenment, 17
  Episcopacy, 221, 222-3
  Theologians, 276
Catholicism, English, 17, 23, 72-4, 80, 99, 104, 168, 225
Catholic Relief Act (1778), 19
Catholics, 14, 81, 164, 174-5, 191, 276
Catholics, Persecution of, 18-22, 39, 99, 115, 175, 191-2, 272
Caveirac, Abbé de, 40
Cecil, William (see Lord Burghley)
Cecil, Sir Robert (1563-1612), 129, 269, 273
Challoner, Bishop, 19
Chancery, High Court of, 182, 221
Charles I (1600-49), 52, 84-5, 100, 104, 129-30, 150-2, 194
Charles II (1630-85), 28, 66, 73, 86-8, 91, 104-5, 196, 203, 261, 275
Charles IX (France), 39-40, 46-9
Charter of the Forests (1215), 103
Charters, 3, 214
Chartley House, 83, 156-7
Chateaubriand (1768-1848), 44-6
Cheney, Professor C. R., 3, 55-6, 58, 102-3, 139
Chetham Library (Manchester), 74
Christ, 192
Christendom, 54, 57, 227
Christian Humanism, 30
Christians, 1, 7, 4, 118, 243
Church, Early British, 21, 204
Church lands, 80
'Citizen of the World', xii, xiv, 17, 33, 54, 61, 89, 95, 210, 245
Civil War, English (1642-49), 32, 130
Clairvaux, Abbot of, 132
Clarendon, Earl of (1609-74; *History of the Great Rebellion*), 64-7, 85, 104, 130, 150, 166, 196, 237
Clarke, Sir George, 87

INDEX

Claude, Queen, 110
Claydon, Dr. T. (*William III & the Godly Revolution*, 1996), 93
Clement VII, Pope (1523–34), 78, 146
Clement XIV, Pope, 250
Clergy, Submission of (1529–30), 112
Clifford Archives, 74, 163
Clifford, Sir Thomas, 74
Cnut, King (c.994–1035), 149
Coins, 3
Coke, Sir Edward (1552–1634), 154, 161
Coldingham (Double-monastery), 239
'Collective Memory', 67, 70
Coligny, Admiral de, 40, 49
Cologne, 65, 256
Commons, House of, 58, 60, 67
Commons' Journals, 65, 105
Confessions, 70, 81, 84, 145, 159–60
Conn (Papal envoy), 104
Conquest, Norman (1066), 242–3
Contextual Criticism, 45
Continent, European, xii, 3–4, 7, 9, 40, 74, 99, 166, 199, 206, 224, 241, 244, 283
Continental Historiography, xiii, xviii, xix, 41, 48, 199
  influences, 4
  politics, 91, 94
  scholars, ix, xviii, 48
  seminarians/priests, 163
  sources, 91
Conway Castle, 153
Corby Castle, 73
Cornelius, Nicholas (alias Gifford), 283
Corpus Christi College library, Cambridge, 221
Cotton Library MSS., 78, 83, 119–20, 220, 230
Council Book, 62
Council of barons, 57
Counter-Reformation, 116
Courcelles Despatches, 83
Court, Elizabethan, 228
Courtenay, Thomas, 147, 165
Covenanters, 27
Coventry, 147
Cranmer, Thomas (1489–1556), 114, 172, 174, 175
Craven, Lord, 94
Criminology, 141
Crispin, Lord of Milherve, 165
Critical techniques/sciences, 2, 76
Cromwell, Oliver (1599–1658), 28, 52–3, 69, 86, 114, 130, 154, 204
Cromwell, Richard, 64

Cromwell, Thomas (c.1485–1540), x, xiv, 14, 75–9, 81, 89–90, 94, 96, 117, 157, 162, 174
Crook Hall (Nr. Durham), 19
Crown lawyers, 144
Croyland, Chronicle, 177, 180, 182–4
Crusades, 135
Culture, 16–17, 241–2, 272
Curle (Secretary to Mary, Queen of Scots), 119, 120, 156

Danby, Earl of (1631–1712), 86, 105
Danes, 149
Danish Invasions, 241
'Dark Ages', 6, 8, 55, 138, 238–9
Darcy, Lord, 77
Darnley, Lord (1645–77), 27, 63, 113, 145, 162–3, 167, 188, 190
Dates, 3, 15, 111, 213, 233
D'Avaux (French ambassador), 92–3, 261
Davies, Geoffrey, 69, 198
Davies, Professor Norman, xii, xv, xxii, 249
Davison, William, 157, 172
Defoe, Daniel (c.1660–1731; *Journal of the Plague Year*), 237
Depôt des Affaires Etrangères (Paris), 92
De Re Diplomatica (1681), xvii, 3–6, 246
D'Estrades, 88
Derrida, Jacques (post-modernist), 30
Despatches/Reports, 53–4
'Development', 209–10, 28
Diceto (Chronicler), 128
Digby, Lord, 166
Dighton (murderer of Princes in the Tower), 183
Diplomatic history, 97
'Divine Right of Kings', 159
Dimmock, A., 160
Diplomatic history, 97
Divine Revelation, 1
'Divorce Question', 24, 75–8, 112, 146, 155, 174
Doctrine, Religious, 10
Döllinger, Dr. Ignaz (1799–1890; German historian), 206, 214
Dolman (Publisher), 76, 214
Domesday Book (1086), 187
Donnington, 270
Dorset, 187
Douai College, xvii, xviii, 19, 74, 121, 135, 150
Double Monasteries, 239
Dover, 187
Dover, Secret Treaty of (1667), 73–4, 104

Index

Drake, Sir Francis (c.1540–96), 82
Drogheda Massacre (1649), 114, 154
Dublin, College Library, 68
Dudley, Arthur, 228
Dudley, Robert (see Leicester, Earl of)
Duffus-Hardy, Charles (editor: Close Rolls), 221
Dugdale, Sir William (1605–86; Monasticon), ix, 7
Du Moulin (Secretary to William of Orange), 92
Duppa, Bishop, 196
Dunstan, St. (c.909–88), 238–44
Durham, xii, 19
Durham, Dean & Chapter Library, 26, 36, 73
Dutch Army, 93–4
Dutch Sources, 53
Dykveldt (Dutch ambassador), 152

Ealdred, Archbishop of York (d. 1069), 25
Eadmer, (c.1060–c.1130; Historia Nova), 138, 242, 287
Eadwig, King (c.940–59), see Edwy
Ecclesiastical History of the English People (731), 10, 54, 207
Echard, Lawrence (1671–1730), 52
Eclectic Magazine (New York), 206
Ecole des Chartes (Paris), ix
Edinburgh, 189, 214
Edinburgh, Treaty of (1560), 223
Edinburgh Review, xix, 22, 26, 41, 239
Edgar, King (c.944–75), 240–41
Edict of Pacification (1570), 48
Education, 76
Edward the Confessor, King (c.1003–66), 162
Edward I (1239–1307), 162
Edward III (13112–77), 58, 60
Edward IV (1442)83), 148, 176–80, 182, 184
Edward V (1470–?83), 179, 182
Edward VI (1537–53), 174, 204, 270
Edwards, Francis, 272–3
Edwy, King (c.940–59), 240–1
Egerton Papers, MXX., 83, 157
Eikon Basilike (1649), 194–6
Eleanor, Dame, 151
Elizabeth I, Queen (1553–1603), 24, 35, 36, 51, 66, 73, 80–1, 104, 114, 119, 124, 126, 129–30, 142, 144–5, 147–8, 153, 156, 158–9, 160–1, 164–6, 188, 191–2, 215, 219–21, 224–30, 260, 270–1, 275, 284

Elizabethan Government, 83, 113, 142, 144–5, 158, 161, 163–4, 188, 191, 193, 220–1, 223–6, 272
Ellis Correspondence, 94, 135
Elton, Sir G. R., 76, 79, 200
Empire, xiv
Empirical truth, 2
England, 55, 61, 86–7, 91, 932, 105, 127, 166, 167, 186–7, 188, 199, 201, 211–12, 219, 238
Englander, Dr. D., 249
English Army, 220
  Attitudes/Perspectives, 70, 90
  Catholicism, 17
  College (Rome), 46, 174
  Constitution, 32
  Crown, 92–3, 240
  Culture, 210
  Freedom, 256
  Gentry, 80
  Government, 70, 78–9, 83, 114–15, 141, 145
  Historical Review, 160
  Historiography, iii, xiii, xiv, 6–7, 9, 31–3, 37, 51, 57, 62, 71, 76, 79–80, 83–4, 89, 94, 99, 100, 102, 107, 116, 131, 138, 158, 160, 163, 171, 188, 191, 198, 201, 202, 205–7, 219, 225, 239, 243, 245, 273
  History, 61, 191–2, 199
  English Institutions, 60
  Monastic Chronicles, 7
  Old, 231
  People, 61, 74, 136, 142, 172, 174, 227, 244
  Politics, 175
  Reformation, xiv, 75, 89, 96, 102, 107–8, 112, 131, 137, 199
  Theatre, 179
  Writers, 162
'Enlightenment', 6, 8, 11, 40, 138, 173
Enquiry Concerning Human Understanding (1748), 9
Epigraphy, 3
Episcopacy, 222
Ermarth, Elizabeth Deeds (post-modernist), 30
Essex, 149
Essex, Earl of, 129, 159, 273
Established Church, 21, 174, 193, 211, 256
Establishment, English, 4, 21, 99, 174, 200, 211
Estates, Dutch, 92–3
Ethelward (Chronicler; d. c.998), 54

Index

Ethelwold, Bishop (d. 984), 241–2
Euro-centric, 54, 56, 89, 108
Europe, xiv, 2, 17, 199, 206, 280
European Ambassadors, 91
    Archives, 44, 48, 75, 91, 199, 253
    Christendom, 135
    Civilization, 12
    Community of Peoples, 61
    Dimension, 90
    Feudal Institutions, 57
    European Framework, 56, 58, 96, 199, 243
    History/historiography, 1, 187, 199
    Perspective, 91, 96
    Politics, 88–9, 91
    Scholarship, 2, 17, 48, 175, 199
    Universities, 24, 77–8
Euro-sceptics, 103
Eusebius, 9
Evans, Professor Richard (*In Defence of History*, 1997), xxv
Evelyn, John (1620–1706), 94, 236
Evidence (non-literary), 3
Evil, 70
Exchequer, 177–8
Execution of Justice (1583), 163, 191
Exhumation, 149–50
Expugnatio Hibernica (The Conquest of Ireland, 1189), 132

Fabyan, Robert (Chronicler, d. 1512), 151
Facts, 30–1, 33–4, 234–7
Falkirk (battle of, 1298), 172
Fascism, 12
Fawkes, Guy, 69, 161
Feiling, Sir K., 178
Feingold, Mordechai (American historian), 90
Fénélon, De La Mothe (French ambassador), 126, 225
Fenwick, Mrs. Anne, 209
Ferdinand, King (Spain, 1452–1516), 108–9, 131
Feudal System/Institutions, 243
'Fine Literature', xii, xvi
Firth, Sir Charles, 11, 28, 203
Fitzosbern, William, 147
Flanders, 241
Flassans, de, 150
Fleetwood (Chronicler), 177
Fleury, 7, 250
Florence of Worcester (Chronicler), 138
Fordun (Chronicler), 146
Forensic Science, 31

Fotheringham, 157
Foucault, Michel (post-modernist), 30
Foxe, John (1516–87), ix, xiv, 62, 71, 75, 137–8, 151, 204
France, xvii, 19, 45, 47–8, 86, 88, 127, 165, 206, 224–5, 229
Franche-comté, 88
Francis I, King (France, 1494–1547), 111
Frederick the Great (Prussia), 204
French Academy, 206
    Government, 154
    Language, 189, 198, 206, 250
    Revolution, 19, 46, 204
    School (of historians), ix, 221, 238
    Sources, 53
Froissart, Jean (Chronicler, c.1335–1404/10), 59, 103, 132, 250, 268
Froude, A. J. (1818–94; *History of England*), ix, 75, 273

Gale, Thomas (editions of Gildas, Nennius and Eddi, 1691), 7
Game Laws, 250
Gardiner, Bishop Stephen (c.1497–1555), 114, 148, 165
Garnet, Fr., S. J., 84, 115–16, 154, 220, 251, 272
Gauden, Dr. (Bishop of Exeter, Worcester), 194, 196
Geneva, 86
Geoffrey of Monmouth (d. 1155; *Historia Regum Britanniae*), 265–6
Gerard, Fr., S. J., 64, 73, 115–16, 220–1, 265
German booksellers, 76
    culture and history, v, 204
    Language, 198, 206
    scholarship, xx, 11, 37–8, 40–1, 48, 75, 98, 118, 120, 121, 173, 203–4
    Universities, 37, 99
    writers, 37, 75, 121, 214
Germany, 37, 47, 92, 98, 190, 204
Gervase of Tilbury (Chronicler, c.1145–c.1210), 103, 128
Ghosh, P., 13, 203
Gibbon, Edward (1737–94), ix, 99, 121, 205–6, 250, 266
Gibson, Edmund, Bishop of London (1669–1748), 148
Gifford, Gilbert, 82, 224, 283
Gildas (*De Excidio et Conquesta Britanniae*, c.541), 133
Giles, Rev. Dr. (*Patres Ecclesiae Anglicanae*), 215

Index

Gillingham, Professor J., 134, 179, 184
Gillow, Henry, 73–4
Gilpin, 25
Glamorgan, Earl of, 152
Glasgow, Archbishop of, 73
Glastonbury, Abbey of, 241
'Global history', 96
'Global village', 96
'Glorious Revolution' (1688), 89–96, 199
God, 1, 192
gods, 1, 37
Godwinstone, H. (*see* Harold II)
Goebbels, J. (1897–1945), 145
González, Tomás (*Apuntamientos*, 1832), 224, 226–7, 229, 284
Gooch, Dr. G. P., 61, 1221, 174, 256
Gordon Riots (1780), 18, 21
Gospels, 4
Göttingen University of, 37, 40, 99, 121, 252, 262
Gradwell, Dr. Robert, 46, 74–5, 101
Grafton, Richard (Chronicler, 1507–73), 180
Grave (Holland), 92
Great Fire of London (1666), 211
'Great Myth', xii–xiv, xxii, 9, 10, 62, 71, 76, 85, 89, 99, 117, 200–1, 206, 250
Great Plague (1665–6), 234–7
Great War (1939–45), 61, 245
Greek, 1
Greek writing, 3
Greenway, Fr., S. J., 64, 73, 115, 154, 220–1
Gregory XIII, Pope, 39, 45
Grey, Lord, 166
Griffiths, Professor Ralph, 178–9, 184
Griffet, Henri (1698–1771, French historian), 101
Grosjean, Père, S. J., 247
Group Scholarship, 99
Guise, Duke of, 150, 154
Guizot, François (1787–1874, French historian), 12
Gunpowder Plot (1605), x, 64, 73–4, 84, 115–16, 128, 154, 161, 220, 251, 272–3
Guy, Professor John, 80

Hagiology, 4
Hague, 86, 93, 105
Haigh, Christopher (*Elizabeth I, Profiles in Power*, 1998), 142, 158
Hailes, Lord, 146
Halford, Sir Henry, 150
Hall, E. (Chronicler 1496/7–1547), 62

Hallam, Henry (1778–1859), ix, 69, 71, 75, 137–9, 200, 205, 238, 256
Hamilton, clan, 274
Hamilton, Duke of, 73, 85
'*Hamlet*, 3
Hampton Court, 52
Hampton Court Conference (1604), 115, 169, 276
Hanover, Elector of, 40
Hapsburgs, 88, 109
Hardwicke, Lord, 73
Hardwicke Papers MSS., 72, 81, 83–4, 164
Harfleur, 134
Hargreaves, Dr. A. S., 194
Harleian MSS., 75, 83, 119–21, 157
Harold II, King (c.1022–66), 24–5, 146, 162
Harwich, 143
Hatton, Sir Christoper (c.1540–91), 130, 164
Hearne, Thomas (1678–1735), 4–7, 38, 83, 101, 116, 231
Hebrew, 198
Hemingford (Chronicler), 59, 146
Helveotsluys (Low Countries), 92–3
Henrician Government, 76–7, 94, 107
 Parliament, 77
 Reformation, 25, 90, 163
Henry II (1133–89), 57, 103
 III (1207–72), 103
 IV (1366–1413), 149, 153, 271
 V (1387–1422), 134
 VI (1421–71), 176–80
 VII (1457–1509), 108–9, 124, 153, 181, 183
 VIII (1491–1547), xiv, 24, 75–8, 81, 89, 101, 107–9, 112, 117, 124–5, 146–7, 151, 155, 161–2, 174, 180, 204, 261
Herald's College Archives, 111
Herbert, Lord, 111, 150
Hermitage Castle, 146
Heroes, 204–5
Heyleyn, Peter (*History of the Reformation*, 1661), 137
Hickes, Dr. George (first *Anglo-Saxon Grammar*, 1689), 4, 7, 38
Histoire Générale de la Civilisations en Europe (1818), 12
Historical Laws, 2
 Novel, 11, 30
 Tradition, 17
 Truth, xi–ii, xvi, xxv, 1–3, 7, 13, 65, 70

Historicism, 12
Historiography, xii–x, xiii, 5
History, 1–2, 5, 11, 16, 30, 37, 70–1, 97, 246
History, Technical, 276
Hitler Myth, 61, 245
Hoak, Dale (American historian), 90
Holinshed, R. (Chronicler, d. c.1580), 62, 81, 180
Holland, 82, 86–7, 91, 105, 127, 176
Holland, Lord, 129
Holmes (of the British Museum), 111, 120
Holyrood House, 189
Hornby, 19–20, 206, 208–10
Hoveden (Chronicler), 107, 128
Howard, (of Corby Castle), 220
Howard, Lord Henry, 129
Howard, Philip, 72
Howard, Thomas (4th Duke of Norfolk), 270
Hughes, Mgr. Philip, xxii
Huguenots, 39, 40–1, 48–9, 105, 154
Hume, David (1711–76), ix, xiv, xvi, 8, 11–13, 31, 52, 55, 71, 104, 117, 121, 136, 151–2
Human Family, 61, 70
Husenbeth, Rev. C., 213
Hyde, Edward *see* Clarendon, Lord

Iceland, 61
Icelandic Literature, 138
Iconography, 3
Ingolsby Regiment, 155
Innes, J., 237
Innocent III, Pope (1161–1216), 56
Inscriptions, 3
International Commission for the History of Representative Institutions, 32
International Politics, 97
International Monthly (New York), 206
Internet, xxiii
Interregnum (1649–60), 130
Ireland, 67–9, 132, 217
Irish, ix
Irish Massacre (1641), 21, 67–8, 168
Irish Rebellion (1641), 26, 69
Isle of Wight, 181
Isabella (Queen of Spain), 131
Italian Archives *see* Archives, European
Italian Language, 49, 198, 200

Jacob, Professor E. F., 178
James I (1566–1625), 73, 115, 126–8, 161, 220

James II (1633–1701), 66, 91, 93–5, 117, 123, 125, 127, 135, 152, 158, 166, 168–9, 217, 256, 261, 275
Jedburgh, 146
Jeffreys, Judge (1648–89), 152
Jenkins, K. (post-modernist), 30
Jesuits, 2, 64, 73, 115–16, 192, 247, 283
Jesuit Archives (England), 154, 221
Jesuit Archives (Rome), 265
Jewish, 160
Joaccino, 78
Joan of Arc (1412–31), 174
Joan of Kent, 174
John XII (Pope), 241
John, King (1166–1216), 23, 55–6, 102–3, 128, 132, 163, 244, 274
John of Gloucester, 183
Jonah, 235
Jones, Professor J. R., 114
Joseph, King (of Spain), 229
Judaeo-Christian, 1
Julius II, Pope (1503–13), 78, 109

Kaye, Mr., 74
Keightley, T. (*History of England*, 1839), 69, 200, 256
Kennet, Bishop, 63–4, 94
Kent, 187–8]
Kenyon, Professor John, 142
Killegrew, 220
King's Bench, 192
King's Library (Paris), 152
Kingship, 194
Kipling, Dr. (Dean of Peterborough), 22
Kirk, Mr. 152
Kirk-o'field, 189
Knowles, Professor Dom D. M., 13, 55, 58, 97, 103, 241
Knox, John (c.1512–72), 25, 81, 260
Kyle, Bishop, 73

Labanoff, Prince A., (*Recueil des Lettres de Marie Stuart*, 1844), 83, 157
Laing, Malcolm (*History of Scotland*, 1800), 177, 182, 3, 188
Lancaster, 19, 209–10
Lancaster (House of), 175–6
Lancaster Library, 74
Lancaster University, 208
Lancastrians, 124, 176, 179
Lancelot, 185
Lanfranc, Archbishop (c.1010–89), 242
Langan, T., 263
Langton, Stephen, Archbishop (c.1156–1228), 55, 57, 102–3

INDEX

Lansdowne, Lord, 75
Landsdowne MSS., 74, 121
Latimer, Bishop Hugh (c.1485–1555), 25
Latin, 7, 19, 189, 198, 212
Latin MSS., 19
Laud, Archbishop William (1573–1645), 84, 151
Lauderdale, Earl of, 27
Lee, Bishop Rowland, 146–7, 270
Legal and Financial, 79
Leges Henrici Primi, 107
Le Grand (French historian), 78, 110
Leicester, Earl of, 81, 164, 220, 227, 284
Leigh, William (of Devonshire), 73, 83, 215, 258
Lenane, Fr. Pat, xxii
Leo XII, Pope, 206, 280
Lent, 148
Leopold, Emperor, 88
Levellers, 52
Lever (Protestant 'reformer'), 25
Lexicography, 37
Lichfield, 74
Lichfield Archives, 74
Lichfield, Bishop of, 240
Liddlesdale, 189
Lincoln, 118, 187
Lingard, John
  Achievements, 198–207
  & Acton, Lord, xv, 49, 70, 97, 254, 279
  & Anglo-centricism, xiv, 88, 198
  Anglo-Saxon Church (1808), xviii, 6–7, 19, 239, 276
  & Archaelogy, 148
  & Bede, Venerable, 10, 55, 117
  & Maurist scholarship, 7
  & Carlyle, T., 204
  Character, 14–15, 17, 19, 30, 95, 140, 197–8, 208, 215, 217–18
  'Citizen of the World', xiv, 17, 89, 95–6, 245
  Classical training, xviii, 13
  & Continental politics, 91
  & Culture, 16–17
  & Döllinger, Ignaz, 206, 214
  & Douai College, 19
  Early life, x, 18–20
  & Ecumenism, 20, 209
  & 'Enlightenment', 17, 95
  Education, Continental, x, xvii–iii
  Euro-centric, 86–9, 95
  European perspective, 91, 243–4
  & Facts, 30–1, 33–4, 61
  as Gardener, 20
  & Guizot, F., 12
  & Hearne, T., 6–7
  as Historiographical pioneer, x, xiii, 1, 141–2
  & Historical truth, xvi, xxv, 7, 14, 30, 169, 172, 198, 221, 231–2
  & History as an independent discipline, 31, 34
  & Hornby, 19–20, 206, 208–9
  & Humanities, 19
  & Hume, David, 11–13, 31, 55
  Humour, 50, 217–18, 243
  Illnesses, 208, 215–17, 280
  Impartiality, 29, 34, 65, 103, 144, 174, 276n13
  Intelligence, 19
  & Judgement, 97
  & Laity, 209
  Languages, 17, 49, 98
  Literary powers, 234–8
  as Liturgist & liturgical reformer, 209
  & Mabillon, Jean, xix, xvii, 1, 14–15, 43, 99, 100
  & Macaulay, Lord, x, 13, 48, 88, 120–1, 203, 218, 234, 236, 237
  & Maitland, F. W., 15, 246, 279
  & Mazure, M., 91
  & More, Thomas, 277
  & Metaphysics, 174
  & Non-Juring scholars, 6–7
  & Pantheon of British historians, xi
  Personality, 17, 19, 20, 146, 197–8, 208, 215
  Perspective, 50, 95–6
  & Philosophic history, 11, 12, 15, 31, 200, 255
  & Philosophy, xviii, 2, 11, 19, 31
  Piety, 19
  Politics, 88–9, 276
  as Priest, x, 19, 21, 30, 70, 97, 99, 140, 174, 209, 216
  & Ranke, Leopold von, 37–8, 49–50, 54, 97, 100, 122, 125, 173, 206, 254, 276
  & Rationalism, 173
  & Raumer, Friedrich von, 119–20
  & Recognition abroad, 31, 245
  & Revisionist history, 31, 245
  & Romanticism, 173
  & Scientific methodology, xii, xiii, 7, 35, 257
  & Second Vatican Council (1962–65), 209–10
  & Sentimentality, 172–3
  & Soames, Henry, 211

Index

& Source criticism, xix, xvi, xviii, xxi, 34, 44, 53, 58, 62, 77–9, 83, 95–6, 99–100, 102, 120–1, 137–40, 166, 173–4, 179, 184–5, 187, 197, 199, 201–2, 205, 221, 232, 234–7, 243–4, 257
& Southey, R., 173, 203, 211
& Strickland, A., 203
& Style, xix, 13, 15, 61, 200, 232, 234–
& Theology, xviii, 11, 19, 31, 221
& Turner, S., 173
& Ushaw College, 19, 208
Lisle, Alicia, 64
Literature, History as, 11, 16, 200, 202, 206
Liturgy, 209
Liverpool, 19
Lloyd, Dr. S. D., 128, 188
Logic, 2
Lomax, Mrs T., 280
London, 19, 93, 118, 176, 215, 275
London Institution, 116
London University, xv
Lonsdale, Lord, 110
López, Dr. Rodrigo, 160–1, 273
Lords, House of, 140
   Commission, 68
Lords Despatches, 67–8
   Journals, 53, 65, 67, 236
   Justices, 67
Lord Treasurer's Accounts, 63
Louis XIV (of France, 1638–1715), 73–4, 87–8, 91, 95, 104–5, 127
Lovell, Lord, 123, 153
Low Countries, 43
Lowther, Sir J., 64
Lucerna, 168
Lucius Brutus (Leuer Mawr), 9, 118, 260
Ludlow, 182
Ludlow (*Memoires*), 53, 63
Ludovisi Papers, 46
Lune, River, 208, 210
Luther, Martin, 132, 290
Lyford (Berks.), 194
Lyotard, Jean-François (post-modernist), 30

Mabillon, Jean (1632–1707), xvi, xviii, 1–7, 14–15, 38, 98, 100, 246, 290
Macaulay, Lord (1800–59), ix, xii, xiv, xvi, xvii, 8, 10, 13, 28–9, 37, 48, 71, 87, 99, 121, 130, 136, 171, 200, 202–3, 20–6, 218, 234, 236–7, 252, 280, 286

MacCulloch, Diarmaid (*Thomas Cranmer*, 1996), 174–5, 196
Mackay, James (*William Wallace*, 2000), 173
Mackintosh, Sir James, 46–7
Magna Carta (1215), 57, 102
Main Plot (1603), 161, 173
Maitland, Earl of, 188
Maitland, F. W. (1850–1906), ix, xvi, 13, 15–16, 107, 202, 244, 246, 287
Malone, Edmund, 177–9
Malmesbury, William of (1095–*c*.1143), 106, 123, 132
Man On His Past (1955), 47
Maltese Archives *see* Archives, European
Manchester, 7, 19, 22
Mann, T. (English ambassador at Vatican), 225–6
Manuscripts, 3, 72, 75
Margaret, Duchess (Netherlands), 43–4
Mariana, Juan de (Spanish historian, 1532–1624), 108–9, 131, 264
Maritain, Jacques (French philosopher, 1882–1973), xiii
Marlborough Papers, 52
Marr, Earl of (Scottish regent), 220
Marx, Karl (1818–83), 12
Marxist historians, 12
Mary I (1516–58), 21, 24, 66, 73, 79, 80, 114, 126, 142, 146–8, 151, 153, 165, 167, 174, 204, 219, 229, 261, 270
Mary II (1662–94), 86
Mary Queen of Scots (1542–87), 27, 63, 73, 75, 81–3, 119–20, 127, 129, 142–6, 151, 155–7, 167, 188, 220–1, 223, 270, 274
Mason, Dr. R. A., 190
Mass, 145, 216
Massacre of St. Bartholomew (1572), x, xx, 15, 21, 38, 39–50, 68, 96, 145, 158, 172, 175, 261
Masterman, N., xxii
Mathew, Rev. David, 250–1
Matthew of Westerminster (Chronicler, *Flores*), 138
Matilda, Queen (wife of William the Conqueror), 185–8
Maurist (Benedictine) monks, xviii, 2, 4, 99
Mawman, J. (publisher), 26, 45, 85, 116, 165
Maxwell, M. P., 69
Maynooth College (Ireland), 19

Index

Mazure, M., (*Histoire de la Révolution de 1688 en Angleterre*), 91–2, 261
Mazure, Mlle., 261
McArdle, Canon Nicholas, 210
Medals, 3
Media, 36
Medieval Chroniclers, 55, 58, 101–2, 121, 123, 131, 138–9
   England, 15
   Period, 8, 17, 57, 96, 101, 208, 238, 243, 269
   Institutes, 243–4
   Statutes, 45, 199
Medievalists, 244
Melville, Sir James, 63
Memoirs, 93–4, 123, 153
Mercia, 240–1
Metaphysical Truth, 2–3
Meteren (Dutch historian), 131, 165
Millennium, First, 234
   Second, 122, 172, 198
   Third, 96, 210
Milner, Bishop, 14
Milton, John (1608–74), 86, 168, 260
Milton State Papers, 53
Minden (Germany), 92
Ministère des Affaires étrangères de France, 91
Missionaries, 9–10, 192, 204
Mitchell (Scottish trial of, 1679), 27
Momigliano, A. (Italian historian), 3
Monasteries/monks, 14, 24, 55, 80, 238–44
Monasteries, Dissolution of (1536–43), 14, 112
Monasticon (Dugdale's, 1655), ix
Monmouth, Duke of, 52, 166
Monmouth's Rebellion, 52, 152
Monte Porzio, 254
Montfaucon (*Palaeographica-graeca*), 2–3, 5, 185
Morality, 57
More, Sir Thomas (1478–1535), 112, 171, 180–4, 192, 209–10, 277
Morland (Cromwell's agent in Piedmont), 86, 168
Morley, Bishop, 196
Morrill, John, 69
Morton, Cardinal (1420–1500), 180
Morton, Earl of, 81, 113, 188
Mostyn, Charles Browne, 45–6, 261
Motley, J. L. (*Rise of the Dutch Republic*, 1855), 273
Mulgrove Earl of, 152
Munck, T., 88

Munich University, 206
Muratori, Lodovico Antonio (Italian historian, 1672–1750), 250
Murimuth (Chronicler), 59
Murray, Earl of, 81, 162–3, 166–7, 271
Muslow, Alan, 30–1
Myth/myths, 9, 31, 67, 172
Myths, Nationalist, 70

Nag's Head Scandal, 221, 282–3
Namier, Sir Lewis (1888–1960), 245
Napoleon (1769–1821), 44–5, 226, 228–9, 253
Nationalism, 56, 69
Nau (Secretary to Mary Queen of Scots), 119
Navarre, King of, 48
Nazi code of communication, 247
Neale, Sir John (*Queen Elizabeth*, 1934), 141–2, 191, 200, 278
Nescience, Ideology of, 1, 33
Netherlands, 44, 81, 224–6
Newbrigensis (Chronicler), 128
Newman, Cardinal J. H. (1801–90), 210, 281
Newmarket Races, 275
Newspapers, 236, 286
New York International Monthly, 206
Nimweguen (Holland), 92
Nismes, 150
Noailles (French Ambassador), 63, 66, 126, 147, 151, 165
Nonant, Hugo (Chancellor), 76
Nonconformists, 115
Non-jurors, 4, 6–7
No-Popery Campaigns, 20
Norfolk, 143
Norfolk, Duke of, 51, 73, 129, 143
Norfolk House Library, 74
Normandy, 25, 134, 146
Norman period, 242
Normans, 24–5
Norris, Admiral, 82
Northumberland, Duke of, 73, 110, 153
Northumbrian scholars, 133
North West Catholic History Society, 209
North Wolds, 18
Numismastics, 3

Odo, Bishop (of Bayeux), 147, 187, 188
Oeuvres de Louis XIV, 88–9
Office (daily prayers of a priest), 209, 216
Oldcorne, Rev., S. J., 220
Orderic (Chronicler), 187
Oriental missionaries, 9

Index

Original documents, xii, 2
Orleans, Duchess of (sister to Charles II), 88
Orleans, Duke of, 151
Osbern (Chronicler), 242, 287
Oscott College Library, 74
Oswald, Bishop (961–92), 241–2
Oxford and Cambridge Review, 174
Oxford Faculty of Modern History, ix
Oxford Histories of England, 141
Oxford University, xv, 99, 136, 246
Oxford and Cambridge Review, 174

Pace, Richard (Secretary to Henry VIII), 77
Palaeography, 3, 5
Palaeographica graeca, 3
Palestine, 135
Palgrave, Sir Francis (Dep. Keeper of Public Records), 74
Pallavicini (Italian historian), 101
Pandulph (papal envoy), 56, 102
Panzani, G. (papal envoy), 104
Paolo, Frao (Italian historian), 80
Papacy, 56–7
Papebranche, Daniel (Maurist scholar), 2
'Papist', 10, 24
Paris, 2, 39, 44–6, 49, 91, 95, 111, 158, 172, 175, 226–7, 253
Paris, Matthew (*c*.1200–*c*.1259; *Historia Major*), 55–6, 58–9, 101, 103, 106, 128–9, 131–2, 138–9, 269
Paris University, 78, 106
Parker, Matthew, Archbishop (1504–75), 55, 138, 221–2, 283
Parliament, 32, 53, 60–1, 80, 84–5, 105, 252
Parliamentary Commissions, 214
  Journals, 53, 62–6, 83
  Rolls, 139, 153, 182
  Writs, 55
Parma, Duke of, 106, 151
Parole evidence, 68
Parry, Dr. (double-agent), 160
Paul IV, Pope, 80, 219
Paulet, A., 82–3
Peardon, T. P. (*Transition in English Historical Writing*, New York, 1933), 103
Peel, Sir Robert, 75
Penal Laws, 20, 212
Pennines, 209
Pepyes, Samuel (1633–1703), 236
Percy, Lord Henry, 110–11
Percy, Sir Thomas, 128

Perousa, 168
Perspective, 95
Perrers, Alice, 58
Peterborough, Dean of *see* Kipling
Peterhouse, Cambridge, xiii, xxii, 77, 97, 242
Petition (for Catholic Emancipation), 140
Philip II (King of Spain, 1527–98), 43–4, 80, 143, 160, 165, 224–7, 229, 250
Philipps, Thomas (decipherer), 82, 127, 155, 157
Phillips, Rev. Dr. Peter, xxii, 269
Philosophers, 1, 3, 8, 30, 40, 50
Philosophic History, 9, 52, 121, 200, 202
Philosophy, xii, xvi, xviii, 1, 9
Physical evidence, 185
Picts, 133
Pictaviensis (Chronicler), 146
Piedmont, 168
Piombino Archives (Rome), 46
Pius V, Pope, 193
Pius VII, Pope, 206
Plague, the Great *see* Great Plague
Platt-Deutsch Language, 165
Pococke, Nicholas, 230
Pogrom, 69
Pole, Cardinal (1550–58), 78, 80, 101, 151, 155
Polemics, 136
Politics *see* Lingard: Politics
Pollard, A. F., 191
Pollock (Judge), 140
'Popery', 90, 212
Porchester Castle, 181
Portsmouth, 143
Portugal/Portuguese, 82, 153, 160
Post-Modernism, ix, 3, 14–15, 30, 33, 252
Powicke, Sir Maurice, 13, 57, 253
Poynter (Bishop), 140, 259, 263
Practical Truth, 3
Praemunire, Statute of (1393), 125, 244
Prescott, W. H. (*Reign of Philip II*, 1855–58), 273
Provisors, Statutes of, 244
Price, Edmund (Editor, *Dolman's Magazine*), 212
'Princes in the Tower', 181–5
Printing Press, 93
Privy Council, 67
Proctor, Mr. (Anglican rector), 19, 209
Progress, Idea of, xiv, 6, 31–2, 89
Propaganda, xiv, 39, 55, 62–3, 72–3, 76, 78, 80–2, 89, 91, 93–4, 96, 103, 115, 124, 138, 142, 157–8, 163,

168, 179, 191–2, 240, 245, 256–7, 275
Protestant Church, 22, 212
Protestantism Establishment, x, 142
Protestant historians/historiography, 23, 102, 109–10, 137, 221, 239
Protestant Landowners, 259
Protestant Traditions, 8
Providence, 276
Prussian School of historians, ix
Psychology, xii, 41, 159
Puritans, 81, 115, 169, 270
Puseyite, 204
Pyrrho (c.360–c.270 BC), 1, 14, 30
Pyrrhonistic thinkers, 2

Quadra, de (Spanish ambassador), 227, 284
The Quarterly Journal, 29
Queen's University, Belfast, xix, xxii, 199

Raleigh, Sir Walter (1554–1618), 130, 161
Rambler, The, 203
Ranke, Leopold von (1795–1886), ix, xix, xx, 37, 41, 47–8, 54, 75, 97–8, 121, 200, 206, 253–4, 276
Rapin, Sieur de Thoyras, Paul de (1661–1725), 105
Raumer, Friedrich von (1781–1873), 83, 104, 118–19, 120–1
Reade, Conyers (*Lord Burleigh & Queen Elizabeth*, 1960), 142, 191, 227
Reason, 1, 6, 8, 11, 138, 222
Rebellion (1745), 18
Recusant, 20
Redgate, A. E., 10
Reflections on the French Revolution (1790), 46, 177
Reformatio Legum Ecclesiasticorum (1552), 174–5
Reformation, xiv, 3, 9, 14, 21–3, 33, 55–6, 75, 89, 95, 112, 131, 223, 231, 238
Reformation Parliament, 94, 112
Reformation Statutes, 89
Reform Bill (1832), 140
Religion, 1, 14–15, 25, 30
Religious Orders, 3
Renaissance, xviii, 1, 209, 238
Renard (Imperial ambassador), 80, 1010, 114, 148, 165, 261
Requesens, 150
Restoration (1660), 28, 194

Revisionist historians, xii, xiv, xv, 32, 95, 158, 199
Revisionism, 5, 31, 33, 57, 60, 14; 2
Rheims, 150
Rhetoric, 184
Rhine, 87
Riccio (Rizzio), David, 167
Richard I (1157–99), 57
Richard II (1367–1400), 59, 149, 176, 221, 262, 271
Richard III (1452–1485), 176–84, 276–7
Richard III Society, 178, 180, 277
Richard of Bordeaux, 148
Ricoeur, Paul (post-modernist), 10
Ridolfi, Roberto, 143, 194
Ridolfi Plot (1570), 143
Rizzio, D. *see* Riccio
Robertson, William (Scottish historian, 1721–93), 104
Rochford, Lord, 153
Rolls, Close, 55, 58
Rolls, Patent, 55, 58
Rolls of Parliament, 59–60
Rome, 19, 29, 45–7, 74–5, 77–80, 100–1, 118, 154, 158, 219–20, 254
Roman Empire, 133
Roman Numerals, 232
Romans, 149, 208, 212
Romantic Movement, 173, 276
Rosetti (Papal envoy), 100, 104
Ross (Ridolfi conspirator), 143
Ross, Professor C. (*Richard III*, 1999), 184
Rouen, 128
Rowse, A. L. (*England Under Elizabeth*, 1950), 141–2, 191
Royal Kings Arm Hotel (Lancaster), 208
Rugge MSS. Collection, 236
Rules of Evidence, 28, 169
Rushworth (*Historical Collections*, 1618–48), 53, 63
Russell, Professor Conrad (*Unrevolutionary England, 1603–42*, 1990), 32–3, 143
Russell, Lord, 106
Rye House Plot (1683), 166, 275
Rymer, Thomas (*Foedera, Conventiones, et Acta Publica, ab anno 110*, 1704–35), 55–6, 59, 63, 102, 194, 146, 178, 182–3, 221

Sabaudiensis (Italian historian), 168
Salviati (Papal nuncio, Paris, 1572), 41–9, 158
San Martino, 168

Index

Sander, Nicholas (*De Origine Progressu Schismatis*, 1585), 65, 137, 146
Saracens, 135
Sausurre, Ferdinand de (post-modernist), 30
Savoy, Duke of, 27, 86
Saxons, 133, 149, 208
Scarisbrick, Professor J. (*Henry VIII*, 1968), 78–9, 112
Scarlett (Judge), 140
Schlözer, August, Ludwig (1735–1809), 121
Scholar monks, 2–4, 98
School of scholars, xii, 3, 40
Science, xviii, 1, 15–16, 30, 252
Scientific history, xix, 4, 10, 20, 75, 97–8, 120, 266
  source criticism, xii, xvii, xviii, 3, 5, 7, 11–13, 20, 29, 35–8, 40–1, 66, 185, 197, 199
  Treatises, 3
  Truth, 2
Scientist, 234
Scorey, Bishop, 221
Scottish history, 220
Scottish Library, 73
Scotland, 84, 145, 166, 172–3, 217, 220
Scots, 85, 171–2
Scott, Sir Walter (1771–1832; Historical novels), 11
Scottish Conspiracy (1565), 81
Scottish history, 220
Scripture, 1, 4
Scrope, Archbishop (c.1350–1405), 149
Seals, 98
Second Vatican Council (1962–65), 209
Seeley, Sir J. (1835–95), 204–5, 280
Seminary, 2
Senatus, 26
Sentimentality, 172–3
Seymour, Jane, 162
Seymour, Thomas (1508–49), 228
Shaftesbury, Lord, 116
Shakespeare, William (1564–1616), 3, 134, 178–80, 277
Sharp, Sir Cuthbert, 51
Shepherd, William (Unitarian minister), 20
Sherburne, Thomas, 225–9
Scholastic humanism, 1
Sharp, Professor Kevin, 246
Shea, D. F., 174
Shrewsbury, Earl of, 72, 83, 110
Signatures, 3, 98

Simancas (Spanish State Archives), 100, 108–9, 160, 224–9, 273, 284
Simeon (Chronicler), 107
Slavery, 250
Sloane, Sir Hans, 291
Smith, Adam (1723–90), 52
Smith, Rev. Sydney, 20, 250, 257
Smith, Thomas, 230
Soames, Henry (*History of the Reformation*, 1826), 71, 136, 138, 21, 240, 256, 274
Society of Antiquaries, 7
Socrates, 9
Solms, Count (Dutch commander), 93
Somerset, Duke of (son of Henry VI), 176
Source criticism, xii, xvi, xxi, 5, 11, 12–13, 29, 33, 35, 36, 53, 62, 66, 71, 98–9, 100, 137, 139, 166, 173, 185, 237
Southey, Robert (Poet/historian, 1774–1843), 173, 211, 276
South Wales, xiii, 208
Soviet Bloc, ix
Spain, 81, 84, 87–8, 105, 109, 131, 225–7, 229
Spanish Archives *see* European Archives
  Armada (1588), 151, 225
  Empire, 88, 224
  Government, 84
  Language, 198
  Monarchy, 88
  Netherlands, 87, 161
  Spanish Sources, 53, 225
  State Papers, 160, 224–5, 227–8
  Treasure Fleet, 224
Spelman, Sir Henry (*Concilia*, 1639), ix, 7, 9, 38, 54, 110–11, 118
Spengler, Oswald (*The Decline of the West*, 1918), 12
Spiegel, Gabrielle (post-modernist), 30
Spittler, Ludwig Timotheus (German historian, 1752–1810), 40
Spandanus (Italian historian), 101
Spurr, John, 90
St. Albans, 131
St. Andrew's, Archbishop of, 274
St. Anselm *see* Anselm
St. Augustine, 204
St. Edmund Campion *see* Edmund Campion
St. Dunstan *see* Dunstan
St. George's Chapel, 150
St. Giles (London), 235
St. Isidore's Archives (Rome), 113
St. John's Epistle, 4

INDEX

St. Malachy, 132
St. Maur-sur-Loire, 2
St. Paul, 204
St. Paul's Cathedral, 149, 176
St. Peter, 204
St. Thomas More *see* More, Thomas
St. Victor, 261
Stafford, Lady, 73
Stafford Papers, 73
Staffordshire, 83, 181, 283
Starkey, David (*Elizabeth: Apprenticeship*, 2000), 147, 228, 274
State Paper Office, 75, 83, 113, 115–16, 154, 157, 190, 219–21, 265
State Papers, 62, 75, 77, 83, 110–11, 177, 183, 219
State Trials, 52, 62, 64, 73, 81, 83, 159–60, 163
Statutes of the Realm, 83, 236
Stenton, Sir Frank, 10, 25, 134, 239–42
Stephen, King (*c.*1096–1154), 76
Stigand, Archbishop of Canterbury (d. 1072), 24–5
Stonyhurst Archives, 64, 73, 116
Stouppe Papers, 168
Stowe, John (Chronicler, 1525–1605), 146, 151, 180
Strada (Spanish historian), 43, 106, 151
Strafford, Earl of (Thomas Wentworth, 1593–1641), 84
Strafford Papers, 84
Strickland, Agnes (*Queens of England*, 1849), 135–6, 203
Strype, John (1643–1737), 71, 75, 83, 107, 139, 175, 268
Stuart cause, 18
Stuart period, 69, 87
Stubbs, William, ix, 58
Style, 13, 15, 234–7
Suffolk, Earl of, 104, 183
Sunderland, Earl of, 158
Supremacy, Act of (1534), 112
Supremacy, Act of (1559), 192, 221
Surrey, 187
Surrey, Earl of, 77, 110
Sussex, 143
Sussex, Earl of, 151
Swansea University College, xiii, xxii
Swift, Jonathan (1667–1745), 260
Sweden, 87, 127
Switzerland, 86
Syria (and Egypt), 135

Talbot, Lady Mary, 110, 111

Talbot, Lord, 82
Talbot, Bishop, 14, 19
Tarbes, Archbishop, 78
Tate, Dr. Robert, 66, 213
Tawney, R. H. (1880–1962, *Religion and the Rise of Capitalism*), 25
Taxation, 80
Temple, Sir W. (English diplomat), 86–8, 92, 127, 200
Temperley, Sir Harold, 97
Tertullian, 118
Tewkesbury, Battle of (1471), 176–7, 179
Texel (Holland), 92
The Historian's Craft (trans. from the French, 1954), 37
Theology, i, xviii, 3, 30
The World of William and Mary: Anglo-Dutch Perspectives On The Revolution of 1688–89 (1996), 90–1
Thomas of Walsingham (Chronicler, *Historia Brevis*), 59, 138–9
Thomas, William, 156
Thucydides (460–400 BC), 236
Thurloe (Oliver Cromwell's secretary), 86
Tierney, M. A., 74, 109–10, 212, 215
Tillemont, de, 2
Tillières (French ambassador), 126
Titus Oates Plot (1678), 20
Torbay, 93
Torture, 145, 160, 194
Tory, 65, 140, 252, 276
Tory historiography, 8
Totalitarian, 158–9
Tower, of London, 176–7, 179–81, 183, 220, 271, 275
Toynbee, Arnold (*The Study of History*, 1934–61), ix
Trade and Commerce, 79
Traditionary Belief, 185–6
Transportation, 250
Transubstantiation, 240
Trasimene, Lake (Italy), 20
Treasury Documents, 6
Trevelyan, Sir G. M. (1876–1962), 62
Trevor-Roper, Sir H., 203
Trinity (Doctrine of), 4
Triple Alliance (1667), 87–9, 127
Truth, Historical, xii, 14, 16, 29, 95–6, 99
  Objective, 252
  Poetical, 14
  Practical *see* Practical Truth
  Scientific, 13–14, 16, 252
  Timeless, 16–17
Tudor Chronicles, 141

Index

Government, 79, 81–2, 141–2, 159
Historians, 103
Monarchy, 62, 159
Propagandists, 58
'Revolution in Government', 76
Tuite, Mr., 263
Turner, Sharon (1768–1847), 71, 75, 136–8, 173, 177, 211, 238, 256, 273
Turold (featuring in Domesday & Bayeux Tapestry), 187
Turks, 250
Tyburn, 194
Tyrrel, Sir James (murderer of 'Princes in the Tower'), 183
Tytler, William (1711–92), 188, 220

Ulster, 168
United States of America, 90, 206
Universe, 1, 14, 30
Universities, 24, 77–9
Upcot, Mr. (of the London Institution), 66, 74, 116, 152, 168
Ushaw College, xii, xxii, 11, 19, 36, 74, 100, 208
Utopia (1516), 184

Valla, Lorenzo (1409–57), xxv
Valladolid (Spain), 100, 108, 225
Vassalage, 57
Vassy (France), 150, 154
Vatican, 44–5, 48, 76, 206
Vatican Archives *see* European Archives
Vatican Library, 77
Vatican MSS., 75, 101
Vaudois, 27, 86, 168
Vaughan, Richard (*Matthew Paris*, 1958), 131
Venetian Ambassadors' Reports, 54, 79, 125
Venetians, 250
Vergil, Polydore (*Anglicae Historiae*, 1534), 63
Vetus, Itala, 101
Versailles, 45
Victorians, 32
Villani, 250
Vincent, Professor John, 245
Vindication (Lingard, 1826), xix, 42, 45–6
Vindiciae Gallicae (Mackintosh, J., 1791), 56
Viking invasions, 242
Virgil, 208
Vital (featured in Domesday & the Bayeux Tapestry), 187
Vitoria (Battle of, in Spain, 1813), 229
Voltaire (1694–1778), 40

Wace (*Roman de Brut*, 1155), 187
Wadard (featured in Domesday & the Bayeux Tapestry), 187
Wales, 147
Walker, Canon John, 202, 213
Wallace, William (d. 1305), 172–3
Walsingham, Sir Francis (c.1532–90), 3, 72, 81–3, 129, 142–4, 155–7, 163, 215, 225, 269, 283
Walpole, Horace (*Historic Doubts*, 1767), 183, 277
Wanley, Humphrey, 291
War (England & France, 1793), 19
War, First World, x
War, Second World, 61
Warbeck, Perkin (1474–99), 183–4
Ward, Sir A. W. Ward, 201
'Wars of the Roses' (1455–85), 125, 174, 179
Warwick, 187
Weir, A., 184
Watson, R. (*Philip II*, 1777), 273
Wellington, Duke of (1767–1852), 229
Welwood, 124
Wendover, R. (Chronicler d. 1236), 55–6, 58, 101, 106, 128–9, 132, 269
Western philosophy, 1
Westminster, 93, 181–2
Westminster (Chronicler), 107, 146
Westminster Review, 21, 29
Wexford Massacre of (1649), 114, 154
Wharton, Henry (*Anglia Sacra*, 1691), ix, 7, 38, 231, 242, 287
Whedall, Mr., 74
Whigs, 323, 65, 140, 252, 256, 276
Whig historians, 8, 11, 32, 73, 90, 96, 191, 203, 255, 278
Whig interpretation of history, x, xiv, 57, 61, 71, 73–4, 85–7, 89–90, 144, 152, 159
Whig Reviews, 61, 191
White, Hayden (post-modernist), 30
Whitehall, 146, 235
Whitelock (Cromwellian 'commissioner'), 28
Wigan, 22
Wiles Lectures, xix, xx, 199
Wilfrid, Bishop of NoSrthumbria (c.634–c.709), 242
Wilkins, David (*Concilia*, 1737), 54
William I, the Conqueror (1027/8–87), 24–5, 185–7

Index

William of Malmesbury *see* Malmesbury
William of Newburgh (Chronicler, c.1135–c.1198), 150–1
William of Orange/William III (1650–1702), 86–7, 90, 92–4, 166
William of Poitou (Chronicler), 187
William the Silent, 273
Winchester, x, 18, 151
Wiseman, Cardinal Nicholas (1802–65), 101, 140
Witan, 240
Wolsey, Cardinal Thomas (c.1472–1530), 77–8, 111, 114, 125, 153, 155
Wood, Anthony (*Athenae Oxonienses*, 1691–2), 66
Wood, Thomas, 154
Wordsworth, Dr. (*Who Wrote Eikon Basilike?*), 194, 196
Wormald, B. H. G., 77

Wray, Sir Bourchier, 72
Wright, Thomas (*Queen Elizabeth*, 1838), 74, 83
Wulfstan, Bishop (c.1009–95; *Life of Ethelwold*), 242
Wyatt, Sir Thomas, 24
Wyatt's Rebellion (1554), 24, 147, 165

York, 19, 110, 118, 177, 182
York, House of, 175–6
Yorkists, 124, 179
York Westminster Conference (1568–69), 188, 190

Zuider Zee (Holland), 92
Zurich Letters, 671
Zurita, Gerónimo de (Spanish historian, 1512–80), 108–9, 131, 264

www.ingramcontent.com/pod-product-compliance
Lightning Source LLC
Chambersburg PA
CBHW071359300426
44114CB00016B/2110